Gender and Judaism

GENDER AND JUDAISM

The Transformation of Tradition

Edited by

T. M. Rudavsky

NEW YORK UNIVERSITY PRESS
New York & London

NEW YORK UNIVERSITY PRESS
New York and London

Copyright © 1995 by New York University
All rights reserved

Library of Congress Cataloging-in-Publication Data
Gender and Judaism: the transformation of tradition / edited by T. M. Rudavsky
    p. cm.
Includes bibliographical references.
ISBN 0-8147-7452-0 (cloth). --ISBN 0-8147-7453-9 (paperback)
    1. Women in Judaism--Congresses. 2. Sex role--Religious aspects-
-Judaism--Congresses. 3. Feminism--Religious aspects--Judaism-
-Congresses. 4. Jewish women--Religious life--Congresses.
5. Jewish literature--Women authors--History and criticism-
-Congresses. I. Rudavsky, Tamar 1951-
BM729.W6G45   1994
296' .082--dc20   94-28518
                    CIP

New York University Press books are printed on acid-free paper, and their binding
materials are chosen for strength and durability.

Manufactured in the United States of America

10 9 8 7 6 5 4 3 2 1

This volume is dedicated to the memory of Samuel Melton, whose devotion to matters of the mind and spirit, and selfless generosity, have enabled a major academic center for Jewish Studies to flourish at The Ohio State University.

Contents

III. Literary Dimensions of Gender and Judaism

IV. The Social Fabric of Gender and Judaism

Acknowledgments

Earlier versions of the chapters in this volume were first presented as papers at a conference on "Gender and Judaism" sponsored by the Melton Center for Jewish Studies at The Ohio State University in April 1993. I want to express my gratitude to Zilla Goodman, Leonard Gordon and Rochelle L. Millen for their role in helping to organize the conference, in helping to enlist the participation of many of the speakers, in joining in the planning process at every stage, and in providing well-needed moral support whenever needed. Judith Stauber was responsible for the administrative tasks relating to the conference; her support enabled the conference to run as smoothly as possible, even in the midst of major power-outages at the start of the conference.

Viktoria Herson Finn, a graduate research assistant at the Melton Center, assumed major responsibilities for the editing and technical preparation of the manuscript. It is no exaggeration to say that without her participation, this volume would not exist; she coordinated all the administrative tasks associated with the preparation of the work. Niko Pfund of New York University Press suggested publishing the papers with the Press, and played a major role in bringing the volume to fruition. Despina Papazoglou Gimbel supervised the copy-editing at NYU Press and did a wonderful job of reading through and editing the papers. And finally, I would like to thank Nathaniel, Miriam and Rich for having lived through the stress-filled hours required to bring this volume to fruition.

Introduction

Judaism, in its many forms, has not been a static religion, but rather a religion influenced by changes in the ideas and practices of its members interacting with the outside world. Throughout history, changes in the characterization of gender issues have both influenced and been influenced by Jewish perspectives. This transformation has been accelerated today, as feminist thinkers attempt to discover how modern women fit into Jewish thought and practice.

The Ohio State University provided an early forum for those concerned with issues of gender and Judaism. In 1981 the Melton Center for Jewish Studies at Ohio State hosted one of the first conferences nationwide devoted to issues pertaining to women and Jewish culture; entitled "Tradition and Transformation," this conference was attended by several hundred individuals and proved to be a seminal event in Jewish women's studies. It was therefore fitting that, after barely thirteen years, a "bat-mitzvah" celebration be held to assess the strides made by women within Jewish thought, culture, and *halakhah*. Hence our most recent conference "Gender and Judaism" was held in 1993 at Ohio State.

Needless to say, much has happened in the field of gender studies in the intervening thirteen years. Numerous books and articles have appeared pertaining to Jewish women's history, literature, the role of women in the Jewish community, and the evolving areas of Jewish law and theology. We need only point to the many ground-breaking works by Jewish scholars published since 1981 in order to appreciate the unprecedented scholarly energy that has been invested in these areas. Works by scholars such as Blu Greenberg (*On Women and Judaism*, 1981), Susannah Heschel (ed. *On Being a Jewish Feminist*, 1983), Susan Weidman Schneider (*Jewish and Female*, 1983), Rachel Biale (*Women and Jewish Law*, 1984), and Judith Plaskow (*Standing Again at Sinai: Judaism from a Feminist Perspective*, 1990) reflect the wide diversity of areas and expertise in recent years.

And yet the struggle over the role of women in Judaism is not over. In her relatively early anthology, *The Jewish Woman* (1976), Elizabeth Koltun noted that the Jewish women's movement faced an uncertain future. "Has the movement already accomplished as much as it can?" she asked in 1976 (p. xiv). In a sense the present anthology is a direct response to Koltun's implicit challenge. Alice Shalvi addresses this question directly in her essay "The Geopolitics of Jewish Feminism." A long-time Jewish feminist activist, and founder of the *Jewish Women's Network* in Israel, Shalvi points to the decided questioning of both the patriarchal and androcentric natures of Judaism by the new Jewish scholars; in a cautionary mode, however, she reminds us that whereas both American and European feminism in general, and Jewish feminism in particular, are alive and thriving, Israeli Jewish feminism is "waiting to be born" (p. 244). It is we, she adjures, who must help to facilitate the birthing process.

It is still true, as was noted by Koltun over a decade ago, that many social, political, and religious roles are distributed within traditional Judaism according to sexual orientation. But in recent years these roles have been questioned, evaluated, and, at times, radically transformed. Aided by methodological tools initiated and refined by feminist scholars, Jewish scholars and activists alike have worked to transform the roles of Jewish women and men. The fields of discourse have been broadened to include wider gender concerns: "otherness" incorporates the concerns of gay and lesbian Jews, as well as the more traditionally marked canons of male and female differentiation. Clearly, as the articles in the present volume amply demonstrate, the Jewish women's movement rides the fine line between maintaining the meaningful components of tradition while at the same time working to transform the more oppressive elements of that tradition. Rabbi Laura Geller's essay is an eloquent testament to the overall tensions inherent in this volume. Highlighting the explicitly measurable gains made by women like herself in Jewish 'power' positions such as the rabbinate and cantorial positions, Geller reminds us of the painful price these pioneers have had to pay.

The strides made by women studying and critically assessing rabbinic texts, a task long reserved for the male sphere within traditional Judaism, are amply reflected in articles by Lori Lefkowitz, Rochelle L. Millen, and Naomi Graetz. Lori Lefkowitz juxtaposes the tendency to emphasize the alterity or absence of woman by defining woman in her unique specificity; in her *midrash* on the biblical account of Sarah's eavesdropping on the angels, the politically subversive role of laughter is examined as a feminist ploy. Both Millen and Graetz grapple with canonical texts that for so many centuries have defined women's restrictive role within a male-defined society, enabling these scholars to propel the *halakhic* re-examination of rulings that may be detrimental to the moral and psychic well-being of women. This re-examination can only intensify the process of transformation within traditional bounds.

But how is the category of "otherness" constructed? A number of papers explore this basic metaphysical construction from different perspectives. Utilizing what he terms the "Buber-Gilligan" model, Leonard Gordon proposes areas for institutional reform which allow for further dialogue between Jewish feminists and *halakhists*. In an innovative appropriation of theoretic models drawn from Chandra Mohanty and Biddy Martin, Laura Levitt offers a creative reading of the *ketubbah* and shows how this document has been used to confine Jewish women to a narrow construction of home embedded in a paradigm of heterosexual domesticity. This narrow construction has been reinforced by the many books written not only by Orthodox men, but by Orthodox women as well. In a ground-breaking and uniquely interdisciplinary study, Jody Myers and Jane Litman examine several such works that, written by Orthodox Jewish women, affirm the social reality of Orthodox women by using the tools of feminist language infused with Jewish mystical symbolism. By focusing on the repeatedly expressed themes of woman as "hidden," woman as power, and woman as exemplar of sanctified physicality, Myers and Litman argue that this new Orthodox women's theology is "yet another creative Jewish response to the challenges of modernity" (p. 70).

The very conflation of gender images with biological functions is rejected by Elliott Wolfson, who utilizes kabbalistic literature to demonstrate the importance of the sociocultural construction of gender. Just as kabbalistic texts emphasize the importance of the female becoming male, Wolfson skillfully incorporates into his study many kabbalistic texts which underscore the ontic importance of the male to "divest himself of his maleness and assume the posture of the feminine" (p. 223). The ambivalences toward traditional gender distinctions are delineated somewhat differently by Harry Brod, who explores cultural images of Jewish men as depicted in popular culture. Drawing on the image of superman and other comic book characters, Brod cleverly demonstrates the many ways in which the Jewish male sees himself and is seen by the outside world. That "otherness" extends to all strata of society is demonstrated in Howard Adelman's study of the role of Jewish servant girls employed in the early modern Jewish family; in this study Adelman juxtaposes the categories of class and race alongside those of gender and religion.

Of striking interest to modern readers is the heightened feminist consciousness of late nineteenth- and early twentieth-century German Jewish women writers. These writers share with contemporary women the struggle to live in two worlds, to partake at two tables, while maintaining one's identity. Nahida Remy, the author of the 1891 best-selling book *The Jewish Woman*, is examined by Alan Levenson, who, juxtaposing Remy's love for Jews as a people with her concern for the Jewish woman, argues that her philo-semitism ultimately subverted her proto-feminism. Similar ambivalences are found in the writings of early twentieth-century university-educated Jewish women; these works are analyzed by both Harriet Pass Freidenreich and Pamela Nadell. Does adopting the values of the prevalent secular culture destroy one's Jewish identity? Freidenreich tries to gauge the "Jewish consciousness" of early university-educated German Jewish women, tracing the extent to which they retained a Jewish affiliation with their communities while at the same time they strove to define more equal roles for women in secular society. And Pamela Nadell examines several such early twentieth-century women who, so consumed by their love for Judaism, embarked upon rabbinical study, a field that was only under duress becoming an option available to women. It is instructive to compare Freidenreich's study with the more explicitly sociological study of Sylvia Barack Fishman, who explores the changing behaviors, attitudes, and "Jewish identities" of contemporary Jewish women, in particular with respect to their connectedness to and alienation from Jewish institutional life. Not surprisingly, perhaps, Fishman's findings reinforce Freidenreich's characterization of Jewish women several generations earlier. As noted earlier, transforming a deeply entrenched culture is no small task.

The literature of this fecund mid to late nineteenth century reflects as well the tensions inherent in the voices of articulate Jewish women writers. Shulamit Magnus details the memoirs of Pauline Wengeroff, one of the only women writers of *maskilic* memoirs. Dagmar Lorenz depicts the writings of four German Jewish women writers (Claire Goll, Veza Canetti, Else Lasker-Schüler, and Gertrud Kolmar), all of whom struggle with their self-definition as prominent Jewish women who have ostensively abandoned their faith. And in a sensitive reading of two poems, one by Y. L. Gordon and the other by Devorah Baron, Zilla

Goodman analyzes the way in which both texts "stretch the construct of the submissive woman to parodic lengths" and depict the ways in which women are demoted "to the status of the subaltern" by the vagaries of the Law (p. 207).

That many of the chapters in this volume have been influenced by developments in contemporary feminist methodologies, literatures, and political agenda should be evident, and Susannah Heschel and Maurie Sacks provide cautionary reflections with respect to the entire feminist enterprise. Susannah Heschel's sober examination of recent German feminist thought is a cautious reminder that ideology can often undermine scholarly integrity. Through the equation of Nazism, classical patriarchy, and Old Testament adherence to divine command theory, which eschews personal responsibility in deference to blind allegiance to divine authority, German feminists have argued that Judaism's patriarchy is analogous to the morality of National Socialism; by inference, they argue, both Jewish victims of the Holocaust, as well as German women, emerge as victims of Judaism. Maurie Sacks adjoins readers to "deconstruct" feminist claims and recognize that American Jewish feminist scholarship is itself a sociological phenomenon and ought not to be regarded as a definitive representation of normative Judaism and its gender hierarchy.

The voices collected in this anthology represent the most recent scholarship in the field of gender studies. Let these voices serve to influence a new generation of scholars committed to the transformation of Jewish life and thought.

T. M. Rudavsky
August, 1994

Part I

Gender and Judaism: Theoretical Concerns

Chapter 1

Toward a Gender-Inclusive Account of Halakhah

Leonard D. Gordon

Halakhah, like most legal systems, has been historically unjust to women in at least two important ways: first, by and large, women have been the objects rather than the subjects of laws, and hence women have been unequal to men under the law; second, women have historically been neither lawmakers nor judges, which excludes them from the processes of legislation. These injustices are, obviously, mutually reinforcing.

Does one conclude that law, with its hierarchies, injustices, and rigidity is "not for women," complete with the implication that women are different? (Different and better, to be sure, but nevertheless different.) In America, stuck as we are at the moment with patriarchal structures, feminist efforts have been directed to changing sexist legislation by changing laws, and to bringing women into the system as lawmakers and jurists. When women are "brought in," many people expect that the processes themselves will change, that a female difference will make itself felt, that just as feminist pedagogy can transform the classroom, so too can feminist legislation transform the meaning and operation of the law itself.

Feminist critiques of Jewish law (*halakhah*) have, for the most part, rejected the law altogether on much the same grounds as liberal Judaism's rejection of *halakhah* as a mode of religious expression. Made neither by women nor with women's historical experience or interests at heart, *halakhah* continues to oppress; feminist critics have read *halakhah* as, at best, irrelevant and, at worst, insidious. Jewish defenders of the law have argued that Jewish law is not what it seems: it may seem oppressive, but it is actually about sustaining and deepening the relationships between men and women. To take a particularly popular example, the menstrual purity laws are said to promote friendship in marriage and to prevent women from being seen as sexual objects. What the feminist critique shares with the Orthodox defense is the assumption that women are different and that *halakhah* is a system designed to respond to and codify that difference in lived behavior.

In a juxtaposition suggested by Judith Plaskow in "*Halakha* as a Feminist Issue," Martin Buber and Carol Gilligan both reject the value of legal discourse as a medium for the expression of the highest human values. Buber writes, "I cannot admit the law transformed by man into the realm of my will, if I am to hold myself ready for the unmediated word of God directed to a specific hour of my life."[1] Gilligan's critique of the role of rule-governed behavior in childhood play is by now well known, and has in fact become the centerpiece of liberal apologetics for the inclusion of women in Jewish professional life. Women as rabbis, cantors, educators, and communal leaders now live under the Gilligan-inspired anxiety of bringing their own distinctive "different voice" to the pulpit and the boardroom. With regard to law, that different voice rejects the ultimate value of law and legal argumentation. According to Gilligan, boys are "increasingly fascinated with the legal elaboration of rules and the development of fair procedures for adjudicating conflicts, a fascination that . . . does not hold for girls."[2] Plaskow then paraphrases Gilligan's position: "rules for girls are largely pragmatic, they can be discarded when a game is no longer enjoyable for its participants."[3] Girls are more tolerant in their attitudes toward rules, more willing to make exceptions, and more easily reconciled to innovations.[4] Girl's play, in the Gilligan model, is about the significance of building relationships and not about the play and its outcome.

The dichotomy articulated by Buber and Gilligan between law and relationship implies that law, and hence *halakhah* in the Jewish context, is necessarily hierarchical and exclusionary, and therefore antithetical to such basic components of contemporary Jewish feminisms as the insistence on openness, fluidity, the building of relationships, egalitarianism, and a heightened concern for spirituality. This dichotomy has won increasing acceptance within the Jewish world. Furthermore, the addition of Gilligan's gender essentialism to Buber's theory of dialogical relationships adds gender markers to the old spirit/law split. Jewish law becomes irredeemably male, and Jewish spirituality becomes the female redeemer for Israel. Women are once again imagined as spiritual, nurturing figures, offering contemporary Israel release from the harsh strictures of God, the law-giving Father. Rather than transforming *halakhah* along the model of the feminist transformations of Jewish liturgy, rabbinic midrash, and communal process, the Buber-Gilligan approach would leave the *halakhah* at the door of the new feminist transformation of Judaism.

Faced with this possibility, it is not surprising that some in the community of those committed personally and professionally to *halakhah* have sought to accomplish a feminist transformation themselves. Beginning as a response to Buber's existential critique of law, and continuing as a response to contemporary Jewish feminisms, the largely male community of Jewish theologians, philosophers, historians of *halakhah*, and historians have rewritten the history of Jewish law, and have thereby laid the groundwork for the creation of the "new *halakhah*" sought by Esther Ticktin, the new "*piskei halakhah*" proposed by Rachel Adler, and the "Halakhic education" that Blu Greenberg writes is "the most important area for reaching final equalization of women in the Jewish community."[5]

After briefly reviewing some highlights of this new revisionist history of *halakhah*, I will suggest how to account for the wide variance between the revisionist account and the lived reality rejected by many Jewish feminists. And finally, I will modestly propose some areas for institutional reform that might enable a broader dialogue between Jewish feminists and *halakhic* traditions. In this way, feminist insights concerning the content, form, and history of Jewish law can help effect change without creating new fixed roles for women as teachers of the Jewish spirit rather than of the Jewish body, and as religious counselors rather than religious decision makers.

Writing in dramatically different contexts, St. Paul, Shmuel Safrai, and Martin Buber all affirm the legal-centeredness of late pharisaic and early rabbinic Judaism.[6] Building on the legal resources of biblical and postbiblical Jewish literature, the early rabbis expanded Judaism's legal framework to meet the challenges of exile and, eventually, of the destruction of the Second Temple in 70 C.E. The Mishnah, and the Talmud, which is structured as a commentary to the Mishnah's legal and exegetical discourses, have been understood as the foundation stones upon which the legal edifice of the later codes and modern responsum literature are based. Written in the rabbinic schoolhouse for the rabbinic elite, these documents reinforce the essential hierarchies of their times. So is articulated the traditional account. The conclusion of the Mishnah's fourth division, *Nezikin*, on Civil Damages, is exemplary:

(Horayot 3:8) A. A priest takes precedence over a Levite, a Levite over an Israelite, an Israelite over a *mamzer* [the offspring of a forbidden union], a *mamzer* over a *Netin* [see Joshua 9:27], a *Netin* over a proselyte, a proselyte over a freed slave.
B. Under what circumstances?
C. When all of them are equivalent.
D. But if the *mamzer* was a disciple of a sage and a high priest was an *am haaretz* [unlearned person], the *mamzer* who is a disciple of a sage takes precedence over a high priest who is an *am haares*.[7]

Thus when the rabbis gathered in the town of Yavneh along the coast of the land of Israel to reflect on the destruction of the Second Temple and the loss of political independence, they worked, first and foremost, to establish order and *stasis* in the midst of the chaos of war. With the boundaries between Israel and the other nations falling around them, with Roman soldiers on the Temple Mount, the rabbis restated and added to the laws mandating separation within Israel, building new and revised social hierarchies. Eventually they also added to the significance of gender difference in the *halakhah* as purity rules — other than those regarding menstrual impurity — were gradually removed from the system.

This view of the history of early rabbinism, supporting as it does the feminist critique of *halakhah*, has been challenged in recent decades on both exegetical and historical grounds. Jacob Neusner has denied that the early rabbinic enterprise centered around division and separation as an end in itself. He posits that "the principal message of the Mishnah is that the will of man affects the material reality of the world and governs the working of those forces, visible or not, which express and effect the sanctification of creation and of Israel alike."[8] For Neusner, the point of early rabbinism was precisely the move away from hierarchy, class status, and a mechanical view of holiness to a human-centered view that places the intention of the individual Israelite at the center of creation. This reading provides a powerful rationale for praying in a circle and decentering rabbinic authority in our modern context.

The historian Shaye J. D. Cohen summarizes the contribution of the rabbis who met in the town of Yavneh in terms even more reminiscent of Gilligan and Plaskow:

The major contribution of Yavneh to Jewish history [was] the creation of a society which tolerates disputes without producing sects . . . No previous Jewish work looks like the Mishnah because no previous Jewish work, neither biblical nor post-biblical, neither Hebrew nor Greek, neither Palestinian nor diasporan, attributes conflicting legal and exegetical opinions to named authorities who, in spite of their differences, belong to the same fraternity. The dominant ethic here is not exclusivity but elasticity.[9]

The goal of the rabbinic movement at its inception was to include the Jewish people under one "big tent" in the aftermath of the divisions that had led to the disastrous wars against Rome. Exemplary of Cohen's reading, though not cited by him, is the following passage taken from the Mishnah's fourth division, tractate *Eduyyot*. This tractate stands out in the Mishnah as an anthology of legal topics arranged around such lists as those matters on which the Houses of Hillel and Shammai reversed their traditional rulings, and lists of matters on which the majority of the rabbis enforced compromise and the principle of majority rule against those who held fast to extreme and divisive opinions. In Mishnah *Eduyyot* 4:8, the Houses dispute matters of marriage and cleanliness. Although they reach no consensus, the Mishnah concludes that:

I. Notwithstanding that these declare ineligible and the others declare eligible, yet the House of Shammai did not refrain from marrying women from the House of Hillel, nor the House of Hillel from marrying women from the House of Shammai.
J. And [despite] all the disputes about what is clean and unclean, wherein these declare clean and the others declare unclean, neither refrained from making clean things with the other.[10]

One might be tempted to dismiss the larger significance I propose for the conclusions drawn by Neusner and Cohen. After all, they may simply be noticing that in its first stages, the *halakhic* system was more metaphor than reality. But certainly by the era of the two Talmuds and the grand codes of the medieval period, the pressures of ruling Israel had turned the rabbis from idealist philosophers to hard-nosed, male lawyers and judges.

Perhaps this is so in reality, but it is not in contemporary scholarship. Thus, David Kraemer finds the Babylonian Talmud's main point to be the impossibility of determining truth in legal cases. Rather than being an attempt to uncover legal principles for the governance of Israel, the Talmud emerges as a document seeking to reconcile reason and revelation through the acknowledgment of the need to compromise even in matters of ultimate meaning. He writes that in the Talmud:

> reason ultimately emerges to claim a well-earned place in the center of the system, and even to become "Torah." As it does, any possible conflict between revelation and reason is eliminated by definition, because, having been included in Torah, reason too is now part of revelation. The two poles become, in the Bavli, complete partners in the promulgation of a much compromised truth.[11]

If the Talmud emerges as a document of postmodernism, relativizing truth, and recognizing the limitations of both reason and revelation, then where can we locate the start of the patriarchal, univocal, hierarchical, closed *halakhic* system? Certainly not in the law code of Maimonides. Menachem Kellner's *Maimonides on Judaism and the Jewish People* assures us that the author of the most comprehensive code of Jewish law intended his code as a companion to the *Guide for the Perplexed*, which in turn was designed to teach philosophically minded Jews of the ultimate union of Jew and Gentile that will precede the messianic world to come. For Kellner's Maimonides: "'The law as a whole '. . . aims at two things: the welfare of the soul and the welfare of the body . . . Between these two aims, one is indubitably greater in nobility, namely the welfare of the soul—I mean the procuring of correct opinions."[12] Unlike Kraemer's Talmud, Kellner's Maimonidean *Code* does not affirm diversity of opinion, but it does teach the ultimate equality of all humanity, an equally important contemporary and feminist value not frequently associated with rabbinic *halakhah* in the feminist imagination.

A few further examples will have to suffice in this brief account. In his study of the rabbinic mindset, David Weiss Halivni points to the exemplary work of the medieval *peshat* exegetes who "systematically and unrestrainedly maintained the freedom to explain the Bible differently from, and in opposition to, accepted *halakhah*."[13] And finally, the late Rabbi J. B. Soloveitchik, in his classic work on the *Halakhic Man*, notes that his "deepest desire is not the realization of the

Halakhah but rather the ideal construction which was given to him from Sinai, and this ideal construction exists forever."[14]

Ultimately, even though almost all of Jewish literary creativity during the rabbinic era is legal in character, it turns out that an entire school, or set of overlapping schools, of contemporary rabbinics scholarship deny that legal discourse in Judaism is about law at all. The *halakhic* classics of medieval Judaism have been re-presented to us as community-building texts, seeking to overcome differences of social class among Israel, to promote compromise in matters of legal dispute, to reconcile the conclusions of reason and revelation, and ultimately to undo even the chasm that has for so long separated Jew from Gentile. We are given a *halakhic* system more concerned with process than results and more focused on bringing communities together than on building the boundaries that might keep them apart. And finally, we are told that the rabbinic system of *halakhah* is human centered, removing the ultimate hierarchical relationship from our active consciousness. The community of rabbis insists on the human prerogative to shape law in an ongoing, fluid process, a process that excludes God as too ultimately other to enter into a renewed role as the guardian of Israel.

In spite of the apparent feminism of these constructions of *halakhah*, this contemporary reading of rabbinism avoids the issue of gender. Neusner's analysis of gender is limited to a footnote defending his use of gender-specific language in describing the Mishnah's laws.[15] Cohen's history of the period avoids all reference to the domestic life of Israel.[16] Kellner's frequent references to the Aristotelian legacy of Maimonides ignores the question of whether, according to Aristotle, the souls of women were in any way equal to those of men. The all-male contributors to *Back to the Sources*, a standard handbook on the glories of classical Jewish literature, also fail to comment on the exclusion of women by this tradition.[17]

Thus we find that male scholars, explicitly and implicitly responding to the critiques of *halakhah* popularized by Buber's existentialism and Gilligan's social psychological feminist theories, have reimagined elements of the classical traditions in ways that may make that tradition usable in a feminist context, but they have done so without confronting the exclusion of women from that tradition. In this way, patriarchal power at once assimilates the feminist critique and domesticates it. The rabbis of the Talmud, we are assured, have always known that which contemporary feminist theorists present as new: they have long since assimilated the critique of heteronomy and hierarchy, striking the perfect balance between unity and difference, between the male emphasis on order and separation, and the feminine stress on connectedness and unity.

Whatever the shortcomings of this new reading of the tradition as scholarship and as a response to the feminist critique of law, it does point out the possibility of a feminist revisioning of *halakhah* for our generation. Perhaps we can accept Gilligan's analysis in order to shake up our assumptions about the universality of *halakhah* as a vehicle for spiritual expression in Jewish communities, and it may be possible to do so without falling into the essentialist trap of saying that male *halakhists* need to learn to value their female, relational side. We can recognize that the *halakhic* system, even during its centuries as an exclusively male domain, functioned along two parallel trajectories, as a system designed to preserve a functioning community, and as a system designed to point to and actualize an ideal of unity. For many centuries rabbinic Judaism worked well within that tension for its men. The challenge before some of us now is to see if a transformed rabbinic system can work both for women and men.

If contemporary Jewish feminists have reclaimed the discourses of midrash, liturgy, and history without insisting, from the first, that these genres account for their role in the oppression of Jewish women in the past, perhaps the language of *halakhah* can be reclaimed as well. Rightly or wrongly, for better and for worse, status in parts of the Jewish community is still based on Talmudic scholarship, and religious commitment is measured by the seriousness with which communities and individuals respond to their *halakhic* systems. Communities that stand outside of the discourse of law in Judaism disempower themselves, whatever their motivations.

To facilitate the incorporation of new communities into the study and practice of *halakhah*, historians of *halakhah* must now enforce gender as a category in their analysis of each Talmudic discussion and each transition in the history of rabbinic authority. What role did women play in the formation of law? How did transformations in the social role of women find expression in *halakhah*? What alternative models of decision making existed within women's communities? No easy answers should be assumed, and scholars should never imagine that it goes without saying that women were, at any given moment, excluded from the *halakhic* process.

However much women may have been excluded from positions of power in law historically, this historical exclusion has ironically led to a self-exclusion in our contemporary moment. Jewish law, like American law, cannot be discarded. When feminism joins liberal Judaism in self-exclusion from *halakhah*, feminism risks reinforcing the characterization of women as "Other" within Jewish systems. *Halakhah*, like American law, still requires feminist revision.

NOTES

1. Martin Buber, "Revelation and Law," *On Jewish Learning*, ed. Nahum Glatzer (New York: Schocken, 1965) , 111. Cited in Judith Plaskow, "*Halakha* as a Feminist Issue," *Melton Journal* (Fall 1987): 5.
2. Carol Gilligan, *In a Different Voice: Psychological Theory and Women's Development* (Cambridge: Harvard University Press, 1982) , 10. Cited by Plaskow, Ibid., 4.
3. Ibid., 4.
4. Ibid., 4, citing Gilligan, *In a Different Voice*, 10.
5. Esther Ticktin, "A Modest Beginning," *The Jewish Woman*, ed. Elizabeth Koltun (New York: Schocken, 1976), 129; Rachel Adler, "The Jew Who Wasn't There: *Halakhah* and the Jewish Woman," *On Being a Jewish Feminist: A Reader*, ed. Susannah Heschel (New York: Schocken, 1983), 17; Blu Greenberg, "Judaism and Feminism," *The Jewish Woman*, 183.
6. In the case of Paul, his view of Jewish law may have been more complex than is generally assumed. See, for example, E. P. Sanders, *Paul, the Law, and the Jewish People* (Philadelphia: Fortress Press, 1983). Shmuel Safrai, "Oral Torah," "*Halakha*," *The Literature of the Sages: First Part: Oral Tora, Halakha, Mishna, Tosefta, Talmud, External Tractates*, ed. Shmuel Safrai (Philadelphia: Fortress Press, 1987) , 35–209; Martin Buber, *Two Types of Faith* (New York: Macmillan, 1951).
7. Cited in the translation of Jacob Neusner, *The Mishnah* (New Haven: Yale University Press, 1988), 695.
8. Jacob Neusner, *Judaism: The Evidence of the Mishnah* (Chicago: University of Chicago Press, 1981), 271.
9. Shaye J. D. Cohen, "The Significance of *Yavneh*: Pharisees, Rabbis and the End of Jewish Sectarianism," *Hebrew Union College Annual* 55 (1984): 29.
10. Neusner, *The Mishnah*, 651. For a more detailed examination of this passage in the context of Mishnah tractate *Eduyyot* and of the Mishnah as a whole, see Leonard Gordon, "Who Were the Rabbis? Why Do We Care?" *Reconstructionist* (Summer 1991): 21–23; and "Law, Theology and Pluralism in Earliest Rabbinic Judaism," *Journal of the Society of Rabbis in Academia* (Summer 1991): 57–60.
11. David Kraemer, *The Mind of the Talmud: An Intellectual History of the Bavli* (New York: Oxford University Press, 1990), 189.
12. Menachem Kellner, *Maimonides on Judaism and the Jewish People* (Albany: State University of New York Press, 1991), 69, citing Maimonides' *Guide for the Perplexed*, III.27.
13. David Weiss Halivni, *Midrash, Mishnah and Gemara: The Jewish Predilection for Justified Law* (Cambridge: Harvard University Press, 1986), 105.
14. Rabbi Joseph B. Soloveitchik, *Halakhic Man* (Philadelphia: Jewish Publication Society, 1983), 23.
15. Neusner, *Judaism*, 270. See also Neusner's discussion of the Mishnah's division of women in *Judaism*.

16. Shaye J. D. Cohen, *From the Maccabees to the Mishnah* (Philadelphia: Westminster Press, 1987).
17. Barry Holtz, ed., *Back to the Sources* (New York: Summit Books, 1984).

Chapter 2

Rejection: A Rabbinic Response to Wife Beating

Naomi Graetz

Introduction

The attitudes of the Jewish tradition toward the plight of battered women have just begun to be explored. In the seventies, two master's theses were written, by Mimi Scarf and by Julie Spitzer. In the eighties, T. Drora Setel, Phyllis Trible and Renita Weems wrote articles exploring the potential for male violence in the context of patriarchal attitudes in the Bible. In 1988, Scarf published *Battered Jewish Wives: Case Studies in the Response to Rage.* Two Judaic scholars in Israel, Abraham Grossman and Mordechai Frishtik, have explored the issue, paying particular attention to the responsa literature of medieval rabbis. In December 1992, Howard Adelman delivered a relevant paper at the Association of Jewish Studies in Boston.[1] But there is a need for more comprehensive study of the Jewish tradition's attitudes toward battered women and the status of battered women in Jewish law.

I am writing a book that gauges the attitudes found in classic Jewish text concerning wife beating. Writing from a feminist perspective, I read and interpret with a hermeneutics of resistance to, and suspicion of, these texts. Writing from a feminist perspective implies that one must do more than analyze; that is, one must actively work to change the system being criticized. In this work I describe and analyze figurative and metaphoric battering in some biblical and midrashic texts. Metaphoric battering is revealed most dramatically in my exploration of the concept of the male God of Israel who is described as

13

an abusive husband or father in relationship to His female, childlike people.[2]

This chapter deals specifically with the problem of wife beating in the responsa literature starting from geonic times (600-1100 C.E.) and continuing through modern time. It focuses on those rabbis in the majority group that reject the legality of wife beating. My research leads me to describe two types of rejection. First there is uncategorical rejection; in this case, rabbis hold that battering is so terrible a thing that in itself it is considered to be sufficient grounds for divorce. Although I plan to focus on this uncategorical rejection, there is also qualified rejection. It too views battering as a terrible thing that shouldn't be done, but takes an evasive attitude. I will refer to unqualified rejection as rejection and qualified rejection as evasion. The stance of rejection first of all confronts the problem of wife beating; it neither denies the fact, accepts it nor apologizes for it. The stance of rejection clearly states that wife beating is wrong and demands some kind of redress or release of suffering for the victim. Unconditional rejection is the approach of those rabbis who face up to the fact that there is a problem and condemn it. Some of them relate creatively to *halakhah*, by use of *takkanot* or creative legislation to change what they perceive to be an immoral practice.[3]

The *Takkanah* of R. Perez b. Elijah of Corbeil

During the thirteenth century, when cases of maltreatment of wives by husbands came before the Ashkenazi rabbis, they were not taken very seriously. Consequently, during this time period, a *takkanah* was proposed that dealt with the subject of wife beating. Not much is known about the *takkanah* of R. Perez b. Elijah of Corbeil that deals with wife beating.[4] It is not known whether the rabbis to whom it was sent approved it. According to Finkelstein, who reproduces the *takkanah*, "It consists of two sections, the first providing that any man might be compelled to undertake by a *cherem* or oath, that he would not strike his wife again. He might be compelled to do so on the complaint of either the wife or one of her near relatives. . . The second part states that if the husband refused to undertake such a *cherem*, the Court should assign the wife alimony as if the husband were away."[5] It begins with a shrill cry of a sympathetic rabbi:

(1) The cry of the daughters of our people has been heard concerning the sons of Israel who raise their hands to strike

their wives. Yet who has given a husband the authority to beat his wife? Is he not rather forbidden to strike any person in Israel? Moreover R. I[saac] has written in a responsum that he has it on the authority of three great Sages, namely R. Samuel, R. Jacob Tam and R. I[saac], the sons of R. Meir, that one who beats his wife is in the same category as one who beats a stranger. Nevertheless *we have heard of cases where Jewish women complained regarding their treatment before the Communities and no action was taken on their behalf.*

We have therefore decreed that any Jew may be compelled on application of his wife or one of her near relatives to undertake by a *cherem* not to beat his wife in anger or cruelty so as to disgrace her, for that is against Jewish practice.

(2) If anyone will stubbornly refuse to obey our words, the Court of the place to which the wife or her relatives will bring complaint, shall assign her maintenance according to her station and according to the custom of the place where she dwells. *They shall fix her alimony as though her husband were away on a distant journey.*

If they, our masters, the great sages of the land agree to this ordinance it shall be established.

Perez b. Elijah

Although Finkelstein, who reproduced Perez's *takkanah* in *Jewish Self-Government in the Middle Ages,*[6] hypothesizes that the reason the *takkanah* never passed is because the "crime was one that rarely, if ever, gave trouble to Jews of the Middle Ages,"[7] one can read the text at its face value: if a rabbi needs to make such a *crie de coeur* it reflects a widespread problem. Apparently, at that time women complained to rabbis in their communities about husbands who beat their wives and received unsatisfactory answers. Either the rabbis ignored their complaints, not taking them seriously, or else they did not consider these complaints as grounds for compelling a divorce.

In the preamble of this *takkanah*, Perez makes clear whose side he is on. Just as no man may hit "any person in Israel," so a husband may not hit his wife who is also a person in Israel. Yet despite the injustice of this, no one is acting to make it clear that the husband does not "have the authority to beat his wife." Therefore to redress this social problem

Perez has proposed a *takkanah* that he hopes will have teeth. Perez is suggesting that the community intervene in the family's intimate affairs and makes it clear that wife beating is a communal not a private affair. The *takkanah* of R. Perez b. Elijah of Corbeil was unusually liberal. First of all it forces the guilty husband to take a solemn oath (*cherem*) that he won't beat her. An oath was not undertaken lightly, and in this case, the word of the wife or one of her near relatives is enough. It is not clear from this *takkanah* if the husband is allowed under any circumstance to beat her. The oath simply is that he will not beat her in anger, mean spiritedness, or contempt, because such a practice is not done in Israel.

If, however, the husband stubbornly refuses to repent and listen to the court, the woman will be allowed to live with relatives without being divorced and he will have to support her as if she were still at home. To allow the abused wife to get alimony from her husband's property and to live separately from him without divorce was a revolutionary measure. Presumably that is why the *takkanah* failed to gain the support of his colleagues.

Finkelstein attributes the *takkanah* to the high economic status enjoyed by the women of Ashkenaz.[8] In the fifteenth century, women's status was declining and, correspondingly, wife beating begins to be dealt with less stringently by the rabbis than it was when women's status was high.

The Responsa of the Tosafist School

Most of the responsa that unconditionally reject wife beating date from the twelfth and thirteenth centuries among the Jews of Ashkenaz in Germany and France. These responsa were produced by the tosafist school.[9] Among the tosafists we find clear-cut instances of an attitude that unqualifiedly rejects wife beating. Besides Perez of Corbeil, there are two other notable examples: Simcha B. Samuel of Speyer and Rabbi Meir of Rothenberg. These European rabbis of the French tosafist school were very severe with wife batterers. They prescribed severe punishment to the wife beater and refused to allow husbands to force their wives to do their required housework or to beat them for "their own good." These rabbis considered battering as grounds for compelling a man to give a *get*.[10]

R. Meir of Rothenberg

One of the great tosafists of this time is Rabbi Meir of Rothenberg (The *Maharam*). R. Meir wrote several responsa about wife-battering. For example:

> Q. A often strikes his wife. A's aunt, who lives at his home, is usually the cause of their arguments, and adds to the vexation and annoyance of his wife.
> A. A Jew must honor his wife more than he honors himself. If one strikes one's wife, one should be punished more severely than for striking another person. For one is enjoined to honor one's wife but is not enjoined to honor the other person. Therefore, A must force his aunt to leave his house, and must promise to treat his wife honorably. If he persists in striking her, he should be excommunicated, lashed, and suffer the severest punishments, even to the extent of amputating his arm. If his wife is willing to accept a divorce, he must divorce her and pay her the *ketubah*.[11]

In another responsum, R. Meir reiterates that "one deserves greater punishment for striking his wife than for striking another person, for he is enjoined to respect her." He then adds:

> Far be it from a Jew to do such a thing. Had a similar case come before us we should hasten to excommunicate him. Thus, R. Paltoi Gaon rules that a husband who constantly quarrels with his wife must remove the causes of such quarrels, if possible, or divorce her and pay her the *ketubah*; how much more must a husband be punished, who not only quarrels but actually beats his wife.[12]

R. Meir says that a woman who is hit by her husband is entitled to an immediate divorce and to receive the money owed her in her marriage settlement. This is significant because a woman who leaves the marriage does not always get her *ketubah* money. Although R. Meir's responsa leans on a much earlier one by Paltoi Gaon (842-857) to make this point, it opposes an earlier responsa by the ninth century Gaon of Sura, Sar Shalom. In this responsa, the Gaon of Sura distinguishes between an assault on a woman by her husband and an assault by a stranger. In the opinion of the Gaon of Sura, the husband's offense was less severe because the husband has authority over his wife.[13]

Rabbi Simcha of Speyer

It is not surprising that the next rabbi who unconditionally rejects wife beating is Simcha b. Samuel of Speyer. According to Agus, R. Simcha may have been R. Meir's teacher for a short time.[14] Simcha was a leading member of the Rabbinical Synod of the Rhine Provinces held in 1223. His responsa was reported by Mordecai b. Hillel, another tosafist, who was one of R. Meir's disciples.

In his responsa Simcha declared:

> It is an accepted view that we have to treat a man who beats his wife more severely than we treat a man who beats a fellowman, since he is not obligated to honor him, but is obligated to honor his wife more than himself. And a man who does this should be put under a ban and excommunicated and flogged and punished with various forms of torment; one could even cut off his hand if he is accustomed to it [wife beating]. And if he wants to divorce her let him divorce her and give her the ketubah payment.
>
> You should impose peace between them and if the husband does not fulfill his part in maintaining the peace, but rather continues to beat her and denigrate her, let him be excommunicated and let him be forced by Gentile authorities to give her a get . . .[15]

Why was R. Simcha so extreme? Whereas R. Meir merely stated that a man has to honor his wife, Simcha, using an aggadic approach, wrote that a man has to honor his wife more than himself and that is why his wife—and not his fellow man—should be his prior concern. Simcha stresses her status as wife rather than simply as another individual. His argument is that, like Eve, the mother of all living (eym kol chai), she was given for living, not for suffering. She trusts him and thus it is worse if he hits her than if he hits a stranger.

Simcha lists all the possible sanctions and if that does not work, he takes the daring leap and not only allows a compelled divorce, but allows one that is forced on the husband by gentile authorities. He is one of the few rabbis who authorized a compelled divorce as a sanction. It is difficult to know what accounted for his liberal attitudes. Perhaps it was simple moral outrage. Perhaps it had to do with a view of marriage that goes beyond the halachic injunction to "serve and honor and feed and maintain" his wife.[16] Unfortunately, his opinions were overturned by most rabbis in later generations.[17] The *Radbaz*, R. David b. Solomon Ibn Avi Zimra (1479-1573) was one of the first to question R. Simcha's responsa. He said that Simcha "exaggerated on the measures to be taken when writing that [the wife beater] should be forced by non-Jews (*akum*) to divorce his wife . . . because [if she remarries] this could result in the offspring [of the illegal marriage according to Radbaz] being declared illegitimate (*mamzer*)."[18]

The Twentieth Century

Now that we have a sense of the best responsa that can serve as models for today, I shall look at two modern responsa—that of R. Herzog and R. Waldenberg. R. Isaac Herzog (1888-1959) was the former Ashkenazi Chief Rabbi of Israel who previously served as a rabbi in Belfast and Dublin. In *Heichal Yitzchak*, which is the collection of his responsa, Herzog discusses the validity of a divorce decree obtained by coercion of the husband. Herzog leans heavily on the Rambam, who said that we assume a *get* is kosher because we assume that every Jewish man wants to observe the Torah and so even if a wrongfully constituted *beit din* forced the man to give a *get*, we uphold it. If it was done by a Jewish court, there is no problem. But what if it was done by non-Jews (*akum*)? Then we do have a problem (in contrast to being forced by the Jewish court), because we have seen that force by the civil court can lead to children being considered *mamzerim* or illegitimate issue.

Herzog introduces the Hatam Sofer's opposition to the Rambam. The Hatam Sofer, who died in 1839, was the spiritual father of modern Hungarian Jewry; his prestige was very great. He pointed out that Rambam was wrong to allow the divorce decree to stand if there were questions about its being coerced. Herzog, however, writes that when there is a doubt, the *halakhah* should follow the Rambam. Herzog's understanding of the real meaning of Rambam's answer is not that Jewish force is more valid, but that once anyone has forced a man to give a *get*, the *get* is final and binding.[19]

There was great willingness on the part of Herzog to take a more liberal stance recognizing a coerced *get*, after the fact, even if it were civil authorities who forced the battering husband (or any husband) to divorce his wife. Unfortunately, the Hatam Sofer's ruling is followed in today's Israeli rabbinical courts; most authorities continue to comply with the Hatam Sofer's, and not with the Rambam's, ruling against forced divorce.[20]

Another liberal reading is that of R. Eliezer Waldenburg. His responsa appears in the collection *Tzitz Eliezer*. The question facing him concerns a husband who battered his wife for years outside Israel. The husband was given five years imprisonment. The wife wanted a divorce because she feared for her life.

According to his responsa, there are two reasons why the husband should be forced to give her a *get*. The first has to do with the fact that he will be in prison for five years and will be unable to support her. Waldenberg quotes Hayim Palaggi (1788-1869) of Turkey, who says the main reason we force him is because he cannot provide for her. He also quotes Moses Trani, author of the Mabit and a sixteenth century rabbi in Safed who said it was permissible to force a husband who deserted his wife (by wandering from town to town) to divorce her because he was de facto not supporting her. The second reason is that we should not permit a permanent situation in which a woman has to live with a cruel husband. Here we are referred to early sources stating that a woman cannot be forced to live with a husband whose breath she cannot stand. And if this is so, surely she doesn't have to be forced to live with someone who beats her. He refers to Rabbi Simcha: if a man habitually beat his wife and abused her in front of others, we force him to give her the divorce bill and her *ketubah*, even if the civil court has to pressure him to do it in accordance with what the rabbinical court decrees. Thus we have two totally different reasons for compelling a divorce.

What would happen if we forced the husband's family to provide for her? Waldenburg argues that even if we can take it from the husband's estate to provide for her, the argument rests on her saying that she can't live in a situation in which she is at the mercy of getting beatings that have no end in sight.[21]

It appears that where there is a will there is a way. Waldenburg quotes Simcha and the Mabit, who are willing to interpret *halakhah* in a way that will help women. Had he wanted to, Waldenburg could have followed a different school that is less favorable to women. For instance, in the case of whether to believe a wife's testimony, there are many distinguished rabbis on both sides. The Rambam says that if the woman claims her in-laws are causing her pain, you must believe her and listen to her immediately. The *achronim*, later authorities from the sixteenth century on, say that it bears "looking into" and overrule the Rambam. This is not just an academic issue, however, because it means that a woman has to wait a long time while they check her testimony.[22]

Conclusion

We have examined some responsa of rabbis who view the plight of the battered wife as an inherent injustice and who have thus been willing to interpret the *halakhah* in order that she be able to get on with her life. We have seen examples of disagreement with those authorities who have opposed a forced divorce and authorities who allowed women to live separately from their husbands and yet be maintained by them. We have seen extreme suggestions of cutting off perpetrators' hands and excommunicating them. Yet despite these precedents, we know there are many women who are running the gauntlet of today's rabbinical court system unable to get a divorce from their husbands. Between eight to ten thousand women are left in limbo in the State of Israel.[23] This after all is the year of the *Aguna*, the anchored wife.

Why is it a problem? Part of the problem is that the rabbinical court system lacks teeth. If it tells the husband to do something—like buy an apartment so that his wife doesn't have to live with her in-laws—it cannot follow it up. Part of the problem has to do with the attitude of present-day Orthodox rabbis to women. I have alluded elsewhere[24] to the underlying misogyny in ancient rabbinic thought that must be faced. Whether or not it can be eradicated is another problem.

Finally, part of the problem is the unwillingness of rabbis to change the *halakhah* or interpret the *halakhah* in such a way that men's rights over their wives are diminished, so that a husband who habitually batters his wife would be forced to give his wife a divorce. This attitude is one of conditional rejection, or evasion of responsibility, because these rabbis say they recognize that the *halakhah* treats women unjustly. They claim they "cannot" by law force those unwilling to change the *halakhah*, Jewish law, in order to take away the unilateral power the husband has to initiate divorce proceedings. There has been some talk of using the *takkanah* procedure, but no action or use of this creative halachic tool has been forthcoming. Remember that where there is a will there is a way. It is up to us to pressure the rabbinate so that it will be forced to find the will.

NOTES

1. Mimi Scarf, "Marriages Made in Heaven?" in *On Being a Jewish Feminist: A Reader*, Susannah Heschel, ed. (New York: Schocken, 1983); Mimi Scarf, *Battered Jewish Wives* (Lewiston, Queenston: Edwin Mellen, 1988) ; T. Drora Setel, "Prophets and Pornography: Female Sexual Imagery in Hosea," in *Feminist Interpretations of the Bible*, Letty Russell, ed. (Philadelphia: Westminster, 1985); Julie Spitzer, *Spousal Abuse in*

Rabbinic and Contemporary Judaism (New York: National Federation of Temple Sisterhoods, 1985, 1991); Phyllis Trible, Texts of Terror (Philadelphia: Fortress Press, 1984); Renita J. Weems, "Gomer: Victim of Violence or Victim of Metaphor?" Semeia 47 (1989): 87-104; Howard Adelman, "Wife Beating in Jewish History," in Association for Jewish Studies: Twenty-Fourth Annual Conference (Boston, 1992); Mordechai Frishtik, "Physical and Sexual Violence by Husbands as a Reason for Imposing a Divorce in Jewish Law, "Jewish Law Annual 9 (1992): 145-69; Avraham Grossman, "Medieval Rabbinic Views on Wife Beating, 800-1300," Jewish History 5 (1991): 53-62.

2. I have written about this topic in "The Haftorah Tradition and the Metaphoric Battering of Hosea's Wife," Conservative Judaism 45, no. 1 (Fall 1992): 29-42. See also Benjamin Scolnic, "Bible-Battering," in the same issue (43-52); and David Blumenthal "Who Is Battering Whom?" Conservative Judaism 45, no. 3 (Spring 1993): 72-89, which are reactions to my article.

3. A takkanah is a halachic amendment that changes an existing law. It usually redresses an existing social problem whose source is in the law as practiced. Takkanot became necessary very early in Jewish history. One of the earliest is the prosbul of Hillel the elder, which has to do with cancellation of debts in the Sabbatical year. One of the better-known examples of a takkanah dealing with women's issues is that of R. Gershom (960-1028), which banned polygyny (having multiple wives) for those who lived in Christian Europe. A takkanah overrides and abrogates accepted halachic rules that precede it. Thus it is a radical revision of an existing practice.

4. According to Louis Finkelstein, Jewish Self Government in the Middle Ages (New York: Jewish Theological Seminary, 1924), the text of this proposed takkanah was taken by Guedemann from a Halberstam manuscript.

5. Ibid., chap. 6, 216.

6. Finkelstein's translation: Ibid., 217.

7. Finkelstein Ibid., 70-71 writes that "there may have been some temporary cause that moved R. Perez to urge the adoption of the Takkanah. . . . We never hear of the Takkanah elsewhere, and it probably failed to gain the support of R. Perez's colleagues because the rarity of the offense made the revolutionary measure seem unnecessary."

8. Some examples of this higher status are women being admitted as witnesses, being counted as members of the quorum to recite the Grace, and being permitted to be called up to the Torah (Ibid., 378-79).

9. According to Marcus, their "methods developed in rabbinic circles in Germany and northern France as an extension of the ancient Talmud's own method of questions and answers" [in Ivan Marcus, "Jewish Learning in the Middle Ages," Melton Journal (Autumn 1992): 24.] The tosafists are commentators on the Talmud named after the additions (or tosafot in Hebrew) they wrote on the Talmud.

10. Grossman, "Medieval Rabbinic Views," 121.

11. Eben HaEzer, no. 297, as translated by Irving Agus, Rabbi Meir of Rothenburg, Vol. 1 (Philadelphia: Jewish Publication Society, 1947): 326.

12. No. 298 as cited in Ibid., 326-27.

13. Otzar Geonim, Baba Kamma, no. 198, 62 as cited by Samuel Morrell, "An Equal or a Ward: How Independent Is a Married Woman According to Rabbinic Law?" Jewish Social Studies 44 (1982): 98.

14. Agus, Rabbi Meir, footnote 34 at 10.

15. As cited and translated by R. Biale, 94. Joseph Karo, *Bet Yosef*, Even Ha-Ezer 154: 15. She erroneously identifies R. Simhah as being Rabbenu Simhah ben Shmuel of Vitri (author of the *Vitri Mahzor*).

16. See the *Ketubah*, the Jewish marriage contract.

17. Much of what we know about these responsa that reject wife beating unconditionally come from Binyamin Ze'ev b. Mattathias of Arta, whose views were also quite liberal. Binyamin Ze'ev, who lived in the first half of the sixteenth century in Greece and Turkey wrote a long review of the literature known to him. He supports his very liberal point of view by referring extensively to Rabbi Simcha. He also was in favor of the *cherem* suggested by Perez and quotes from his proposed *takkanah*. He considers the story of the Concubine of Gibeah and the story of Hagar as cases of battered women. His views are considered to be controversial and certainly unusual for the sixteenth century. Most rabbis base themselves on the Mishnah,which says that when a woman knows that something is wrong with her husband, prior to her marriage, she is more or less stuck in the situation. Binyamin Ze'ev, however, writes: "If we cannot find another solution for the situation, we compel him to divorce her and give her the *ketubah* payment even if she had accepted the situation knowingly." (Responsa no. 88).

18. *Responsa of Radbaz*, part 4, 157, the Bar Ilan Responsa Project.

19. *Heichal Yitzchak*, Eben HaEzer, 1, 3.

20. All is not black, for Shaar Yashuv Cohen, a candidate for the Chief Rabbinate of Israel, in a recent ruling, followed Herzog in order to force a husband to divorce the wife he habitually battered. Note, however, that Cohen lost the race for the Chief Rabbinate to Rabbi Lau, who does not normally rule in favor of women.

21. Free translation of Eliezer Waldenburg, *Responsa of Ztitz Eliezer*, 2nd ed. (Jerusalem, 1985): Part 6, 42, chaps 3, 7.

22. See *Piskei din rabaniyim*, part 1, 201, 1953 as it appears in the Bar Ilan Responsa Project for the entire discussion.

23. Daniela Valensi, founder of the Israel-based Organization for Agunot and   Wives of Get-Refusers, estimates that these are the numbers. *The Jerusalem Post Magazine* (12 March 1993): 8.

24. Naomi Graetz, "Miriam: Guilty or Not Guilty?" *Judaism* 40 (Spring 1991): 184-92.

Chapter 3

An Analysis of Rabbinic Hermeneutics: B. T. Kiddushin 34a

Rochelle L. Millen

Introduction

The feminist struggle within Judaism over the last decades has moved from the battle for access to public ritual and leadership roles,[1] to analyses of primary documents,[2] to an examination of the broad theoretical and theological constructs affecting both feminist theory and Judaism.[3] In the development of Jewish feminism, each aspect has been present simultaneously, yet one in particular has tended to dominate at specific stages.

This chapter proposes to explore an overlapping between the latter two categories. I am interested in unraveling some basic presuppositions of rabbinic hermeneutics using as a paradigmatic text a Talmudic passage that relates to the status of women in *halakhah*. An analysis of Talmudic logic and rabbinic method in regard to crucial feminist issues will at the same time contribute toward a reconstruction of Jewish theology that incorporates full recognition of female autonomy.

The well-known exemption of women from time-specified *mitzvoth* is presented and analyzed the text of B. T. Kiddushin 34a. Contemporary discussion of this text has focused on whether this is a sociological or theological issue. Cynthia Ozick proclaimed the dispute over the status of women in Judaism—and hence her interpretation of this determinative text—to be sociological.[4] And whereas Judith

Plaskow has cogently argued for theology as the point of definition,[5] Joel Roth concurs with Ozick.[6]

The dispute engendered in the literature by the sociological-theological debate leads us to focus once again upon the textual source of the conflict, B. T. Kiddushin 34a. Can we glean insight from this text, which has been dissected, analyzed, pulled apart, inveighed against, and even acclaimed by so many in the last decades?

The Mishnah proclaims the general principle that women are exempt from time-specified *mitzvoth*. The *halakhic* literature in the centuries following the editing of the Babylonian Talmud time and again makes reference[7] to what women actually did. Religious practices of women as a group—the Mishnah designates women as a group—become a significant factor in the arguments both for and against female participation in various aspects of Jewish observance. That the structure of the *halakhic* argumentation assumes women as Other is obvious; what is perhaps less clear is that legal discussion is guided not only by theoretical analysis based on rabbinic hermeneutics, but also by what one might call "the reality factor." Do women say *birkhat hagomel*, or *kaddish*, or *hallel*, or hear the *shofar*? The things people do create a social reality the that legal experts cannot ignore. This seems to be an unarticulated assumption both of the text itself and of its subsequent interpretations over the centuries. It is time to revisit Kiddushin 34a and examine both its premises and implications from the perspective of 1993.

The principle of women's exemption from time-specified *mitzvoth*, perhaps more than any other, has over the centuries determined the status of women in *halakhah* and the sociocultural locus of women in Jewish society. It is this principle that establishes and/or confirms women as outside the public domain and on the periphery of the religious, intellectual, and ritualistic aspects governing that domain. This chapter will analyze the structure of the proof for this rule in light of several underlying questions: is the proof, which is constructed according to the hermeneutical rules of Talmudic derivation, compelling; does it have weaknesses and fallacies? It obviously was sufficient to establish a fundamental and far-reaching category in mishnaic law. Was it sufficient on logical-legal grounds, on a sociocultural basis, or a combination, in some proportion, of both?

Analysis of the Proof

The Mishnah states: Women are exempt from all positive *mitzvoth* that are time-specified. The Baraitha[8] asks; what are some examples of this category? And it responds: *Succah, lulav, shofar, tzitzit,* and *Tefillin.*[9] And, the Baraitha continues: where are examples of positive *mitzvoth* that are not time specified? And it responds: *Mezzuzah, maakah, aveidah,* and *sheluakh hakan.*[10] None of these commandments is performed at a particular time.

The Gemara begins by questioning the Mishnah's ruling about women. Is it an unqualified and general rule, the text inquires, that women are exempt from all positive time-bound *mitzvoth*? It does not seem so, because, on the one hand, the *mitzvoth* of matzah, rejoicing on the festivals and assembly[11] are positive time-specified *mitzvoth* and women are obligated to perform them. On the other hand, the *mitzvoth* of *limud Torah, peru v'revuh,* and *pidyon haben*[12] are not time-specific bound *mitzvoth*, yet women are exempt from them. The question of the Gemara here can be seen from two perspectives. First, it is clearly inquiring as to the nature of the mishnaic formulation: what is this rule and how does it work in concrete instances? But second, the concrete examples, which form empirical evidence in this analysis, seem to be derived not from a legal principle but rather from a description of that which women in fact did. Perhaps the text in some way is out to formulate a principle that would explain what women actually did rather than establish a new a priori rule.

R. Yochanan responds in the Gemara to the question of whether or not the ruling of the Mishnah is absolute. It is not, proclaims R. Yochanan, because *ayn lemadim min haclalot*; that is, we cannot extrapolate categorical principles from general rules, because these rules were often taught without including a list of their exceptions. In addition, R. Yochanan continues, even in instances where specific exceptions are enumerated, it cannot be assumed that the list of exceptions is complete; the list may — and in fact often is — only partial. R. Yochanan is thus putting forth the following interpretation: the principle regarding women and time-specific *mitzvoth* as expounded in the Mishnah is a general principle, but not a categorical, universal or absolute principle. This is certainly logical; that exceptions to general legal principles exist in general cases is common sense. However, even when exceptions are then noted,[13] no enumeration of exceptions is to be regarded as exhaustive and complete. The general rule, then, is open-ended with regard to exceptions. It applies to all women as a class, regardless of individual circumstance, yet legal authorities viewed the rule as observed more in the breach than in its fulfillment. The exemption applies categorically to its subject (i.e., all women) but not to its object, (i.e., all positive time-bound *mitzvoth*).

The Gemara validates R. Yochanan's analysis by offering one proof taken from the Mishnah Eruvin 26b. Here the Mishnah lists two foods unacceptable for use in an *eruv* or *shituf,*[14] probably, as noted by Rashi, because they are not nourishing. Other foods (the examples given are mushrooms and truffles) are also disqualified for use in an *eruv*, yet are not included in the Mishnah's list. This would confirm R. Yochanan's claim that general rules, often given without a complete list—or any list—of exceptions, cannot be regarded as categorical, that is, true in all (other) cases. The general principle, while affecting the relation of all women to *mitzvoth*, is not inclusive after all. Having thus established the legitimacy of women's exemption from time-specified *mitzvoth* as a general although not unqualified rule, the Gemara then proceeds to inquire as to its source. Although this principle does not apply in many cases, in what way can its validity be proved in those instances when it does apply? This question in the text assumes familiarity with that which women do and intends, so it seems, to justify the status quo. How is this rule derived? The Gemara asserts its source is from the *mitzvah* of *tefillin* and uses the hermeneutic rule of *binyan av,*[15] or inference from a particular to a universal; in the same way as women are exempt from performing the *mitzvah* of *tefillin*, which is time-specific, are women similarly not obligated to observe any positive, time-specific *mitzvoth*?

But this means the principle, formulated through a *binyan av*, is based on a known entity, that is, the exemption of women from *tefillin*. Now the source of the exemption from *tefillin* must be established. To do this the Gemara uses a *hekesh*, or analogy.[16] Women's exemption from *tefillin* is derived from the *mitzvah* of *limud Torah* or Torah study: just as women are exempt from the latter, are we exempt from the former, the two being linked by a type of analogy or *hekesh* called *semukhin*, or juxtaposition?[17] This process makes the exemption from *limud Torah* the foundation on which the argument is being constructed. Yet women's exemption from Torah study is based on a seemingly tenuous proof. *Limud Torah* is a constant obligation,[18] women being excluded because *levanekha* (to your "sons" or "children") in the verse "And you shall teach them [the laws of the Torah] *levanekha*"[19] is understood in its male, rather than generic meaning. As Rashi says, "to our sons [not children], to the exclusion of your daughters."[20] We shall return to this grammatical twist.

The text continues: if a *hekesh* is made between *tefillin* and *limud Torah*, perhaps one can legitimately make a *hekesh* between *tefillin* and *mezzuzah*.[21] Such an analogy would lead to the opposite conclusion, that because women are obligated in *mezzuzah*,[22] we are similarly obligated in *tefillin*. However, the Gemara supports the first analogy on the grounds that it is made twice in the *Shema*[23] whereas the latter appears only once. Thus *tefillin* is more strongly linked to Torah study.

The Gemara continues to analyze all logical possibilities and objections to its original inference between *limud Torah* and *tefillin*, which was used to validate the claim of the Mishnah and establish the general rules of women's exemption. What if, it suggests, we make a *hekesh* between *mezzuzah* and Torah study? In that case women would be exempt from the former as they are in the latter.[24] This suggestion brings a sharp response of rejection. Because length of days is the express reward for fulfilling the *mitzvah* of *mezzuzah*,[25] it cannot be claimed that women need the possibility of that recompense any less than men. Therefore the analogy of *mezzuzah* to Torah study cannot hold, for women would thus be exempt from a life-prolonging commandment.

At this point in the argument, the Gemara appears to let stand the analogy between *tefillin* and Torah study, bringing no more challenges to the derivation of the rule of female exemption from positive time-bound *mitzvoth*. The discussion now shifts to the degree of inclusion of the rule: all positive time-specified *mitzvoth*? Some? Which ones? It is important to note at this juncture that the Gemara rests its case on a three-pronged argument: (1) Because all women are exempt from *tefillin*, we are therefore exempt from positive time-specific commandments (inference, or *binyan av*); (2) The exemption from *tefillin* is derived from an analogy with Torah study (analogy or *hekesh*); And (3) the exemption from Torah study is based on the interpretation of *ben* as "son" rather than "child."

The structure of this argument is not problem free. Its central difficulty lies in the question as to whether or not *tefillin* is a time-bound *mitzvah*. That this is an issue,[26] even though the conclusion is that *tefillin* is time-specific, considerably weakens the proof. For the original inference is derived from a *mitzvah*, the status of which itself is subject to dispute. And the analogy used to buttress the exemption from *tefillin* (i.e., the *hekesh* with *limud Torah*) is itself based on an exegetical reading of *ben* that may be open to question. The argument as formulated thus far insists that women have the opportunity to merit length of days from performance of the *mitzvah* of *mezzuzah*, but those days will not involve the obligations of study of Torah or putting on *tefillin*.[27]

Challenge to the Mishnah's Ruling: "All . . ."

The Gemara now proceeds to challenge the Mishnah's rule that women are exempt from "all" time-specific positive commandments. Here are its arguments: Why does the Mishnah claim that women are exempt from *Succah* because it is a positive time-specific *mitzvah*? In fact, according to Baraitha in *Succah* 28a, women are exempt because in the determinative verse[28] those who are required to sit in *succah* are designated "*Kol haezrah*," "all the citizens," or "all the native born." The definite article before "*ezrah*" is said to specifically exclude women. That is, were the verse to have read "*ezrah*," men and women would be equally obligated in *Succah*. The addition of the definite article, however, designates the obligation as incumbent only on the more "prominent" group, that is, the men.[29] If not for this exclusionary word, women would be obligated in *Succah*. Abaye and Rava answer this objection, showing that *haezrah* is needed to counter two other interpretations that would otherwise require women to perform the mitzvah of *succah* even though it is time-specific.

Women would be obligated in the *mitzvah* of *reiyah* or *aliyat haregel*, although time-bound, were it not for the word *zehurkha* ("your males") in the verse from Deuteronomy 16:16-17: "Three times a year all your males shall appear before the Lord your God in the place He shall choose, on the festival of Matzot, on the festival of Shavuot and on the festival of Succoth." Thus the Gemara once again challenges the Mishnah. And once again it counters the objection by showing that the word *zehurkha* is indeed needed to preclude the possibility of mistakenly including women based on a comparison of similar expressions[30] between the *mitzvoth* of *hakhel* and *reiyah*.

Having shown that the principle of the Mishnah can meet these specific challenges, the Gemara returns to the initial question of the derivation of the general exemption from the *mitzvah* of *tefillin*. Rather than maintaining this derivation, perhaps the exemption should be learned through the rule of *binyan av* from the mitzvah of *simcha*, or rejoicing, that in fact women are obligated to perform all positive time-specific *mitzvoth*. If both derivations are equally valid, why prefer exemption over obligation? Abaye asserts that in fact a woman does not have an obligation to rejoice,[31] although Rashi clearly understands an obligation developing from Deuteronomy 16:14. Perhaps then the general exemption should be derived from *hakhel* or assembly? Again the Gemara shows this cannot be done because of the rule that any two biblical passages that come as one to teach the same law do not teach that law in other contexts.[32] In other words, the more one has to state a rule the less universal it is; the very repetition indicates that it needs to be specified and is therefore not a general rule.

The text is thus examining every possible objection to the original derivation of the rule of exemption as formulated in the Mishnah. The discussion reaches an impasse when (on page 35b,) the Gemara states that refutation works according to one who accepts the opinion that two biblical passages that come as one do not teach their common law in other contexts. But what is the conclusion according to those who claim two such passages do teach their common law in new circumstances? Perhaps it may be derived from the *mitzvoth* of Torah study and *pidyon haben* that women are exempt from all positive *mitzvoth*, even those that are not time-specific?

At this point the Gemara finds a new source for (both) the exemption of women from positive time-specific *mitzvoth* and our obligation in those that are not time-bound. It is extraordinary that close examination of the text shows four derivations for the exemption of women from positive time-specific *mitzvoth*. Four are necessary because no one is sufficient to establish the principle. The first derivation is *binyan av* from *tefillin*. This is the main argument that is analyzed. As we have seen, it runs into some difficulties and leads to seemingly undesirable conclusions. Those who accept this derivation also accept the rule that if two passages come to teach one law, that one law cannot be generalized into other contexts. But what if one understands the hermeneutical rule to mean that in the case of two such passages one can apply their common teaching in new circumstances? The Gemara responds to potential weaknesses in this form of its hermeneutical armor by assuming a new position. This derivation is espoused by R. Acha bar Yaacov.

R. Acha's derivation, while also concerning *tefillin*, is quite different methodologically from *binyan av*. He quotes Exodus 13:9: "And it shall be a sign for you on your arm and a memorial remembrance between your eyes, so that the instruction of God (*Torat Hashem*) may be in your mouth." R. Acha uses an analogy, a *hekesh*, found in this verse. The entire *Torah*, he claims, is analogous to the *mitzvah* of *tefillin*. Then he continues with a second *hekesh*, or analogy. Even as *tefillin* is a positive time-bound commandment from which women are exempt,[33] so are women exempt from all positive time-specific *mitzvoth*. In addition, the fact that women are so exempted implies that we are otherwise generally obligated in positive *mitzvoth* that are not time-bound.[34] Thus, R. Acha's position works for those who accept that two passages teaching a common law can be applied in new contexts and who want to affirm women's exemptions from positive time-specific *mitzvoth* (and want to do so through the *mitzvah* of *tefillin*).

Those espousing the third position posit that *tefillin* is not a positive time-specific *mitzvah*. In this instance the general exemption of women from obligation in *mitzvoth* in that category is accomplished through a *binyan av* with *reiyah*.

According to the fourth group, the *Torah* explicitly obligates women in *matzah*; and *hakhel* implies that we are exempt from other commandments in that general category that are positive time-specific *mitzvoth*. Tosafot formulates this position based (as is the first derivation), on *ein melamdin*—that is, that one does not apply in a wider context that which two biblical passage come to teach. Therefore, Tosafot asserts,[35] the statements of specific obligations become exclusionary.

There are three technical matters that warrant discussion. First, the *binyan av* from *tefillin*—upon which the first position is based, and which is discussed most prominently in the Gemara—is different from its usual form. Generally, in a *binyan av*, the fundamental assumption or postulate is itself present in the verse from which the *binyan av* is constructed. A typical example would be *"ez ben shenata"* from Numbers 46:27, or *"melekhet okhal nefesh"* from Exodus 12:15. Here, however, the *binyan av* is a two-step process. First, *tefillin* acquires its status in the inference through a *hekesh*, or analogy with *limud Torah*.

Second, in the third position discussed earlier, *tefillin* is not a positive time-specific *mitzvah* and women would therefore be obligated in *tefillin*. R. Meir and R. Yehudah take this position. But in this argument, why isn't the *hekesh* of *limud Torah* to *tefillin* used to exempt women from *tefillin*; that is, whereas *limud Torah* is not time-specific and women are exempt, in this argument *tefillin* is not time-bound and women would also be exempt. The same hermeneutical rule used in the first position, which forms the basic analysis of the exemption principle, could be used here to exempt women from *tefillin* even though it is not regarded as time-bound. This would only apply to *tefillin*, found in the same verse as *limud Torah*, and would not be construed as a general rule.

Why wasn't this done? As we have seen, the *hekesh* to exempt women is used only in the argument that begins with the premise that women are generally exempt from time-specific *mitzvoth*, but not in the position with the premise that women are obligated. The hermeneutical rules, in my view, do not seem to have been applied consistently in each of these cases. Thus the following conclusion may be drawn: Apparently, the use of the rules of hermeneutics was determined by the underlying assumptions, previously accepted premises, and empirical sociological facts in the contexts of which the arguments themselves were constructed. And, as a corollary, refraining from the use of the *hekesh* in this case affirmed the real possibility of women's obligation in *tefillin*.

A third technical matter involves Rashi's insistence that a *binyan av* is the same as a *meh matzinu*; others make a distinction.[36]

That four different derivations are required to maintain the universality of the exemption principle, even with its many and diverse exceptions, indicates the strength of unarticulated assumptions within the hermeneutical scheme the Gemara presents. Rabbi Yochanan responded that "we cannot learn from general principles, even where exceptions are stated," which allows the exemption principle to stand valid, its integrity not threatened by the many exceptions made on an ad hoc basis.

Why was it so important to maintain this principle when the issue could have come to very different conclusions? What lies behind it? Is the text based on accepted differences between male and female legal status, spiritual-religious status, or social and cultural roles? The categories of exceptions to the general exemption rule imply that, historically, this principle probably did not determine the religious practices of women. It seems unlikely—and this is of course speculation—that this was an a priori rule governing female behavior. Rather, it is more feasible to hypothesize a gradual development within the culture as to what women did and did not do.[37] The existence of the principle in the Mishnah may in fact be a legal corroboration of the cultural status quo. Certainly within a patriarchal society the needs of both individual and community were thus met. It is therefore understandable that many exceptions to the general principle existed, for the texts were perhaps written into the law books of an accepted social reality. The far-reaching power of the text, as we all know, is not to be underestimated. If this hypothesis is accurate, the descriptive, one might say, became the prescriptive.

Why then are the arguments in the text, despite demonstrated weaknesses, accepted as convincing? They confirmed the sociocultural reality of the time. Deeply embedded notions of tradition and authority, of woman as Other and man as normative, of social hierarchy, lie beneath the surface of B. T. Kiddushin 34a. The tradition made assumptions in which the exemption from positive time-specific *mitzvoth* could be based primarily on a connection between *tefillin* and *limud Torah* and be understood to make sense. That women of the time were infrequently, if at all, involved in either made it unlikely that applying the rules of hermeneutics to those *mitzvoth* would result in their entry into the domain of public religious life. The circumscribing and restricting of women to the private realm—except when deemed otherwise by convenient exceptions—remained the central barrier within *halakhah* to full autonomy for women.

However, as seen by revisiting this fundamental text, the rules of rabbinic derivation are not hard and fast. Change is an ongoing process, spurred by sociological and cultural circumstances. This text, despite its obvious aim of upholding the Mishnah at all costs, nevertheless provides a general framework that allowed (and still allows) for innovation. The very category of women's exemption can be overcome and transformed by the sociological fact of women's practice. The move from optional to obligatory status of *tekiat shofar* for women is perhaps the best-known example of this strategy; another is the counting of the *omer*. We might also inquire why the *mitzvoth* of Purim and Chanukah are made obligatory, so they thus become exemptions to the so-called general rule? The standard reasons given are written as if to accord to the rabbis the authority of decision: *"hein hayu beoto haneis,"* that is, the national character of these festivals. An additional reason given is the role played by women.

But is it not entirely possible that women simply refused to be excluded and insisted on participation? In other words, perhaps women created a sociological reality the male lawmakers could not ignore. The transformation of option, or *reshut,* with all its psychological liabilities to obligation, or *chiyuv*, was accomplished primarily through the alteration of actual behavior. In that way, observance moved from a second-class level to the very establishment of *halakhic* norms.

Women, then, have come to do more and more in terms of the public domain of religious ritual. At the same time, we have become much more knowledgeable about and educated in the tradition. In order to effect change, we must know and understand; we can only bring a new perspective if we have an excellent grasp of the old. Even the aspects of change that have come and will come about through theological formulation will continue to derive from a transformed sociological reality to which all of us contribute. Cynthia Ozick, I believe, was correct that the problem is sociological. Yet Judith Plaskow unveils another facet of the complex truths of religious traditions: sociology that is objectified as absolute truth becomes theological. The question, then, is also theological.

NOTES

1. See Elizabeth Koltun, ed., *The Jewish Woman: New Perspectives* (New York: Schocken, 1976), and Susannah Heschel, ed., *On Being a Jewish Feminist: A Reader* (New York: Schocken, 1983).
2. For example, Judith Romney Wegner, *Chattel or Person: The Status of Women in the Mishnah* (New York: Oxford University Press, 1988). From a completely different perspective, see the more recent volumes by Tikva Frymer-Kensy, *In the Wake of the Goddess: Women, Culture and the Biblical Transformation of Pagan Myth* (New York: Fawcett Columbine, 1992); and Ilana Pardes, *Countertraditions in the Bible: A Feminist Approach* (Cambridge: Harvard University Press, 1993).
3. See Judith Plaskow, *Standing Again at Sinai: Judaism from a Feminist Perspective* (New York: Harper & Row, 1990).
4. Cynthia Ozick, "Notes Toward Finding the Right Question," originally published in *Forum*. Reprinted in *On Being Jewish Feminist: A Reader*, ed. Susannah Heschel, (New York: Schocken, 1983), 120-52.
5. Judith Plaskow, *Standing Again at Sinai*, op. cit. esp. 1-25, 32-38, 51, 95-107.
6. Joel Roth, "On the Ordination of Women as Rabbis," in *The Ordination of Women as Rabbis: Studies and Responsa*, ed. Simon Greenberg (New York: Jewish Theological Seminary of America, 1988), 127-87. See esp. section 4: Roth's discussion, while veering toward and to an extent supporting a sociological analysis of the issues, is nonetheless problematic. For its result would be to create a three-tiered system within Judaism: all men are obligated in ϕ; women who have so chosen are obligated in ϕ; women who have so decided are not obligated in ϕ. The public rights of those in this third category are thereby diminished.
7. For example, the discussion in *Tosafot* on B. T. Berahot 45b and Aruhin 3a.
8. Baraitha is Aramaic for the Hebrew *hizonah* ("outside") and refers to every *halakhah*, *halakhic Midrash* and tradition not included in the Mishnah edited by Judah ha-Nasi. The *Babylonian* Talmud employs the term baraitha mainly to delineate a view opposed to that of the *Mishnah*. See *Encyclopaedia Judaica*, Vol. 4, 1989, 195.
9. Sitting in the *succah* during *Succoth*; the taking (or waving) of the *lulav* together also on *Succoth* with the *etrog, hadasim* and the sounding or hearing of the requisite number of sounds from the *shofar* on Rosh Hashanah; the wearing of a fringed garment; the wearing of phylacteries during morning prayer. Each of these *mitzvoth* is preceded by a *birkhat hamitzvah*, emphasizing the obligatory nature of each specific act. For a discussion of how and why women can and according to some cannot, make a *birkhat hamitzvah* on optional (i.e., non-obligatory) *mitzvoth*, see the summary in Elikim

Ellenson, *Haishah Vehamitzvoth* (Hebrew) (Jerusalem: Torah Education Dept. of the WZO, 1989), chap. 2-3. Also see Rachel Biale, *Women and Jewish Law* (New York: Schocken, 1984), Chap. 1.

10 . The small encased scroll put at the doorposts of one's home; protective fence required on a flat roof; return of lost articles; the obligation to send away the mother bird when taking the eggs.

11 . The obligation to eat unleavened bread at the Passover seder; the requirement to rejoice on the three main festivals; the gathering of all the congregation, once every seven years, to hear the reading of the Torah.

12 . The study of Torah; the obligation to propagate; the redemption of the first-born male child.

13 . An *eruv* cannot be made with water or salt. See B. T. Kiddushin 34a.

14 . *Eruv* is a boundary that creates a public domain in which carrying is permitted on the Sabbath; it is created through shared foodstuffs (*eruv* meaning to combine). *Shituf* is a partnership.

15 . *Binyan av*, one of the Thirteen Rules (of hermeneutics) of R. Ishmael, is an inference from a single verse or from two verses.

16 . *Hekesh*, or analogy, is also one of these hermeneutic principles.

17 . *Semukhin* refers to the juxtaposition of two laws in adjacent verses. For a good general discussion (in English) of the Thirteen Rules of R. Ishmael, see *Encyclopedia Judaica*, Vol. 8, 366-71.

18 . Based on Joshua 1:8: "This book of the Torah shall not depart from your mouth, but you should contemplate it day and night."

19 . Deuteronomy 6:5-9. Here too the analogy is based on verses 7 and 8.

20 . The unstated principle in Rashi's comment seems to be: *ben* means male progeny except when *bat* (daughter) is mentioned. Considering the difficulty in ascertaining a consistent principle that a priori would determine when the use of *ben* is generic and inclusive or male and exclusive, one might speculate that Rashi's interpretation is ex post facto: because women don't study Torah, *ben* in this verse must refer only to males. The logical deduction would thus be based on sociological fact. See Kiddushin 29A, 31A. The general comment in the *Encyclopaedia* Talmud*it* (Hebrew) is: "*Ben*" always means 'male' or 'son' except in a place where there is a special derivation to include 'daughters'" (Vol. 3, 347-348).

21 . Thereby linking verses 8 and 9 rather than 7 and 8.

22 . Women are obligated in *mezzuzah* because the obligation is on one's residence and is thus not time specific. However, *halakhah* requires *mezzuzoth* to be affixed within thirty days. Is this not even more of a limit than *limud Torah*? Yet women are exempt from the latter and obligated in the former.

23 . Deuteronomy 6:7-8 and Deuteronomy 11:18-19.

24 . Note that in this discussion the exclusion of women from Torah study is neither scrutinized nor questioned.

25 . Deuteronomy 11:20-21. "And thou shalt write them upon the doorposts of thine house and thy gates. That your days may increase and the days of your children. . . ."

26 . It is discussed in Menahot 36b. See Tosafot on Kiddushin 34a.

27 . Note that both *mitzvoth* for women remain optional; there is exclusion from obligation, not prohibition of performance. Here one encounters once again the sociological reality that not having to do X leads to the attitude of why bother to do X?

28 . Leviticus 23:42.

29 . The men of course were editing the Mishnah and writing the commentaries, thus making their designation as "prominent" seem to fit. Also, the implication clearly may have been "prominent in the public domain" or "prominent in the culture." See essays by Orther and Rosaldo in M. Z. Rosaldo and L. Lamphere, eds., *Woman, Culture and Society* (Stanford, CA: Stanford University Press, 1974) , and Elizabeth Janeway, *Man's World Woman's Place: A Study in Social Mythology* (New York: Delta, 1974). Also see Moshe Z. Sokol, ed., *Rabbinic Authority and Personal Autonomy* (Northvale, NJ: Jason Aronson, 1992), esp. Chaps. 4- 6.

30 . *Gezerah shavah*, another of the Thirteen Principles (of hermeneutics) of R. Ishmael.

31 . See, however, Saul Berman, "The Status of Women in *Halakhic* Judaism," *Tradition*, 14, No. 2 (Fall 1973): n. 12. Cf. B. T. Pesachin, 109a.

32 . "*Shnei ketuvim habaim Ke-ehad ayn melamdim.*"

33 . The original analogy with Torah study is maintained.

34 . That is without a specific inclusionary verse.

35 . T. B. Kiddushin 35a, discussion of Tosafot beginning with *elah.*

36 . See Rashi on B. T. Shabbat 26b and Baba Kama 73b; *Sefer Hakritut*, Bayit 3 and the short reference in *Encyclopedia Talmudit* (Hebrew), Vol. 4, 2.

37 . For an interesting, if bizarre, parallel in contemporary historical research, see Christopher R. Browning, *The Path to Genocide: Essays on Launching the Final Solution* (Cambridge: Cambridge University Press, 1992), esp. chap. 5. See also Talya Fishman, "A Kabbalistic Perspective on Gender-Specific Commandments: On the Interplay of Symbols and Society," *AJS Review*, 17, No. 2 (Fall, 1992), 199-245. Fishman concludes, "The treatises' introduction of kabbalistic explanations into the 'universal solvent' of halakhic discourse brought new images into mainstream Jewish culture. . . . Through their very linkage to the realm of halakhah, kabbalistic works like *Sefer Hakanah* may well have influenced everyday notions about women's ineffectiveness, or even destructiveness, in aspects of Jewish ritual life."

Chapter 4

Reconfiguring Home: Jewish Feminist Identity/ies

Laura S. Levitt

Introduction

> Cultural identity is a matter of "becoming" as well as "being." It belongs to the future as much to the past. It is not something which already exists, transcending place, time, history, and culture. Cultural identities come from somewhere, have histories. But, like everything which is historical, they undergo constant transformation. Far from being eternally fixed in some essentialized past, they are subject to the continuous "play" of history, culture and power. Far from being grounded in a mere "recovery" of the past, which is waiting to be found, and which, when found, will secure our sense of ourselves into eternity, identities are the names we give to the different ways we are positioned by, and position ourselves within, the narratives of the past.[1]

I am interested in the ways that Jewish women are "positioned by, and position ourselves within, the narratives of [our various Jewish] past[s]." This chapter will focus on precisely this notion of positionality by drawing a connection between notions of "home" and "identity." Using Chandra Mohanty and Biddy Martin's essay "Feminist Politics: What's Home Got to Do with It?[2] to frame my discussion, I will make connections between their reading of Minnie Bruce Pratt's essay "Identity: Skin, Blood, Heart," and my reading of certain aspects of my

Jewish tradition. I will argue that like Pratt, Jewish feminists must also struggle with the traces of our Jewish pasts as they both remain with us and demand to be reinterpreted in the present. As Martin and Mohanty argue: "Pratt's own histories are in constant flux. There is no linear progression based on 'that old view,' no developmental notion of her own identity, or self. There is instead a constant expansion of her 'constricted eye,' a necessary reevaluation and return to the past in order to move forward to the present."[3]

Thus, building on a notion of "identity" much like that described by Stuart Hall, Mohanty and Martin offer a powerful framework that will allow me to expand my vision of how Jewish feminists might begin to reconfigure our cultural identities. In order to do this, I will do a critical reading of a section of the *ketubbah,* the Jewish marriage contract. I will explain how and in what ways it has been used to confine Jewish women to a particularly narrow construction of "home." More specifically, I will challenge the institution of heterosexual domesticity created and perpetuated by this contract. I will then do a reading of Judith Plaskow's Jewish feminist approach to marriage. In this section, I will raise questions about what this arrangement continues to mean for Jewish feminists in our ongoing attempts to reimagine our Jewish identities in less confining terms.

Jewish Feminist Identity/ies: What's Home Got to Do with It?

By presenting a reading of Mohanty and Martin's critical essay,[4] I am bringing my discussion of Jewish feminist identity/ies into a broader series of debates about "home" and "identity" in feminist theory, cultural studies, and lesbian and gay theory. The connection between these discussions is intertextual. Martin and Mohanty's text has been used by critics within these various fields of study. As one of the first critical commentaries on Minnie Bruce Pratt's now classic "Identity: Skin, Blood, Heart," her contribution to the volume *Yours in Struggle: Three Feminist Perspectives on Anti-Semitism and Racism,*[5] Mohanty and Martin have helped focus critical attention on Pratt's work. They make clear the importance of this text. Mohanty and Martin explain that "one of the most striking aspects of 'Identity: Skin, Blood, Heart' is the text's movement away from the purely personal, visceral experience of identity suggested by the title to a complicated working out of the relationship between home, identity, and community that calls into question the notion of a coherent historically continuous, stable identity and works to expose the political stakes concealed in such equations."[6]

In other words, throughout her essay, Pratt interrogates her privileged history, noting its emergence and reemergence in the present specifically in the forms of racism and antisemitism. Constantly in motion, Pratt again and again calls into question the often violent exclusions upon which those safe places she called home were based. Leaving the "security" of her white middle-class Christian south, Pratt struggles as an out lesbian feminist living with her Jewish lover among African Americans in Washington, D.C. Choosing to live on the edge, in a neighborhood that is not her own, Pratt remains unsettled.

It is precisely this unsettled and yet deeply grounded stance that has drawn me to Pratt and, more specifically, to Mohanty and Martin's reading of her essay. Their reading has allowed me to make connections between Pratt's reworking of her relationship with "the home she grew up in" and my reevaluation of the place of Jewish women within rabbinic and liberal Judaism. Like Pratt who returns and reevaluates her relationship with her father, I hope to show that it is possible to radically critique the traditions of my Jewish fathers and take as my focus the legacy of Jewish marriage. I focus on marriage because it is the major institution that has and continues to define and confine Jewish women to a particularly narrow definition of home. I will argue that it is both possible and important for Jewish feminists, as Pratt suggests, to return to and reevaluate this institution "in order to move forward to the present."

We must not only critique the legacy of our fathers but continually reassess the work of our mothers and sisters as well. As my reading of Judith Plaskow will make clear, we must critique not only the traditional *ketubbah* but Jewish feminist reconfigurations of marriages as well. Jewish feminists need not confine our vision of home to the institution of marriage.

My reading of a section of the *ketubbah* and a portion of Plaskow's "New Theology of Sexuality" will be modeled on Mohanty and Martin's reading of Pratt. I will focus on particular passages that are "characterized not by chronological development but by discontinuous moments of consciousness."[7] Through a close reading of these discontinuous passages, I will explain their "built-in contradictions" as well as their "fundamental instability."[8] I will then use these passages to offer a somewhat different approach to marriage than those offered by other Jewish feminist scholars.[9] Out of a close reading of these passages, I, like Pratt, will call for radical change while recognizing that the legacy of Jewish marriage continues to inform even my desire for change. In other words, as Martin and Mohanty explain:

Change is not a simple escape from constraint to liberation. There is no shedding the literal fear and figurative law of the father, and no reaching a final realm of freedom. There is no new place, no new home. Since neither her [Pratt's] view of history nor her construction of herself through it is linear, the past, home, and the father leave traces that are constantly reabsorbed into a shifting vision.[10]

This is the model I will use in my reading of texts on Jewish marriage.

The *Ketubbah*: The Naturalization of the Heterosexual Contract

The *ketubbah* is a written contract that sets out the terms of an exchange. The document, in the Babylonian tradition, followed a particular prescribed formula and enactment. In this tradition, the text is written and signed prior to the marriage ceremony. It sets out the monetary terms of the exchange as well as the legal stipulations that make the contract binding. In this very brief space, I will focus on the opening section of the text and describe how I read its affirmation of a particular form of "compulsory heterosexuality."[11] I will then demonstrate how this passage might be read as "fundamentally unstable." The text reads as follows:

> Be my wife according to the law of Moses and Israel. I will work, honor, feed and support you in the custom of Jewish men, who work, honor, feed and support their wives faithfully. I will give you a settlement (*mohar*) of virgins, two hundred silver zuzim, which is due you according to Torah law, as well as your food, clothing, necessities of life and conjugal needs, according to the universal custom.[12]

This passage follows immediately after the identification of the bride and groom. Here the text shifts to the first person and is written in the voice of the groom. Although there are many things to say about this passage, I want to focus on just one aspect of the text—its repetitiveness. Why does the text say essentially the same thing in a number of different ways? It is this excess that interests me. I am struck not only by the repetition of the groom's obligations, but the various ambiguous references to Jewish law as well.

In the opening clause, becoming a wife is connected to "the laws of Moses and Israel." This legal reference is initially ambiguous, its meaning contested. It has been argued that it refers to biblical and/or rabbinic law. The tension between these readings also says much about the status of what it means to be a "wife." Beyond this, there is yet a second reference to Jewish law that parallels this opening statement. Unlike the first, this second reference is quite specific. A biblical practice, the *mohar* or bride price, is presented as "Torah law."[13] Given the parallel, Torah law and the law of Moses and Israel are equated. But what interests me are the differences between these two references to law. What does it mean to go from a general, albeit ambiguous statement, to a very specific reference to a legal practice? Moreover, what does it mean to move from a law associated with Moses and the Jewish people to a statement of textual authority? The need to secure authority on all these fronts suggests contestation. In other words, the legal definition of the relationship between a husband and a wife is not self-evident. What these references highlight instead is the fragility of these claims to authority.

In the second part of this passage, the groom invokes the custom of Jewish men. He adds their practice to the authority of Moses and Israel. In this instance, custom and law are equated. And yet, is the law of Moses and Israel the same as the custom of Jewish men in relation to their wives? The gap between these two assertions is quite revealing. Even more striking is the precise repetition of the following obligations: "to work, honor, feed and support." The first reference appears to be tied to the initial invocation of the laws of Moses and Israel. The second time this formula appears it is more clearly tied to the practice of Jewish men. By means of this exact repetition, the gap between law and custom is filled. Law and practice become one and the same thing. Thus, what God demands of Jewish men is precisely what Jewish men are already doing. If these statements were reversed, their ideological agenda would become more apparent. In other words, they tell us that Jewish men's power over Jewish women through the institution of marriage is divinely sanctioned. Through parallelism and repetition this dependent relationship takes on a self-evident quality. And yet, by going out of its way to state and restate this definition of marriage, the text also reveals its vulnerability. Thus, instead of reflecting common practice, it might make more sense to read this text rhetorically. In so doing, its insistence on making and remaking the same point may be better read as advocating a particular type of relationship that was, by no means, normative.[14]

This statement is then followed by yet another rendition of the groom's obligations. And, as I have already indicated, this portion of the text parallels the previous one in two ways. First, it too begins with an invocation of Jewish law and then specifies yet another reading of the rule of custom. In this second statement, however, the formula includes additional obligations, "your food, clothing, necessities of life and conjugal needs."[15] This time, along with food and clothing, the groom spells out his obligations in even more detail. Most importantly, he pledges to provide for his wife's "necessities of life" as well as her sexual needs.[16] Why does the text essentially repeat itself? But, more importantly, what do the variations from the aforementioned formula signify?

To begin with, is repetition again used to make a connection between law and custom. This time the custom invoked is not just the custom among Jewish men, but presumably universal practices. Universal custom is juxtaposed to a very specific Torah law. In this case the specificity of the biblical law of the bride price is equated with a universal practice. The assumption of a bride's virginity upon marriage as well as her subjugation within the institution of marriage are, therefore, brought together. In this final parallel, sexuality is highlighted. The references to virginity and conjugal needs, make clear the husband's sole access to his wife's body as part of his overall control of her life.

In various ways, therefore, this passage presents male dominance and heterosexuality as both commanded and natural. The institutional arrangement set up and reenforced by these two powerful statements is a relationship of domination. Two unequal parties are involved, a man with power and a woman who presumably needs this man to take care of all her most basic needs. Despite the paternalistic logic involved, the text nevertheless advocates an asymmetrical power relationship. What is especially disturbing, and perhaps liberating, about this particular passage is its excess. Through repetition, it ironically reveals what Mieke Bal has called the "burden of domination."[17] As fundamentally unstable, Bal suggests that domination can be challenged: "Insecurity is not a prerogative exclusively of the dominated. Traces of the painful process of gaining control can therefore be perceived in those very myths."[18] Thus, by highlighting the traces of this process of securing control in the construction of the *ketubbah*, we begin to unravel its mythic claims to authority and disrupt its continuity in practice.

Plaskow and Marriage: Toward a Reconfiguration of Home

In her Jewish feminist theology, Judith Plaskow argues that the institution of marriage need not continue to replicate and reenforce asymmetrical power relationships between Jewish men and women. In response to a legacy of domination, Plaskow offers a more respectful and loving model for right relationships. This is most articulated in her discussion of sexuality. Informed by Audre Lorde's notion of the erotic,[19] Plaskow's theology of sexuality begins from the premise that the erotic is a source of empowerment capable of transforming relationships of domination. In the brief space remaining, I will present a critical assessment of Plaskow's reconfiguration of the institution of Jewish marriage. She begins as follows: "A first concrete task, then, of the feminist reconstruction of Jewish attitudes towards sexuality is a radical transformation of the institutional, legal framework within which sexual relations are supposed to take place."[20] With this in mind, according to Plaskow, "Marriage will not be about the transfer of women or the sanctification of potential disorder through the firm establishment of women in the patriarchal family, but the decision of two adults — any two adults — to make their lives together, lives which include the sharing of sexuality."[21] Plaskow then goes on to note that: "This redefinition of the legal framework of marriage is based both on rejection of the institutionalization of heterosexuality and on the important principle that sexuality is not something we can acquire or possess in another."[22]

In these ways, Plaskow thus critiques the institutional arrangement so precariously secured in the opening section of the *ketubbah* and reestablishes marriage on presumably different grounds. Appealing to the language of the liberal contract, she calls for an egalitarian relationship based on mutual consent.

As a critique, her position is, at first glance, quite persuasive. It appears to be a bold reassessment of the legacy of the *ketubbah* and its confining of Jewish women to a relationship of heterosexual domination. The question is, does Plaskow's appeal to "mutual consent" alleviate the problem of domination? By using the language of liberalism, does Plaskow radically alter the terms of the rabbinic contract? Even taking her at her word, it appears that the promises of a liberal contractual arrangement are themselves fundamentally unstable. Directly after presenting "marriage" as a decision between any two adults, Plaskow writes the following: "In the modern West, it is generally assumed that such a decision constitutes a central meaning of marriage, but this assumption is contradicted by a religious (and secular) legal system that outlaws homosexual marriage and institutionalizes inequality in its basic definition of marriage and divorce."[23]

According to this statement, there is a clear tension between the assumption of meaning and the institutionalization of marriage in the modern West. As in the *ketubbah* passage, here again there is a built-in contradiction this time between the "meaning" and the "definition" of marriage. Despite the fact that mutual consent is central to the meaning of marriage, it remains an asymmetrical heterosexual power relationship. Liberal marriage is thus ambivalent. What is striking about this admission is that it directly follows Plaskow's own advocacy of liberal marriage. Although overtly claiming liberal "meaning," she does not fully account for this ambivalence, nor does she redress the institutional failings of the liberal contract. Her own position, therefore, cannot avoid participating in this ambivalence because she offers no means to actually reject this legal framework. Instead, her liberal position only serves to mask the ongoing inequities within the modern West. As Tania Modleski, a feminist cultural critic, has recently noted, it is precisely this kind of well-meaning and yet fundamentally benign gesture in the right direction that serves to reenforce the asymmetrical power relationships it appears to overtly challenge.[24] This means that, on a deeper level, Plaskow's efforts to critique the institution of Jewish marriage by appealing to the liberal contract only serve to reenforce current Jewish marital practices. In other words, as in the modern West, here too the centrality of mutual consent in the meaning of marriage will do nothing to alleviate the ongoing institutionalization of both heterosexuality and gender inequality.

Critical Imagining: Toward Some Tentative Conclusions

By remaining committed to the perpetuation of an institution called marriage, Plaskow does not offer Jewish feminists a new vision of home. Her constructive move, at its best, offers a better rendition of marriage, remodeled but not reconstructed. Returning to a notion of cultural identities, I want to conclude by suggesting that Jewish feminists can both critically and imaginatively claim a different legacy. Through a careful reevaluation of some pieces of the textual tradition of Jewish marriage, I have tried to make clear the traces of its construction. By focusing on discontinuous moments in these texts, I have tried to show that "far from being eternally fixed in some essentialized past, [Jewish feminist identity/ies] are subject to the continuous 'play' of history, culture and power."[25] In other words, the authority claims made by these texts can be challenged.

Although I do not advocate any simple "shedding [of] the literal fear and figurative law of the father" as embodied in the institution of Jewish marriage, I have tried to reposition myself in relation to specific texts. In so doing, I have opened these texts to "the 'play' of history, culture and power." It is in the midst of this play that I have tried to show that it is possible for Jewish feminists to begin to position ourselves within these narratives. Even as we stand in one particular place and claim a position, a home, we can also continue to acknowledge that we have other options. Thus, it is the fundamental instability of our cultural identities that allows us to reconfigure home, to claim both singular and plural, Jewish feminist identity/ies.

NOTES

1. Stuart Hall, "Cultural Identity and Diaspora," in Jonathan Rutherford, ed., *Identity, Community, Cultural Difference* (London: Lawrence and Wishart, 1990), 225.
2. Chandra Talpade Mohanty and Biddy Martin, "Feminist Politics: What's Home Got to Do with It?," in Teresa de Lauretis, ed., *Feminist Studies, Critical Studies* (Bloomington: Indiana University Press, 1986), 191-212.
3. Mohanty and Martin, 196.
4. It should be noted that the title for Mohanty and Martin's essay seems to owe much to a very different source, Tina Turner's pop music hit "What's Love Got to Do with It." Terry Britten and Graham Lyle, "What's Love Got to Do with It," *Private Dancer*, Tina Turner, Capitol Records, 1984.
5. Elly Bulkin, Minnie Bruce Pratt and Barbara Smith, *Yours in Struggle: Three Feminist Perspectives on Anti-Semitism and Racism* (Brooklyn: Long Haul Press, 1984). Along with Mohanty and Martin, other readings of Pratt's essay include Nancy K. Miller, "Dreaming, Dancing and the Changing Location of Feminist Criticism, 1988," *Getting Personal: Feminist Occasions and Other Autobiographical Acts* (New York: Routledge, 1991), 72-100. Miller writes about Mohanty and Martin's essay while also doing a reading of Pratt. For a critical reading of Miller on these texts, see my "Reconfiguring Home: Jewish Feminist Identity/ies," 1993 dissertation, Emory University, Chap. 4. Other readings of Pratt, Mohanty, and Martin include: Susan David Bernstein, "What's 'I' Got to Do with It?" *Hypatia*, 7:2 (Spring 1992): 120-47, and Ed Cohen, "Who Are 'We'? Gay 'Identity' as Political (E)motion (A Theoretical Rumination)," in Diana Fuss, ed., *Inside/Out: Lesbian Theories, Gay Theories* (New York: Routledge, 1991), 71-92.
6. Mohanty and Martin, 195.
7. Mohanty and Martin, 197.
8. Mohanty and Martin, 197.
9. On precisely this question, see my analysis of Judith Plaskow later. Other Jewish feminist readings of the institution of marriage in various texts and various periods

include: Rachel Biale, *Women and Jewish Law: An Exploration of Women's Issues in Halachic Sources* (New York: Schocken, 1984); a number of historical accounts in essays included in Judith Baskin, ed., *Jewish Women in Historical Perspective* (Detroit: Wayne State University Press, 1991); Judith Romney Wegner, *Chattel or Person? The Status of Women in the Mishnah* (New York: Oxford University Press, 1988); and Marion Kaplan, *The Making of the Jewish Middle Class: Women, Family, and Identity in Imperial Germany* (New York: Oxford University Press, 1991). Although these accounts vary and are often quite nuanced, my point is that none of these texts use the category of cultural identity as a way of understanding the impact of this legacy on Jewish women.

10 . Mohanty and Martin, 201.

11 . Adrienne Rich, "Compulsory Heterosexuality and Lesbian Existence," *Blood, Bread, and Poetry: Selected Prose 1979-1985* (New York: W. W. Norton, 1986), 23-75.

12 . Aryeh Kaplan, *Made in Heaven: A Jewish Wedding Guide* (New York: Moznaim Publishing, 1983), 105.

13 . The *mohar* is the biblical "dowry of virgins" referred to in Exodus 22, and the sum of 200 *zuzim* reflects biblical specifications. Exodus 22:15-16 refers to the bride-price, the *mohar*, the payment in silver that is due a virgin. What is especially disturbing about this proof text is the context of the discussion. For an extended discussion of these issues, see my " Reconfiguring Home: Jewish Feminist Identity/ies" 1993 dissertation, Emory University, especially Chap. 1, "The Ketubbah: Jewish Women Under Jewish Law, The Legacy." At the end of this chapter, I argue that there is a disturbing connection between marriage and rape laws not only in rabbinic texts but biblical texts as well. We see this, for example, in Genesis 34, where Dina is made to marry the man who raped her. This is also true in the text before us, which reads as follows: "If a man seduces a virgin for whom the bride-price has not been paid, and lies with her, he must make her his wife by payment of a bride-price. If her father refuses to give her to him, he must still weigh out silver in accordance with the bride price for virgins" (Exodus 22:15-16) *Tanakh* (Philadelphia: Jewish Publication Society, 1985), 119.

14 . Employing a "hermeneutic of suspicion," the self-evident quality of this asymmetrical relationship may not be so obvious. See Elisabeth Schüssler Fiorenza, *In Memory of Her: A Feminist Theological Reconstruction of Christian Origins* (New York: Crossroad Publishing, 1988).

15 . Kaplan, 105.

16 . Another question worth asking is why these two are separated. Are we to assumed that sex is not a necessity for women? This seems to reenforce my argument that the specification of sexuality parallels the reference to virginity that precedes it.

17 . "The burden of domination is hard to bear. Dominators have, first, to establish their position, then to safeguard it. Subsequently, they must make both the dominated *and* themselves believe in it." Mieke Bal, *Lethal Love: Feminist Literary Readings of Biblical Love Stories* (Bloomington: Indiana University Press, 1987), 110.

18 . Bal, 110.

19 . Audre Lorde, "Uses of the Erotic: The Erotic as Power," *Sister Outsider: Essays and Speeches* (Trumansburg, N. Y.: Crossing Press, 1984), 53-60.

20 . Judith Plaskow, "Towards a New Theology of Sexuality," in Christie Balka and Andy Rose, eds., *Twice Blessed: On Being Lesbian, Gay and Jewish* (Boston: Beacon Press, 1989), 145.

21 . Plaskow, 145.

22 . Plaskow, 145.

23 . Plaskow, 145.

24 . "This is a space, as we shall see, increasingly occupied in a post feminist, post civil rights era by a mass culture that must on one level acknowledge the political struggles of the last few decades and on another, deeper level would ward off the threat these struggles pose to the white male power structure." Tania Modleski, "Cinema and the Dark Continent, Race and Gender in Popular Film," *Feminism without Women: Cultural Criticism in a "Postfeminist" Age* (New York: Routledge, 1991), 122.

25 . Hall, 225.

Chapter 5

The Secret of Jewish Femininity: Hiddenness, Power, and Physicality in the Theology of Orthodox Women in the Contemporary World

Jody Myers and Jane Rachel Litman

It is not unusual to find books written by Orthodox Jewish men instructing women how and why to uphold a traditional lifestyle. It is notable that currently there are a number of these works written by Orthodox women. Addressed specifically to women and designed for mass appeal, these books attempt to articulate a woman's philosophy of Judaism. We examined a number of these works in order to determine just how the authors dealt with the challenges facing contemporary Jewish women, and what this could reveal to us about religion's role in modern society.[1]

The field of Jewish Studies has dealt extensively with the transition of European Jewish society from premodern existence to modernity. We are adding to this research by evaluating a particular kind of Jewish response to modernity: one that uses and responds to contemporary gender theory to buttress traditional gender roles. Consequently, our particular study is explicitly interdisciplinary: history, textual analysis, religious studies, sociology, and gender theory are necessary to our evaluation of this phenomenon. Our analysis will include an evaluation of the authors' use of feminist theory and their claim that Orthodoxy empowers and values women. This critical analysis is crucial to fully understand their work.

Orthodox Judaism is not one denomination, but many, including a range of behaviors and many factions. What all Orthodox Jews share is the conviction that service to God involves the strict observance of the moral and ritual laws of the Torah; this entails accepting the authority of rabbis who maintain that their interpretation and rulings can be traced back to the original revelation on Mount Sinai. The Orthodox women that we examined focused on the three commandments of the Torah that postbiblical tradition teaches are unique to women: *challah* (burning a piece of dough from bread before baking, in symbolic reference to the ancient priestly portion), *nerot* (lighting Sabbath candles), and *niddah* (following the ritual purity laws specific to women).[2] The writers agree that these three commandments (*mitzvot*) govern their religious lives.[3] They give special prominence to the third commandment, euphemistically called the family purity laws. Of the three, this commandment is the most elaborate, the most at odds with modern culture, and therefore the most in need of explanation.

What we have learned corroborates the findings of feminist scholars researching other cultures. The Orthodox women we have studied are utilizing in defense of their gender roles nearly the same symbols that women from a variety of religious cultures—Protestant, Catholic, Muslim—have put forward in their apologetics: the notion of separate spheres, and similar ways of describing women's power and physicality. Furthermore, we note that the very process of constructing an apologetic, that is, taking on one's own defense, changes the women. These Orthodox women are affirming their social reality by using new tools: feminist language, mystical symbolism previously known only to men, and their own novel theological exegesis. Because of their contact and immersion in nontraditional or formerly masculine enterprises, their very conservative intent moves them away from traditional female roles and conceptions and the result contains within it the stirrings of social change.

In our examination of this literature, we were not surprised to learn that the writers believe that when women adopt the values and behaviors they find inherent in the commandments of *challah* and *nerot*, but especially *niddah* the problems facing women in contemporary non-Orthodox society diminish. This is not only because they believe that a traditional lifestyle rectifies the inadequacies of secular society. It is also because they believe these commandments have a spiritual healing effect on the world; they believe the family purity system, in particular, is so reflective of the divine that its very existence infuses harmony into the realm of creation.

What did surprise us in our research was our discovery that, for certain circles of Orthodox women, the system of family purity serves as a paradigm for Jewish theology. Even when the authors do not set out to discuss this ritual, they invariably use the behaviors, symbols, and tensions within the family purity system to illustrate what they believe are deep truths about the cosmos and God's relationship to it. They project onto God their own social reality: God has regular times of withdrawal from the world—periods of *niddah,* so to speak—followed by reemergence and more evident creativity. Not only does this identification confirm the necessity of women's religious observance; it also reflects the women's estimation of their own importance, for when women can imagine God in their own likeness it testifies to their own sense of worth.[4]

The self-respect of these women is also evident in their boldness to write books and articles about Judaism. Not only is this an activity reserved to men, but it implies the inadequacy of preexisting literature.[5] These authors want a type of Judaism that acknowledges women's concerns as they are defined by women. And, judging by the popularity of this literature among their peers, their sentiments are shared by many others.

The Family Purity System

A brief description of the family purity system, and the issues that have become intertwined with it, will be helpful in understanding this contemporary literature.

The primary source of the purity laws is in the Pentateuch, particularly the book of Leviticus. There God instructs the Israelite priests that they must guard the public, holy spaces in the Israelite camp from contamination with impurity.[6] Several purity laws relate to men's and women's genital discharges. Men and women experiencing genital discharges due to ill health (*zav, zavah*) are instructed to stay out of the sacred space for seven days after the end of the discharge and then undergo a ritual water immersion to restore purity. Menstrual fluid is among the healthy discharges. The laws stipulate that the menstruating woman is ritually impure (*niddah*) for seven days (including her menstrual period), contaminating anything upon which she sits or lies, or any man with whom she has intercourse. At the end of this seven-day period, she is considered ritually pure, as are the men with whom she has had intercourse. According to the Levitical laws, the priests are obligated to enforce this quarantine. It is not clear, however, if any of the ritual impurity laws were operative outside of the priesthood or the ritual realm or if they were associated with immorality or sexuality.[7]

Eventually, however, these laws became associated with sexuality and personal morality. The first suggestion of this appeared during the Babylonian Exile (586–538 B.C.E.), when the menstruant served as a metaphor for Israel's violation of the covenant.[8] By the early rabbinic era, shortly after the Second Temple was destroyed (70 C.E.), this evolution was complete. All of the extensive Levitical system of bodily contamination and purification, which was part of the Temple's sacrificial system, fell into disuse *except for* the purity laws relating to menstruation and sexual relations.[9] They were explicitly applied to the nonpriestly communal and familial arenas. This change is illustrative of the rabbinic transformation of priestly, Israelite religion; the rabbis "democratized" sanctity, making it available to those outside of the priestly class by developing rituals in the home and synagogues and other modes of religious fulfillment in the study houses. Furthermore, the length and type of impurity was redefined. Now the menstrual impurity (*niddah*) lasted only as long as the menstrual flow, but in order to guard against the possible contamination from an unhealthy discharge (*zavah*), an additional seven days without any type of discharge were required.[10] The woman's state of impurity would then be lifted by an immersion in water (*mikveh*). The rabbis invoked the legacy of priestly legislation to fortify a new rationale for the laws: that God in his wisdom ordained these laws to preserve marital love.[11]

Once the link between ritual purity and sexual behavior was established, the family purity laws became interwoven with the general attitudes about sexuality.[12] Over the ages, the rabbis maintained a fairly moderate stance on sexuality. Within the prescribed framework of marital relations conducted in accordance with the family purity laws, sex was considered good even if it bore no connection to procreation. There were those who were less positive, however; particularly among philosophers and mystics, there were those who evinced a more negative attitude toward sexuality. The positive attitude toward marital sex became a mainstay of rabbinic Judaism until the present time.[13]

A noteworthy development occurred in circles connected to Kabbalah, medieval Jewish mysticism. There sexual intercourse became a metaphor for divine creativity. The myriad texts from medieval mystical literature describe sexual intercourse in one or more of the following three ways: as a reflection of divine creativity, as an influence upon divine creativity; or as a contemplative model for the mystic attempting to cling to the Godhead.[14] Eighteenth-century Hasidic mysticism, specifically that of the Lubavitch Hasidim (Habad), added a new element to this: God's creation of the world was understood to include the bringing into being of the finite within divinity, as well as the total negation of the finite within divinity, that is, divine creativity involved creation as well as negation (*bitul*).[15] This had its earthly parallel, according to Habad thought, when the boundaries of each person become dissolved, and their distinct selves are nullified during the sex act. Within all these forms of Jewish mysticism, menstrual impurity became associated with demonic forces, while semen became sacralized. The family purity laws became invested with tremendous importance as guardians and enhancers of God's power and purity.

At the present time, these laws are part of an intricate system adopted to varying degrees of stringency by contemporary Orthodox women. The following is the accepted *halakhic* (legal) standard within Orthodox Judaism. Twelve hours before her menstrual period is expected, a married woman ceases physical contact with her husband. Until she is ritually pure again, all touching is prohibited, the couple must sleep in separate beds, avoid handing objects one to another, and avoid other behaviors that could tempt them into sexual relations. One day after her flow ceases, she begins to do an internal vaginal check for discharges, twice daily for the next seven days. If she finds no evidence of discharge, she immerses herself in a *mikveh*, and physical contact may resume. Trained female counselors may guide her in the entire process, and all questionable matters are referred to a rabbi.[16]

Orthodox Women's Writings

The women's literature we examined represents authors from the left and right wings of Orthodoxy and one point somewhere in the middle. We believe we have examined the most important and influential writings available in English. The following is a description of our sources.

1. Tamar Frankiel, *The Voice of Sarah: Feminine Spirituality and Traditional Judaism* and her article, "Sex and the Spirit," *Tikkun* 5 (6), November/December 1990. She has a doctorate in the history of religions, has taught at universities, and edited textbooks on Christianity and world religions for an academic press. Frankiel accepted Judaism and Orthodoxy as an adult. She characterizes her transformation as moving from being a single, career-oriented feminist to a traditional Jewish wife and mother of five. Nevertheless, she

continues to teach in secular institutions and those affiliated with the
non-Orthodox Jewish community. Of all the authors, she is the most
familiar and comfortable with non-Orthodox culture.[17] Her book is
widely available within the Orthodox community, in Judaica sections of
general bookstores, and through academic publishing mail-order
catalogs. *Tikkun* is a bimonthly Jewish critique of politics, culture, and
society, and purports to be one of the voices of the Jewish Left.

2. Tehilla Abramov, *The Secret of Jewish Femininity: Insights into the
Practice of Taharat HaMishpachah*, translated from the Hebrew. This
book is widely available in bookstores catering to Orthodox Jews and is
also distributed through mail order by Feldheim Publishers. Abramov
is from Israel and is representative of a non-Hasidic branch of
Ashkenazic Orthodoxy. She is the most conservative of the authors
represented here. She is affiliated with the *Ohr Somayach* Yeshivah,
which maintains a department for training rabbis to bring secular or
non-Orthodox Jews—in particular, the younger cohort of the Jewish
community—to Orthodoxy; this process is commonly called "outreach"
(Hebrew *kiruv*). Abramov teaches the wives of these rabbis how to
attract secular or non-Orthodox Jewish women to a traditional lifestyle.
This book is a summation of her teaching. It is a technical guide to the
observance of the family purity laws, as well as her testimony of their
many benefits: increased fertility, health, marital happiness, nice
children, and good sex. She conveys these benefits through "*mikveh*
lore"—anecdotes transmitted from woman to woman, plus
unreferenced scientific studies. The book contains many approbations
by Israeli and American rabbis certifying its acceptability for Orthodox
Jews. Thus, the book was meant for an audience that is already
Orthodox, as well as for those who are potential members of the
community.

3. Publications by the Hasidic sect known as Lubavitch, or Habad,
including *Aura: A Reader on Jewish Womanhood; The Modern Jewish
Woman: A Unique Perspective*; and "Exploring the Hidden," by Shimona
Krengel, in *Wellsprings* 31 (vol. 6, no. 3, February-March 1990), an
outreach magazine for women. Habad is distinguished among Hasidic
groups for its aggressive program of outreach to assimilated Jews, with
careful concern to appeal to women who have been exposed to
feminism. *Aura: A Reader on Jewish Womanhood* is a book of testimonies,
by women, regarding the benefits to women of a traditional lifestyle.
Most of the authors seem to be college graduates or hold higher
professional degrees, and so probably grew up outside the Hasidic
community. Several of them begin their testimonies with an admission

that they have happily abandoned their careers or career aspirations and are occupied solely in the home as wives and mothers. *The Modern Jewish Woman: A Unique Perspective* contains testimonies from women as well as men. We paid particular attention to the writings of Shaina Sara Handelman, a professor of English literature, in *Aura* and *The Modern Jewish Woman*. Both Handelman and Shimona Krengel's article in *Wellsprings* rely heavily on Habad mystical symbolism. Both books are available in bookstores in the Orthodox community and are distributed by the Lubavitch organization.

Findings

There are many of ways of living an Orthodox Jewish life. It cannot be assumed that Orthodox women share the same extent of physical or cultural insularity from secular culture, or that their self-understanding or religious conceptions are identical. The fine distinctions which we have uncovered in these women's literature are integral to an understanding of how their literary expression relates to their particular social position.

Orthodox women who live in a cloistered environment where Orthodoxy is the norm need no apologetics referencing external culture to support their Jewish practice. They can comfortably argue that the sole reason for observing the laws is to obey God; and, as traditional Jews have done over the ages, they may enhance their observance by searching for "reasons" for the commandments that testify to the Torah's wisdom.[18] This is generally the approach taken by Abramov, for whom all the marital and other benefits that accrue from the laws are clearly tangential to the duty of obedience to God. Her particular Orthodox community is the most removed from secular society; she is doubly insulated by her position within ultra-Orthodox circles in Israel. Furthermore, there are no indications in her book or in the publisher's comments pointing to her life experience outside of the Orthodox community. Although she is involved in outreach, her work is not as aggressive an effort as that conducted by the Lubavitch movement; when non-Orthodox people appear, they have already presented themselves as prospective followers. Not surprisingly, her explanations and reasoning are the least sophisticated of the authors. It is significant that even she felt the need for a woman-authored guidebook.

In contrast, women who are more involved with the secular and non-Orthodox world are in greater need of apologetic literature. Unquestioned obedience is rarely enough for either newly Orthodox

Jews or for those who make it their mission to bring non-Orthodox Jewish women into the fold. Newly Orthodox Jews need to explain to themselves and others why they rejected one lifestyle and accepted another, particularly a lifestyle that imposes distinctive limitations and obligations upon them. Those women engaged in outreach work may have these same needs, because they are often formerly non-Orthodox, but in addition they have to promote traditional Judaism in terms that will appeal to secular or non-Orthodox women. Both types may want to construct a counter-ideology: a religious ideology that utilizes concepts and symbols from the secular world, but reverses their underlying values and conclusions in order to buttress Orthodoxy. This is the approach taken by Frankiel (who still describes herself as a feminist[19]) and to a lesser extent by the Habad women.

Three themes repeatedly appear in this literature that are central to the apologetic and that play important roles in each philosophy of Judaism: women's hiddenness, women as exemplars of sanctified physicality and women's power.

Women as Hidden

The authors do not deny that Orthodox women are absent from the communal realm of Jewish life, and restricted within their marriages by their withdrawal from physical/sexual contact with their husbands during the period of *niddah*.[20] Rather, they attribute great value to this status, which they call "the hiddenness of women."[21] This term is used because of its connection to mystical concepts, but also we should not overlook the effect that the passive usage ("women's hiddenness," rather than "removing women from the public sphere") has on the reader. The absence of women from the public sphere is conceptualized as a state of being rather than as an act of will. Of course, this "hidden" state of being is the mirror of the biological hiddenness of her sexual organs. The paradigmatic woman is a vessel, whereas the paradigmatic man is an active, projecting creature.

All authors argue that the "hiddenness" that operates within marital life increases women's attractiveness as well as their feminine powers. Because the Jewish wife is not always available to her husband, she cannot be taken for granted. The couple can continually relive the erotic excitement of the wedding night, when religious tradition (which frowns upon premarital sex) finally permitted sexual relations between the lovers. The authors have adopted the language and dynamic of the romantic ideal: the necessity of seduction and tease, the lure of mystery and the exotic, the sweetness of deprivation when it is followed by fulfillment, and the facade of female passivity and male aggression. They also point out that the period of *niddah* allows women the opportunity to tend to their own needs rather than the needs of their husbands.[22] This rationale transforms a system of prohibitions and obligations into a psychosocial strategy of emotional sustenance and marital health. It gives traditional women the feeling that they are in control of their sexual lives.

Frankiel and the Habad women, who are attuned to the loss of status that secular women will experience by being excluded from the public sphere, assert that the "hiddenness" of Orthodox women actually attests to their preciousness. On its simplest level, this is an affirmation of the Orthodox ideal of modesty for women, often expressed in the phrase "the honor of a king's daughter is within."[23] However, these authors invest this ideal with theological meaning and denigrate the nonprivate sphere. They argue that the public sphere is less sacred and important than the private. The public sphere was undesirable from time immemorial even for men, Krengel explains, for "the greatest leaders of the Jewish people invariably wished to avoid their appointment as leaders."[24] In arguments reminiscent of the nineteenth-century cult of domesticity, they elevate the private sphere as the repository of purity and the guardian of the sacred.[25] Frankiel illustrates this distinction in the following manner:

> Legends often tell of the "mysteriousness" of women, of our "secret" lore. These are not merely reactions to patriarchy: out of fear or self-protection we hide our real selves. Rather, we know deeply that some forms of power are best kept secret, guarded from public scrutiny, and used with great care. Esther's name is sometimes interpreted as meaning "hidden," as in *hester punim* [sic] — the "hidden face" of God; and God's name is never mentioned in the Megillah — the divine is hidden too. This is one of the deep dimensions of women's lives.[26]

Here women's hiddenness is not only defended as an element of age-old female wisdom, it is also likened to divinity. God sometimes remains hidden, but this does not diminish divine sanctity or power; actually, it may enhance it. So, too, it is with women.

Krengel develops this notion of women's separate sphere into a critique of modernity. She illustrates the public realm with phenomena that appear only in the modern period and that are associated with corruption, egoism, and greed. For example, she identifies the public sphere with billboards, pop stars, publicity columns, and election campaigns; and the private realm with the Holy of Holies (the guarded center of the ancient Temple) and the unknowable essence of the Godhead. This is clearly a "stacking of the deck."[27] The slanted nature of the examples is not immediately obvious because they are presented in flowing, evocative prose. The argument is designed not for its balanced logic, but for its emotional effect: to provoke disgust with the public realm so sought after by modern, secular women and men. The author is establishing an ironic contrast between past and present that is central to conservative ideology: the present is only momentarily liberating and holds only false promises for the future, whereas the past already established all that is enduring and sustaining. Frankiel, in contrast, does not engage in an explicitly antimodern approach in her discussion of the separate spheres; she is too beholden to modern culture to denigrate it so absolutely.

Evaluating the public and private realms as a dichotomy between pure and impure is also an attempt to undermine the problematic association of woman and pollution; that is, one wonders why, if the private is so good, it is linked with menstrual impurity. Even with the best of translations, the family purity laws abound with the language and symbolization of contamination and pollution. The woman who observes these laws is trained to detect and evaluate the stains on her clothing and other evidence of menstrual and genital discharge. She knows that the problem comes from within her body. What the authors are doing is directing the stigma of pollution away from women. Frankiel explicitly denies that *niddah* has anything to do with pollution.[28] But Krengel argues this point more subtly. She explains that the realm of hiddenness must be carefully guarded from the contagion of the outer world, a contagion inseparable from public life.[29] It is not women, but the male and public spheres that are impure. The reason she is restricted is to protect her body from the impurity of the outer world, not to protect the outer world from her impurity.

The authors' reversal of the pollution theme marks a crucial change from the usual descriptions of menstruation in religious literature. Works written by men dealing with the family purity laws will typically include the late biblical and rabbinic associations between *niddah* and immorality, unbridled lust, and human imperfection. It is not difficult to understand why women, especially modern women, would be offended or uninspired by these explanations. The women authors are rectifying the problem. They defend the existing ritual, but reconstruct its rationale. When women are responsible for describing their own bodily functions, they avoid the negativity ascribed by men.[30]

The hiddenness theme is developed theologically in the writings of the Lubavitch women and Frankiel, who utilize concepts drawn from mystical literature. According to the medieval Kabbalah, there is an aspect of divinity that can be known and approached through prayer and contemplation; this is imagined and named in the ten *sefirot* that together form the dynamic of revealed divinity. However, the unknowable essence of God (the *ein sof,* infinite) remains beyond human comprehension. Paradoxically, the *ein sof* is most manifest in the lowest *sefirah,* called *malchut,* which "has nothing of its own," but receives its content from the other *sefirot.* Krengel points out that *malchut* is associated with women and the physical world. Also, "in this absence of any independent existence, it parallels the true nothingness of G-d."[31] In other words, the hidden, inaccessible essence of God—which is more holy than the more manifest elements of divinity—is more akin to women and women's spirituality than to men and their spirituality.

According to teachings articulated by Habad mystics, true cleaving to God involves the self's attainment of *bitul* (negation), "the perception of the world as nonexistent and of divinity as possessing the only true existence."[32] *Bitul* is essential in order to ascend from one spiritual level to the next.[33] Thus, humanity finds its source in God, and indeed, imitates God through a cycle of negation and manifestation. Handelman explains that *bitul,* the losing of one's own independent existence, going out from oneself, occurs in the ritual of immersion in the *mikveh,* which transforms ones status from *niddah* to *tahor* (ritually pure). "Elevating oneself by becoming a vessel for *kedushah,*" actually an *empty* vessel, is the height of woman's spirituality.[34] This pattern is concretely manifested in the mystical concept of sacred time, in which God's presence is imagined as less apparent during the six days of the week and more manifest on the Sabbath. World history is conceptualized in this pattern, too: during the era that began with the destruction of the Temple in 70 C.E. (the Exile, or *galut*), God's presence is barely evident, and it will appear in its full effulgence in the Messianic Age.[35]

The authors point out that a woman observing the family purity laws experiences a similar cycle within her own marital life: she withdraws from sexual relations during the time in which she is *niddah* and *zavvah,* and then reemerges and participates in full sexual relations until prior to her next menstrual period. In her own body and in her sexual relationship with her husband, she is mirroring the relationship between God and the universe. Handelman explains that

> these . . . absences of *kedusha* which G-d has created within the monthly cycle of a woman, of the weekly cycle of Shabbos, the nightly cycle of sleep, or the entire life-cycle of the Jewish People as a whole are, in their innnermost sense, all parts of the process of spiritual ascent. Nor is the connection between these different cycles artificial. The Talmud compares the Jewish People to the moon, for just as the moon waxes and wanes every month, so too do the Jews undergo phases of concealment and renewal in *golus* [*galut*, Exile] and *geula* [redemption, Messianic Age].[36]

A woman who experiences the ritualized monthly cycle, then, is granted a special connection to history and nature.

Handelman even more explicitly draws the parallel between a woman in *niddah* and God. In the previous quotation, she preserves the identification of women with the symbols of the Jewish people and the moon. Thus, the implicit parallel is God as the male beloved and the sun, which corresponds to the classical Jewish symbology. However, Handelman also subtly shifts symbolic identities to women's advantage. She quotes a previous Habad leader, the Tzemach Tzedek, who wrote, "The Hebrew letters of the word *niddah* also mean '*nod hay*,' God wanders." Handelman ties this divine wandering to the feminine manifestation of divinity, the *Shechinah*, who accompanies the Jews in their exile.[37] That is, a woman in *niddah* is like the *Shechinah*. By identifying God as female, Handelman is reorienting the traditional gender categories. Again, *niddah* no longer has a negative connotation of expulsion, but it represents a cosmological stage necessary to creation and history. Just as God withdraws and then creates, so too a woman in *niddah* withdraws and then procreates.

In a similar fashion, Frankiel links women's cycles to the greater cosmic enterprise. She notes that the physical changes within a woman's body are actually superficial compared to the more important reality they point to: "The entire process is something else: a scale drawing, so to speak, of the creativity of the universe."[38] In attempting to understand what the author means by creativity, we must note that a woman is least fertile during the roughly fourteen days that, according to rabbinic law, she is a *niddah* and *zavvah* and thus prohibited from having intercourse. She is then likely to enter her most fertile period, and this coincides with her immersion in the *mikveh*, after which, according to rabbinic law, her husband is obligated to initiate sex. Conception—creation—is likely to occur. A Jewish woman who follows the family purity laws and attempts to become pregnant, then, is being likened to God, who undergoes the divine version of *niddah* followed by a manifestation through creativity.[39] She, along with her husband, is also reenacting the grand drama of Jewish history. This theology assigns to women, more than men, the power of reproductivity. It enhances, above all else, their religious role as child bearers.

Women as Sanctified Physicality

All three sources equate the female with the physical. They are proud that Judaism has adopted a stance toward physicality that, according to them, grants women's bodies deep respect. This contrasts with Christianity, which in their minds denigrates the value of the material world; and it is superior to Greek culture, which, in its hedonistic materialism affirms the value of all physicality.[40] In Judaism, however, the material world can be sanctified by making specific connections between it and divinity. These connections involve the commandments, which are concrete deeds that involve the physical world. The authors explain that women, being physical, are closer or equal to nature; indeed, they assert that the menstrual cycle is the specific sign of the close harmony of women and nature. Women are thus more in tune with divine creativity and possess great power "to elevate the potential of the physical world."[41]

All of the authors maintain that the commandments in general have the effect of sanctifying the physical. Women's *mitzvot* do this more directly than men's because, they assert, the performance of women's *mitzvot* do not merely involve the physical world, but effect a change in it. This notion is explained elsewhere by a Habad rabbi, as follows:

> [Although] every mitzva brings light, purity, and sanctity into the world, not every mitzva possesses the physical properties which parallel the spiritual effects of the mitzva. The mitzvos of lighting the Shabbos candles, challah, and family purity, are obvious exceptions. Here the very physical phenomenon of lighting the candles creates light . . . And the mitzva of family purity is the obvious physical channel to introduce purity into one's life, family, and home.[42]

This repeats the earlier theme that the woman who follows the family purity laws is like God. When she lights candles, she is reenacting God's primordial creation of light, and in going to the *mikveh* she is assuming the godly task of sanctifying the profane.[43]

However, this symbolic construction of the menstrual cycle is out of sync with the biology of real women. A woman who follows rabbinic law is actually unlikely to be governed by this monthly rhythm. Orthodox women of childbearing age who accept the *halakhic* prohibition on birth control[44] will be pregnant soon after marriage, or nonmenstruating after childbirth. Upon commencement of menses, they will likely become pregnant again shortly. Actually, the family purity laws will not regulate women's sexual lives each month unless they are infertile or using birth control. It is clear that these authors are not addressing postmenopausal women; girls; unmarried women; lesbians; women with irregular periods, hysterectomies, or other deviations from the stereotype of the regularly menstruating heterosexual married woman. They are appealing to young women, married or hoping to marry, with child-bearing capability.

The authors who argue from the basis of mystical assumptions exacerbate this problem. They equate women's marital lives with divine creativity. How, then, are we to understand sexual behavior that cannot possibly result in pregnancy? It seems to fall short of the ideal. With their theology they have linked sex and procreation in a manner similar to Christianity, a linkage they scorn.

For all these positive references to women as equal to the physical, none of the three authors accepts the value of woman's sexual pleasure in and of itself. This would be an imitation of what they call Greek, hedonistic values. Yet, it is noteworthy that in our sources, which purport to address women's concerns, women's sexual sensations are not discussed.[45] The Israeli Orthodox author comes the closest; she is firmly rooted in the Talmudic tradition, and she echoes the rabbis by affirming the force of women's erotic impulses. However, she too diminishes the importance of women's sexual desires by insisting that "a total woman" is not content with merely the fulfillment of her sexual desires, as is a man, but seeks through her sexuality holiness and love as well.[46]

Furthermore, the use of certain mystical concepts seems to imply that a woman's orgasm is actually irrelevant to sanctified sexuality. The Hasidic concept of *bitul*, the self-negation that is a prerequisite for spiritual attainment, exemplifies this problem. The woman who seeks the religious ideal of the negation of self is surrendering all those aspects of herself that indicate her own uniqueness. From a Hasidic point of view, these unique elements are merely egotistic or trivial barriers to ultimate reality. Of course, the authors, unlike feminists, do not understand this self-negation as a loss of power. Yet, this emphasis on self-negation, we would argue, lessens the likelihood of women's sexual satisfaction. The authors describe women's behavior during the sex act in very passive terms. They liken women to the *sefirah malchut*, which is like an empty receptacle awaiting penetration. Furthermore, they describe sexual relations in explicitly *nonphysical* words, as if physical pleasure is unimportant, perhaps even irrelevant, to the sex act. For example, Krengel writes the following:

> It is only when we enact self-nullification and surrender ourselves to our Creator that we can reveal our source beyond creation and become truly active beings. Unity occurs when both giver and receiver are ready to assume their roles. The Zohar says that precisely through the union of Male and Female, the essence is revealed. Birth and creation arise out of Bitul and receiving.[47]

The woman and man "assume their roles": he gives, she receives, and then she conceives. Sexual feeling is not mentioned here. Frankiel's writings exhibit the same tendency to write about sexuality in phallocentric terms:

> We must acknowledge that we are attracted by the power of sexuality not only for our own pleasure but for the holiness that we, as Jews, know it holds. But we need to use that power wisely . . . . What then is the goal? Here I can only speak for myself, as I try to reflect on my own experience and the stories of women of our heritage. I seek the focused intensity, the white hot point of contact with God that can emerge from a life dedicated to holiness. I want to be able to tap the reservoirs of passion and vitality, courage and clarity, that I know are available there.[48]

Physical sexual pleasure, then, is sublimated in a spirituality that potentially disregards women's needs.[49]

Women as Powerful

Another prominent theme in the literature is women's power. It is clearly important to the authors that, despite women's public invisibility and the taboos surrounding their persons, the readers understand that Jewish women are, in their unique way, still powerful.

These authors approach the issue of power from a romantic ideology; they maintain that women's power is located in their ability to be alternately modest or seductive. Abramov, the author of the guidebook, explains that the family purity laws give the wife the power to keep her husband interested in her and the marital relationship strong. She quotes a non-Orthodox thirty-something career woman who adopted the family purity laws after experiencing marital tensions: "Every visit to the *mikveh* gave us a sense of renewal and a chance to recapture wedding night magic."[50]   Abramov argues that the power held by modern, liberated women is illusory and ultimately not fulfilling.[51]   Furthermore, it has not solved the problem of unwanted sexual contact for married women. According to her, women have a physiological disinclination to engage in sexual relations during and immediately after their menstrual period. Because men do not have a "natural" inhibitor during the period of *niddah*, women cannot help but insult their husbands or hurt their feelings by refusing sex at that time. The family purity laws solve this delicate dilemma, guaranteeing "a woman's right to privacy while preserving a spirit and harmony within the home."[52]

We question the reasoning that holds that these laws are indicators of women's power. The women in this system have access to strategies that are full of guile and manipulation; this is typical of power in an underclass. Those with prerogative, in contrast, have authority, their time-honored right to wield explicit power. Initially, it does appear that the family purity laws give women some degree of personal control. The women determine if they are ritually pure and sexually available, and the requirements of vaginal examination may give them greater knowledge and consciousness of their body. However, the laws are constructed by a male elite, and rabbis are the ultimate authorities on the woman's status and the only ones who may make exceptions to the rules. Thus, whereas women following the family purity laws may have some added power, they do not have any additional authority. A cycle of alternating modesty and explicit sexuality may give women more control than unrestricted sexual access, but it is disturbing that woman's power cannot be attained through their own internalized desire and ability to act on it. Nevertheless, the authors clearly do not see it this way; they live within a religious framework in which all are limited by laws, and women seem to have greater power than their husbands in the couple's sex life.

Another development of the power theme is in the notion that this covert feminine power is superior to power held by men. Frankiel develops this notion at length. She locates women's power within a cycle of modesty and sexuality, a contrast that in itself she finds exciting. She identifies the dualistic tensions of sexual power in almost all biblical women who she describes as manipulating (although she rejects the use of this term) men with their beauty for higher ends. For example:

> Esther, then, gives us a clue as the role of female sexuality in establishing our own identity. Sexual power is part of a woman's inherent power—differing in degree, quality, and extent for each woman. But it cannot remain a viable source of power when squandered: it must be guarded and used in its own proper time.[53]

A woman's sexual power has the potential for holiness, according to Frankiel, when the end she wishes to achieve is "holy . . . not just to get married, but to fulfill a special destiny; not just to wield power, but to save the Jewish people."[54] This is not the mode of power common to men, whose power is manifest publicly and who do not undergo such extended delay of ego gratification. Yet, it is the best and holiest manifestation of human power, and it is this that will redeem the world: "The woman who knows her sexuality, and her inner, spiritual self, can recognize her true purpose in life, can act with power and confidence at any moment, and can thereby affect her own destiny, the destiny of her people, and that of the whole world."[55] According to Frankiel, this power is part of women's psychology and biology. Jewish women reinforce this innate power by their unique *mitzvot*, specifically the family purity laws.[56]

Finally, and most important, women's power is in their enactment of private rituals like the family purity laws. According to an old Jewish tradition, conception that takes place when a women is in *niddah*, or while the couple is having impure thoughts, will result in a spiritually or physically deformed baby. The authors put this in a positive light by explaining the beneficial impact of the family purity rituals on the cosmos. Abramov explains that the Exodus from Egypt was the result of "women observing the laws of Family Purity in the depths of slavery."[57] Handelman notes that these laws "have direct spiritual and physical consequences on the health of one's children and the health of the entire House of Israel."[58] It is important to note that Frankiel, as she describes the power of these rituals, cannot help but contrast it to modern forms of women's political power:

> As women, then, we are in a privileged position in opening the channels of the world to the divine flow. At the beginning we may not see what is the direct benefit to the world of all the rituals we can perform. It is tempting to push aside davening [prayer] and run to a political action meeting or sign up for a Saturday class on economic theories that will end poverty. These may be valuable actions, but we must learn to think twice before we relegate ritual practice to second priority. What happens through our Jewish practice is nothing less than a realignment of the world, preparing the world to accept goodness and truth that have never before been revealed. Women are spiritual midwives in rebirthing the world. Just how is a mystery. . . [59]

Although Frankiel does not explicitly tell women to forego political activism in their effort to improve the world, she does imply that a woman performing her specific commandments will have a far greater impact on the world.

Conclusion

The existence of a counter-ideology (feminist arguments transformed) reflects the wide acceptance of feminist thinking, but also the failure of modern society to enable Jewish women to meet their social, emotional, and economic needs. Lynn Davidman has shown in *Tradition in a Rootless World* that many secular women are drawn to Orthodoxy not primarily because of religious belief, but because within the Orthodox community women are more likely to find husbands, female companionship, community concern for their economic well-being, a framework within marriage that gives women "space," and respect for bearing and raising children. The newly Orthodox women she studied repeatedly emphasize that they feel less, not more, burdened as Orthodox women.[60] Feminism had given them great expectations for what they could achieve, but in an untransformed society these expectations could not be met. The women's philosophies of Judaism studied here were designed partly to address women who are or were once caught in this dilemma. The authors are motivated by concern for their Jewish sisters in whom they recognize themselves.

This woman's philosophy puts at its center the woman who wants to be or is child-bearing and married. Her body is the mirror of divine creativity, and her status—if expressed within the framework of the family purity laws—resembles the sacred dynamic in nature and in Jewish history. She becomes a metaphor for God, nature, and the Jewish people. She is continuing the sacred deeds of the Jewish heroines of old. Who could resist such a grandiose role?

For all of this philosophy's borrowing from the contemporary world, it is a deeply conservative outlook. Authenticity resides in the past. In contrast to this type of Orthodox women is the cohort that is advocating greater female participation in the communal Jewish sphere: women who advocate Talmud study for women, who want women to constitute their own *minyan* (prayer quorum), and who urge women to regularly observe *mitzvot* that have been traditionally left to men. This latter group is struggling with existing gender roles, even as they are firmly committed to Orthodox Judaism. They pose a serious threat to the status quo, and have been severely criticized from within. Not surprisingly, Frankiel rejects this opinion in the opening pages of her book.[61]

Women's Orthodoxy that revolves around *challah, nerot,* and *niddah* is proudly nonrational. Truth is found not in critical examinations of power relations and of inherited behaviors and beliefs, but in traditions that cannot be rationally encompassed. Thus, the authors stress nature, mysticism, and intuitive knowing.[62] That they cannot establish the truth of their convictions with the usual indices of causality does not seem to bother them. They are pleased that they are part of what they refer to as the great mystery of the universe. Rationality is, after all, not necessary to a religious truth claim, and mystery is closely tied to the concept of revelation. Reason, as such, is suspect because it is the foundation of empirical, scientific thinking associated with modernity.

Instead of relying on human reason, the authors enjoy citing Jewish mysticism, or *Kabbalah,* in their apologetics. The attraction to mysticism is, in itself, a testimony to an alienation from modernity. These Jewish women accept that mysticism is nonrational and incomprehensible from a modern vantage point—but that is its very strength as a source of religious truth. They pridefully relate that these teachings emanate from God at Mount Sinai and were faithfully transmitted for thousands of years, in secret. The hidden, private nature of mystical teachings is the essence of its authenticity. *Kabbalah* is particularly helpful for those engaged in outreach to women. It contains many diverse and highly conflicting teachings about woman, purity, and sexual relations (real or metaphorical) that match the equivocal character of these women's identities. It deals explicitly with gender issues in sometimes daring ways, but it ultimately contains them within a traditional Jewish framework. However, the manner in which the authors use *Kabbalah* in their apologetics illustrates their low status within their community. When they speak of Jewish mysticism, they inadvertently reveal their ignorance of it. They describe Jewish mysticism as if it were a monolithic entity. It is clear that they know of it only through present-day male interpreters who present one particular strand of mystical teachings, and not through direct study of mystical texts, an activity that, in Orthodox circles, is still reserved to men. Other research indicates that in many Orthodox communities, learned men prepare lectures on Jewish mysticism specifically for women.[63]

This new Orthodox women's theology is yet another creative Jewish response to the challenges of modernity. Religion is a rather elastic cultural force. When social and political changes forced the Jews out of their insular communities and corporate existence, religion had to restructure itself in order to survive. Orthodoxy is one of many new forms of Judaism. It should not be mistaken for simply the survival of premodern Judaism, even though Orthodox Jews make this claim. The very existence of this literature, women's theology written by women and institutionally supported by communal organs directed toward Jewish insiders and outsiders, testifies to its novelty. It is indeed unprecedented to find in Jewish literature the elevation of child-bearing women not only above senior women in the community, but above Jewish men who study Torah and dominate the communal Jewish realm. This outlook marks a substantive divergence from the premodern conceptions of both woman and theology.[64]

We should not discount the demographic concerns of the Orthodox community that undergird this theology. Like many Jews, the Orthodox mourn the loss of Jews during the Holocaust and are worried about the continued survival of the Jewish people. Ashkenazic Orthodox Jews strongly identify with the Eastern European Jewish communities and heritage that were essentially obliterated during the Holocaust. They, especially, feel the pressure to replace the losses.[65] Perhaps of greater and more immediate concern, though, is their acute consciousness of the losses stemming from the assimilation of Jews in the modern era. They are particularly desirous of increasing the proportion of Torah observant Jews within world Jewry—to them, the only authentic way of being Jewish.

Relevant to this study are two methods that the Orthodox employ in their attempt to remedy the current demographic crisis. The first is vigorous outreach to non-Orthodox Jews. These efforts are focused almost exclusively on young Jews: college-age youth, young marrieds, and parents of school-age children. Lubavitch Hasidim have established preschools and supplementary and all-day elementary schools not only to teach young children, but to bring their parents to Judaism as well. Because the focus on the young offers the greatest "return" on the investment of time and effort, outreach efforts to the elderly and middle-aged are not that common. Another way of dealing with the problem of assimilation—and it is not distinct from the first—is the direct appeal to Jewish women through formal and information education. This women's theology serves an extremely crucial function: it helps ensure that Jewish women are willing to bear many children and raise them within an Orthodox framework. Not only sociologists are aware of the finding that increased secular education for women and women's career aspirations lead women to restrict the size of their families. An ideology that sanctifies traditional Jewish motherhood and negates the value of women's public and secular pursuits may counteract the modern pressures that continually erode the triumphant future of Orthodoxy.

The inclusion of Orthodox women as leaders in the outreach enterprise demonstrates their increased importance within their community. Although their creative endeavors are still limited by traditional norms, they are not just passive recipients, even in such traditionally male spheres as the creation of theology. It will be interesting to see just how far they are willing and allowed to take their novel interpretations of Torah.

NOTES

1. Earlier versions of this chapter were presented at the Western Region American Academy of Religion and the Jewish Feminist Research Network. We are grateful for the many helpful and insightful comments by our colleagues, including Elizabeth Say, Bruce Phillips, Shoshanna Gershenzon, David Ellenson, Fredelle Spiegel, Robin Goldberg, and Tamar Frankiel.
2. In a household without a woman, however, the adult male is obligated to fulfill the first two commandments; and he is likewise obligated to observe those elements of the *niddah* laws that devolve upon him as husband. *Challah* is a *mitzvah* that is performed only when baking bread, although it can be observed by purchasing only those breads

carrying certification that "*challah* is taken." Orthodox women often interpret this commandment broadly to encompass their role in maintaining a home that operates in accordance with *kashrut*, the dietary laws. *Nerot* is also interpreted broadly to refer to the women's role in enabling her household to uphold the Sabbath laws and to enjoy the Sabbath day. *Niddah* will be explained in detail later.

3. This is not to argue that an Orthodox woman's philosophy of Judaism needs to have this focus. Within Modern (left-wing) Orthodoxy, there are women who articulate something closer to an equal-rights/equal-duties approach. They are not the subject of this chapter.

4. Rita Gross, "Female God Language in a Jewish Context," *Womanspirit Rising: A Feminist Reader in Religion*, eds. Carol P. Christ and Judith Plaskow (San Francisco: Harper & Row, 1979), 167-74.

5. We thank Shoshanna Gershenzon for bringing our attention to one denunciation of the new women's writings in an Orthodox women's magazine distributed throughout the English-speaking world. Rabbi Yosef Neumark criticizes rather sharply these works for being "besides the point," as well as being patronizing and too transparent for intelligent Orthodox women. See his "Feminism vs. Judaism," *The Jewish Woman's Outlook: A Perspective for the Torah Woman*, 6, no. 2 (April-May 1984/Nissan-Iyar 5744): 13-18.

6. These are detailed throughout Leviticus, but chapter 16 describes most concisely this priestly function. The cultural anthropologist Mary Douglas in *Purity and Danger: An Analysis of Concepts of Pollution and Taboo* (London: Routledge and Kegan Paul, 1966), 115, pointed out that Levitical impurity was associated with conditions of the body that indicated a non-intact state: skin disorders, unhealthy genital discharges, infections, seminal emissions, menstruation, and childbirth. She suggests that this concept of impurity manifests the belief that the body is a reflection of the sacred community; any disturbance in the intact nature of the body is symbolic of a breakdown of the social order. Thus it was imperative to prevent the intrusion of these problematicized bodies—and those who had touched them—into the community's sacred spaces.

7. See Leviticus 15, the most detailed treatment of the *niddah*. There is another priestly source that appears to contradict this rather neutral treatment of the *niddah*. Leviticus 18 lists the sexual abominations of the surrounding nations, including sexual relations with a *niddah*, that the Israelites should not practice. The punishment is *karet*, capital punishment inflicted by God. Traditional exegetes harmonize these texts by arguing that the former refers to intercourse with a woman unaware that she is a *niddah*, whereas the latter refers to deliberate intercourse with a *niddah*. Rachel Biale, *Women and Jewish Law: An Exploration of Women's Issues in Halakhic Sources* (New York: Schocken, 1984), 154-58, argues convincingly for a historical approach to these texts; namely, that the latter emerges from the exilic period.

8. Ezekiel 36:17; Ezra 9:10-11.

9. In addition to the menstrual-connected laws that are described in this paragraph, there were two practices observed in some, but not all Jewish communities during late antiquity and medieval times: a man's immersion after experiencing a nocturnal emission (the next morning, or prior to the commencement of the Sabbath); and a man's (and less frequently, a woman's) immersion following sexual intercourse; "Purity and Impurity, Ritual," in *Encyclopaedia Judaica* (Jerusalem: Keter Publishing, 1972), vol. 13, 1405-14. Kabbalistic literature attributes demonic and divine creative power to seminal fluid, and communities in which *Kabbalah* assumes great authority (e.g., Hasidic)

encourage the observance of these rituals. The authors of this chapter observe that these customs are becoming more widely practiced.

10. Babylonian Talmud, Niddah 66a attributes this stringency to the insistence of Jewish women, who in their piety preferred to restrict themselves rather than err and return too early to a state of ritual purity. For a discussion of this attribution, see Judith Plaskow, *Standing Again at Sinai: Judaism from a Feminist Perspective* (New York: Harper & Row, 1990), 65.

11. Babylonian Talmud, Niddah 31b.

12. This new connection amounts to a visible shift in Jewish religion from a religious emphasis on a state of being to an emphasis on a state of doing. Under the rabbis, the "doing" was participating in the whole cycle of rituals and social behaviors of a Jewish woman: marrying, going to the *mikveh*, pregnancy, and so forth.

13. See David Biale, *Eros and the Jews: From Biblical Israel to Contemporary America* (New York: Basic Books, 1992).

14. Moshe Idel, "Sexual Metaphors and Praxis in the *Kabbalah*," *The Jewish Family: Metaphor and Memory*, ed. David Kraemer (New York: Oxford University Press, 1989), 197-224.

15. This is a theme that, in medieval times, was found only in Christian and Gnostic sources. See Rachel Elior, "HaBaD: The Contemplative Ascent to God," in *Jewish Spirituality: From the Sixteenth Century Revival to the Present*, ed. Arthur Green (New York: Crossroad Publishing, 1989), 167. It should be noted that the process of *bitul* involves the dissolution of the finite world, in all its multiple aspects, into the infinite, unified divinity—that is, many are transformed into one.

16. This is spelled out in Abramov's guidebook, cited later in the text.

17. "Modern Orthodoxy" refers to the left wing of the spectrum of Orthodoxy and exhibits the greatest level of receptivity toward non-Orthodox culture. Within Orthodox circles it is regarded as a pejorative, indicating a certain shallowness of commitment to Jewish law; the left wing prefers to call its version of Judaism "Centrist Orthodoxy." See Samuel Heilman and Steven M. Cohen, *Cosmopolitans and Parochials: Modern Orthodox Jews in America* (Chicago: University of Chicago Press, 1989). Frankiel conforms to the Modern Orthodox ideal in her intellectual openness and occupation; however, her position on woman's status in Jewish society (specifically, her rejection of new opportunities for women in the synagogue service) puts her to the right of Modern Orthodoxy as it is usually defined.

18. This type of literature is called *taamei ha-mitzvot* (reasons for the commandments). Theoretically, apologetics takes as its framework the external value system and shows that Judaism competes favorably with it, whereas *taamei ha-mitzvot* literature is constructed from a narrower Jewish world view. In the contemporary context, the distinction between the two has broken down; see "Apologetics," *Encyclopaedia Judaica*, vol. 3, 200.

19. See her preface to *Voice of Sarah: Feminine Spirituality and Traditional Judaism* (New York: Harper & Row, 1990), xi - xiii.

20. Obviously, their husbands are restricted, too; however, the impetus for this comes from within the woman's body, and it is she who performs elaborate rituals in response.

21. We are not claiming that the authors are the first to coin this term or to present all of these interpretations. For example, Moshe Meiselman, *Jewish Woman in Jewish Law* (New York: Ktav Publishing, 1978), 11-14, refers to women as hidden and contrasts the Jewish respect for private spaces to the ancient Greek's value of public display. His

treatment of this, however, is not as developed or complex as that found in the books we are examining here.

22. Abramov, *Secret of Jewish Femininity: Insights into the Practice of Taharat Ha Mishpachah* (Southfield, MI: Targum Press, 1988), 97-109. The testimony on this subject of Yehudis Groner can be found in the Habad book, *The Modern Jewish Woman: A Unique Perspective* (Brooklyn: Lubavitch Educational Foundation for Marriage Enrichment, 1981), 59-60. Frankiel, *Voice of Sarah*, 80-81.

23. This phrase, originally from Psalms 45:14, *kol kevudah vat-melech penimah*, is central to later rabbinic discussions about the role of women. See references in Meiselman, *Jewish Woman*, 14.

24. Shimona Krengel, "Exploring the Hidden," *Wellsprings* 31 (6) 3, February-March, 1990: 4.

25. The key elements of the cult of domesticity are summarized in Elizabeth Say, *Evidence on Her Own Behalf: Women's Narrative as Theological Voice* (Savage, MD: Rowman and Littlefield, 1990), 11-26.

26. Frankiel, *Voice of Sarah*, 31. This interpretation of Esther can also be found in Krengel, "Exploring the Hidden," 5. It appears quite often in Habad interpretations of the holiday of Purim, and it is a key prooftext in the contemporary Habad insistence that, despite the apparent eclipse of divinity, the Redemption is imminent.

27. One could just as easily identify the private sphere with child abuse, embezzlement, conspiracy, and earthquake faults; and identify the public sphere with weddings, communal worship, and distributing food at a homeless shelter.

28. Frankiel, *Voice of Sarah*, 81: "While the descriptions of the time of *niddah* are usually translated 'impurity' or 'uncleanness,' they do not connote magical danger or pollution, let alone dirt. The time is viewed negatively only from the point of view that now creative union cannot properly take place. No other pollution is involved, no other relationships are forbidden. The only things not permitted at this time are entering into sexual relations, and gestures between husband and wife that might lead to such relations." This point will be raised again later, in the discussion of physicality.

29. Krengel, "Exploring the Hidden, " 5, "No matter how much integrity the person has, being in the public eye generates some degree of compromise, of assuming masks or roles, of molding one's self to meet requirements however subtle. . . . The reason that the degree of concealment is a barometer, so to speak, of esteem, is because that which is hidden is both closer to the source of emanation, and more unified. Although God's Oneness defies description, his manifestation in the material world is diversified. . . . Thus it is that concealment connotes preciousness. Something which can be seen is already removed from its source and part of the plurality of the world. That which is hidden is both closer to source and more intrinsically contained and unified."

30. A widely published Orthodox rabbi, Aryeh Kaplan, in *Waters of Eden: The Mystery of the Mikveh* (New York: National Conference of Synagogue Youth/Union of Orthodox Congregations of America, 1976) describes the menstrual cycle as "inefficient, uncomfortable, and unesthetic [sic] "(42), and explains that "Niddah represents the state of expulsion from Eden" (44). The authors are reminded here of Rachel Adler's observation: "Women were taught disgust and shame for their bodies and for the fluid which came out of them, that good, rich, red stuff which nourished ungrateful men through nine fetal months. The *mikveh*, instead of being the primal sea in which all were made new, became the pool in which women were cleansed of their filth and thus became acceptable sexual partners once more. Nor did it help when rabbis informed offended women that their filth was spiritual rather than physical." From editorial

notes to her article, "Tum'ah and Toharah: Ends and Beginnings" *Response*, no. 18 (Summer 1973): 126. (See the next section for our discussion of the Orthodox women's transformation of the concept of *niddah*.)

31. Krengel, "Exploring the Hidden," 7. It should be noted that women are compared to an empty vessel, or the state of *bitul*, both during *niddah* (when they are hidden from view) and during intercourse. In both cases, they are likened to God, in the former case to the *ein sof* itself, and in the latter case to the *sefirah malchut*.

32. Elior, "HaBaD," 186.

33. This corresponds to the notion of liminality: that transformation of identity requires a phase of chaos, nothingness.

34. Saina Sarah Handelman, "Niddah and Mikvah—A Chassidic Approach," *Aura: A Reader on Jewish Womanhood* (New York: Lubavitch Women's Organization, 1984), 62. Frankiel, *Voice of Sarah*, 83, echoes this without the explicit Kabbalistic terminology: "We move from inwardness to transformation and renewal, then to the willingness *to give ourselves to another* in a coming together that mirrors the union of the world with its source. Individuality and independence are balanced at a deep level with interdependence and *mutual surrender*" (italics added).

35. This concept is not unique to Habad mysticism. On this subject, see Elliot Ginsburg, *The Sabbath in Classical Kabbalah* (Albany: State University of New York Press, 1989).

36. Handelman, "Niddah and Mikvah," 61-2.

37. Handelman, "Niddah and Mikvah," 62. The original text of the Tzemach Tzedek's sermon is in *Sefer HaLikutim*, Dach "Tzemach Tzedek," vol. 6, 38-40.

38. Frankiel, *Voice of Sarah*, 81. She writes further (83), "We move from inwardness to transformation and renewal, then to the willingness to give ourselves to another in a coming together that mirrors the union of the world with its source."

39. See Robin Goldberg, "Imagining History as Herstory through the Story of Esther: Restoring and Restorying the Feminine among HaBaD Women" (unpublished manuscript of paper delivered at the 1991 Association for Jewish Studies Annual Conference). We agree with Goldberg's statement, 20, that "the body of God is imagined as the body of Woman as well." She also points out that, despite this re-imaging, the Kabbalistic terminology for "God's body" remains male.

40. Abramov, *Secret of Jewish Femininity*, 30; Frankiel, *Voice of Sarah*, 22; Krengel, "Exploring the Hidden," 5.

41. Krengel, "Exploring the Hidden," 5-6.

42. This is the statement of Rabbi Heschel Greenberg, "Mitzvos as Purification," *Aura*, (op.cit.).

43. Abramov, *Secret of Jewish Femininity*, 31. Krengel, "Exploring the Hidden," 6. Frankiel "Sex and the Spirit," *Tikkun* 5 (6) November-December 1990, 34: "When so channeled [by following the *mitzvot*, including the restrictions on sexual partners], sexuality becomes not only acceptable but actually holy."

44. We do not mean to imply that there is an absolute prohibition on birth control. The contemporary tendency among Orthodox decisors of Jewish law has been to issue a general rule against birth control, but to be flexible in individual cases. An individual woman can appeal for (and will likely receive) permission to use birth control under certain conditions; for example, if pregnancy would endanger her medical or psychological condition, or if she already has borne several children.

45. This can be only partly explained by the religious value of modesty, which limits free discussion of sexuality as well as imposing restrictions on dress. See discussion later.

46. The comparison of men and women, and the discussion of the total woman (her phrase), is found in Abramov, *Secret of Jewish Femininity*, 32-33.
47. Krengel, "Exploring the Hidden," 7.
48. Frankiel, "Sex and the Spirit," 107. We also note that she tends to write about spirituality in a similar manner (107): "Focus, clarity, and the intensity of holiness are what we require in our sexual and our spiritual lives, in our communities and in our relation to the world. And these sprout forth when at last, despite all obstacles, we commit ourselves to a person, a community, a way of life."
49. We wonder how these authors address the matter of female masturbation. Do they consider it permissible? Is it an option during the time of *niddah*? We wonder how they would react to the practice of Ethiopian Jewish women during the time of their menstrual seclusion, when physical intimacy between women is socially sanctioned.
50. Abramov, *Secret of Jewish Femininity*, 100.
51. She explains this at greater length earlier (37) in reference to another woman: "She began to feel that a Torah lifestyle would enhance her ability to express her femininity, whereas the values modern society held out as the ideal for women ignored this aspect of her personality."
52. Abramov, *Secret of Jewish Femininity*, 105.
53. Frankiel, *Voice of Sarah*, 31.
54. Frankiel, *Voice of Sarah*, 35.
55. Frankiel, *Voice of Sarah*, 36.
56. Frankiel, *Voice of Sarah*, 83.
57. Abramov, 39. She quotes the *Midrash* that the Jewish people were redeemed from Egypt due to the merit of the righteous women, and interprets it to refer specifically to these laws.
58. Handelman, "Niddah and Mikvah," 65.
59. Frankiel, *Voice of Sarah*, 56.
60. Lynn Davidman, *Tradition in a Rootless World: Women Turn to Orthodox Judaism* (Berkeley: University of California Press, 1991).
61. Frankiel, *Voice of Sarah*, xi-xii, describes how she once felt rage at the limitations of woman's place in Orthodox Judaism and found incomprehensible Orthodox women's rationales. She now finds herself speaking in much the same way to others. What convinced her that the system was truthful and nourishing was the experience of performing the rituals and "the evidence of the deep inner strength of the women" around her.
62. It is interesting to note the parallel development of neo-pagan women's spiritual expression. Goddess worship, magic, and Wicca, for example, that identify women with natural forces and a symbolic Neolithic religious past actually share many features with this Orthodox women's theology.
63. Goldberg, "Imagining History as Herstory," 12. See also Handelman, "Niddah and Mikvah," 61.
64. From our admittedly unscientific and anecdotal survey, it appears that men do not read this material or pay much attention to it. Several male Orthodox rabbis told us that they recommended it to their female congregants, but had never read it. The text of Abramov's book, however, is preceded by the statements of seven rabbis testifying to its worthiness.
65. According to American Orthodox population estimates from 1965, there were 1 million individuals, one-fifth (200,000) who actually conduct their lives within the framework

of *halachah*. The remaining four-fifths are what sociologists call the *residual* Orthodox (remnants of the traditionally observant Eastern European immigrants "who remained Orthodox in name and are responsible for the statistical picture that shows a higher percentage of older persons among the Orthodox") and *non-observant* Orthodox (those who have no commitment to the practice, but affiliate for other reasons); see Shubert Spero, "Orthodox Judaism," *Movements and Issues in American Judaism,* ed. Bernard Martin (Westport, CT: Greenwood Press, 1978), 85. Population estimates from 1989, according to Jack Wertheimer, "Recent Trends in American Judaism," *American Jewish Year Book* (1989), 81, show a decrease, reporting 540, 000 individuals. Many are in the 18 to 34-year-old group, but (except for N.Y.C.) two or three times this number is in the over-65 age group. There is still a significant proportion that do not practice, but an increasing number of observant Orthodox. Thus, the residual Orthodox has been decreasing (through death) and is still a heavy percentage of the total. It will continue to offset the gains made by the younger childbearing cohort. Still, according to the sociologist Charles S. Liebman, "This is the first generation in over 200 years—that is, since its formulation as the effort by traditional Judaism to confront modernity—in which Orthodoxy is not in decline" (quoted in Wertheimer, "Recent Trends, "108). Orthodox Jews feel themselves to be a denomination with staying power and appeal to a wide range of Jews, but there still remains a deep concern with diminishing numbers.

Part II

Gender and Judaism: The History of a Tradition

Servants and Sexuality: Seduction, Surrogacy, and Rape: Some Observations concerning Class, Gender, and Race in Early Modern Italian Jewish Families

Howard Adelman

Introduction

This chapter will examine the role of servants in the Jewish family in an attempt to test class and race in combination with gender and religion as categories of analysis in the study of the Jewish family in early modern Italy. These cases come from the rabbinic literature (responsa, letters, and contracts) of early-modern, northern Italian Jewry, mostly of German, French, and local Italian origins.[1]

Servants and the Family

The nature of Jewish domestic relations is seen in "A contract for taking possession of a young woman in the house and providing her with food and beverage." Dated 1577-78, the contract was between two men: the venerable David, son of the late Rabbi Moses Leshis, and the sage Reushav Mordechai, son of Rabbi Gamaliel of Foligno. The young woman, the orphan daughter of the late son of David, was called "Pelonit," or "Jane Doe." The most important aspects of the contract involved those who were not party to it, namely Reushav's wife, Simhah, who would do most of the training and supervision, and Pelonit, who would do much hard work. The contract acknowledged that its fulfillment was based on Reushav's ability to prevail upon Simhah to nurture the young woman, "like a mother for her children." Simhah must teach her how to read Hebrew and Italian "according to the ability of the teacher (*hamelammedet*) and the student." In addition to teaching her needlework, to the extent that she was able to do so, she must instruct her in "all the needs of the house that are suitable to be known by every enlightened woman": sweeping, mopping, making beds, washing dishes, dancing, kneading, rolling, baking, salting, porging, cooking, roasting, and playing music (*niggun*).

This list shows the way certain activities such as dancing, music, and porging—which may seem of particular interest to us today, were embedded in a larger context. Dancing and music may indicate to some the high degree to which secular Renaissance culture entered into the domestic life of Italian Jewish women. Porging, or *nikkur*, the process of removing the fat, veins, nerves, and sinews from the hindquarters, is an intricate ritual procedure requiring certification beyond that necessary for kosher slaughtering. The involvement of women in kosher slaughtering and porging has been construed, erroneously, by some as proof of what they called "feminine emancipation" among Italian Jews. Robert Bonfil has argued against this position by showing that the reason women were allowed to slaughter was not emancipation but so that in isolated locations they could provide food for their families.[2] His argument is confirmed by the inclusion of porging in this list of routine domestic activities. The literature on women and porging also indicates that from the time of the Talmud (Hag. 5a) until modern Italy, marriage often qualified a woman for porging.[3] There may have been an economic motivation for allowing domestic porging if, because of their isolation or local laws, Jews could not sell the hindquarters to non-Jews.

The contract explained that the young woman must learn to do all these tasks with great haste, a minimum of discussion, and purity of heart. She must learn the virtues of silence, modesty, humility, and proper cleanliness; arrangement and decoration of her head, body, and clothing; thriftiness with money; and the appropriate respect for all creatures. The contract thus shifted from matters of domestic service to a mentoring relationship between an established woman and a young adolescent, explicitly comparing it to the way a mother must educate, guide, and train a daughter. Further, Simhah was specifically urged to rebuke, afflict, discipline, and chastise Pelonit according to the standards for proper daughters, while having compassion on her at all times. Reushav, to the extent that it would be suitable to his honor, must make sure the young woman obeys his wife. If not, he should treat their young charge harshly so that she would learn humility and good behavior.

The central aspect of the finances discussed in the rest of the contract was that the costs borne by the young woman's family were to cover the effort, education, supervision, and (listed last) food provided by the host family. The hosts, noted for their piety and devotion to their students, may not have had young children of their own at home because no child-care duties were stipulated. They must not treat this orphan as a female slave (*shifchah*), or as a foreign woman (*ishah zarah*), but rather only as a Jewish daughter, praiseworthy and holy. She must respect, honor, and serve them and their house as if she had been born to them. This section of the contract ended with a prayer for the couple: "May it be acceptable that the divine presence will rest upon the deeds of their hands and they will rejoice in their students. . . . Amen."[4]

The positive sentiments toward Jewish servants in this contract are found in other documents from this period. For example, there is a case where a male servant of one Jew fell in love with the female servant of another Jew. The male servant approached her employer to ask for her hand, a common custom in Christian Europe. Her employer was touched by the man's request, saw the marriage as a good arrangement, and wanted to cooperate. He offered a financial contribution for her marriage and noted that she would provide her husband with services as a housekeeper and a companion, in that order. Moreover, he felt this would be a better arrangement than his sending her off to what he characterized as a foreign people (*am nokhri*, Exodus 21:8), by which he seems to mean a more distant Jewish family, who would have sex with her, rape her, and treat her cruelly. However, before consenting to the marriage, he asked the woman what she thought. In approaching her he reviewed his relationship with her; she was an orphan without any living relatives, whom, as a father, he had nourished, taught the ways of modesty, defended from the advances of men, and preserved her reputation and honor. Also mentioned was her friendship with his daughters. Now that she was a mature young woman, he hoped to lead her to marriage with one of the many men who expressed interest in her, and hoped as well that her husband would be the source of her progeny, especially a son who would provide for her. In what he believed was the way of every Jewish woman, she would bless her family by doing weaving or other work, especially if in his travels her husband became unable to provide for his family; this is evidence that servants were not expected to stay servants forever and that this stage of their lives may have ended with marriage, which also might not last forever. The employer stressed to her that the young man was from a good people, again meaning a local Jewish family, and he would protect her, respect her people, crave her beauty, and perpetually ravish her with love. However, after he told her the man's name, she screamed with utter panic:

> How is it that you have hastened to find for me violence and destruction, to bring me under the heel of this vile man, whom I have long known as a whoremaster, a gambler, and a fool, burdened by every evil blemish, he has the teeth of a lion. . . . It would be a disgrace for me to become his wife and to serve him. Who would come up from the garbage, yearning to be a servant betrothed to this evil man? Against me he will turn his hand, again and again, all day, while after the whore he winks his eyes and gestures with his fingers openly in public.

The employer, as well as his family, showed affection and a feeling of kinship for the young female servant in his home, even though he may not have been the best judge of character. The servant had no difficulty expressing her views frankly to her employer.[5] Ultimately, she was going to be serving a man; whether it would be her husband or her employer was still her choice to make.[6]

Sexual Relations between Servants

Two other cases provide further insight into relations between employers and servants, and between male and female servants. In one letter, the writer chided the recipient who had recommended a male servant to him on account of the man's loyalty, honor, and reticence with women. On the basis of this recommendation, the writer brought the servant into his house and appointed him to rule over his people, again meaning his family and his affairs: "I made him a member of my household and I did not withhold from him anything." One day, about a month after this arrangement began, when the employer returned home he heard a sound like a kettle going off. This sound, he soon discovered, was made by this servant and a Jewish woman servant. The employer turned against her, calling her a scoundrel, even though for ten years he had been providing her a lordly larder while she worked in his house as a cook. He then warned this male servant not to have anything further to do with her. However, the next day

(Shabbat), while the whole family, except for the servants, was at synagogue, the two servants took advantage of the opportunity to continue where they had left off. In a few months her employer found out that she was pregnant and he became furious at the man who had recommended the male servant, at the male servant for violating his instructions, and at the female servant for succumbing to what he described as the frivolousness and simplemindedness of women.[7] She too was angry because, afraid of their employer's wrath, none of the men of the household had paid any attention to her. This shows the assumption that companionship for servants was likely with others in the same household and that marriage or pregnancy marked the end of service for a servant. This employer had been able to keep his trusted female servant for ten years because he had fended off all men.

In another case, a man had recommended a young male servant for a position in a household where he soon made a female servant pregnant. The man who had recommended him was reproached by the employer. To defend the servant and himself, he responded with a sarcastic and graphic attempt to blame women for provoking sexual promiscuity. He defended the young male servant's character, arguing he had made only one small mistake in his life by making this woman pregnant and noting that the male servant recognized the child as his own and that he would raise it whether it would be a son or a daughter. The writer further recommended that if the pregnant servant were noisy or rebellious, her present employer should not allow her to stay in his household.[8] Here male solidarity transcended class lines and the result was to reproach women for the behavior of men.

Sexual Relations between Servants and Employers

Several cases of sexual relations involved a married Jewish woman and her male Jewish servant.[9] "Reuven," a rabbinic scholar and businessperson, was married and had two sons and a daughter with his wife, unnamed here. "Shimon" was their Jewish servant. Once Reuven was out of town, Shimon was home with Reuven's wife, and members of the community became suspicious of their conduct together. The rabbis of the city sent instructions through the sexton to Reuven's wife not to let Shimon stay with her in the house while her husband was away. Although the rabbis had started no formal proceedings against her, she protested that the charges, instigated by her enemies, were unsubstantiated. Shimon soon stopped working for her. When Reuven returned from his trip, he stated that he was not suspicious of his wife on account of Shimon or any other man. Reuven and his wife stayed together for at least another year and a half without incident, even though, at Reuven's request, Shimon had returned to his job on a daily basis. Reuven died on his next business trip. Shimon soon proposed marriage to the widow; she accepted and together they drew up an engagement contract. Two rabbis objected because Shimon was suspected of having committed adultery with her while she was married to Reuven, a relationship that would render marriage forbidden. The rabbis sent the sexton to her three times to warn her not to marry Shimon and to threaten that if she did, they would force him to divorce her. Nevertheless, they were married in a Jewish wedding ceremony.

Some rabbis challenged this marriage and Mahalalel Hallelyah of Civitanova, a rabbi in Ancona in the mid-seventeenth century, wrote a lengthy responsum drawing on rabbinic precedents in support of the marriage. His views were endorsed by Simchah Luzzatto and Jacob leveit Halevi, both distinguished rabbis in Venice.[10] Hallelyah argued that witnesses to a woman's indecent conduct with a man (*edei davar mekhu'ar*) were not sufficient proof to convict her of adultery. There had to be witnesses to the actual intercourse (*edei teme'ah*).[11] Such a decisive proof would prevent her from remaining with her husband or ever marrying her lover. Without decisive proof she could remain with her lover after her husband divorced her. Hallelyah also argued that because the charges of adultery had never been adequately investigated, that the warnings had been given to her and not to Shimon, and that a man cannot be forced to divorce his wife, her marriage to Shimon must be allowed. Thus traditional impediments to women's autonomy were used to her benefit. Hallelyah also argued that the legitimacy of the children she had with Reuven should not be endangered by investigating charges of adultery against her. Such caution was a common reason that the rabbis of Italy did not prosecute adultery, putting the stability of the family ahead of personal considerations of honor or legal sanctions against adultery.[12] The fact of a marriage between an employer and a servant attracted little attention.

Another case from around 1571 involved a woman who was married with several children. When her husband suspected that one of the servants made her pregnant, he became jealous and began to insult and abuse her. The servant soon left their house. But before doing so, he told the woman that he wanted to marry her and so she should get help to free herself from her husband. He then wrote her letters in which he described their past intimacies together (*devarim mekhu'arim*), which are proof of her infidelity as well as her literacy.[13] Her brother intercepted one of these letters and gave it to her husband, which is another indication that male solidarity could transcend family ties. Her husband confronted her with it as proof of her adultery, to which she happily confessed. He believed her and divorced her, including in the bill of divorce the stipulation that she could not marry the corespondent. She threatened that if she could not marry him in Judaism, she would marry him in another religion. Her father, who once before had prevented her from apostasy by bringing her back to her husband, appealed to the rabbis to find a Jewish way to allow her to marry her lover; he was sure that otherwise she would commit apostasy.

Moses Provencal (1504-76), a rabbi in Mantua,[14] wrote a responsum addressing her father's request. He began by referring to the servant as a member of the household, *ben bayit* and *mibeito*. Although the letter and the confession may have seemed like straightforward proofs of adultery, he was not willing to concede they were sufficiently incriminating because there had been no eyewitnesses to the actual sexual intercourse. He advised the father to inform the couple that a married woman who committed adultery may never marry her lover. Nevertheless, he stressed that this couple should be treated gently so that she would not convert because the Jews do not have the power to enforce harsh decrees for the benefit of Jewish survival. If they did, he would handle the case differently by abusing and afflicting the couple to make an example out of them to prevent others from doing what they had done. An interesting case of relations between a young master who was ten years old and maidservants is found in Leon Modena's autobiography: "But on account of two of Mordecai's maidservants who hated me and embittered my life by their wickedness—may their master forgive them—I returned home at the end of the year."[15]

Cases also involved male employers who had extramarital relations with female servants. For example, when Samuel Rieti's wife became pregnant, he received a letter of congratulations with the added warning not to keep a female non-Jewish servant in the house.[16] In another case, a man had intercourse with his female servant several times. When she became pregnant, he threw her out of the house. Although she was suspected of then having sexual relations with other men, her former employer recognized the daughter as his own.[17] Another man was seen tumbling on a bed with a female servant; exactly nine months later she gave birth to a son. In the course of the rabbinic investigation of the child's paternity it was also learned that this woman

was engaged to another man who had been out of town, that she had
intercourse with him before he left town, and that she already had a
child with her employer.[18] These cases do not provide sufficient
information for understanding the potentially complex nature of
relationships between servants and employers, including often the basic
fact whether or the servant was Jewish. Some further cases may
provide more extensive detail.

Servants as Surrogates

Two cases provide a poignant look at marriage through the vantage
point of a sexual encounter between a man and his female servant.[19] A
Jewish priest, a *kohen*, and his wife had been married for ten years
without having any children. According to Jewish law (Yevamot 6:6
and 64a) at this point the man must take another wife for purposes of
procreation. During the Middle Ages, the ban against polygyny
attributed to Rabbenu Gershom (960-1028) may not have applied in
cases of infertility.[20] During the early modern period, several Italian
rabbis argued that when taking another wife because a marriage had
been infertile it was not necessary to divorce the first wife; others wrote
that divorcing her was necessary.[21] In this case, the man loved his wife
very dearly and he would not consider divorcing her, nor did she want
to be divorced. He argued that he could not be forced to divorce her
and he did not want to be pressured into taking an additional wife
because he was afraid the two women might become adversaries,
leaving little doubt that polygamy was a realistic possibility.
Nevertheless, he wanted to fulfill God's commandments by producing
Jewish offspring. He therefore joined with a young Jewish woman
(*na'arah*) who was a servant in his house, with the knowledge of his
wife, and, the document noted, "perhaps with her permission."[22] The
servant became pregnant and gave birth to a son. "Then his wife took
the child to her breast and he became a son to her."[23] This seems to
have been a ritual of adoption with biblical resonances. The boy grew
up and began executing the priestly prerogatives, such as reading first
from the Torah and administering the priestly blessing. Some rabbis
tried to stop him, viewing his lineage as defective because of their
understanding of Leviticus 21:7: "They [priests] shall not take a woman
that is a harlot [*zonah*], or profaned [*halalah*]; neither shall they take a
woman put away from her husband [*gerushah*]; for he is holy unto his
God." Most rabbis, however, felt that his mother did not belong to any
of these categories. Some were concerned that as a single woman his

mother had not gone to the ritual bath at the end of her menstrual period so that her son, conceived in impurity, may not be suitable for the priesthood.[24]   Other rabbis countered that conception during menstrual impurity would not be a sufficient reason to alienate a person from the priesthood.   There was no discussion concerning the permissibility of the surrogacy arrangement; if the father had not been a priest it might not have been discussed at all.[25]

Charges of Rape

I have found only one case where a female servant accused her male employer of rape.   It is from 1716, somewhat later than the other materials discussed here.   Nevertheless, like many of the other cases described, it may provide insight into similar behaviors or structures in the Jewish family and community that were not documented or, if they were, I have not yet found, although such cases figure regularly in the records of the period.[26]   The graphic and disturbing details, often from the mouth of the female victim testifying before a Jewish court, are important for finding the woman's voice in history and seeing that women could be witnesses in Jewish courts.   A rumor circulated that Rachel, the daughter of Joshua Isaac Foa, became pregnant having sex with her married employer, "Reuven" (Jedidiah Luzzatto).   Her father protested to the Jewish leaders of the city (*havaad hakaton*), who immediately launched an investigation by a Jewish court.   The court threatened Rachel with dire punishments if she did not tell them the truth.   She stated that it was Reuven who impregnated her and that he had intercourse with her in his house on the first night of Passover, during the intermediate days of Passover, and again on the night of Shavuot.   As proof, she gave a complete description of his body.   She testified that Reuven was the only man, Jewish or Christian, with whom she ever had relations.   The court then cross-examined Rachel's father, her mother, and other men and women who knew her.   The court received vague and divergent replies.   They then summoned Reuven.   There was no mention of any threats being made to intimidate him.   Nevertheless, he responded with anger and arrogance, admitting only that he had unnatural sexual relations with her, including oral and anal intercourse, from which he could not understand how she could have become pregnant.   He then claimed that several other men had been intimate with her.   The court investigated these men and anybody who knew them, but could learn nothing further.   They then summoned

Rachel and Reuven together for cross-examination. The responsum includes a Hebrew transcript of their exchanges with the court:

Are you acquainted with Reuven? I am acquainted with him. Why and how? I am acquainted with him because he betrayed me. How did he betray you? He removed my honor. When did he remove your honor? Before Passover. How much time before Passover? Four days approximately. During the day or during the night? During the day. In his house or where? In his house. In which room of his house? In his room upstairs. Was he alone and nobody else was with him? He was by himself. Tell how it happened. I went upstairs to do my work and he called me so I went to his room and he had intercourse with me.

Reuven interrupted and asked her:

How did I do it and how did it happen? I wanted to go and you grabbed around my body and would not let me go. You revealed my nakedness but I did not consent. So I placed one thigh on top of the other. I wanted to scream but you placed one hand on my mouth and with the other hand you separated my thighs and did what you pleased. Were we on the bed or lying down? I was on your bed the way that you placed me down. Did I stay for long on the bed with you? For about a half hour and for the duration your hand was covering my mouth. After the deed did you go downstairs and not tell anybody about it? I went down but I was too ashamed to tell anybody about it. Afterwards did I have intercourse with you a few more times or not? Did you not have intercourse with me on the first night of Passover, or not? What did I say to you when I had intercourse? You said that you wanted to have intercourse with me. Why did you not scream—so that my wife would have heard and saved you? I replied to you in a loud voice that I did not consent and your wife was asleep and did not hear.

This inquest included further charges, countercharges, and much screaming between the two of them. Reuven denied everything to which he had already confessed and described other activities so offensive to the rabbis that they refused to record them. To protect

Rachel from further abuse, they asked her to leave the proceedings. Reuven claimed that a man had heard from a woman that she saw someone else hugging Rachel. The court then sent for the father of this woman to testify. He charged that this man was a liar. They then sent for this woman who denied everything. Finally, Reuven was excommunicated in the synagogue for raping a Jewish woman who worked in his house. He then grabbed a Torah scroll and vowed that everything that Rachel said was a lie and that any man who would have intercourse with her would be afflicted by all the curses in the Torah. When Rachel was on the birthing stool, the rabbis sent the sexton of the community to command the midwives to interrogate her further. As her birth pangs increased, they told her that she hovered between life and death and that she should confess the truth. She maintained that the only man with whom she ever had intercourse was Reuven. The rabbis thus ruled that Reuven was the father and he must support the child. Rachel's father requested the traditional damages for the shame brought to his daughter, the injury done to his family, his expenses, and his further costs. Many rabbis responded to this case. Some of the key issues included Reuven's paternity, confirmed not only by his confession but because Rachel was a servant in his house; his obligation to support his child; the extent to which this could be considered rape, including the principle that even if a relationship began with compulsion and ended with compliance, it was still considered forced; her not screaming; the event taking place in a city, as opposed to the countryside; the lack of witnesses; and questions about Reuven's ability to hold her mouth, pry her thighs apart, and rape her while she struggled for a half hour; and his assertion that he had tried hard not to make her pregnant but somehow it still happened. This case follows a pattern found in other contemporary rape cases between a master and his servant in which the violent rape was followed by continued prolonged sexual relations and a return to "normality," often because of necessity and a lack of redress.[27] Rabbi Joseph Fiameta condemned Reuven:

> And further, because he is an armed robber robbing the creatures in his house and between his walls, because he shed the blood of war in peace (II Kings 2:5), because the father and mother of the young woman entrusted her to him to serve him and to be under his protection, but, following his evil designs, he seduced her and overpowered her, profaned her, and committed fornication with her, and because it is known to him

that, when they start out, virgins do not know the way of the world . . .[28]

Several punishments were suggested for Reuven. These included forcing him to row a galley ship, expelling his children from school, barring his wife from the synagogue, separating him from the Jewish people, and fining him as a rapist rather than a seducer. In the latter case he must pay for her shame, injury, pain, and a fine—perhaps as much as a dowry because he cannot marry her—which is the customary punishment for a rapist.[29]

Black Servants in Jewish Homes

Finally, on occasion there was a racial component to early modern Jewish domestic life.[30] One case involved a Jewish man who bought a Black, female, non-Jewish slave (*shifchah kushit*). He bought her from a prince who had bought her from the master of a ship, who had plundered a boat owned by Arab merchants containing dates and other merchandise—including Black men and women—headed for market. Following what was characterized as a common pattern, this women established a special relationship with the man and soon gave birth to a son. Neither the mother nor the child had ever immersed in a ritual bath and hence had not converted to Judaism. When the man died and the slave and her son were acquired by his heirs, the question arose, concerning whether conversion by immersion to Judaism would be adequate alone or whether she also needed a document of manumission. In a responsum about this case, Samuel Aboab (1610-1694)—a rabbi in Verona and Venice, among other places—included a document that had been used for freeing slaves in his community for the past forty-five years. Clearly this had not been an isolated case and there may have been a regular transition of slaves, including Black women, into membership in the Jewish community.[31]

In another case involving the conversion of slaves, a Black, non-Jewish, female slave had regularly gone to the ritual bath. Her immersion was not for the purpose of conversion but for ritual purity after menstruation so that she could have religiously correct sexual relations with her Jewish owner. Yehiel ben Azriel Trabot of Ascoli (d. 1591), a rabbi in Ferrara, whose daughter Rivkah was responsible for bringing some of his teachings to the attention of his colleagues who then recorded them for posterity, ruled that the child was her son (but not his) and could not be considered Jewish until he was properly converted.[32] Thus, whereas there may have been a reluctance for single Jewish servant women to go to the ritual bath that would publicize their premarital sexual activity, their offspring with their Jewish employers were considered Jewish because both biological parents were Jewish. This was not the case, however, when the mother was not Jewish.[33] I have not yet found any cases where only the father was not Jewish, which suggests that most Jewish servants worked for other Jews.

Conclusions

My first reading of these cases led me to think that in writing about Jewish servants I had an excellent opportunity to study Jewish history from the bottom up and to explore the relations between different classes of Jews. Further study of the materials, however, led me to the realization that in many respects servants were really a part of the family for which they worked, a finding that is reflected in other periods. Thus the emotional and sexual relationships between employers and servants were an extension of this intimacy as well as a threat to it rather than merely the oppression of one class of Jews by another. The study of this very limited number of cases about the role of servants in Jewish households offers an opportunity for investigating the extended nature of the early modern Jewish family. As in much of Christian Europe, servants were usually young and single, often from families that had fallen on hard times once of the same class as their employers (sometimes even from the same family).[34] Such servants, serving as a temporary stage between leaving home and getting married, are sometimes called "life-cycle servants."[35] When they married, servants could join, or rejoin, the same class as their employers. These servants often, but not always, lived in the same house as their employers, who treated them with affections ranging from paternalistic protection to exploitative abuse. Servants who maintained close contact with their own families turned to them for protection when wronged. The marriage or pregnancy of a servant was highly inconvenient for both the servant and the employer.[36]

The inclusion of servants as part of the family did not produce a sense of taboo concerning sexual liaisons with them. In fact, it seems that the home and family were particularly common venues for sexual escapades and long-term relationships, sometimes considered concubinage. Catholic tradition vacillated on whether concubinage based on marital affection constituted an unofficial marriage. In Italy, while living together without benefit of marriage, Catholic couples often established contractual obligations in matters of fidelity and finances. Even though not sanctioned, or because they were not sanctioned, concubine relationships protected the assets of the woman's family when it could not provide a large enough dowry; thus they often allowed the woman to enter into a relationship with a man of higher status than her family could have afforded her to marry.[37]   Among Catholics, inheritance for the children of concubines was problematic, but certainly not impossible, especially in local courts. Some medieval lay legal authorities were more willing to treat the children of these relationships as legitimate heirs.[38] This tendency was found in the early modern period, but was opposed by the Church, possibly to limit possible heirs so that more unclaimed property would accrue to the Church.[39]   Although there was some tolerance of permanent and monogamous concubinage, polygynous relationships involving both a concubine and a wife were banned by Church law and practice.[40] There is, however, evidence that the children of these relationships were raised and supported by the man and his wife, with varying degrees of enthusiasm.[41]

Jewish law, unlike Catholic law, did not oppose nonmarital and extramarital relationships for men. The concubine was not only called a *pilegesh*, but an *ishah meyuchedet*, a woman who had a long-term, special, intimate relationship with a man. The man may or may not have been married to another woman. The relationship could be terminated without divorce because there had been no betrothal. The relationships explored here between Jewish men and servants show many functional similarities to concubinage, polygyny, and levirate unions among the Jews of the early-modern period, especially in Italy.[42]   These relationships produced offspring that among Jews were regarded as legitimate heirs, presenting very few difficulties.[43] These cases indicate that polygyny had not been eliminated among the Jews, including Ashkenazic Jews, even by the ban attributed to Rabbenu Gershom. Thus for Jews, polygynous relationships could also be a source of legitimate children, especially in infertile marriages. The *ketubah* did not usually protect women when the marriage was affected by infertility or strife. Ironically, the opportunity for men to fulfill religious needs with women other than their wives may have had a salutary effect on the stability of the Jewish family system.[44]

Gender, race, and class as categories of historical analysis provide much insight into the structure of the Jewish family and some appreciation of the intentions and motivations of the men and women involved. Before generalizing from these limited cases, however, further investigation is required to ascertain if the men and women studied here are truly representative of the intentions and motivations of other Jews.

NOTES

1. On the relationship between gender, race, and class in feminist thought, see Elizabeth Spelman, *Inessential Women: Problems of Exclusion in Feminist Thought* (Boston: Beacon Press, 1988). For another treatment of this subject, see the paper presented by Elliott Horowitz at the conference on the family sponsored by the Zalman Shazar Center and the Israeli Historical Society in July 1993. I would like to thank Benjamin Ravid, Arnold Adelman, Mordechai A. Friedman, and Jody Myers for their suggestions.

2. Robert Bonfil, "The Historian's Perception of the Jews in the Italian Renaissance: Towards a Reappraisal," *Revue de etudes juives* 143 (1984): 71-75; and idem, "Qavim lidmutam hachevratit veharuchanit shel yehudei eyzur venetziah hameah hatetzayin," *Tzion* 41(1976): 90-93.

3. See my "Rabbis and Reality: The Public Roles of Jewish Women in the Renaissance and Catholic Restoration," *Jewish History* 5:1 (1991): 27-40.

4. Ms. Jerusalem, Benayahu, vav, 9, vols. 8a-9b. I would like to thank Binyamin Richler, director of the Institute for Microfilmed Hebrew Manuscripts at the Jewish National and University Library in Jerusalem, for bringing this manuscript to my attention and for making a copy of it available to me, Meir Benayahu for his gracious permission to use this manuscript, and the Smith College Committee on Faculty Compensation and Development for the funds for acquiring a microfilm of this manuscript and the others cited here. On the contracts of Christian women domestic servants in fifteenth-century Italy see Christiane Klapisch-Zuber, *Women Family, and Ritual in Renaissance Italy* (Chicago: University of Chicago, 1985), 80.

5. For an instance where maidservants exercised some control in a household, see Leon Modena, *Autobiography of a Seventeenth Century Venetian Rabbi: Leon Modena's Life of Judah*, vol. 8a,. ed. and trans., Mark R. Cohen (Princeton: Princeton University Press, 1988), 86.

6. Yacob Boksenboim, ed., *Iggerot beit rieti* (Tel Aviv: Chaim Rosenberg School of Jewish Studies, Tel Aviv University, 1987), no. 298.

7. Boksenboim, *Iggerot beit rieti*, no. 296

8. Boksenboim, *Iggerot beit rieti*, no. 297

9. All possible combinations of sexual relations between servants and employers are discussed by Cissie Fairchilds, *Domestic Enemies* (Baltimore: Johns Hopkins University Press), in her chapter, "Sexual Relations between Master and Servant," 164-92.

10. The most legible version of this document is in "Halel gamur," Ms. UCLA 779, bx 7.2, no. 28; another version, harder to read and missing several sections, is in Ms. UCLA 779, bx 8.7, no. 8. See also Ms. JTSA 7228, no. 28.

11. On the concept of *tumah*, see Lev. 18:20, Num. 5:13, 14, 20; Dt. 24: 1-4.

12. For instances, see Isaac Lampronti, ed. *Pachad yitzhaq* 2 (Venice, 1750-Berlin 1888), fols. 59b-67b, s. v. "gillui arayot," and the critical edition of Barukh Mordechai Cohen, ed., vol. 5 (Jerusalem: Mosad Harav Quq, 1961), 385-468.

13. For another case of adultery where the wife is incriminated by letters she sent to her lover, see Isaac Lampronti, ed., *Pachad yitzhaq* 5 (Lyck, 1866), fols. 13a-16a.

14. The more legible version is Ms. Jerusalem 8° 1999, no. 114 (Ms. Livorno, Talmud Torah, Bernheimer, no. 23); another version is available in Ms. JTSA 7214, no. 114. For the published summary, see Isaac Lampronti, *Pahad yitzchaq* 5 (Jerusalem, 1986), cols. 430-31, a critical version of the original vol. 3 (Venice, 1753, reprinted in Benei Barak, n.d.), fols. 63b-64a, s. v. "gillui arayot."

15. Leon Modena, *Autobiography*, 86. Also see Fairchilds, *Domestic Enemies*, 174.

16. Boksenboim, *Iggerot beit rieti*, no. 10.

17. Azriel Diena, *Sheelot uteshuvot*, Yacov Boksenboim, ed. (Tel Aviv: Chaim Rosenberg School of Jewish Studies, Tel Aviv University, 1977), no. 138.

18. Meir Katzenellenbogen, *Sheelot uteshuvot* (Krakow, 1842; Reprint Jerusalem, 1980), no. 33.

19. Ms. Jerusalem 8° 1999, nos. 111-12.

20. For a discussion of this topic and further references, see my "Custom, Law, and Gender: Levirate Union among Ashkenazim and Sephardim after the Expulsion from Spain," *The Expulsion of the Jews: 1492 and After*, R.aymond B. Waddington and Arthur H. Williamson, eds.;(New York and London: Garland Publishing, 1994), in addition, see Mordechai A. Friedman, *Ribbui nashim beyisrael* (Jerusalem: Mosad Bialik, 1986), 44.

21. Judah Minz, *Sheelot uteshuvot*, no. 10 (Cracow, 1842; Jerusalem, 1980); Katzenellenbogen, *Sheelot uteshuvot*, nos. 13, 19; Yehiel Trabot, Ms. Jerusalem 8° 194, no. 48; Yehiel Nissim ben Samuel of Pisa, in Yavov Boksenboim, ed., *Sheelot uteshuvot matanot baadam*, no. 157, (Tel Aviv: The Chaim Rosenberg School of Jewish Studies, Tel Aviv University), 1987.; cf. Ms. JTSA 7084, nos. 158 and 144; Ms. Jerusalem 8° 1992, no. 24 (illegible); Leon Modena, *Ziqnei yehudah*, nos. 2, 3, 7, ed. Shlomo Simonsohn,(Jerusalem: Mosad harav ququ, 1956), argued for divorcing the first wife.

22. Ms. Jerusalem 8° 194, no. 48, reports that the wife desires her husband to take another woman in addition to her: *ishto chaftzah yikach acheret aleha.*

23. The prose here follows Exodus 2:10, 1 Kings 3:20, and Ruth 4:16.

24. This concern was also raised in Ms. Jerusalem 4° 617, no. 17, fol. 29b.

25. Similar arrangements are found among the Jews of Spain; see Yom Tov Asis, "'Herem derabbenu gershom,'" *Tzion* 46 (1981): 267-69.

26. *Pachad yitzhaq* 1 (Venice, 1750), cols. 301-61; 1, fols. 31b-37b, s. v. *"ones noten arbaah devarim."*

27. Rape of Servants in Venice is discussed by Guido Ruggiero, *The Boundaries of Eros: Sex, Crime, and Sexuality in Renaissance Venice* (New York: Oxford University Press, 1985), 101, 151.

28. *Pachad yitzhaq* 1, cols. 338-39.

29. For a literary discussion of a rape, see Abraham Yagel, *A Valley of Vision*, David Ruderman, trans. (Philadelphia: University of Pennsylvania Press, 1980), 18, 191-202. See also Emmanuel Le Roy Ladurie, *Montaillou: The Promised Land of Error*, Barbara Bray, trans. (New York: George Braziller, 1978), 169-78.

30. For the nature of racial considerations in Italian Hebrew literature, see my "Finding Women's Voices in Italian Jewish Literature," *Women of the Word: Jewish Women and Jewish Writing*, Judith Baskin, ed. (Detroit: Wayne State University, forthcoming). For further information on black servants in Italy, see Dennis Romano, "The Regulation of Domestic Service in Renaissance Venice," *Sixteenth Century Journal* 22 (1991): 676; Christine Klapisch-Zuber, "Women Servants in Florence in the Fourteenth and Fifteenth Centuries," *Women and Work in PreIndustrial Europe*, ed. Barbara A. Hanawalt (Bloomington: Indiana University Press, 1986), 80.

31. Samuel Aboab, *Devar shmuel*, no. 369 (Venice, 1702; Jerusalem, 1983).
32. For examples of married Spanish Jewish men converting non-Jewish slaves after they became pregnant, see Yom Tov Asis, "'Herem derabbenu gershom,'" 267-69.
33. "Matanot beadam," Ms. JTSA 7084, no. 142; "Ma'arivei nachal," Ms. JTSA 7085, no. 132; see Yosef Green, "Mishpachat trabot," *Sinai* 79 (1976): 153-54; Friedman, *Ribbui nashim*, s. v. *pilegesh*.
34. For example, after the death of her husband, one widow from Constantinople lived with her *yavam* for three years as a hired servant without having received *chalitzah* or *yibbum*. Then he tried to throw her out. The rabbis saw this as an affront to his people. Concerned that she might destroy herself (by suicide or apostasy) because of lack of financial support, a wealthy Venetian rabbi put her up in a hotel at his expense, Modena, *Iggerot yehudah areyeh mimodena*, ed. Yacob Boksenboim (Tel Aviv: The Chaim Rosenberg School of Jewish Studies, 1985), no. 228.
35. See J. Hajnal, "Two Kinds of Pre-industrial Households," *Family Forms in Historic Europe*, Richard Wall et al., eds. (Cambridge: Cambridge University Press, 1983), 92-99; and Miriam Slater, *Family Life in Seventeenth Century London* (London: Routledge and Kegan Paul, 1984), 112-17; Marjorie K. MacIntosh, "Servants and the Household Unit in an Elizabethan English Country," *Journal of Family History* 9 (1984): 20-21; Romano, "The Regulation of Domestic Service," 661-78.
36. See for example, Lawrence Stone, *The Family, Sex, and Marriage in England 1500-1800* (New York: Harper & Row, 1977), 404; See also S. D. Goitein, *A Mediterranean Society* 1, (Berkeley and Los Angeles: University of California Press, 1967), 130-47.
37. James A. Brundage, *Law, Sex, and Christian Society in Medieval Europe* (Chicago: University of Chicago Press, 1987), 446, 516-17.
38. David Nicholas, *The Domestic Life of a Medieval City: Women, Children, and the Family in Fourteenth Century Ghent* (Lincoln, NB: University of Nebraska, 1985), 104-6 and 154-72.
39. Jack Goody, *The Development of the Family and Marriage in Europe* (Cambridge: Cambridge University Press, 1983), 68-82.
40. See Brundage, *Law, Sex, and Christian Society*, 98-103, 245, 297-300, 341-43, 444-47, 514-17; see also Heath Dillard, *Daughters of the Reconquest* (Cambridge: Cambridge University Press, 1984), 127-33.
41. Christopher Brooke, *The Medieval Idea of Marriage* ((Oxford: Oxford University Press, 1991), 33.
42. For a discussion, see Elikim Ellenson, *Nissuim shelo kedat moshe veyisrail* (Tel Aviv: Devir, 1975), 54, 56-62 and Friedman *Ribbui nashim*, xiii and xiv. See also Ms. Jerusalem 4° 617, no. 17, fol. 29b; Yagel, *Valley of Vision*, 226, cf. 309-10; and Judah Sommo's introduction to his *Magen nashim*, in Schirmann, *Tzechot bedichuta dekiddushin*, (Jerusalem: Sifrei Tarshish-Devir), 128.
43. On succession in Jewish law, see Louis M. Epstein, *The Jewish Marriage Contract* (New York: The Jewish Theological Seminary, 1927), 123-25.
44. See also Friedman, *Ribbui nashim*, 28-46, and also Ellenson, *Nissuim*, 83-96. Many of the traditional rabbinic sources on *pilagshim* and sex with servants (both Jewish and Christian) from both Spain, Germany, and Italy have been reviewed by Ephraim Kanarfogel, "Rabbinic Attitudes toward Nonobservance," *Jewish Tradition and Nontraditional Jews*, J. J. Schacter, ed. (Northvale, NJ: Jason Aronson, 1992), 17-26. The one problem with Kanarfogel's excellent presentation is the title. Many of the behaviors he documents, as we have tried to show, are neither nonobservance nor nontraditional, but accepted aspects of rabbinic practice and Jewish tradition.

Chapter 7

An Adventure in Otherness:
Nahida Remy-Ruth Lazarus (1849-1928)

Alan T. Levenson

Nahida Remy began her popular 1891 book *The Jewish Woman* with two striking and methodologically conflicting observations.[1]   First, Remy stated that "in order to comprehend woman, one must study the history of her slavery." Her readers might have expected from such an opening sentence a striking manifesto for the emancipation of Jewish women, doubly oppressed by gender and by religion—and they would not have been disappointed.   Remy passionately defended the "pure," "noble," and "innocent" Eve on the grounds that, having no power to discern good from evil, she had no reason to heed God's command and reject the serpent's tempting offer.   In a misreading of the biblical text worthy of the *midrashists,* Remy rendered God's final punishment of Eve, *"v'hu yimshal bach,"* (Genesis 3:16) as "and he shall be like unto thee," which is departing from a tradition that consistently read in the verse "and he shall rule over thee" a divine mandate for male dominance.[2]   With many acerbic asides, Remy lampooned the need of men to control women instead of summoning up the self-control to master their own sexual selves.[3]

Yet Nahida Remy's second sentence, "to correctly judge the Jewish woman, one must compare her with the women of other nations," introduced her prevailing method.   In chapters titled "Antiquity," "the Christian Idea about Woman and Marriage," "Jewish Literary Women," "Jewish Benefactresses," Remy argued the superiority of Jewish tradition

99

over its pagan, Graeco-Roman, Christian, and contemporary German counterparts, both in portraying woman nobly in literature, and also in assigning women a meaningful role in life. As we shall see, Remy's Jewish apologetic crowds out her feminism, and we are left with an essentially conservative prescription for the modern Jewish woman, to wit, "the only way to an honored and prominent position is the practice of the virtues of their foremothers."[4] This chapter attempts to reconstruct, through a reading of Remy's life and work, the path by which her philo-semitism subverted her proto-feminism. As these two impulses compete and intertwine in Remy's life and work, a brief consideration of each term seems appropriate.

Certainly, contemporary standards of feminist consciousness cannot be imposed on the earliest period of the movement, and this is especially true of German feminism. Despite the presence of political liberalism, a growing middle class, and a Protestant majority—the conditions typical of countries that spawned feminist movements in the nineteenth century—German feminists generally enunciated a more conservative agenda than their American or English counterparts.[5] Bismarckian Germany's conservatism and authoritarianism alike checked the radicalism of the organized feminist movements. German women were slow to win rights of property ownership and marriage without parental consent, slow to gain admission into the universities, and slow to overcome occupational discrimination. The battle for suffrage, a sine qua non of feminism elsewhere, was hotly debated among German feminists. The *Allgemeiner Deutscher Frauenverein* (1865) and the *Bund Deutscher Frauenvereine* (1894) fought mainly for better educational and occupational training, usually with the spectre of spinsterhood and prostitution in the background. It would simply be erroneous to assume that German feminists aimed at equality between men and women.[6] The bulk of bourgeois feminists agreed with Friedrich Naumann's statement that "all other woman's work makes way for the work of motherhood."[7] Remy's lauding the role of the Jewish woman as wife and mother, consequently, cannot be offered as evidence of "subverted" feminism. I wish to highlight, rather, Remy's consistent subordinating of the interests of women to the "higher" consideration of the interests of Judaism, and her privileging the model of the traditional Jewish woman as a paradigm for the future.[8]

Although feminism—Jewish and German—has recently received considerable scholarly attention, the opposite is true of philo-semitism. Tentatively, philo-semitism may be defined as "that sentiment or action which supports Jews on the grounds that being Jewish, they possess certain desirable traits."[9] Like antisemitism, philo-semitism manifests a wide range of forms, motives, and degrees of intensity in the individual philo-semite. Like antisemitism, philo-semitism needs to be defined within a particular place and time. Studying the German context after World War II, Frank Stern noted that philo-semitism was a necessary veneer calculated to prove rehabilitation to the Occupation Forces and to cleanse one's past of the taint of Nazism, and by implication, complicity in the destruction of one's former "Jewish fellow-citizens." Individual guilt also played a role, but the political needs of German society provided the main bulwark of philo-semitism. When those needs evaporated, so too did favorable attitudes toward the Jews.[10]

Nahida Remy, however, came to intellectual maturity in a time when the prevailing "cultural code" was not philo-semitic.[11] In Wilhelmine Germany, antisemitism permeated the court, the churches, and university life. Thus it comes as no surprise that philo-semitism in this society evidenced profound ambivalence. Political philo-semitism in Remy's Germany, far less organized and less popular than its antipode, found expression in the Abwehrverein, an organization that defended the Jews as either fully German already or shortly on the way to becoming so. One spokesperson for this aforementioned group termed intermarriage the "best sort of mission to the Jews." Christian philo-semitism rarely existed without a concomitant program of conversion.[12] Only a handful of Christian clergy objected to Jewish baptism without Christian faith, the cynical path by which, year-in and year-out, hundreds of German Jews left their second-class community.[13]

Antisemitism, of course, contains potentially philo-semitic positions: the fantasy of a Jewish world conspiracy bespeaks their formidable organizational prowess, their domination of national cultural life, and Jewish intellectualism. Only a few examples are required to demonstrate how adept the German intelligentsia was in its ability to both praise the Jews and to bury them. On his seventy-fifth birthday, the novelist Theodor Fontane, after poking fun at his enthusiastic Jewish readership, concluded:

> *Abram, Isack, Israel,*
> *Alle Patriarchen sind zur Stell'.*
> *Stellen mich freundlich an ihre Spitze,*
> *Was sollen mir da noch die Itzenplitze!*
> *Jedem bin ich was gewesen,*
> *Alle haben sie mich gelesen,*
> *Alle kannten mich lange schon*

Und das ist Die Hauptsache . . . "kommen Sie, Cohn."

Despite their avid support, a striking contrast to his preferred Junker audience, Fontane could not overcome his innate prejudices that were easily kindled into anti-Jewish expressions. Throughout his life and despite a large number of Jewish acquaintances, Fontane oscillated between applauding and detesting his "semitic" audience.[14] The economist Werner Sombart became a sought-after speaker in German Jewish intellectual circles on the strength of his pseudo-scholarly *The Jews and Modern Capitalism*. The credit Sombart gave to Jewry as innovators of a capitalistic ethic contained a thinly veiled condemnation of German Jewry. Among the many scholarly licenses that he granted himself, Sombart found hidden Jews at every turn of the road toward capitalism. Jews and their baptized descendants "still retained Jewish characteristics"; "again and again men who contribute to the development of capitalism appear as Christians, who in reality are Jews." Sombart, and his reception in Jewish circles, provides another startling example of the ambivalence of German philo-semitism.[15]

Even the most ardent philosemites in Wilhelmine Germany seem to have been unable to purge themselves of a patronizing attitude toward Jews and unable to overcome the intense "otherness" of the Jew. Take, for instance, these comments of Paula Winkler, a woman who devoted her energies to the career of modern Judaism's most famous religious thinker, who spoke out publicly in favor of Zionism, and who converted to Judaism:

> You ancient people! You wonderful people! Just see how strong your blood is even in the worst of you, and how it will rise up again despite your will. . . .
>
> How I love you, people of sorrow! How strong your heart is and how young it has remained! No, you shall not go under in the confusion of alien peoples. In being different lies all your beauty, all happiness and joy of earth remain your own!. . .
>
> How I love you, you people of people, how I bless you![16]

Remy's philo-semitism, which led to her conversion to Judaism and her adoption of the name Ruth Lazarus, was remarkably free from the ambivalence, patronizing, and stereotyping characteristic of German philo-semitism. While several features of *The Jewish Woman* merit elaboration, the most remarkable feature of this work is the author herself. Remy, a Catholic by birth, had become a Judaic scholar, had mastered Hebrew, and within a few years after the publication of *The Jewish Woman*, had authored three additional studies about Jewish culture. In 1895 Remy married Moritz Lazarus, a renowned Berlin University professor and Jewish communal leader, and completed her own spiritual quest by adopting Judaism. Remy related her singular path to Judaism in the autobiographical *Ich suchte Dich!* (I sought you!). This revealing memoir offers the key to understanding *The Jewish Woman*, published seven years earlier.[17]

Desertion formed the central motif of Nahida Sturmhoeffel's childhood. Abandoned by her father, Nahida's mother left her — whether for reasons of health or money is never made clear — with an aristocratic Italian Catholic pietist. This woman, referred to only as "the Countess," imposed a rigorous and at times physically abusive regimen on the intelligent and sensitive Nahida. She was removed from her hometown, her mother tongue, and her mother, and so waiting for her mother's rescue occupied a large part of the fantasy life. In both *The Jewish Woman* and *Ich suchte Dich*, Nahida Remy recalled the boisterous, capable and good-natured butcher's wife in her hometown of Flatow.[18] Early on, perhaps, this Jewish woman represented a caring female role model and an important counterexample to her own dysfunctional family.

Nahida probably received a more tangible push toward philo-semitism after a beating by "the Countess" and a comforting by a Jewish servant named Amalie.[19] Once again, the theme of Jewish able pragmatism surfaces. For Amalie, who also lives apart from her mother and her family, sends them a portion of her earnings to help with their support. The event that occasioned Nahida's beating is also significant. Nahida was not reading the racy Italian and French classics that the Countess suspected. She was pouring over the Hebrew Scriptures, her favorite book. What the young Nahida loved about the Bible — even if she did not articulate it as clearly as the writer Nahida Ruth Lazarus recollected years later — strikes me as believable; namely, the great emphasis placed on family life and the strong role of the mother that typifies the Hebrew Bible generally and the family narratives of Genesis in particular. The intense loyalty of Sarah, Rivka, Joheved, and Hannah to their favored child struck Nahida as a forceful contrast with statements of Jesus, such as "Who is my mother? Who are my brothers?" and, to his own mother, "Woman, what have I to do with you?" When

Amalie comforted the bleeding Nahida, she also pronounced a benediction recalled as follows:

> What did you speak to me Amalie?
> It was Hebrew
> Hebrew?
> Yes! The language in which your "God of Love" also spoke.
> Nahida regarded her closely. She did not understand her, but she felt that Amalie meant well.
> And what did it mean?
> It is simply an exclamation: "God should protect you" [Gott shaumeir sein].[20]

Finally, she was taken back to Germany by her mother, but Nahida's childhood became easier only by degrees.   Estranged from her classmates by dint of her nonconformist tendencies and independent thinking, Nahida recalled conversations with her school's Protestant pastor.   Confronting Pfarrer Tobold, the first sympathetic Christian figure in Ich suchte Dich, with her preference for the Old Testament, and her disbelief in the need for an intercessor, Nahida guaranteed his refusal to confirm her in the Evangelical (e.g., Protestant) Church. Associating Roman Catholicism with the hated Countess, Nahida now shut the doors to Protestantism too. In her own words, "she was to one and the other a stranger."[21]

Whereas Nahida Remy obviously experienced her familial situation as a deprivation, it removed a major encumbrance to her personal autonomy as an artist.   Unlike the majority of the thousands of nineteenth century German female writers, Remy did not use a pseudonym, nor did she need to submit to the control of a male authority.[22]   In fact, Remy made her way in the world quite successfully. In 1873, the 24-year-old actress, playwright, and free-lance writer met and married the noted theatre-critic Max Remy. Details in her autobiography are sparse, but the couple clearly did not live happily ever after. Max Remy became ill shortly after their marriage and died in 1881, as a major debate over the "Jewish Question" raged in the German press.[23]

Once again Nahida Remy had been abandoned. Her successful career—for she was now the well-known author of Sicilian Sketches— apparently did not end her spiritual longings. At this point, however, Remy found the path that would resolve her perpetual otherness. The medium, once again, would be a combination of female bonding and

Judaism. Prompted by an interest in the "Jewish Question," Remy immersed herself in the Jewish histories of Isaac Marcus Jost and Heinrich Graetz, and she devoured Moses Mendelssohn's *Jerusalem*. But the decisive push toward claiming a Jewish identity came through Remy's acquaintance with Frau Zerline Meyer, an intelligent, aged Berlin Jew.

Through Zerline Meyer, Nahida's Jewish circle had expanded considerably to include, among others, Rabbi Solomon Kohn and Moritz Lazarus. At Lazarus' prompting, Leipzig publisher approached Remy to write *Das juedische Weib*. With her usual industry, Remy immersed herself in the task. Her emotional fondness for Judaism was bolstered with the sources of tradition, and Remy augmented her storehouse of Jewish experiences by frequent visits to Berlin's Potsdamerbruecke synagogue, the site of Franz Rosenzweig's famous Yom Kippur conversion of 1913. Describing her project as she usually did, in the third person, Remy wrote, "She learned to know and understand this people, and because she learned to understand them, she had to love them."[24] Would that it were, that every investigation into Judaism at that time had such ineluctable results!

The intellectual colloquy between these two women developed into a warm emotional bond; Frau Meyer had also been abandoned in a certain sense: as Remy related, alone among her large family, Zerline Meyer had remained true to Judaism.[25] Shortly before her death Zerline Meyer presented her Judaica library to Nahida Remy. In a moving elegy, Remy commented: "One is only a true, good Jewess who learns, loves and honors Judaism. One not need be a scholar, but one must cleave to Judaism with one's whole heart." And, I would argue, Nahida saw herself as the true inheritor of Zerline Meyer—and the proof of her being a worthy heir, a worthy daughter—was her loyalty to Judaism. With the search for a mother completed, the erstwhile actress and novelist found a new vocation: "The struggle against Christian prejudice against the Jews and the elevation of a noble self-consciousness among the Jews themselves."[26] Writing *The Jewish Woman* provided Remy with the opportunity to realize that vocation and to confirm her Jewish legitimacy. Her chapter "Jewish Apostates" is highly revealing. Whereas Remy assigns the role of seducer to the Protestant pietist Friedrich Schleiermacher, she directed her anger at the salonnieres who succumbed to his wiles. Although it may be fair play to focus only on female apostates in a book dedicated to the subject of Jewish women, in her autobiography Remy's shock that some modern

Jews were oblivious to their Judaic heritage was directed solely at women. In a series of exclamations, Remy chastised Jewish women:

> She saw Jewesses impatient to cut short discussion, when it came to the history of their coreligionists. . . . She saw Jewesses who drew back from her because they "feared" that the discussion would return to the three great prophets, whose names they had forgotten. . . . She saw Jewesses, who only waited until the death of their mothers or fathers, in order to have themselves baptized.[27]

To describe Jewish apostasy as a female practice at a time when more males than females apostasized, and to say that it is purely a matter of character, with no reference to the enormous pressures on German Jewry to conform to the majority religion or to the weaknesses of the German-Jewish subculture's nurturing of Jewish identity, cannot be considered a balanced treatment.[28] I hazard a psychological guess here that touches on the limits of Remy's feminism and philo-semitism alike: her (volitional) redefinition of Jewishness that "one is only a true, good Jewess who learns, loves and honors Judaism," which allowed Remy into the fold, also required that some Jewesses be read out of the fold. As an avid reader of Genesis, Remy knew that the firstborn was frequently supplanted: inheritance entailed disinheritance.

Although her formal conversion to Judaism came four years after its publication, *The Jewish Woman* represented a psychological breakthrough for Remy. Before discussing the impact that her unique path to Judaism had on her presentation of Jewish women, we must briefly ask: what sources did Nahida Remy have at her disposal? Alongside the historical and philosophical works already mentioned, and Remy's knowledge of biblical Hebrew, she quoted specialized monographs on the role of the Jewish woman, and the aggadic sections of Talmud translated by August Wuensche and Ignaz Goldhizer. It seems likely that Moritz Lazarus's understanding of Judaism as "Sittenlehre als Gottesdienst" (ethical teachings as Divine service) had a profound impact on Remy.[29] Whereas Lazarus's liberalism imparted his *Ethics of Judaism* with an abstract flavor typical of the "essence of Judaism" approach; his role as a founder of Voelkerpsychologie (ethno-psychology) as well as his small-town Posen upbringing, attuned his ears to the organic life, folkways, and humor of the Jews.[30] Already inclined by her personal encounters to view Judaism as a living, breathing entity rather than an abstraction, the reader of *The Jewish*

Woman, is struck, to quote Yosef Yerushalmi's description of the ex-Marrano Isaac Cardozo, "not by its erudition *per se*, but the manner in which it was acquired. For we see here, how largely by means of translations, a man like Cardozo was able to receive not merely the content but *the very texture* of Jewish tradition" (my italics).[31] The case of Cardozo, like that of Remy, offers testimony to the degree to which one can identify with a tradition (even one as daunting as Judaism) to which one was born a stranger. The challenge for a Marrano like Cardozo—to reclaim an identity that has been alienated from the individual—strikes me as apropos for Remy, despite her self-association with the Moabite Ruth, the classic "convert" of the Hebrew Scriptures. The many examples of Remy's ability to capture the very texture of Judaic tradition may be summarized in her treatment of prayer in the Hebrew Scriptures. Probably working from the original Hebrew, she focused on confidence, gratitude, and devotion—not faith, hope, and charity—as the language of Jewish devotion. In the following quotation, note not only the way in which Remy captures the intimacy that the traditional Jew felt toward the Almighty, but also her willingness to turn the woman's experience into the norm: "This ever-recurring praising, a calling to the Lord, and this continual thinking of the Eternal, this referring to Him [sic] the great and the small, the joyful and the sorrowful events, this is a characteristic trait of Biblical woman-nay, of all the Jewish people."[32]

To make a case for Remy as a feminist, consider her unusual ability to convey a world in which female experiences were cognitively central rather than peripheral. The attention given to women in Lazarus's massive *Ethics of Judaism*, for instance, is minimal. The studies of Gustav Karpeles and Meyer Kayserling, published around the same time as Remy's *The Jewish Woman*, presented little more than a "connect the dots" of famous Jewesses from Deborah to the present.[33] But Remy's works represented not only the rich and famous but also women in the setting of marriage, family, and the workplace. Nor did Remy overlook the venues where women cultivated their personal piety, characterizing visits to the *mikveh* as providing the "freedom and time to develop the inner religious life."[34] Not surprisingly, Remy's portraits of Jewish women approach idealization. In the chapter titled "The Jewish Mother," after relaying a few stories of children abused by their Christian mothers, Remy wrote, "I can safely assert that no Jewish mother would be guilty of such unnatural conduct. I do not believe that a Jewish mother would even send her into a factory."[35] One wonders what Bertha Pappenheim, who founded the Judischer Frauenbund in order to combat Jewish white slavery, would have thought of Remy's depiction![36] Idealization is also a form of stereotyping; yet Amalie's benediction years earlier led Remy to master Hebrew, not to glamorize or to demonize it. And, as far as her Jewish apologetic allowed, Remy remained committed to presenting the social *realia* of Jewish women, including the drudgery, labor, and disappointments.

Remy's feminist tendencies evaporate when the subject threatens a positive appraisal of Judaism. On the biblical view of divorce, Remy contended that the Talmud, rectified "the incomplete Bible text." As a philo-semite and Bible enthusiast, she could not believe that the deuteronomic law actually says "when a man finds something shameful in her, he writes her a note of divorce, gives it to her and dismisses her."[37] Remy also defended the test of the bitter waters for the *sotah* (the woman suspected of adultery) as a psychologically acute way to force an admission of guilt. That men were never forced to drink such waters, despite what Remy said elsewhere about their "tendency" to stray, seems not to deserve mention. Remy joined male apologists in blaming the discrepancy between Jewish ideals and current realities on women: they alone had the task of preserving "a pure and spotless family life." Likewise, Remy's praise of the Talmud for interceding on the part of the "weak and helpless" (women, in the case of divorce) is taken as proof of idealism, not as a situation demanding redress.[38]

During the Imperial period, German women made substantial inroads as wage earners in the burgeoning industrial economy, in the school systems, and even in some of the free professions. New vistas opened for middle-class Jewish women as well, and they soon occupied a notable place in the universities, which were previously an all-male domain. In the 1890s, moreover, German feminism became more assertive in demanding that greater attention be paid to the right of the woman to cultivate her individuality. Who could have been better positioned to effect a synthesis of feminism and Judaism than a gifted autodidact with a key to a critical bastion of Jewish male authority-control of the normative texts? Yet, for the psychological reasons described earlier, Remy insisted that they must define themselves first and foremost as wives and mothers. Remy warned that the Jewish woman should not imagine that "she acts wisely and well if she imitates in everything the non-Jewess, and obliterates every distinction between the latter and herself."[39] Remy encouraged other Jewish women to study Judaism, but only in order to identify, not to revise it. Quite typically, this extraordinary woman with an extraordinary career delimited her feminism sharply. And, though her path to Judaism was unique, like many other Jewish women in German society, she needed to choose between the competing claims of religion and gender.

I have argued that Remy's philo-semitism developed in tandem with a resolution of her abandonment by her mother; yet it cannot be overlooked that Nahida Remy had been abandoned by her father first. There is insufficient evidence to demonstrate that her marriage to Lazarus closed the circle of abandonment-redemption, yet it seems plausible, given that Lazarus, who was twenty-five years older than Remy, was first introduced to her as a mentor and played a catalytic role in her gravitation toward Judaism. Whatever the psychodynamics behind their marriage, it proved to be happy but brief; after seven years, Moritz Lazarus's died in 1902.[40] The bulk of Ruth's efforts, from that time until her death in 1928, were devoted to the publication of Lazarus' voluminous writings, little read today either by scholars of cultural anthropology or of Judaic thought. Lazarus' villa in Merano needed to be sold as postwar inflation eroded Ruth's savings. The publicist Julius Brodnitz, in a short obituary titled "Nahida Remy: A Word of Remembrance and Thanks," recalled meeting her in a small flat, paid for by the "Central Organization of German Citizen of the Jewish Faith," yet speaking with enthusiasm about publishing Lazarus's work. Brodnitz concluded, that "if one would honor our great Moritz Lazarus, one must not forget Nahida Remy." I suspect that our hero might have found that eulogy less sexist than we do; indeed, I imagine that she would prefer to be remembered not only as Nahida Remy, but also as Ruth Lazarus.[41]

Nahida Sturmhoeffel Remy Lazarus was an exception. Consequently, her principal historiographic value inheres in what light she can shed on the rule. In Imperial Germany it took courage to say; "Your people shall be my people; and your God my God" (Ruth 1:17). Remy articulated a monolithic agenda for Jewish women that few would endorse today. That she was able to identify with Judaism to such an extent as to articulate a Jewish agenda at all fixes one pole of the continuum of German attitudes about Jews that ranged from virulent antisemitism on one end, to the philo-semitism of Nahida Remy on the other.

NOTES

1. Nahida Remy's *Das jüdische Weib* (1891) went through at least four editions in German between 1891 and 1922, and was twice published in English. All citations are from Louise Mannheimer's translation, Nahida Remy, *The Jewish Woman* (Cincinnati: C. J. Krehbiel, 1895).
2. Remy, *The Jewish Woman*, 63-64.

3 . Remy, *The Jewish Woman*, 90.
4 . Remy, *The Jewish Woman*, 249.
5 . Richard J. Evans, *The Feminist Movement in Germany, 1894-1933* (London: Sage, 1976), 1-30, and passim.
6 . Evans, *The Feminist Movement in Germany*, 26.
7 . Cited in Amy Hackett, *The Politics of Feminism in Wilhelmine Germany, 1890-1918* (New York: Dissertation, Columbia University, 1976), 333. Helene Lange, one of the leaders of German feminism, also emphasized occupational training as a means of improving mothering skills. Evans, *The Feminist Movement in Germany*, 27-28.
8 . Hackett, *The Politics of Feminism*, xvii; Susannah Heschel, "Introduction," *On Being a Jewish Feminist* (New York: Schocken, 1983).
9 . Alan Edelstein, *An Unacknowledged Harmony: Philo-Semitism and the Survival of European Jewry* (Westport, CT: Greenwood Press, 1982).
10 . Frank Stern, *The Whitewashing of the Yellow Badge. Antisemitism and Philosemitism in Postwar Germany*, William Templer, trans. ,(Oxford-New York: Pergamon Press, 1992).
11 . Shulamit Volkov, "Antisemitism as a Cultural Code,." *Leo Baeck Institute Yearbook* 23 (1978): 25-46 (hereafter, *LBI Yearbook*).
12 . The nexus between Christian philo-semitism and conversionary (even millenarian) expectations deserves further investigation.
13 . The "philosemite" was Sanskrit authority Albrecht Weber, quoted in Barbara Suchy, "The *Abwehrverein* I," *LBI Yearbook* 28 (1983): 227-28. See Todd Endelman, "The Social and Political Context of Conversion in Germany and England, 1870-1914," *Jewish Apostasy in the Modern World* (New York: Holmes and Meier, 1987).
14 . Wolfgang Paulsen, "Theodor Fontane-The Philosemitic Antisemite." *LBI Yearbook* 26 (1981): 312-13.
15 . Paul Mendes-Flohr, "Werner Sombart's 'The Jews and Modern Capitalism'." *LBI Yearbook* 21 (1976): 87-107. My reading is based purely on Mendes-Flohr's.
16 . Paula Winkler, "Betrachtungen einer Philozionistin." *Die Welt* 36 (6 Sept., 1901). See also Maurice Friedman, *Martin Buber's Life and Work: The Early Years, 1878-1923* (Detroit: Wayne State Press, 1988), 50-52
17 . Nahida Ruth Lazarus, *Ich Suchte Dich! Biographische Erzaelung* (Berlin: Siegfried Cronbach, 1898). The name Nahida Remy appears in parentheses beneath Nahida Ruth Lazarus. This autobiography was translated into Hebrew in 1932 under the title *Bikashtikha*. The title reflects the roots of Remy's quest. Putatively, the "Dich" is God; psychologically, the "Dich" seems also to be her lost mother.
18 . Lazarus, *Ich Suchte Dich*, 10-11; Remy, *The Jewish Woman*, 247.
19 . Remy always refers to "Die Grafin" by her title, never her proper name.
20 . Lazarus, *Ich Suchte Dich*, 66-67.
21 . Lazarus, *Ich Suchte Dich*, 168-69.
22 . Patricia Herminghouse, "Women and the Literary Enterprise in Nineteenth-Century Germany," in Ruth-Ellen Joeres, ed., *German Women in the Eighteenth and Nineteenth Centuries* (Bloomington: Indiana University Press, 1986), 78-93.
23 . Nahida's first meeting with Max Remy contains an interesting detail: Remy's mother was at his office and the conversation took place between the two women--the evident affection at this meeting was between Nahida and Mrs. Remy, not between Nahida and Max. It was also at this meeting that we learn two more interesting family facts: that Nahida's mother was also named Nahida, a name taken from a novel; Nahida tells Mrs.

Remy that she "never speaks of her father" because he "made my mother very unfortunate/unhappy." Lazarus, *Ich Suchte Dich,* 180.

24. Lazarus, *Ich Suchte Dich,* 194.

25. Lazarus, *Ich Suchte Dich,* 207.

26. Lazarus, *Ich Suchte Dich,* 211.

27. Lazarus, *Ich Suchte Dich,* 206.

28. Of course, Nahida Remy was not the only contemporary to lay the blame for Jewish apostasy at the feet of Jewish women. See Deborah Hertz, *Jewish High Society in Old Regime Berlin* (New Haven: Yale University Press, 1989), 7-22.

29. "Sittenlehre als Gottesdienst" is a phrase Remy used in her *Culturstudien über das Judenthum* (Berlin: C. Dunker, 1893). Only the first volume of Lazarus's massive two-volume work on Jewish philosophy, *The Ethics of Judaism* (Philadelphia: Jewish Publication Society, 1899) appeared during his lifetime. The second volume appeared posthumously in 1911. We know from letters that, after their marriage, Remy aided Lazarus in bringing this work to light. See David Baumgardt, "The Ethics of Lazarus and Steinthal," *LBI Yearbook* 2 (1957): 205-17.

30. Lazarus' s attention to the people of Israel was an unusual one for a Jewish thinker in the German Kulturbereich, whether liberal (Hermann Cohen) or Orthodox (Samson Raphael Hirsch).

31. Yosef Hayim Yerushalmi, *From Spanish Court to Italian Ghetto* (New York: Columbia University Press, 1972), 266. As Baumgardt, "The Ethics of Lazarus and Steinthal," noted many years ago, Lazarus was the first Jewish scholar to alert the non-Jewish world to humor contained within traditional sources.

32. Remy, *Prayer in the Bible and the Talmud* (New York, 1894), 6-20.

33. See for instance: Gustav Karpeles, *Die Frauen in der jüdischen Literatur: Ein Vortrage* (Berlin, 1889); Meyer Kayserling, *Die Jüdischen Frauen in der Geschichte, Literatur und Kunst* (Leipzig, 1879).

34. Remy, *The Jewish Woman,* 156.

35. Remy, *The Jewish Woman,* 160.

36. Initially, Remy had neglected to write a chapter on the Jewish mother. Remy needed to be prompted by Moritz Lazarus to rectify this oversight, his sole substantive criticisms of her work. Lazarus, *Ich Suchte Dich,* 204-5. On Bertha Pappenheim, see Marion Kaplan, *The Jewish Feminist Movement in Germany: The Campaigns of the Jüdischer Frauenbund, 1904-1938* (Westport, CT: Greenwood Press, 1979).

37. Remy, *The Jewish Woman,* 50.

38. Remy, *The Jewish Woman,* 50-51.

39. Remy, *The Jewish Woman,* 251.

40. That Ruth was happy in her second marriage seems clear from her devotion to publishing Lazarus' posthumous works. In a letter to his cousin Johanna Berendt, Moritz Lazarus writes: "Taken all in all — this excellent woman is my light and my life. That she is a talented, successful writer, you know; but she is also a highly cultivated soul, and enthusiastic. . . . How can I describe her? Take a look at Song of Solomon 31:31." Quoted in Ingrid Belke, *Moritz Lazarus und Heymann Steinthal: Die Begruender der Voelkerpsychologie in ihren Briefen,* Vol. 1 (Tubingen: J. C. B. Mohr, 1971), 242-43.

41. Julius Brodnitz, "Nahida Remy" *CV Zeitung* (20 January 1928): 28-29.

Chapter 8

Jewish Identity and the "New Woman": Central European Jewish University Women in the Early Twentieth Century

Harriet Pass Freidenreich

In her memoirs, entitled *Der dreifache Fluch* (The Threefold Curse), Käte Frankenthal identified the three strikes she had against her in Nazi Germany: she was a Jew, an intellectual, and a socialist. Frankenthal was born in 1889 into an affluent German-Jewish family; her father was a successful businessperson and her mother a devoted housewife. Although she remained deeply attached to her parents, she rejected their middle-class Jewish lifestyle and values. Whereas her father was president of the Jewish community of Kiel, religion lacked importance in her life and she found associating with other Jews too restricting. She decided at an early age not to marry, dismissing the possibility of intermarriage but claiming to have no love for Jewish men and to be "turned off by anything Jewish in appearance or manner." Rejecting the idea that Jews should have a monopoly on her interest, she formally left the Gemeinde and declared herself *konfessionslos* in 1923 after both of her parents had died. Frankenthal was a Jew by fate, but a medical doctor and a socialist politician by choice.[1]

In many respects, Käte Frankenthal was an exceptional and unconventional woman; she learned fencing and boxing for self-defense, often wore men's attire, smoked cigars, and drank whisky. But her lack of a strong, positive Jewish identity was by no means unusual among the 400 Central European university women of Jewish origin whose lives I am presently studying. Like most of these women, she came from an upper-middle-class family and received an excellent secular education, but very little formal Jewish training other than required religious knowledge classes at school. Her family was involved in the Jewish community and socialized primarily with other Jews, but observed few Jewish practices in the home and was largely assimilated into German culture. She had little desire to create a traditional Jewish household of her own, consciously refusing to follow her mother's example as a Jewish homemaker and disdaining cooking, washing, cleaning, and child-care. Instead of taking the expected path of Jewish womanhood as wife and mother, she turned to a professional career as a physician and political involvement as an Social Democratic Party (SPD) deputy on the Berlin Municipal Council.[2] Like many other educated Jewish women in early twentieth-century Germany and Austria, Käte Frankenthal considered herself a Jew by descent, but not by religion or by nationality.

Despite their shared socioeconomic background, university-educated women in pre-Nazi Germany and Austria nevertheless demonstrated a spectrum of Jewish personal, religious, and national identity. For convenience, I have divided them into three broad groupings: the "Former Jews" who left the Jewish community, the "Just Jews" who remained affiliated, and the "Jewish Jews" who actively affirmed their Jewishness. Membership in the Gemeinde by itself is not necessarily a very meaningful criterion for women, however, because in many instances the decision concerning whether to remain in the community was made not by the women themselves, but by their fathers or husbands who paid the mandatory taxes as heads of the household.

Ascertaining and measuring the identity of modern Jewish women is by no means an easy task. For men, one can utilize public indicators of Jewish involvement, like participation in synagogue and Jewish communal activities, as well as religious behavior and life-cycle events, such as circumcision and Bar Mitzvah. For women, who were largely excluded from the public domain of synagogue and community and whose documented Jewish life-cycle events were most likely to be marriage and burial, Jewish identity was mainly expressed in the private sphere of the home and was often hidden from general view. Although I realize that much of a woman's Jewish identity was personal and based on values and attitudes that defy quantification and can change over a lifetime, I have tried to develop a rough scale of measurable behaviors upon which to evaluate these women as Jews. My ascending ladder of Jewish consciousness consists of the following eight levels: (1) women whose parents were Jews; (2) those who acknowledged their Jewish origins; (3) members of the Jewish community; (4) those who associated primarily with other Jews and/or married Jews; (5) women who observed major Jewish holidays, whether in the home or the synagogue; (6) members of Jewish youth, women's, or Zionist organizations; (7) those who sought further Jewish education as adults or did research on Jewish topics; and (8) those who observed Shabbat and Jewish dietary laws.

At the bottom of this ladder are the "Former Jews," often referred to as apostates, who constitute about twenty percent of my sample.[3] They are Jews by descent who might acknowledge their Jewish origins but who largely reject their Jewish identity by formally leaving the Jewish community, whether through baptism or by becoming officially *konfessionslos* (without religion). Thirty-five women, roughly half of this group, became Christians; most were baptized as Protestants, but others became Catholics and a few eventually joined the Unitarian Church. In some cases, these women were already baptized as children, but in other instances they converted as adults. (In two rather exceptional cases, women who had been baptized as children and whose mothers were also baptized returned to Judaism as adults.[4]) Most of these women knew very little about Judaism from their homes or their formal education. Their families had often celebrated Christmas with trees and exchanges of gifts. Raised in an extremely assimilated environment, it is scarcely surprising that such women no longer identified themselves as Jews.[5]

But in several cases at least, adult baptism resulted from a quest for spiritual fulfillment. Alice Salomon, a pioneer in social work education and an active feminist, turned to Protestantism for solace and sustenance during World War I after the death of her mother.[6] Edith Stein, the philosopher and educator who became a Catholic nun, was influenced by the examples of other baptized Jewish intellectuals, like Husserl, who served as her mentors and role models. In her memoir (interestingly enough entitled *Life in a Jewish Family*), which she wrote in a convent in the mid-1930s, she describes her mother as a pious woman who attended synagogue quite regularly. Yet Stein found Judaism as she knew it religiously and intellectually unsatisfying and rejected her mother's traditional Jewish piety.[7]

Others left the Jewish community less for spiritual than for practical reasons, such as marriage or job prospects. An academic or even a public school teaching career proved extremely difficult for unbaptized Jews. With a few notable exceptions, the women who managed to achieve untenured academic positions had left the Jewish community beforehand. Most of these women came from highly assimilated backgrounds and some refused even to acknowledge their Jewish origins. Although most female academics remained single, those who married tended to marry Protestants or other "Former Jews."[8]

Very few Jewish women with higher education demonstrated strong religiosity. Instead they tended to reject religion in nearly all forms and were more likely to consider themselves humanists and adopt a left-wing ideology. Twenty percent of my total sample (or eighty women), including twenty-five percent of those born after 1900, either sympathized with or were actively involved in Social Democratic or Communist politics in Central Europe. Most of these leftist women retained at least nominal affiliation with the Jewish community, but some of the more prominent activists — such as Käte Frankenthal, Toni Sender, and Käthe Leichter — like their male counterparts, opted to become *konfessionslos* for political as well as personal reasons.[9]

The overwhelming majority of the university women of Jewish origin never formally left the official Jewish community. In certain cases, they remained Jewish simply because they did not consider it honorable to abandon a minority group in distress.[10] These "Just Jews," the roughly two thirds of my sample who were located on the middle rungs of the ladder, accepted their Jewishness as a fact of life, even though this aspect of their personal identity did not always play an important role in their lives before the advent of Nazism.

Much like Jewish men, Jewish women were very much a part of the general process of assimilation into the middle-class German culture in Central Europe in the late nineteenth and early twentieth centuries. Marion Kaplan has argued that women in Imperial Germany often served as the bastions, maintaining a Jewish lifestyle and traditional values in the home.[11] Whereas this might have been true for many of their grandmothers and some of their mothers, for the most part the two generations of Jewish women who attended university before and after World War I were not interested in perpetuating the role of traditional Jewish homemaker. Except for some of the women who married early, especially those who dropped out of school before completing their degrees, university-educated Jewish women attempted to carve out new personal and career roles, rather than follow in their mothers' footsteps.

In many families, decreasing levels of Jewish observance among women can be traced over several generations. As one unmarried woman with a doctorate in chemistry expressed it: "My grandmother went to synagogue and was involved in Jewish organizations, my mother observed the high holidays, we did not deny being Jewish."[12] Another woman with a doctorate in economics and three children refers in her memoirs to an Orthodox grandmother who observed dietary laws and Zionist parents who went to synagogue twice a year, but states that "somehow, any observance of the Jewish holidays has disappeared from my life."[13] Both memoirs and questionnaire responses clearly indicate that the Jewish observances that women recalled from their childhood homes were in most cases no longer a part of their lives as adults.

Roughly one quarter of my sample never married. Some of these women continued to live with their parents and occasionally shared in family Jewish observances. But, when they lived alone, they rarely, if ever, followed Jewish religious practices. Unmarried women had a very difficult time fitting into the framework of organized Jewish life. There was little place for them within Jewish institutions, although some worked as social workers in the Jewish community and others taught in Jewish schools, especially during the thirties. A few single women, such as the lawyer Margarete Berent, became involved with the Jüdischer Frauenbund, the moderate Jewish feminist organization, and attempted to fight for more rights for women within the community—but they were clearly exceptions.[14]

Among those university women who married, many did so fairly late in life and at least a third had no children. Most of these women married Jewish men with similar backgrounds, but they did not necessarily consciously raise their children as Jews. Aside from the small group of women who came from modern Orthodox backgrounds (fewer than ten in all), it is unclear how many of these married women observed Jewish festivals in their own homes or lit candles on Friday night, let alone followed Jewish dietary laws.

Women rarely attended synagogue, except perhaps for the High Holydays.[15] Few women even mentioned synagogue attendance in their memoirs, although at least one woman, Charlotte Wolff (a physician and a lesbian), expressed her indignation at the separate seating of women that characterized virtually all synagogues in Central Europe, whether Orthodox or Liberal:

Both the atmosphere and the happenings in the Synagogue almost suffocated me. The religious service was held on the ground floor, which was reserved for males. Women did not participate in it, and had to sit in a gallery above. . . . The women, second-class citizens of God, chatted about children, house and clothes, and paraded their fineries to one another. They didn't understand Hebrew anyway; neither did most of the men I believe. . . . I accepted neither the discrimination between the sexes nor the hollow holiness of the religious services.[16]

Seeing no likelihood of changing the synagogue, Wolff and many other educated Jewish women simply stopped attending services.

Whereas university-educated Jewish men, including several of the fathers and husbands of women in my data base, provided the leadership within the Jewish community, women with similar education and commitment played virtually no role in communal governance. In some cases, tax-paying female heads of household gained the right to vote in communal elections, but they could not be elected to communal office. Several university-educated women, including Käte Frankenthal, served on municipal councils and in provincial legislatures, but none could become representatives in the Gemeinde. Middle-class German-Jewish women were typically expected to become involved in Jewish women's volunteer service organizations—such as the Jüdischer Frauenbund, B'nai B'rith Women's auxiliaries, or Women's International Zionist Organization (WIZO)—but relatively few university women ever became actively involved in such organizations.

Most of these women were not joiners; they were individualists who sought intellectual fulfillment in their academic studies, professional careers, or personal family lives as wives of professionals. Unlike their male counterparts, Jewish women students rarely established their own societies even though they formed a disproportionately large group among female students. They were more likely to join mixed-sex socialist or even Zionist student societies than to belong to women's organizations, although some affiliated with women's professional groups.

Although being Jewish in Central Europe was generally viewed as a matter of religious rather than national affiliation, measured by identification with Jewish institutions or by the presence or absence of ritual practices, for many women being Jewish was simply a matter of descent and fate, because they no longer performed Jewish ceremonies these "Just Jews" associated primarily with other Jews, not necessarily by choice, but as a result of social ostracism. They were Jewish simply because they "looked Jewish" or were known to be Jewish, whether or not they wanted to acknowledge this fact. Some of these women have claimed that "Hitler made me a Jew," but most indicate they were aware of antisemitism long before the rise of Nazism, even if it was not directed at them personally.

The fairly small minority of "Jewish Jews" within my sample provide exceptions to many of these general rules. This group, at most fifteen percent of the total, approached the top rungs of the consciousness ladder and actively affirmed their Jewishness, whether by perpetuating Jewish observances in their homes, involvement in Jewish organizations, acknowledgment of a Jewish nationality, or seeking to acquire more advanced Jewish knowledge. Some were raised in traditional or modern Orthodox households and received supplementary Jewish educations from local rabbis.[17] Others grew up in a Zionist milieu or else rebelled against their assimilated backgrounds by becoming Jewish nationalists.[18] Even for many of the Orthodox women, identifying themselves as Jews by nationality and involving themselves in Zionist activities provided a vehicle for a more positive and modern identification as Jews. As one woman with a doctorate in history, born in 1900, wrote me in a recent letter, "Why did I become a Zionist, although I was raised in the [S. R.] Hirsch [Orthodox] community [in Frankfurt]? This was not a common event in those days, but it was not unusual either. Those were the happy and hopeful days after World War I and being Jewish was a matter of pride and joy."[19]

Women rarely had opportunities for advanced study of Judaica, because European universities did not offer Jewish Studies courses and rabbinical seminaries proved an inhospitable environment for women. Nevertheless, a small contingent of women sought out both formal and informal means of acquiring more knowledge about Jews and Judaism to supplement their higher general education. Some attended lectures by Hermann Cohen or participated in Franz Rosenzweig's Lehrhaus; others took courses on ancient Israel or chose to write dissertations on specifically Jewish topics in fields such as German literature or economics. A few, including Hannah Arendt and Selma Stern-Täubler, pursued research on Jewish issues after receiving their doctorates. Such women tended to develop a stronger than average Jewish consciousness and commitment, although they rarely adopted a traditional Jewish lifestyle.[20]

Rahel Goitein Straus, one of the first women to earn a medical degree at a German university, and later the mother of five children, provides an example of a new Jewish superwoman of the early twentieth century. Born in 1880 in Karlsruhe, the daughter of an Orthodox rabbi, she was raised by her widowed mother in a very observant household. She received an unusually thorough Jewish education and became an ardent Zionist while still a teenager. Straus did not rebel against the role of Jewish wife and mother, but ran a fairly traditional, kosher Jewish household, graciously welcoming many visiting Zionist dignitaries as well as numerous Jewish students into her home. She organized and led various women's Zionist groups in Munich, was active in feminist organizations, and served on the national executive board of the non-Zionist Jüdischer Frauenbund. In addition, she maintained a private medical practice, gave lectures to women on proper nutrition and birth control, and wrote a pamphlet for mothers explaining how to discuss sex with their daughters. Whereas her lawyer husband served as vice-president of the Munich Gemeinde in charge of welfare, Straus limited her activities largely to the women's sphere.[21]

But committed Jews like Rahel Goitein Straus were far more exceptional among Central European Jewish university women in the early twentieth century than socialists like Käte Frankenthal or the many others who either rejected their Jewishness or only allowed it to play a minimal role in their lives until Hitler appeared on the scene. By acquiring a higher education equal to that of men, these "new women," the products of the first generation of feminism, strove to define new and more equal roles for women in society but not necessarily within the Jewish community. University women were dissatisfied with the traditional middle-class Jewish woman's role as homemaker. But although most of these women retained nominal Jewish affiliation, they rarely attempted to reform their community or the position of women within it. Prior to the Nazi era, Germany and Austria certainly produced a very large number of "new women" of Jewish origin, but the "new Jewish woman"—a modern woman with a strong, positive Jewish identity—had scarcely begun to emerge.

NOTES

1. Käte Frankenthal, *Der dreifache Fluch: Jüdin, Intellektuelle, Sozialistin* (Frankfurt: Campus Verlag, 1981).
2. Ibid.

3 . Percentages of sample and generalizations are drawn from a data base of 400 Jewish university women compiled from memoirs, questionnaire responses, interviews, biographical dictionaries, and other available published and unpublished sources.

4 . Emily Melchior Braun, Unpublished memoir, LBI Memoir Collection, ME 231; interview with GSLF, Yardley, PA, September 1990.

5 . Marie Munk, Reminiscences/Memoirs (1961), LBI Memoir Collection; Else Gerstel, Grandma, Times have changed!, Unpublished memoir, LBI Memoir Collection, ME 184; Hilde Spiel, *Die hellen und die finsteren Zeiten: Erinnerungen, 1911-1946* (Munich: List, 1989); Marie Langer, *Von Wien bis Managua: Wege einer Psychoanalytiker* (Frankfurt: Kore, 1986).

6 . Alice Salomon, "Character Is Destiny: An Autobiography," *LBI Memoir Collection*, AR-3875, 120-24.

7 . Edith Stein, *Life in a Jewish Family, 1891-1916, Collected Works of Edith Stein, Sister Teresa Benedicta of the Cross, Discalced Carmelite,* L. Gelber and Romaeus Leuven, eds., Vol. 1 Washington, D. C.: Institute of Carmelite Studies Publications, 1986.

8 . Elise Richter, "Summe des Lebens": Lebensfreuden, Lebensleid, Unpublished memoir, 1940, Nachlass Elise und Helene Richter, MA 9, 336/47, 3, Landes- und Stadtsarhiv, Vienna; Hedwig Hintze, Lebenslauf, Habilitationen #1243, HUzBA, Berlin; "Charlotte Bühler," in Ludwig Pongratz et al., eds., *Psychologie in Selbstdarstellungen* (Bern: Huber, 1972), 9-42; Larissa Bonfante, "Margarete Bieber (1879-1978): An Archaeologist in Two Worlds," in Claire Richter Sherman, ed., *Women as Interpreters of the Visual Arts, 1820-1979* (Westport, CT: Greenwood Press, 1981), 239-73.

9 . Stella Klein-Löw, *Erinnerungen: Erlebtes und Gedachtes* (Vienna: Jugend und Volk, 1980); Gisela Konopka, *Courage and Love* (Edina: Burgess Printing, 1988); Frankenthal, *Der dreifache Fluch*; Toni Sender, *The Autobiography of a German Rebel* (New York: Vanguard, 1939); Herbert Steiner, ed., *Käthe Leichter: Leben und Werk* (Vienna: Europaverlag, 1973).

10 . This attitude is sometimes attributed to their fathers, e.g., Johanna Philippson, *Fragments from an Autobiography* (courtesy of F. Lustig, London); Elisabeth Moore (Beate Clara Berwin), My Own Development, bMS, Ger91, 26, Houghton Library, Harvard University, Boston; Klein-Löw, *Erinnerungen*.

11 . Marion A. Kaplan, *The Making of the Jewish Middle Class: Women, Family and Identity in Imperial Germany* (Oxford: Oxford University Press, 1991), 64-84.

12 . Questionnaire completed in 1992 by EE, b.1909 in Breslau.

13 . Ruth Feitelberg Hope, "The Story of My Family," (ME Collection 770), LBI Memoir 21, 51, 86-87.

14 . Tilly Epstein, Einige Erinnerungen aus Philanthropin in Frankfurt am Main, LBI Memoir Collection, ME 378; Margot Pottlitzer, Interview of Kate Freyhan (1974), LBI Memoir Collection, ME 242; Margarete Berent Collection, AR-2861/2862.

15 . Charlotte Popper in Monika Richarz, ed., *Jewish Life in Germany: Memoirs from Three Centuries* (Bloomington: Indiana University Press, 1991), 266-67.

16 . Charlotte Wolff, *Hindsight* (London: Quartet Books, 1980), 47-48.

17 . Frieda Hirsch, Mein Weg von Karlsruhe über Heidelberg nach Haifa, 1890-1965, unpublished memoir, LBI Memoir Collection; Popper op. cit.; Yaakov and Hadassah Wehl, *House Calls to Eternity: The Story of Dr. Selma Wehl* (Brooklyn: Mesorah Publications, 1987).

18 . Rudolfine Menzel, My Life in Germany, #155, bMS, Ger91 Collection, Houghton Library, Harvard University, Boston.

19 . Letter from RBB, b.1900, Frankfurt, 28 May 1992.

122 *HARRIET PASS FREIDENREICH*

20 . Frieda H. Sichel, *Challenge of the Past* (Johannesburg, 1975), 59-61; Minna Lachs, *Warum schaust du zurück: Erinnerungen 1907-1941* (Vienna: Europaverlag, 1986).
21 . Rahel Straus, *Wir lebten in Deutschland* (Stuttgart, 1961).

Chapter 9

The Women Who Would Be Rabbis

Pamela S. Nadell

In 1977 Mary Roth Walsh wrote in the preface to *"Doctors Wanted: No Women Need Apply,"* that historians had by and large neglected the study of the entry of women into the male-dominated professions.[1] Since then, however, a number of fine books have documented the history of women's efforts to become physicians, lawyers, scholars, and scientists; the institutional, social, and psychological barriers they faced in their struggles; and the various strategies they employed to cope with the roadblocks they encountered as they pursued their careers.[2] The histories of American Protestant women's efforts to join the clergy became part of this new interest in American women's entrance into the male-dominated professions.[3] What these works collectively uncovered was a largely forgotten record of the struggles of individual women over the course of the nineteenth and twentieth centuries to enter the "brotherhoods" of the male-dominated professions.[4]

Toward the end of the eighteenth century, as Carl Degler has shown, some women (in Europe represented by Mary Wollstonecraft), began to espouse the idea of individualism, assuming that "women, like men, had interests and lives that were separate and different in purpose from those of other members of a family."[5] As significant numbers of women embraced this idea, it augured dramatic changes in their lives and helped launch the women's rights movement. For some, one goal of that movement was entrance into the professions. Inspired by the joint ideals of individualism and feminism, small numbers of American women gradually won entry into the male-dominated professions, first in medicine and the ministry, and then in law and the academy.[6] In some cases these pioneers were successful in opening the doors, however marginally, for others to follow. In other cases, such as the women who failed to achieve ordination in certain Protestant denominations and those denied admission to Harvard University Medical School before 1945 and its law school before 1950, they kept the issue of women's access alive.[7]

In the late 1960s and 1970s unprecedented numbers of college-educated, American middle-class women flocked to the seminaries and medical, law, and graduate schools that would launch them into careers in the professions. They sensed, as Anna Quindlen has written of those years, "that all over America and indeed the world women were beginning to feel this same way, beginning to feel the great blessing and the horrible curse of enormous possibility."[8] Although these women were by and large unaware of those who had gone before them to open the gates to the professions, their efforts proved to be, as these histories have shown, but the latest stage in a long struggle for women to enter and to advance in the professions.

The movement for women's rabbinical ordination rightly belongs within this developing historiography of women in the professions. By the time Sally Priesand was on the verge of becoming the first woman to be ordained a rabbi in America, she had learned that she was not the first woman to try to enter the rabbinate. In her 1972 rabbinical thesis, written in the same year of her ordination, she wrote briefly about a handful of women who had preceded her in the attempt to achieve rabbinical ordination, including—Regina Jonas, who was privately ordained in Germany in 1935.[9] Since then, Ellen Umansky has illuminated some of the names of the women who tried for and failed to become rabbis.[10] But if the histories of women's entrance into the other professions are paradigmatic, the history of the emergence of female rabbis merits a fuller analysis.

The subject raises a number of significant questions and suggests three approaches. The first is to explore, as I have begun to do elsewhere, in what ways women's roles in the American synagogue changed over the course of the late nineteenth and twentieth centuries, paving the way for women to assume new leadership roles in their congregations. In particular, this requires an examination of the emergence of synagogue sisterhoods and how they afforded women opportunities for new roles in their congregations.[11] It also requires examining women who may be considered the "functional equivalents" of rabbis; that is, those who led services in the small-town congregations that could not afford regular rabbis, those who served as synagogue presidents before that position opened to women in the wake of feminist challenges to circumscribed female roles within the synagogue, those whose careers as educators afforded them opportunities to fulfill roles typically associated with rabbis; and those who filled in for their rabbinical husbands when they were ill and after their death.[12] The second approach is to examine the elite institutions that have granted women's ordination (the Hebrew Union College-Jewish Institute of Religion, Reconstructionist Rabbinical College, and Jewish Theological Seminary of America), and their rabbinical alumni associations to consider what internal changes and external forces propelled their leaders to break with the tradition of male ordination. And the third is to explore the pioneers, to study the handful of women who by enrolling in courses in the rabbinical schools raised in real, not in abstract, terms the question of female rabbinical students and the issue of women's ordination.

This last approach, the focus of this chapter, which in the short space allotted here can but touch upon the subject, raises a number of additional questions. Who were these women? Where and how did they manage to become students in the various rabbinical programs? What were their aspirations? What happened to sidetrack their ambitions away from the rabbinate or to stop them from achieving their goal? What then did they do with their lives? In what ways did the choices they made in terms of family and careers reflect on their initial aspirations for Jewish leadership and draw on the educations they received? To what extent did they remain advocates for the expansion of women's roles in the synagogue and for women's ordination?

Prior to the early 1970s, the chief arena for women attempting to pioneer women's ordination lay within the institutions associated with Reform Judaism: Cincinnati's Hebrew Union College and New York's Jewish Institute of Religion. Yet the more traditional institutions of American Judaism were by no means entirely isolated from the debate. One of the first women to study in rabbinical school, albeit with no intention of seeking ordination, was Henrietta Szold. From 1903 to 1906 she attended the Jewish Theological Seminary, Conservative Judaism's rabbinical school. And she reported with glee the consternation this aroused in the Yiddish press that assumed she would use her training to adjudicate questions of Jewish law.[13] After 1909, the Seminary channeled women who wished advanced Jewish educations to its Teachers Institute. In 1941, when Zionah Maximon found that its courses would not give her the education in Talmud and Midrash she wanted, Seminary faculty granted her special permission to attend classes in the rabbinical program with the caveat that she receive no credit of any kind or be listed as a special student.[14] Later, in 1957, Seminary Chancellor Louis Finkelstein replied to Gladys Citrin's request to study for the rabbinate: "Perhaps you would come to our Teachers Institute and become a teacher."[15] Although these examples suggest an awareness of the issue of women's ordination that went well beyond the Reform movement, the pioneers who attempted, albeit unsuccessfully before 1972, to challenge the male hegemony over the rabbinate by and large turned to Reform settings.

The extent to which they were aware of Reform's commitment to liberalism and its long history of statements supporting women's equality within Judaism and steps taken to ameliorate women's status within Jewish law is unclear.[16] Nevertheless, women interested in the rabbinate entered Reform institutions. From the 1890s forward, in almost every decade, there were one or more women studying for the rabbinate at these schools. Some of their names are familiar; others are not. At Hebrew Union College in Cincinnati, they included Ray Frank, Martha Neumark, Avis Shulman, and a number of the female students at the University of Cincinnati who took advantage of the undergraduate program launched by Hebrew Union College in 1957. In New York at the Jewish Institute of Religion, their ranks included Irma Lindheim, Dora Askowith, and Helen Levinthal. While Reform leaders in the Central Conference of American Rabbis and synagogue sisterhood members united in the National Federation of Temple Sisterhoods would from time to time raise the question of women's ordination in the abstract, these women, like those who pioneered in the professions in the nineteenth century, attempted on their own and unsuccessfully to push the question from the "bottom up."[17]

When Isaac Mayer Wise opened Hebrew Union College in 1875, one of the approximately dozen students, in what was then really "little more than an intensive religious school," was eleven-year-old Julia Ettlinger.[18] Although Ray Frank, the "girl rabbi of the West," apparently studied there in 1893, and some young women completed the College's Preparatory Department, earning Bachelor of Hebrew Letters degrees while they finished high school, the debate over women's ordination erupted within Reform Judaism in the early 1920s.[19] In 1921 seventeen-year old Martha Neumark, a student in the Preparatory Department and daughter of its professor David Neumark, launched a two-year-long debate among the College faculty, its rabbinical graduates, and its

Board of Governors over whether or not the College would ordain women as rabbis. As the deliberation over Neumark's efforts to become a rabbi was reaching its negative conclusion,[20] Irma Lindheim began raising the question, this time in New York City at the Jewish Institute of Religion.

The Jewish Institute of Religion had been founded by Rabbi Stephen Wise, the noted orator and Zionist, in 1922. Wise, after deciding against matriculation at Hebrew Union College, had been privately ordained by Adolf Jellinek, the liberal rabbi of Vienna. When his negotiations with New York's premier Reform synagogue, Temple Emanu-El, broke down over its lay leaders efforts to muzzle his freedom of speech in the pulpit, he founded the Free Synagogue, which joined Reform's Union of American Hebrew Congregations. Increasingly dissatisfied with the quality of Hebrew Union College and especially with its anti-Zionist stance, Wise, who was unquestionably associated with Reform or what is elsewhere called liberal Judaism, determined to act on a dream to found his own school. With the aid of the Free Synagogue, the Jewish Institute of Religion opened in 1922. The nontraditional nature of the seminary and its dedication to the free expression of all forms of Judaism marked the school as liberal while avoiding the label Reform.[21] Just as its was registering its first class, a chance meeting with Stephen Wise brought Irma Levy Lindheim to its doors.[22]

Born in New York City in 1886, Irma Levy was the daughter of well-to-do German Jewish immigrants. In 1907 she defied her father's wishes to arrange a suitable marriage and wed Norvin Lindheim, who was socially her peer but whose career as a fledgling attorney was deemed unsuitable by her father. Together the Lindheims raised five children and made their New York City home a center "for a mixture of important people from the worlds of business, diplomacy, finance, and the arts," many of them Germans her husband had met in his growing international law practice.[23]

Yet raising a family and the life of hostess were not enough to absorb Irma Lindheim, a woman of apparently remarkable energy and talent. Her fourth child was but five weeks old when she enlisted for active service in the Motor Corps of America, an organization established when the United States went to war with Germany to recruit female volunteers to drive and do odd jobs for the military. Quickly she rose to first lieutenant, the only Jewish woman to become one of its high officers. In the midst of her service, Lindheim became increasingly aware of "the disgrace of [her] basic ignorance as a Jew." While on weekend leave from the Motor Corps, she visited Baltimore, spending an evening at the home of the ardent Zionist Harry Friedenwald. Returning on the train to New York, she had what she later described as a "conversion," the moment when her life mystically changed, and she determined to use her vast energies on behalf of Zionism. She met Henrietta Szold and began to work for Hadassah. She became Chairperson of the Seventh District of the Zionist Organization of America and used her monies (her father's death in 1914 had left her independently wealthy) to buy a brownstone on 74th Street in which to establish its educational and cultural center. Her involvement in Zionist work helped distract her from what came to be a family tragedy—her husband's wrongful conviction of conspiracy in making a false report concerning the registration of German property in America during World War I.

Her Zionist work made Lindheim increasingly aware of her woefully inadequate knowledge of Jewish history, tradition, and culture. Although as a child she had attended religious services with her grandmother and Sunday School, she recognized how little she knew of Judaism and all things Jewish. Not only did the Lindheims not celebrate Jewish holidays—they crafted their first Chanukah celebration in 1918—when told that she had to serve her dinner guest, the Zionist Herbert Bentwich, kosher food, she prepared smelts stuffed with lobster.

Running into Wise, Lindheim asked if he would accept her as a special student at the Institute. His enthusiastic response led her to pause in her work for Zionism and to enroll at the Institute in October 1922, beginning a three-and-a-half-year period of intensive study. As with her earlier work for the Motor Corps and Zionism, Lindheim threw herself wholeheartedly into her studies. She sent her children out of the city to the family's twenty two-room mansion in Glen Cove, Long Island, and set up a small studio apartment a block from the Institute. She then devoted herself to ten-hour days of classes and study, pausing only to cook dinner in the evenings for her husband and to spend weekends with her family.

Lindheim succeeded in school as she had elsewhere. She was accepted for a special graduate course at Columbia University, taught by the influential educator John Dewey, despite the fact that she lacked the bachelor's degree necessary for admission. Both the faculty and the students voted her best in scholarship two years in a row, she later claimed.

By February 1923, Lindheim determined to change her status from that of special student and petitioned the faculty to admit her as a regular student in the rabbinical program. At first the professors decided that the lack of proper facilities, such as dormitories, obviated against the admission of women to the Institute. Worried that the question of women's ordination might add to the burden of establishing the Institute on a firm ground and sensing that many of the present students lacked "seriousness," which would be more easily developed without the presence of women, the faculty voted to admit women only as auditors to Extension courses — what today we would call adult education classes — while allowing the three women already enrolled in Institute classes (including Lindheim), to remain. But the discussion continued. In March the faculty again debated the question. At a third meeting in May, the faculty changed its mind and unanimously recommended the admission of women to the Institute on the same basis as men. While the Institute's original catalogue described it as a school for training men for the Jewish ministry, its 1923 charter of incorporation stated that it had been founded "to train, in liberal spirit, men *and women* for the Jewish ministry, research and community service" (italics mine).[24] Much later Lindheim wrote of her ambition: "It was not that I had any plan to function as a rabbi. I simply believed, in a time of women's gradual emergence as individuals in their own right, that if I prepared myself in accordance with the requirements of being a rabbi, the door would be opened for other women, should they wish and have the gift to minister to congregations."[25]

In the midst of her studies, in March 1924, the personal crisis that had tested her family since her husband's trial and conviction in 1920 came to a climax. Norvin Lindheim, whose conviction on conspiracy would be subsequently overturned, was called to serve his jail term. The month in jail and the long haul of the legal battle took its toll on the Lindheims. The seemingly unflappable Irma Lindheim sagged under the burden. In 1925, on the verge of collapse, she was ordered by her doctor to rest. The change of scenery he prescribed led her to make her first trip to Palestine, a journey recorded in the letters she wrote home and published as *The Immortal Adventure*.[26] When at last Lindheim returned to New York, she decided that she could no longer indulge herself in the luxury of being a student, that she had to act upon what she had seen and learned. Later she wrote that Wise was disappointed that she would not complete her final year at the Institute and become a rabbi, but that as a devoted Zionist he understood that it was more important for her to work for Palestine than to receive ordination.

With renewed energy, Lindheim once again threw herself into Zionist work. In 1926 she succeeded Henrietta Szold as National

President of Hadassah and was reelected to a second term in 1927. As its president she traveled around the country, speaking from synagogue pulpits, both Reform and Conservative, and meeting with rabbis and lay leaders. She and others, including Wise, were angered by what they deemed to be the disastrous leadership of the Zionist Organization of America (ZOA) under Louis Lipsky. They were especially bothered by its refusal to grant Hadassah women, which was a constituent agency of the ZOA, representation on its committees commensurate with their numbers; she became embroiled in a public controversy to reorganize the ZOA, which spilled over onto the pages of the *New York Times*. In the midst of that campaign in the spring of 1928, her husband died at the age of forty seven. Lindheim refused reelection as Hadassah president and turned once again to Palestine to recover her spirit. In 1933 she settled there, eventually selling the family mansion in Glen Cove to join Kibbutz Mishmar Haemek and turn to Labor Zionism.

Yet she retained her passionate interests in American Jewish life. In her later years she tried to push Hadassah to develop a Jewish youth farm experience modeled on her work with the Volunteer Land Corps during World War II; to sell copies of her autobiography, *Parallel Quest* (1962); and to develop "Gramsie's Hour," a program of Jewish education she created to train Jewish mothers and grandmothers to imbue their children with a sense of Jewish identity. She died in 1978.[27]

Lindheim's story, although of interest in and of itself, must be set in context and compared to the accounts of others who attempted to crash the barriers for women in the rabbinate. Doing so will reveal how her history illuminates a number of themes common to those women who challenged the male hegemony over the rabbinate from the bottom up.

The first common thread concerns the seriousness with which her efforts to be admitted to rabbinical school were met. Martha Neumark saw Hebrew Union College faculty, administration, Board of Governors, and alumni in the Central Conference of American Rabbis respond thoughtfully to her raising of the question of women as rabbinical students; Lindheim's challenge was similarly deemed worthy of serious deliberation. Undoubtedly, the timing of the raising of this question explains in part the consideration both Neumark and Lindheim received. The early 1920s heralded an era of great expectations concerning the emancipation of women. In the wake of the passage of the suffrage amendment, many believed all other barriers to women's emancipation would easily fall. The fact that they did not revealed, as William Chafe has shown, that "discrimination against women remained deeply rooted in the structure of society—in the roles women and men played and how those roles were valued."[28] Despite all the attention given to the new jobs open to women—attention shared by the Anglo-Jewish press—career women in the 1920s remained clustered in traditionally female occupations rather than breaking down barriers to professions excluding them.

Yet equally important to the regard that both Neumark and Lindheim received was their position as insiders to their seminary communities. Neumark was the daughter of Hebrew Union College Professor David Neumark. The Lindheims not only belonged to Stephen Wise's Free Synagogue but were apparently long-standing supporters of Wise and the Institute. Norvin Lindheim was one of the Institute's trustees and presumably, as trustees elsewhere do, supported the school financially.[29] It was one thing to dismiss another Institute student of the 1920s, Dora Askowith, who held a doctorate from Columbia University and taught history at Hunter College, as unsuitable for the rabbinate. It was quite another to refuse admission to the wife of a trustee—even when she lacked the formal academic credentials requisite for admission.[30]

Finally, what Lindheim did after her years at the Institute reveals just how firmly entrenched male and female roles were for the Jewish community. Perhaps she was right when she wrote in her autobiography that Wise was disappointed that she did not become a rabbi. But until the 1970s the Jewish Institute of Religion never ordained a woman. When Helen Levinthal (the daughter and granddaughter of prominent rabbis and thus another insider), completed the curriculum in 1939, she received a Master's of Hebrew Letters degree, not ordination.

Instead, as Lindheim's story shows, Jewish women, gifted with knowledge and education and skilled in leadership, were to serve American Jewry, but they were to do so as "professional" volunteers. That was their calling. If they reached high office, that was their ordination. Lindheim understood this. In writing to Henrietta Szold of her nomination to the national presidency of Hadassah, of the call to lead its thirty thousand women, she claimed: "If, at the Convention, the decision of the National Board is confirmed, I shall feel that I have been ordained, more truly so, even, than had I been confirmed as a rabbi."[31]

Lindheim's journey from rabbinical school to volunteer service would be matched by some of the other women who tried to crash the barriers to the rabbinate. Only in a new era when a resurgence of feminism began in the late 1960s to spill over into American Jewish life would the battle fought by Lindheim and the other pioneers end in victory. After nearly a century of debate and discussion Jewish women would at last have the choice—of serving their community as volunteers and as rabbis.

NOTES

1. Mary Roth Walsh, "*Doctors Wanted: No Women Need Apply*": *Sexual Barriers in the Medical Profession, 1835-1975* (New Haven: Yale University Press, 1977), xi.
2. In addition to Walsh, "*Doctors Wanted*," see Joan Jacobs Brumberg and Nancy Tomes, "Women in the Professions: A Research Agenda for American Historians," *Reviews in American History* 10 (June 1982): 275-96; Margaret W. Rossiter, *Women Scientists in America: Struggles and Strategies to 1940* (Baltimore: Johns Hopkins University Press, 1982); Karen Berger Morello, *The Invisible Bar: The Woman Lawyer in America, 1638 to the Present* (New York: Random House, 1986); Penina Migdal Glazer and Miriam Slater, *Unequal Colleagues: The Entrance of Women into the Professions, 1890-1940* (New Brunswick: Rutgers University Press, 1987); Lynn D. Gordon, *Gender and Higher Education in the Progressive Era* (New Haven: Yale University Press, 1990).
3. Emily C. Hewitt and Suzanne R. Hiatt, *Women Priests: Yes or No?* (New York: Seabury Press, 1973); Priscilla and William Proctor, *Women in the Pulpit: Is God an Equal Opportunity Employer?* (Garden City, NY: Doubleday & Co., 1976); Virginia Lieson Brereton and Christa Ressmeyer Klein, "American Women in Ministry: A History of Protestant Beginning Points," in *Women of Spirit: Female Leadership in the Jewish and Christian Traditions*, eds. Rosemary Ruether and Eleanor McLaughlin (New York: Simon and Schuster, 1979), 301-32.
4. In 1915 the influential educator Abraham Flexner characterized a profession as a brotherhood; cited in Glazer and Slater, *Unequal Colleagues*, 175.
5. Carl N. Degler, *At Odds: Women and the Family in America from the Revolution to the Present* (New York: Oxford University Press, 1980), 189.
6. The following examples highlight landmark dates for women's entrance into the professions. They reveal first the gradualness of the movement of women into the professions over the course of the nineteenth century. Second, they demonstrate the various paths women pursued to enter the professions, first engaging in apprenticeships and then as professional education and licensure became more formalized, gaining admission to institutions granting the required degrees. In 1835 the sisters Harriot K. and Sarah Hunt completed their medical apprenticeships. Elizabeth Blackwell was the first woman to graduate from medical school (1849); Walsh, "*Doctors Wanted*," 1. In 1853 Antoinette Brown was ordained a Congregationalist minister at Oberlin College; Barbara Miller Solomon, *In the Company of Educated Women: A History of Women and Higher Education in America* (New Haven: Yale University Press, 1985), 34-37. In 1870 Lemma Barkaloo became the first woman to graduate from law school; Morello, *The Invisible Bar*, 44. At Mount Holyoke the "shift from the nineteenth-century faculty of pious, Christian ladies to the twentieth-century faculty of productive scholars and intellectuals" began in the 1890s; Glazer and Slater, *Unequal Colleagues*, 27. In 1904 Jessica Blanche Peixotto became the first female faculty member appointed at the University of California at Berkeley; Gordon, *Gender and Higher Education*, 62-63.
7. In 1847 Harriot Hunt applied unsuccessfully to Harvard Medical School; Walsh, "*Doctors Wanted*," xiv. In 1868 Lemma Barkaloo applied to Harvard Law School; Morello, *The Invisible Bar*, xiii.

8. Anna Quindlen, *Living Out Loud* (New York: Random House, 1988), xvii.
9. Sally Jane Priesand, "Toward a Course of Study for Reform High School Youth Dealing with the Historic and Changing Role of the Jewish Woman" (Rabbinic Thesis: Hebrew Union College-Jewish Institute of Religion, 1972). This was subsequently published, with some revisions, as *Judaism and the New Woman* (New York: Behrman House, 1975). The date for Regina Jonas's ordination comes from Ellen M. Umansky, "Women's Journey towards Rabbinic Ordination," paper presented at the conference, "Exploration and Celebration: An Academic Symposium Honoring the Twentieth Anniversary of Women in the Rabbinate," Hebrew Union College-Jewish Institute of Religion, 31 January 1993, and is based on the work of Katharina Kellenbach.
10. Ellen M. Umansky has published a number of articles touching on this subject, beginning with "Women in Judaism: From the Reform Movement to Contemporary Jewish Religious Feminism," in *Women of Spirit*, 333-54. Among her other works touching upon the same theme are "Spiritual Expressions: Jewish Women's Religious Lives in the Twentieth-Century United States," in *Jewish Women in Historical Perspective*, ed. Judith R. Baskin (Detroit: Wayne State University Press, 1991), 265-88; "Piety, Persuasion and Friendship: A History of Jewish Women's Spirituality," in *Four Centuries of Jewish Women's Spirituality: A Sourcebook*, eds. Ellen Umansky and Dianne Ashton (Boston: Beacon Press, 1992), 1-30.
11. Pamela S. Nadell and Rita J. Simon, "Sisterhood Ladies and Rabbis: Women in the American Reform Synagogue," in *Women in Jewish Culture: An Active Voice*, ed. Maurie Sacks, (University of Illinois Press, forthcoming).
12. I am indebted to Professors Michael Meyer and Jonathan Sarna for suggesting the term "functional equivalents" at a seminar during my fellowship at the American Jewish Archives in May 1989. Examples of these functional equivalents were Beatrice Sanders, who succeeded her husband Gilbert as president of Trinidad, Colorado's Temple Aaron in 1952 and for more than two decades conducted its weekly and High Holiday services; Lenell Goodman Ammerman, president of Washington, DC's Temple Sinai from 1965 to 1967; Cleveland Jewish educator Libbie Braverman; and Paula Ackerman who, in 1950, succeeded her husband William Ackerman as rabbi of Beth Israel in Meridian, Mississippi.
13. Jewish Historical Society of Maryland, Microfilm #3/1 Hebrew College, Letters from Henrietta Szold, 1866-1944. Henrietta Szold to her mother, 2 December 1904.
14. Jewish Theological Seminary of America, Joseph and Miriam Ratner Center for the Study of Conservative Judaism. Jewish Theological Seminary Records, RG 3A, Faculty Minutes, Box 2, 1940-41, 8 January 1941, 16
15. Jewish Theological Seminary of America, Joseph and Miriam Ratner Center for the Study of Conservative Judaism. Jewish Theological Seminary Records, RG 1M, Box 153, Letter from Gladys Citrin to Dr. Finkelstein, 20 May 1957; Letter from Louis Finkelstein to Miss Citrin, 28 May 1957.
16. For a discussion of aspects of this, see Nadell and Simon, "Sisterhood Ladies and Rabbis."
17. In 1956 the Central Conference of American Rabbis (CCAR), Reform Judaism's rabbinical association, began to study once again the question of women's ordination. In 1963 at its fiftieth anniversary convention the women of Reform Judaism at the biennial conference of the National Federation of Temple Sisterhoods resolved in favor of having the College and the CCAR take up the matter once again.

18. American Jewish Archives, Nearprint. Special Topics: Rabbis, Women. Jacob R. Marcus, "The First Woman Rabbi," Press Release, 1972; Samuel S. Cohon, "The History of the Hebrew Union College," *American Jewish Historical Quarterly* 40 (1950-51): 25-26; the assessment is Michael A. Meyer's in "A Centennial History," in *Hebrew Union College-Jewish Institute of Religion at One Hundred Years*, ed. Samuel E. Karff (n.p.: Hebrew Union College Press, 1976), 18.

19. Those who completed an additional four years in the Collegiate Department, along with attendance at the University of Cincinnati, were ordained rabbis. For two different assessments of Ray Frank, see Reva Clar and William M. Kramer, "The Girl Rabbi of the Golden West: The Adventurous Life of Ray Frank in Nevada, California and the Northwest," *Western States Jewish History* 18 (1986): 99-111, 223-36, 336-51; Umansky, "Women's Journey towards Rabbinic Ordination."

20. Umansky, "Women's Journey Towards Rabbinic Ordination."

21. Meyer, "A Centennial History," 137-69. The Jewish Institute of Religion merged with Hebrew Union College in 1950.

22. Irma L. Lindheim, *Parallel Quest: A Search of a Person and a People* (New York: Thomas Yoseloff, 1962), 106.

23. This and what follows are taken from Lindheim, *Parallel Quest;* 106-14 cover, her years at the Institute.

24. American Jewish Archives, Mss Collection, #19, 9/7, Faculty Meetings, Minutes 1922-1951, 2 February 1923, 7 March 1923, 4 May 1923; *Jewish Institute of Religion Preliminary Announcement, 1923-1924*, 6; *Jewish Institute of Religion Catalogue 1946-47, 1947-48*, 24.

25. Lindheim, *Parallel Quest*, 112.

26. Lindheim, *The Immortal Adventure* (New York: Macaulay, 1928).

27. On the controversy with Lipsky, see Hadassah Archives, RG #4 Zionist Organizations and Zionist Institutional History, Box 1, Folders 3, 4, 7. On her later activities, see Hadassah Archives, Microfilm Reel #16 Zionist Political History, Hadassah President's Correspondence Series, RG #7 Irma Lindheim Correspondence, 26 July 1943-1 August 1963, 16 January 1964-10 February 1977.

28. William H. Chafe, *The Paradox of Change: American Women in the Twentieth Century* (rev. ed. of *The American Woman, 1972*; New York: Oxford University Press, 1991), 44, 100. On the Jewish press' celebration of Jewish women in new roles, see for example, Libbian Benedict, "Jewish Women Headliners—XLVIII: Clarice M. Baright—Magistrate," *American Hebrew*, 1 January 1926; "Business Women in Industry," *American Hebrew*, 5 November 1926.

29. Ralph Marcus, "In Memoriam: Norvin R. Lindheim," *Jewish Institute Quarterly* 4, 2 (January 1929; misdated January 1928).

30. Jewish Institute of Religion, Faculty Meeting Minutes, Vol. 1 (September 1922-July 1928); 2 (September 1928--July 1932); 3 (1933-43). Askowith, who entered the Institute in its first year, is discussed in a number of meetings. The faculty concluded that Lindheim's lack of a bachelor's degree was more than made up for by her "background of information and culture" and her work at the Institute that warranted admitting her as a regular student; 11 December 1924.

31. Lindheim, *Parallel Quest*, 201.

Chapter 10

Configurations of Patriarchy, Judaism, and Nazism in German Feminist Thought

Susannah Heschel

Introduction

Defining the relationship of German women to National Socialism emerged as a problem within the German feminist movement during the 1980s and has remained a challenge. One of the first difficulties to arise was why German women initially supported the National Socialist German Workers' Party (NSDAP), given its retrogressive attitudes toward women's role within society and the state. German feminist historians who have examined Nazi policies toward women have concluded that National Socialism succeeded not only in eliminating women from the public realm of German life and banishing them to "Kinder, Küche, Kirche," but had even developed a "final solution" in regard to women, the first step of which was the forced sterilization program. Female leadership within the NSDAP, the role of women at concentration camps, and the acquiescence of women, including feminists, to Nazi ideology are issues that have been investigated primarily by non-German historians. As a result, the myth has emerged that women were not active as Nazis, but were victims of Nazism.

In recent years German feminists have begun to analyze the "mentality" of Nazism and the Holocaust as patriarchal phenomena. Patriarchy and the rape, war, and violence it spawns, they argue, were initially introduced into Western civilization through the Old Testament, which presents a God of vengeance and violence who advocates genocide against nonbelievers. The Old Testament's religious commandments demand certain behaviors, rather than beliefs or attitudes, producing a morality of obedience to divine authority, rather than a morality based on thoughtful consideration of right and wrong. Later developments in Judaism strengthened that approach, the argument continues, resulting in a religion characterized by legalism, authoritarianism, and an absence of personal responsibility for one's actions.

Such stereotypes of Judaism's patriarchy and authoritarianism are not new, but continue older motifs prominent in modern antisemitic ideology. German feminists, however, have drawn the unique conclusion that Judaism's patriarchy is analogous to the morality of National Socialism. German women emerge not as responsible for Nazism, but as victims of it and, by extension, as victims of Judaism. Even the Jewish victims of Nazi crimes are by implication victims of their own religion.

These feminist arguments must be seen within the broader context of German debate about the Holocaust, which first became an intense topic of discussion after West German television showed the American TV mini-series, "Holocaust," in 1979.[1] The discussion began to retreat after the Bitburg Affair in 1985, which sparked an upsurge in antisemitism within West Germany as various German media proclaimed "the power of the Jews" behind the anti-Bitburg protests.[2] The ongoing conflict among historians concerning interpretations of Nazism and the Holocaust, the so-called *Historikerstreit*, gave credence to arguments that Hitler should be viewed not as an aggressor, but as the defender of Western Europe against the threat of Bolshevism; it also legitimated a widespread view that the Holocaust was only one of numerous occasions of suffering during the course of World War II, including the dislocation of German refugees in Eastern Europe and Stalin's murder of millions of Soviet citizens.[3] The unification of the Germanys in 1990 was widely used as a pretext to declare an end to the postwar era, and discussions of the Holocaust began to seem backward.[4] The time had come for Germany's "normalization" within NATO and as an international leader. Finally, feminist failure to provide a responsible analysis of Nazism and antisemitism should be seen within the larger context of a rise in antisemitism within the German Left.[5] A steady shift to the Right within Germany during the past decade should not diminish the seriousness of leftist antisemitism as the German Left finds itself in a philosophical as well as political crisis.[6] Limiting itself to "philosophical forebears who provide the solid tradition they affirm and reject," the German Left has failed to develop the necessary new categories to analyze antisemitism on the Left as well as the Right of the political spectrum.[7]

Apart from contextual influences, however, antisemitism within the feminist movement is disturbing because of the feminist claim to hold all inherited traditions suspect. German feminism has reacted to discussions of the Holocaust during the last two decades with a mixture of jealousy and resentment, which have led to its own anti-Jewish expressions. Instead of contributing a discussion of antisemitism informed by feminist theory, German feminists have developed theories of patriarchy's responsibility for Nazism and Judaism's responsibility for patriarchy.

Edith Kurzweil correctly notes that "in contrast to their parents' generation, and to their cohorts on the right, German leftists live with Nazi history. . . in order to avoid its repetition."[8]   Yet Nazism is a particularly troubling issue for German feminism, not only because of its challenge to German identity, but also because Nazism conflicts with feminist claims to women's powerlessness within a male-dominated historical order.   The generation of fathers may easily be held responsible as the perpetrators of evil, but how can German feminists understand the role of their mothers?   Although much of feminist theory seeks to emphasize the positive power of the mother-daughter bond over the frequently destructive father-daughter struggle, Susan Linville remarks that German feminists experience the additional difficulty "of seeing and representing the mother when her powerlessness includes her failure actively to resist fascism."[9]   At most, the failure of resistance, not the crime of active participation, becomes the trope explored as feminists theories are formulated to explain the victimhood of German women.   But that failure, in turn, is understood as the result of women's oppression under patriarchy.   Indeed, the greater the suffering of German women under National Socialism can be demonstrated, the more women can be exculpated from responsibility for Nazi violence and can even emerge as unsullied heroes.

The Old Testament and Judaism as Sources of Violence

That patriarchy entered Western society with the Old Testament is a common notion among German feminists, especially among those engaged in research on ancient matriarchal cultures.   These feminists argue that the Old Testament eliminated goddess worship and egalitarian social structures by introducing a male monotheistic deity whose demands for exclusive loyalty led to religious intolerance, violence, and war. The argument is popularized by Gerda Weiler's *Ich Verwerfe im Lande die Kriege* (1984). She writes:

> Patriarchal monotheism developed through the elimination of the cosmic Goddess; there is no father in heaven without the murder of the mother. . . . It was inevitable that together with the development of patriarchal religions, the position of woman in society would also be upset. . . . The victorious march of the deuteronomist ideology in Judeah accomplished the radical oppression of woman. The scope of misogynous polemic in the Old Testament reaches from instructions of petty restrictions of women's rights in everyday life to the justification of the brutal murder of women. . . . [The history of Israel shows] how this people leaves the tolerant *Weltanschauung* of its mothers, how it demonizes the penetrating love of matriarchal religion, splits off destructive aggressions and fights for dominance in the Near East with a brutal extermination program. On the reverse side of power waits powerlessness. Israel is destroyed and ceases to exist as a state. . . . Total claim to power must lead to disaster and total destruction.[10]

Brutality, power, and destruction are terms that recur frequently in feminist descriptions of the God of the Hebrew Bible. Feminist theologian Christa Mulack writes, "The omnipotence of the new God Jahwe had to gradually prove itself, in a terribly gruesome way. The books of the Hebrew Bible are full of the calls of Jahwe to murder non-believers,"[11] thus inaugurating genocide. This gruesome God set an example for all men, Mulack continues, by teaching them to exert power over others, especially women, "as Jahwe had done." She blames the Hebrew Bible for creating a mentality that leads West German men annually to rape and abuse about a quarter of a million daughters and girls, as young as six months old.[12]

Blaming Jewish texts for contemporary sexual violence in Germany was also the theme of the 1989 political pamphlet, "Violence against Women and Girls" published by the Green Party of North Rhine-Westphalia in 1989 which describes the history of abuse: "Sexual violence against girls has taken place in all cultures and times. Especially drastic is the outlook of the Talmud." There follows a passage from the Talmud, in German translation, which permits the betrothal of a girl child by her father, followed by a discussion of Maimonides' alleged permission for the rape of a girl under the age of three years. The next sentence states that according to Christian canonical law, marriage between children was forbidden. In other words, however misogynous Christianity might be, it is nonetheless an improvement over Judaism. Whereas the Talmud may be viewed as a sexist document, as are the documents of most religious traditions, it is scapegoated by being the only text cited in the entire discussion of the history of violence against girls and women, as though it were the root cause of contemporary Germany's sexual violence, and as though German Christian men through the centuries gained "permission" from the Talmud for their rape of German women.

German Women as Victims of Nazism

What involvement did German women have with the Holocaust? According to some noted German feminist historians, German women are not responsible. They were, in fact, victims of the Nazis, not fellow perpetrators. Feminist historians' appeal to a "grace of female birth," as Karin Windaus-Walser has critically termed it,[13] is an example of the attitude articulated by German Chancellor Helmut Kohl at his official state visit to Yad Vashem, when he expressed thanks that the "grace of late birth" meant that he held no responsibility for the Holocaust, having been only a teenager during the Nazi years. For some German feminists, Jews and women were targets of Nazi aggression and destruction, giving them the "grace" of victimhood, rather than the guilt of perpetrators.

In her important study of Nazi sterilization policies, feminist historian Gisela Bock argues that the Nazis' goals included women as their targets of murder. "As little as the women's politics of National Socialism, its sexism, was racially neutral, its racial politics, that is, its racism, was just as little gender neutral."[14] All women were victims of National Socialism and its racial war because women were a minority, "not so much in a numerical sense . . . but in the sense of being of lesser worth, that is, in the sense of racism."[15] Bock has established that one percent of women in Germany capable of giving birth were sterilized during the Third Reich.[16] Although equal numbers of men and women were sterilized, ninety percent of those who died from sterilization procedures were women, forty-five hundred in all.[17] Of those who survived sterilization, women suffered more than did men, because, according to Bock, "being without children bears a different meaning for women than for men."[18]   These deaths, she writes, were a form of "planned and deliberate mass murder" that differs only in degree, not in kind, from the genocide of the Jews. The distinction between forced sterilization of women and the genocide of the Jews was, according to Bock, "in the perspective of the victims . . . only relative": "Their death was not an errant 'by-product' of a birth policy limited 'only' to sterilization and 'not' aimed at murder, but rather a planned and conscious mass murder. For women the sterilization policy was not a prior step, but the beginning and first step of the mass murder of women and men. "[19]

Not only does the grace of female birth exonerate German women from responsibility for Nazism, it also suggests that they bear no responsibility for antisemitism.   The distinguished German psychoanalyst Margarete Mitscherlich, co-author of an important study, *The German Inability to Mourn*, has contributed the claim that antisemitism is a male phenomenon that cannot arise in women due to their psychic structures.[20]   Mitscherlich argues that women suffer fewer castration anxieties, psychic conflicts, and projections, and therefore do not generate antisemitism. At most women may become antisemitic through their identification and adjustment to the racism and antisemitism of men.

In other efforts to relativize the significance of the Holocaust, the persecution and murder of women as witches in the course of Western European history is termed a women's holocaust. Over and over, the women's holocaust is presented as the murder in Europe through the centuries of 9 million, occasionally 30 million, women as witches. In some cases, the contemporary situation of German women is termed a holocaust. The feminist theology journal, *Schlangenbrut*, declared 1988 as the year in which the women's holocaust, defined as the "dissolution of our self-consciousness, the angst that still burns today in us as a result of patriarchy," must become the central theme for women. The question is whether such comparisons succeed in convincing Germans to take women's suffering seriously, or convey an attitude denigrating Jewish suffering.

It is striking to note that German feminist historians have written relatively little on the history of women perpetrators in Nazi Germany, compared to feminist historians in other countries, such as Claudia Koonz, Renate Bridenthal, Marion Kaplan, Rita Thalmann, Sylbil Milton, or Atina Grossman. At most, German feminists speak of the "humanizing function" of German women within the Nazi system.

German feminist discussion of fascism emphasizes the role of misogyny within National Socialism, but frequently fails to mention antisemitism.

Nazism as Judaism

What is unquestionably the most disturbing motif of German feminism is the connection made between Nazism and Judaism. Nazism is identified by certain German feminists as the outgrowth of patriarchy. German women do not bear responsibility for Nazism because they are its victims, as they are victims of patriarchy. Moreover, because patriarchy, they argue, originated with Judaism, Nazism is ultimately the result of Judaism.

One of the most active spokespersons for this argument is Mulack, who argues that Nazism is characterized by a morality of blind obedience to authority, which also characterizes Judaism. Both, she claims, typify male attitudes. Using as her sources primarily the New Testament's caricatures of the Pharisees, rather than Jewish literature, Mulack portrays Jesus as an opponent of Jewish morality who strove to overcome Judaism and introduce a feminist religion. Jesus' failure to bring an end to Judaism has meant the continuation of patriarchy and all of its consequent immoralities, which led ultimately to Nazism. Mulack writes:

> We can say that the relations of Jesus with the law corresponded to typically female ideas, while those of the Pharisees and Scribes were at home in a typically male mental world. . . . It is always the same thing: Within patriarchy no man takes responsibility for his deeds, because he acts on the command of someone higher. The men themselves wash their hands in innocence. These men would have done exactly as Pilate, if Jesus had let them, but also exactly like Rudolf Hess or Adolf Eichmann, who pleaded "not guilty," because in the last analysis they had only followed the command of a Führer. And if this Führer commanded murder, then his followers would certainly have to murder. With all the differences that are certainly present here, the inner methods of argumentation are still the same. It always shows the same obedience to authority that is so typical for the male gender.[21]

Mulack suggests that an ethics based on law characterizes Judaism and represents patriarchal thinking. Rejection of external authority is the female mode of ethics, a mode that Jesus also possessed, although he happened to be male. Judaism is male, patriarchal, and misogynist; Christianity is female, feminist, and liberating. The conclusion that Mulack draws is that Hess and Eichmann are typical examples of patriarchal morality that disclaims responsibility by appealing to a "higher authority," a morality that characterizes Judaism. Mulack maintains that Jewish adherence to divine commandments is equivalent to Nazi obedience to the criminal orders of their superiors. Ultimately, Nazism is the result of the triumph of Jewish patriarchal morality over Jesus' feminist morality. German Christians are thus in no way responsible for the Holocaust; Jews are made by Mulack into victims of their own religion. And who is washing her hands in innocence?

Mulack's arguments received a broader audience in Germany through Franz Alt's recent book, *Jesus: der erste neue Mann*,[22] which Micha Brumlik has described as "the first antisemitic best-seller since 1945."[23] Alt repeats feminist claims that Jesus represents an "androgynous" spirituality, in sharp opposition to the Jewish environment in which he was raised. Patriarchy is identified with Judaism, and Jesus is said to have rejected both, in the name of an ethic of sensitivity, relationship, and love. Alt writes in support of feminism, and of the renewal of Christian faith, using feminist anti-Judaism to rescue Jesus for the twentieth-century German bourgeoisie, and encouraging the identification of Nazism with Judaism. Alt cites Mulack to "explain" the Nazi murder of Jewish women and children in August 1941:

> The murder of children at Biela-Zerkov happened because there was a command for it. The near stoning of the adulterous woman [described in the gospels] happened, because there was a law for it. But where was the conscience in both of these stories about men? Christa Mulack: "It is always the same thing: Within patriarchy no man takes responsibility for his deeds, because he acts on the command of someone higher. The men themselves wash their hands in innocence."[24]

Through highly popular writers, such as Alt, even the most outrageous feminist claims can find uncritical approval and widespread dissemination.

Women Versus Jews as Victims

The resentment of German feminists toward the attention to Jews evoked by remembrance of the Holocaust is expressed in a short story by a prominent leader of the German women's movement, Helke Sander. The story describes a telephone conversation in which a German feminist researcher is asked by a male friend if she would help an Orthodox Jewish man to obtain a research grant from a German foundation. She refuses. In the internal monologue that follows she thinks:

> The will to destruction which we receive in the five books of Moses has already poisoned and perverted enough people in the last few thousand years. The literally murderous patriarchy of the Old Testament, the intolerance, contempt for women, the prohibition against thinking and the authoritarianism and ideology of extermination are filled with the same spirit as the ideology of those who killed the Jews.[25]

She goes on to condemn the Germans' concern with the Holocaust because it blinds them from seeing other atrocities, such as nuclear arms, the killing in Iran and Cambodia, and the genocide during the colonization of America. Yet her plea is not simply for attention to other horrors, but a plea to cease making the Holocaust a primary concern: "I got sick and tired of your Jewish issues long ago," the narrator thinks. Her greatest resentment is that abuse of women is treated as marginal in comparison to the Holocaust: "But why get all worked up about Bitburg when the Pope was able to travel the world without there being a public outcry at the crimes of his institution?"

Sander's story is remarkable for its authentic rendering of an attitude predominant among many Germans, especially within the feminist and peace movements. It is a mentality unwilling to recognize distinctions between suffering and death, one that demands attention to other, legitimate issues only by denigrating the Holocaust. The narrator asks, "When would it be permissible to talk about 'Jewish pet issues' with the same impunity as it seems already possible to talk about 'women's pet issues'?"

Throughout the narrative the protagonist becomes repeatedly engulfed in tears, which are explained as the result of her frustration at her failure to achieve recognition for her position and be taken seriously, particularly by her male friend. The suffering of "women" becomes her own, because her tears are tears of self-pity. Throughout, "women" and their suffering seem not to include Jewish women. "Jew" appears in the story as male and Orthodox; Jewish women are absent, whether as co-feminists or as co-victims of patriarchy. The Holocaust of the Jews is classified under patriarchal concerns, not feminist concerns, as if all Jews were male and all feminists were Christian.

The Feminine Jesus as Holocaust Victim

Depicting Jesus as feminine has come into vogue in German popular writings. The Gospel stories—read as portraying Jesus as a sensitive, forgiving teacher—combined with the Sermon on the Mount—read as glorifying "female" values of gentleness and compassion—are used as evidence that Jesus taught and embodied female values. According to the feminist theologian and Jungian psychoanalyst Hanna Wolff, the historical Jesus was in fact the first woman-identified, "anima-integrated" feminist male.[26] Wolff's Jesus is presented in sharp contrast to the Jews of his day, who preferred their stagnant, regressive religion to the progressive, psychologically healthy spirituality offered by Jesus.[27] She further argues that his femaleness has been thoroughly misunderstood and distorted through the centuries, with disastrous consequences for women and men. The human failure to distinguish between the historical Jesus and human projections onto him has made Jesus, according to Wolff, the greatest of all Holocaust victims. She writes, "But we should certainly not forget the greatest victim of the Holocaust, and that is Jesus Christ, distorted for two thousand years through our projections, martyred and repeatedly pronounced dead."[28] Jesus as the ultimate embodiment of female values becomes the greatest victim of the Holocaust, the ultimate patriarchal event.

Women as Heroes of National Socialism

There is no question that the National Socialist regime is regarded by today's German population as at least partially evil, even if over sixty percent of adults questioned in 1992 also saw some positive accomplishments to the Third Reich. Despite its evil effects, Nazism is not viewed as having destroyed all German values, political, social, and moral. Nonetheless, the challenge to reaffirm Germany despite Hitler has been difficult. An early feminist response is demonstrated in the 1979 film by Helma Sanders-Brahms, *Deutschland: Bleiche Mutter* (Germany: Pale mother), which depicts the sufferings of the filmmaker's parents who saw themselves as indifferent to Nazism, but who nonetheless fell victim to its politics and militarism. The father is almost immediately drafted into military service, precisely because, the film explains, he refused to join the NSDAP. A sensitive man, he weeps after killing civilians and is humiliated by his fellow soldiers for refusing to visit prostitutes, out of commitment to his marriage.

The absence of the father allows an intense bond to develop between mother and daughter, left alone to struggle for survival after their home is destroyed in an air bombardment. They go to live in the countryside. The simplicity of their life and the loving gentleness of their relationship remain unaffected by the militarism of the regime, even by the mother's rape by American soldiers, which the young daughter witnesses. Indeed, the war, by removing men from the domestic sphere, actually fosters the matriarchal idyll.

The father's return from war, however, brings home the evil. The film's narrator states, "The return to family life. War started inside whilst outside there was peace." The father is hardened by the violence of battle, and vents his rage on his wife, abusing her emotionally and physically. She suffers a sudden paralysis that affects half her face, and her husband complains bitterly of his difficulties in achieving success at work. Although the daughter attempts to preserve the family's relationships, the mother turns away from her and the father shows her no love. The film concludes with the mother's attempted suicide, witnessed by her daughter.

This film narrates National Socialism as a split phenomenon: in its essence a male event of brutality in which German women play no role, for its duration it permits the freedom and independence of women, because their men are preoccupied. The greatest victims of National Socialism are Germans; in the metonymy of the film's mother, the Nazis ultimately caused a paralysis of Germany, now unloved by the rest of the world, while the "good" Germany was affirmed by the women on the sidelines. Alone with her child, away from the air raids and bombs of the city, the mother can preserve the values of German life. Those values are coded in the film using clichés common to nineteenth-century German romanticism and the twentieth-century volkish movement, and that were recapitulated in Nazi kitsch: the peaceful German countryside; a sensitive, desexualized German mother; Germans creating community by rebuilding their land together.

As is common in postwar German cinema, Jewish deportations are alluded to, but antisemitism is absent. Without the larger context that gave rise to the deportations, these appear in the film as momentary events, unconnected to the film's protagonists, who are merely bystanders. Because the central theme of the film is reconstitution of the shattered relationship between daughter and mother, the narrative voice of the daughter comments on the mother's utter indifference to the deportation of the Jewish owners of the local sewing shop: "It is true. I believe you. You didn't want it. But you also didn't stop it. I accuse you. But with what right? How am I better? I was just lucky to be born later." Here, as in so many other feminist texts, there is no accountability because women were simply uninvolved. Patriarchal history belongs to men; women are not responsible for it.

In the story of *Deutschland: Bleiche Mutter* Nazism is not an antisemitic war against Jews, but a patriarchal war against women. In this film the female victims manage to transform themselves into Germany's heroes. While the men march off to self-destruction in Nazi uniforms in a display of German nationalism, it is the women who embody and thereby preserve the meaning of being German. Seduced to enter the "house of murderers," German women are no more the perpetrators of Nazism than the innocent girls betrayed by evil men in the Grimm's fairytale, "The Robber Bridegroom" narrated in the film by the mother to her daughter as an explanatory parable of Germany's fate.

Responses to Charges of Anti-Judaism

Outraged denial has been the typical response to charges of German feminist anti-Judaism. Negative depictions of Judaism are accepted as legitimate evaluations of it, rather than as part of a systemic misrepresentation endemic to Occidental culture. By ignoring the history of antisemitic stereotypes and their effects, typical anti-Jewish images — for instance, Judaism's alleged lack of a moral system — cannot be evaluated properly. Instead, feminist views of Judaism are defended by arguing that the author's intention was not antisemitic; that contrasts drawn between Judaism and Christianity are not anti-Jewish, but simply aimed at depicting differences; or that the analogy between Judaism and Nazism cannot be viewed as defamatory to Judaism because it in fact represents the truth.

Discussions of anti-Judaism in Christian feminist theology began in the United States in the early 1980s, and in Germany in 1986. The topic was discussed in feminist periodicals, including the feminist monthly *Emma*,[29] the feminist theological quarterly *Schlangenbrut*,[30] the Swiss feminist annual *Fama*,[31] and in two anthologies of articles: *Verdrängte Vergangenheit die Uns Bedrängt: Feministische Theologie in der*

Verantwortung für die Geschichte,[32] and *Weil Wir nicht Vergessen Wollen.*[33] Anti-Judaism in feminist theology was also discussed at conferences of feminist theologians sponsored by several of the Evangelische Akademien of various regions and in Jewish-Christian dialogue groups, including the Arbeitsgruppe Jüdisch-Christliches Dialog at the Berlin Kirchentag in May 1989, and at the European Society of Women for Theological Research in September 1989. Within East Germany, the issue was discussed at a meeting sponsored by the Evangelische Akademie of Berlin-Brandenburg in March 1987.

Christian feminist theologians whose work was criticized also responded. In a widely publicized statement printed in 1988 in the distinguished journal *Evangelische Theologie,* seven women (including Dorothee Soelle, Elisabeth Moltmann-Wendel, and Luise Schottroff) counterattacked, charging that anti-Judaism was embedded in all Christian theology, a problem they deplored, but that feminist theologians should not be isolated as targets for criticism. A critique of feminist theologians, they wrote, constituted "an attempt to discredit the Christian women's movement."[34]

To date, however, whereas numerous Christian feminists in Germany condemn antisemitism and anti-Judaism in principle, very few have either published criticisms of specific feminist writings or clarified the nature of theological anti-Judaism. As a result, there is frequent denial of anti-Judaism within any given feminist text.

Elisabeth Moltmann-Wendel, for example, insists that her depiction of Judaism is not anti-Jewish, but is an effort to differentiate it from Christianity. Efforts to avoid anti-Judaism, she argues, might lead to an inability to recognize "the new" within the early Jesus movement, such as Jesus' abolition of Judaism's "blood taboos."[35] Rather than present the relationship between Christianity and Judaism in terms of oppositions, she calls for viewing the relationship in terms of differences: "From the perspective of the early Christians and of many Christians until today Jesus really did bring something new. The 'new' is always the new in relation to my old experience of living under coercions, unfreedoms, legalisms, and imperatives."[36] According to Moltmann-Wendel, Jesus liberated women from the "ghetto" of Judaism, but that liberation was lost to later Christianity due to the suppression of women's equality by the early Jewish Christians, who distorted Jesus' teachings with Judaism's patriarchy. That precisely those stereotypes of Judaism have functioned negatively for centuries is not noted by Moltmann-Wendel, nor does she cite Jewish literature in drawing her conclusions concerning religious experience within Judaism.

Defending a text against charges of anti-Judaism by claiming that the author's intention was not anti-Judaism has become common. For example, Judith Plaskow has criticized Carter Heyward's description of Jesus' "radical shift in consciousness" from Judaism's emphasis on ritual to Christianity's emphasis on right relationship. Dorothee Soelle criticizes Plaskow for demonstrating "total suspicion toward a theologian."[37] Reading Heyward's distinction in the context of anti-Judaism strikes Soelle as "unfair, because it is not contained in Heyward's tendency of thought."

In another example, Jürgen Moltmann, perhaps the most internationally respected Protestant theologian alive today, has condemned anti-Judaism but defends the efforts of Christian feminists to "differentiate" between Judaism and Christianity. The critique of anti-Judaism is, according to Moltmann, "anti-Christian," and can be "deathly" for a Christian theologian. Further, Moltmann argues that Jews who formulate the critique are motivated by their own lack of Jewish identity.[38] He does not clarify the significance of Christian scholars engaged in the critique.

In separate responses published in *Emma* and *Schlangenbrut*, Elga Sorge and Christa Mulack contested charges against their work, whereas Gerda Weiler attempted an apology. In an essay entitled "To Hell with Antisemitism," Sorge wrote that if her critique of Judaism's sexism were considered anti-Jewish, Jesus himself would have to be considered an antisemite.[39] By contrast Weiler wrote, "Antisemitism has absolutely nothing to do with my self-understanding and my life history. I regret that I formulated false claims and assumptions in my book."[40] She cites a Jewish woman in Jerusalem who was fascinated by her interpretation of the biblical narrative concerning Tamar and who told her, "If more women studied in this way, then one day the Bible will have to be re-written."[41] Weiler has recently issued a newly revised edition of her book, in which she claims to have eliminated its anti-Judaism.[42]

On the other hand, Weiler has been defended by Heidi Göttner-Abendroth, who claims that the critique of anti-Judaism is a malicious effort to suppress the independent research efforts concerning matriarchy.[43] Göttner-Abendroth has gone further, arguing that the critique of Gerda Weiler is unjust, serving to "discriminate against an independent, fearless, pioneering work." The critique demonstrates, she continues, that "it has nothing to do with 'anti-Judaism,' but with an assault against research on matriarchy that is autonomous and free from institutional, male interpretations."[44]

Christa Mulack defends her comparison of Judaism and Nazism:

I see no difference whether God the Lord in Ezekiel 9 commands the extermination of women, children, and old people on the grounds of their different religious practices, or whether Hitler and his executioners called for the murder of the Jews. . . . Finally the Holocaust is only one of the innumerable effects of patriarchal structures of thinking, which we find not only in the Hebrew Bible and to which not only Jews fell as victims, but . . . above all women. They are all similarly tragic victims of patriarchy.[45]

More recently, Mulack wrote that she did not intend "to place the mass murder of the Jews on the same level as the planned murder by Jewish men of the adulterous woman reported in the gospels [John 8]. The points of comparison were rather the readiness of both [the Nazis and the Pharisees], on the basis of a command, to become murderers, without feeling guilty or even feeling any responsibility."[46]

There is nothing new in Mulack's supposedly radical feminist theology, because precisely these stereotypes concerning the Pharisees and Jewish morality abound in the history of German antisemitism, and that German Jews (and some Christians) since at least the middle of the nineteenth century have struggled to counter. Basing her arguments on the story of John 8 as an authoritative source for a depiction of Pharisaism is illegitimate: the story appears only in late manuscripts of the New Testament; it was written as a polemic, not as a neutral historical account of an event; and it does not represent the voice of Pharisaic Judaism. Comparing a fictional caricature of the Pharisees with the historical reality of the Nazi murders suggests that either the Pharisee clichés of the New Testament are accurate representations, or that the Nazi murders were fictive exaggerations.

Support for the critique of feminist anti-Judaism has emerged in Germany in particular from Siegele-Wenschkewitz. She has criticized feminist historians writing on women in the Third Reich for interpreting evidence of remorse and protest against the death of a friend or neighbor as a sign of a fundamental rejection of National Socialism. She calls instead on feminist historians to recognize that the "majority of the women in Germany found an arrangement with National Socialism and in that way National Socialist antisemitism was carried along by women as well."[47] In regard to anti-Judaism in Christian feminist theology, Siegele-Wenschkewitz has argued that the "hermeneutics of suspicion" developed by feminist theologian Elisabeth Schüssler-Fiorenza to reveal multiple meanings within patriarchal texts concerning women's history should also be applied to Christian texts in the effort to reveal hidden layers of anti-Judaism.[48] Marie-Theres Wacker, a Catholic theologian in Germany, has been particularly critical of feminist accusations that Jews "killed the Goddess." She has also warned that Christian churches "have done nothing to prevent" the antisemitic "outrages" committed by Germans, but have instead "contributed daily to anti-Judaism in their sermons and religious instruction so that little resistance has arisen."[49]

Conclusions

Blaming Judaism for Nazism and the Holocaust did not originate with feminists, but can be understood as a continuation of Nazi propaganda that claimed Jews were responsible for instigating World War II. Accordingly, Germans were fighting a defensive, not offensive, struggle against the Jews, and antisemitism became a principle of revolutionary liberation of the German people from a degenerate "Judaization" of their society.[50] Certainly during the Nazi years antisemitic propaganda made it clear that the Jews were deservedly suffering discrimination and persecution: the Jews had brought their suffering upon themselves, through their own faults. Blaming the Jews continued in the earliest postwar Protestant church response to the Holocaust, the Darmstadt Declaration of 1948, according to which the Jews were put to death during World War II as the result of their original and continuing crucifixion of Christ.[51] Because antisemitism is illegal in postwar Germany, it has become common to avoid blaming Jews and instead to hold Judaism responsible for Germany's evils. The polyvalence of the German word "Judentum," which means Judaism, Jewry, and Jewishness, creates an ambiguity that permits the shift from blaming Jews as corrupt individuals to blaming Judaism as a religion.

Theodor Adorno once remarked that the one thing Germans will never forgive Jews for is Auschwitz. Numerous commentators have noted that contemporary antisemitism has grown in Germany not despite, but because of Auschwitz. German guilt, we are told, is so unbearable that it results in blaming the Jews for it, making it seem justified to hate them for this guilty conscience. The constant reminders today by German Jews of the Holocaust and of antisemitism have evoked the response that Jews must be an especially evil people because even the concentration camps failed to teach them *Friedfertigkeit*, or peacemaking. This inability in turn is blamed on Judaism itself, a religion of vengeance rather than reconciliation.

German feminists' refusal to assume responsibility for Nazism can also be seen as a continuation of the utter failure and collapse of the postwar de-Nazification efforts. Very few of the doctors, lawyers, judges, SS officers, or murderers had to appear before the courts for trial, and those who did received mild punishments, often from judges who themselves had been Nazi party members. From the outset the German public protested the de-Nazification proceedings and demonstrated their sympathy not for those who had been murdered, but for the murderers, whom they tried to protect from detection and prosecution.[52] Even statements of complicity, such as the Stuttgart Declaration of 1945 published by the Lutheran church, declared the shared guilt of all Germans, thereby implying that the few should not be singled out for punishment, and said not a word about the fate of the Jews, nor about antisemitism. Similarly, feminist versions of Nazism renounce women's responsibility for the evil, instead portraying misogyny (rather than antisemitism) at the heart of National Socialism, thus making women its victims rather than its collaborators. Yet feminist analysis does not become feminist only by "proving" the independence of women and their resistance against patriarchy.[53]

Indeed, a romance with victimization plays a central role in German feminist antisemitism. Inherent within feminist theory, and especially emphasized within German feminism, is the view of women as victims of patriarchy, rather than subjects of history.[54] Women are said to lack a history, a religious tradition, an identity, even a language. Although feminists declare their goal to be the attainment of women's subjecthood, they simultaneously emphasize women's status as victims. Such theory can be used to define an extreme position of women's victimhood and lack of agency or moral responsibility. This perspective is combined with a tendency to divide a historical event between victims and perpetrators. The case of the Holocaust lends itself justifiably to that division: it was not a war, but a mass murder of people who had no prior enmity toward their murderers, but on the contrary, felt warmth, affection, and even love for Germany. German feminists identify with the Jews not only to avoid responsibility, but also because the model of the Holocaust as a neat distinction between victims and perpetrators seems well-suited to some aspects of women's experience. For example, violence against women is perpetrated mainly by those who are supposed to love them—husbands, fathers, brothers, and lovers. The problem is that in Nazi Germany German Christian women were not Jews, and there is no evidence that any factions within the National Socialist movement ever called for the extermination of all women. Defining the relationship between contemporary German women and the National Socialist past will only succeed when that history is confronted directly.

NOTES

1. See Friedrich Knilli and Siegfried Zielinski, eds., *Holocaust zur Unterhaltung. Anatomie eines internationalen Bestsellers* (Berlin: Verlag für Ausbildung und Studium, 1982).

2. Cover of *Quick* magazine, 25 April 1985. See Hajor Funke, "Bitburg, Jews, and Germans: A Case Study of Anti-Jewish Sentiment in Germany during May, 1985," *New German Critique* 38 (Spring/Summer 1986): 57-72.

3. See Charles Maier, *The Unmasterable Past: History, Holocaust, and German National Identity* (Cambridge: Harvard University Press, 1988).

4. "Special Issue on German Unification," *New German Critique* 52 (Winter 1991).

5. See Henryk M. Broder, *Der Ewige Antisemit: Über Sinn und Funktion eines beständigen Gefühls* (Frankfurt am Main: Fischer Taschenbuch, 1987).

6. Andrei S. Markovitz, "Germany: Power and the Left: A New Political Configuration," *Dissent* 38 (Summer 1991) : 354-59.

7. Edith Kurzweil, "An American in Frankfurt," *Partisan Review* 51, 4, and 52, 1 (1984-85) : 828-33.

8. Ibid., 829.

9. Susan E. Linville, "The Mother-Daughter Plot in History: Helma Sanders-Brahm's Germany's, Pale Mother," *New German Critique* 55 (Winter 1992) : 53.

10. Gerda Weiler, *Ich Verwerfe im Landes die Kriege: Das verborgene Matriarchat im Alten Testament* (Munich: Frauenoffensive, 1984), 33.

11. Christa Mulack, *Am Anfang war die Weisheit* (Munich: Kreuz Verlag, 1988) , 22-23.

12. Ibid., 33.

13. Karin Windaus-Walser, "Gnade der weiblichen Geburt? Zum Umgang der Frauenforschung mit Nationalsozialismus und Antisemitismus," *Feministische Studien* 6 (November 1988) : 102-15.

14. Gisela Bock, *Zwangssterilisation im Nationalsozialismus: Studien zur Rassenpolitik und Frauenpolitik* (Opladen: Westdeutscher Verlag, 1986) , 17 and 380.

15. Ibid., 13-14.

16. Ibid., 456.

17. Ibid., 12.

18. Ibid.

19. Ibid., 380.

20. Margarete Mitscherlich, *Die friedfertige Frau* (Frankfurt: Fischer Verlag, 1985).

21. Christa Mulack, *Jesus: der Gesalbte der Frauen* (Stuttgart: Kreuz Verlag, 1987) , 155-56.

22. Franz Alt, *Jesus:Der erste neue Mann* (Munich: Piper Verlag, 1989).

23. Micha Brumlik, *Der Anti-Alt* (Frankfurt am Main: Eichborn Verlag, 1991).

24. Alt, *Jesus*, 84.

25. Helke Sander, *The Three Women K.*, trans. Helen Petzold (London: Serpents Tail, 1991).

26 . Hanna Wolff, *Jesus der Man: Die Gestalt Jesu in tiefenpsychologischer Sicht* (Stuttgart: Radius Verlag, 1975).

27 . Hanna Wolff, *Neuer Wein: Alte Schläuche* (Stuttgart, 1981).

28 . Cited by Bettina Decke, "Christlicher Antijudaismus und Feminismus," in Albert Sellner, ed., *Der sogenannte Gott* (Frankfurt am Main, 1988) , 105.

29 . Susannah Heschel, "Töteten 'die Juden' die Göttin?" *Emma* (December 1988) : 26–31.

30 . See articles, interviews, and readers' letters in *Schlangenbrut* 16 (March 1987) ; 17 (May 1987) ; and 18 (August 1987).

31 . *Fama: Feministisch-theologische Zeitschrift* 6 (March 1991).

32 . Leonore Siegele-Wenschkewitz, ed., *Verdrängte Vergangenheit die Uns Bedrängt: Feministische Theologie in der Verantwortung für die Geschichte* (Munich: Christian Kaiser, 1988).

33 Christine Schaumberger, ed., *Weil Wir Nicht Vergessen Wollen: Zu einer Feministischen Theologie im deutschen Kontext* (Münster: Morgana Frauenbuch Verlag, 1987).

34 . "Zur Situation: Stellungnahme Feministischer Theologinnen zum Vorwurf des Antijudaismus," *Evangelische Theologie* 48, 2 (1988): 158.

35 . Elisabeth Moltmann-Wendel, "Jesus, Die Tabus und das Neue," *Dialog der Religionen* 2 (Fall 1992) : 130–45.

36 . Ibid., 140.

37 . See Dorothee Soelle, "Warum brauchen wir eine feministische Christologie?" *Evangelische Theologie* 53, 1 (1993): 86–92. Plaskow's critique is published in "Feminist Anti-Judaism and the Christian God," *Journal of Feminist Studies in Religion* 7, 2 (Fall 1991): 99–108.

38 . Jürgen Moltmann, "Verletzte Gewissen," *Publik-Forum* 10 (21 May 1993) : 16.

39 . Elga Sorge, "Zur Hexe mit dem Antisemitismus," *Emma* (February 1989) : 50–51.

40 . *Schlangenbrut* 17 (May 1987) : 31.

41 . Ibid.

42 . Gerda Weiler, *Das Matriarchat im Alten Israel* (Stuttgart: W. Kohlhammer Verlag, 1989).

43 . Heide Göttner-Abendroth, *Das Matriarchat I: Geschichte seiner Erforschung* (Stuttgart: Verlag W. Kohlhammer, 1988).

44 . Ibid., 169–70.

45 . Christa Mulack, "Kontrovers diskutiert," *Schlangenbrut* 22 (1988): 40–43.

46 . Christa Mulack, "Jesus, die Nazis und die Männer," *Publik-Forum* 4 (26 February 1993): 21–22.

47 . Leonore Siegele-Wenschkewitz, "Die Wiederkehr des antijüdischen Stereotyps in feministischer Theorie und Theologie," *Metis: Zeitschrift für historische Frauenforschung und feministische Praxis* 1, 2 (1992) : 29–32.

48 . *Publik-Forum* 4 (22 May 1993).

49 . Marie-Theres Wacker, "Feminist Theology and Anti-Judaism: The Status of the Discussion and the Context of the Problem in the Federal Republic of Germany," *Journal of Feminist Studies in Religion* 7, 2 (Fall 1991) : 109–16.

50 . Lawrence Rose, *Revolutionary Antisemitism in Germany: From Kant to Wagner* (Princeton: Princeton University Press, 1990).

51 . Christoph Matthias Raisig, *Der Rheinische Synodalbeschluss vom 11. Januar 1980, "Zur Erneuerung des Verhältnisses von Christen und Juden": Seine Vorgeschichte, seine Inteiton und die ersten Reaktionen.* Inaugural Dissertation, Göthe University Frankfurt, 1992.

52 . See Frank Stern, *The Whitewashing of the Yellow Badge: Antisemitism and Philosemitism in Postwar Germany*, trans. William Templer (Oxford: Pergamon Press, 1992).

53 . See Leonore Siegele-Wenschkewitz, "Frauengeschichte im Nationalsozialismus: Eine 'Frauenpraxis aus Liebe'? Zur Diskussion mit Annette Kuhn," *Metis: Zeitschrift für historische Frauenforschung und feministische Praxis* 2, 4 (October 1993).

54 . Maria Baader, "Zum Abschied: Über den Versuch, als jüdische Feministin in der Berliner Frauenszene einen Platz zu finden," in Ika Hügel, Chris Lange et al., eds., *Entfernte Verbindungen: Rassismus, Antisemitismus, Klassenunterdrückung* (Berlin: Orlanda Frauenverlag, 1993), 82–94.

Part III

Literary Dimensions of Gender and Judaism

Chapter 11

Eavesdropping on Angels and Laughing at God: Theorizing a Subversive Matriarchy

Lori Hope Lefkovitz

Introduction

Considerations of gender and Judaism, including my own efforts, have tended to examine Jewish law and ritual practice; the characterization of the sexes and of sex in the textual tradition from biblical narrative through the documents of rabbinism and contemporary culture; and the history of women's and men's roles, privileges, and burdens. Judith Plaskow's *Standing Again at Sinai* is exemplary in many regards and in this regard as well; as its subtitle indicates, it approaches "Judaism from a Feminist Perspective," and in doing so, it uses the categories of Jewish theology—in this instance, Torah, Israel, and God.

This chapter represents a preliminary attempt to theorize Jewish feminism, borrowing categories of analysis from French feminist theory. What might be said about Judaism if our primary categories were, for example, "fluids" and "voices"? And for voices I think not of the articulate voice of patriarchal order and reason, but woman's more anarchic voices, metaphorically represented in Hebrew Scriptures by Miriam's singing, Hannah's unintelligible whispering that was confused for drunkenness, the ambiguous screams of childbirth and the laughter of Sarah. For fluids, I think of water, of course: Rebecca at the well, and Miriam, who is especially associated with water. Miriam's name is perhaps translatable as "bitter sea"; there is the river into which she places the baby Moses and beside which she hides, the Red Sea where she leads the people in song, and the water that leaves the camp with her death and for the absence of which Moses strikes the rock.[1]   I think too of mother's milk, the celebration at Isaac's weaning and Yael's gift of milk to Sisera before she murdered him.   And there is blood of course, with its monthly presence and the levitical purity laws of *niddah*, the blood of childbirth, and the absence of blood lamented by Sarah when she doubts that she can conceive after her menopause.

Voices and fluids provide metaphors for feminist ritual practice as well: *Miriam's Well*, a title that alludes to the midrash that a well accompanied Miriam in the desert and because of which the people were spared thirst, names a book of women's ceremonies, and Plaskow describes women's ritual with words appropriate to female anatomy; these rituals are, she writes, "fluid" and "open," not "rigid."[2]   One might go on to examine the pattern in Hebrew Scripture of using the female body as a habitual site of representation, a divine drawing board upon which are written messages to and about the Jewish body politic.   And now I am thinking, for example, of Miriam's leprosy and of the fragmented female body in Judges 19, the female corpse that is cut into twelve pieces that signify the fragmented relationship among the twelve tribes under the rule of Judges, the pieces functioning as multiple, mobile signifiers.   The Jewish woman's body (well, ill, bleeding, lactating or fragmented, the maternal body and the Jewish American Princess body), her fluids, and her voices (her laughter, her muttering, her screams) provide bases already inscribed in the Jewish textual tradition for a theory of woman's subversive powers.

I cannot explore all of these possibilities here, but I will exemplify with a discussion of Sarah's enigmatic laughter when she overhears God's promise that she will bear a child late in life.   In considering the difficulty for God and reader alike of interpreting Sarah's laughter, I suggest that God's respect for Sarah's unorthodoxies—her eavesdropping, her laughter, and her reference to menarche—can provide a basis for imagining an empowered matriarchy on terms different from those privileged by the heirs to rabbinic Judaism.   I preface my attention to Sarah with an articulation of some of the problems that attend this enterprise, and I conclude by placing Sarah's laughter in a larger theoretical context meant to justify both my use of laughter as a category of analysis and my making so much of this particular textual moment.

This effort is a navigation between Scylla and Charybdis: on the one side, to celebrate the power available in representations of women risks justifying a subconscious terror of female sexuality that provides the very excuse for the oppression of women; on the other side, to lament the absence of power in the constructions of woman as Other within traditional Jewish categories implicates us in the perpetuation of a classification system that reifies stereotypes of masculinity and femininity.[3] I see the first problem by analogy to the Victorian trick of elevating woman to the pedestal that becomes her prison.[4] Biblical heroines in the bedroom, as I have suggested at greater length elsewhere, exemplify the negative, overwhelming power of the slave in the Hegelian master-slave relationship. Delilah, Yael, Esther, or Judith do battle in the bedroom, the one place where men always lose; a little seduction and a man literally loses his head (his eyes, hair, or limbs—all symbolic castration). It is small wonder that men wanted women to stay in the tent.[5]

The second risk is celebrating woman's differences in ways that can be used to keep her tied to man by the energy of opposition. This tendency to see Woman constructed as Other is evident in Jewish feminist research as well. For example, in her essay "*Mizvot* Built into the Body: *Tkhines* for *Niddah*, Pregnancy, and Childbirth," Chava Weissler reminds us that "one of the important insights of feminist theory is the alterity, the otherness of women. Men are the rule, women the exception. . . . The female body, like the female person, is the exception."[6] From such classic statements as the essays in Susannah Heschel's *On Being a Jewish Feminist* through Plaskow's most recent work, this research frequently begins by positioning woman in her alterity or her absence. Whatever the field of investigation—biblical narrative, rabbinic midrash, *halakhah*, myth, ritual, shtetl life, or contemporary life—woman can be located as Other within the male normative discourse that names her, defines her, legislates for her, and restricts her.

I prefer Denise Riley, who echoes Desdemona's question to Iago in her book *Am I that Name?: Feminism and the Category of "Women" in History*, and Patti Lather in *Getting Smart*, both of whom demonstrate that the history of feminism is a dialectical history of efforts to define woman in her specificity and to expose unjust definitions of woman as different from person. Attempts to absolutely define woman are ultimately and inevitably falsified. Riley cautions: "For 'women' are always differently re-membered, and the gulf between them and the generally human will be more or less thornily intractable."[7]

I will try to read Woman as represented in tension with the normative, embodying an empowering Derridean *différance*: mysterious, ambiguous, multivalent, and acting outside of verbal language. My own title exemplifies this point to the extent that there is a tension between the usual connotations of "eavesdropping on angels and laughing at God" and the different connotations that these activities have when they describe the matriarch. I mean to imply heresy: eavesdropping is at best rude; it is more usually manipulative, an effort to discover what one is not meant to know, and in political contexts, the activity may of course be treasonous. Eavesdropping on angels conjures up Lucifer in Milton's *Paradise Lost*, who illicitly acquires divine knowledge and whose response of seditious laughter is brazen, inappropriate, and disrespectful. "Laughing" is always potentially ambiguous: it may be mirthful, skeptical, contained, or hysterical; ironic, nervous, delighted, humored, or mean; but when the object of laughter is God, surely this laughter is loud and demonic, at best profoundly embittered, and at worst frankly evil.

My title alludes instead to Sarah. Eavesdropping on her spouse's conversation with the messengers of God who came to declare her fate, the first matriarch of Hebrew Scriptures heard the promise of a child still to be carried, borne, and suckled by her, though she is aware, the text tells us, of her own body and its stages: she is beyond receiving monthly periods, and, as she herself says, her husband Abraham is old. As immediately as one recognizes the reference to Sarah, one loses the connotations of heresy that are otherwise implied by "eavesdropping on angels and laughing at God." Sarah's listening at the tent may be read as an allegory of women's experience in history and especially in religious history; denied direct access to power—sacred or otherwise— women position themselves to "overhear" the plans of gods and men as a survival strategy. To the extent that men "live" within institutions and women "survive" them, we see a distinction built into the etymology of "survival" itself, "over" living, or living "over," like "overhearing" as opposed to simply living and hearing. What is insidious behavior for men is normative for women.

Sarah at the tent suggests for me an alternative discursive possibility to woman as Other. Instead we see Woman as outsider looking in, with powers and privileges that accrue from distance. To return to my allegory: Sarah laughs. Whether she laughed because she finds the idea of conceiving a child in old age ludicrous, or whether she laughed with delighted surprise, or whether she laughed with bitterness—having longed all of her life for a child, and having God's promise come so very late—the text does not say. Why Sarah laughed is mysterious to God as well because He asks Abraham why Sarah laughed. Because Sarah is afraid, she denies having laughed, but God—

who evidently sees what we do even if He, like Sigmund Freud after Him, is not fully clear about woman's motives—declares, without apparent reproach, "but you did laugh." If you indulge me in the allegory, the first Matriarch represents Woman as eavesdropping and laughing, and it represents God in relation to her as deferential to her psychic complexity, as if God (and for "God" one may read "Man" or "History") speaks with clarity, and Woman responds with ambiguity. He inquires, receives no satisfying response, and He shrugs. Later God gives Sarah authority over Isaac's future, as well as authority over the bondswoman Hagar and her son Ishmael. "Listen to Sarah," God tells Abraham, whom the rabbinic tradition by and large imagines is too naive to accurately understand Hagar and their son.

The other matriarchs are also devious and subversive, and they too are approved of by the God of Hebrew Scriptures. Without too much elaboration, let me simply allude to Rebecca eavesdropping on Isaac and Esau, after which she tells Jacob how to steal the blessing of the firstborn. When Jacob says that he is afraid, Rebecca answers with evident self-confidence and in stereotypically maternal fashion, "I'll accept the blame." Rachel steals; Leah tricks Jacob in the marriage bed. Women are often represented as subverting male intentions in the very process of fulfilling God's mysterious plans.

In *Countertraditions in the Bible: A Feminist Approach*, Ilana Pardes characterizes the Bible as "a heteroglot text," and she strives to "explore the tense dialogue between the dominant patriarchal discourses of the Bible and the counter female voices which attempt to put forth other truths."[8] Contrasting the Bible with modern fiction, she writes that "dealing with a text that is not divided into chapters and parts composed by sundry authors during approximately a dozen centuries requires a different hermeneutic suspicion." For Pardes, "the confounding mixture of dispersed language . . . best represents the art of biblical narrative."[9]

Exposing heteroglossia is Pardes's strategy for discovering feminist countertraditions in the Bible. But perhaps we over-interpret biblical ambiguity. Perhaps biblical characters—heroines especially—are so inadequately drawn that the reader cannot know how to evaluate them. When I offered my reading of Sarah's laughter and God's response to another reader of biblical narrative, he demurred. This reader dislikes Sarah, especially her callous treatment of Hagar and Ishmael, and he thereby departs from the commentaries that assume Sarah's wisdom and judiciousness. Accordingly, he offers an alternative reading of Sarah's laugh.

Because the Hebrew allows for multiple connotations of the word that I have translated as "laughed," some commentators who are unhappy with the implication that God does not understand Sarah's motivations translate this as "Sarah mocked" or "derided." God's question is then rhetorical, a reproach in the syntax of a question: "Why do you mock, woman, am I, God, not capable of anything?" The answer is implicit in the question. I accidentally found support for this reading when I looked over these chapters in the new *Oxford Study Bible* (1992). A footnote indicates that "Sarai" means "mocker" and that when God changes Sarah's name from Sarai to Sarah, it is a change in meaning from "mocker" to "princess." I have spent some time with Sarah and her stories over my years as a reader, and I don't remember having seen that translation before. I went to the standard dictionary, Brown, Driver, and Briggs's *Lexicon*, and there is no suggestion of mockery in any variant of Sarai or Sarah, only variants of "noblewoman." I went to the *Midrash Rabbah* convinced that if there was a "mocker" to be found in Sarai, surely one of those medieval exegetes would have found her. Again, there was only nobility.[10]

I am left wondering how "mocker" infiltrated itself into "Sarai" and became so codified by *Oxford*. I make much of this translation ambiguity because of the tension between God's apparent acceptance, even love of Sarah in the biblical narrative, and the efforts of readers to expose the possibility of regarding her as a rebel.

Sarah's laughter does not end there. If Sarah laughs at first with the mirth of skepticism, she does later bear the child who will inherit the covenant of Abraham. Sarah names her son both in memory of her own laughter and with a promise of laughter; she names him "Yitzchak," which means "he will laugh," and in turn makes the whole tradition heir to laughter.

Abraham, the first patriarch, gives us monotheism, faith, and duty. We remember Abraham, above all, as the knife-wielding father ready to sacrifice the son named for laughing. The commenting tradition has spent less time asking what the matriarchs bequeath to their tradition, but one might notice here that Sarah's bequest can be construed as the opposite of duty, something more anarchic and illogical than the obedience connected with Abrahamic faith and made emblematic by Kierkegaard's critical attentions. Her narrative, by contrast, displays a consciousness of her own and her husband's sexual bodies, with its oblique reference to menarche, intercourse, and male potency—all coded as liminal or doubtful because associated with the sexual bodies of the aged. Sarah eavesdrops. She laughs, and the next patriarch is named in association with her laughter.

It is through this word again, the root letters of which give us "to laugh," "to mock," "to play," and "to sport," complete with the ambiguous renderings of "play," that we are asked to understand Sarah's banishment of Ishmael and Hagar. Sarah sees the older brother "playing with" (some translations render it "mocking") the younger. But we remember that the verb "to play" or "to mock" comes from the same root as Isaac's name; so in playing with Isaac, Ishmael "isaacs Isaac." Midrashim speculate about what Ishmael did. Did he play the part of the favored younger child, and Sarah banishes her son's would-be usurper? A less innocent reading is that in isaacing Isaac, Ishmael plays dirty, plays with Isaac, and Sarah responds with appropriate necessity to banish the boy. It is indeterminate of course, but that finally is my point. Sarah's laughter, and Isaac as heir to her laughter, yields only ambiguity, and in so doing it participates in the mystery of God's working in His history book.

A Gloss on Laughter: Mothers, Witches, and Hysterics

I have made much of Sarah's laugh. As a way of justifying this excess, I want to gloss that laughter with other laughter in the hope of demonstrating that woman's laughter resonates with associations in the Western textual tradition, associations that have been wonderfully illuminated by feminist criticism. It is commonplace that language constitutes the distinguishing feature of humanity. But Umberto Eco, following Aristotle, reminds us that laughter is also distinctively human.[11] It is laughter, not reason, that Kathleen Norris requests in her poem "A Prayer to Eve." She begins: "Mother of fictions and of irony, help us to laugh." A resonant sentence from Hélène Cixous's "The Laugh of the Medusa," reads: "You have only to look at the Medusa straight on to see her. And she is not deadly. She's beautiful and she's laughing." Why does Norris petition first for laughter? What does Cixous mean when she says that the Medusa is not deadly but is laughing? Carol P. Christ, in her "reflections on a journey to the Goddess," which is the subtitle of her book *Laughter of Aphrodite*, writes self-reflexively about "Gavriel's laughter" entering her bones. The reference is to Elie Wiesel's *Gates of the Forest*, which begins with mythic laughter rising above the corpses of angels who had entered into mortal struggle. In this laughter, as in the laughter of Aphrodite that she hears on a personal journey in Lesbos, Christ finds a "mediator of transformation."[12] Not mirth, this laughter distances Christ from pain.

Catherine Clément, in *The Newly Born Woman*, writes that "all laughter is allied with the monstrous." She catalogues the laughter of hysterics and witches, alluding to a power that is "petrifying and shattering constraint," and she generalizes that laughter "breaks up, breaks out, splashes over."[13] With reference to this laughter, she quotes Mary Douglas's *Purity and Danger*:

> Each culture . . . attributes a power to some image or another of the body, according to the situation of which the body is the mirror. . . . The things that defile are always wrong one way or another, they are not in their place or else they have crossed a line they never should have crossed and from this shift a danger for someone results.[14]

Douglas identifies that which defiles as that which is outside of recognized category boundaries: obvious examples in Judaism include bodily emissions. Blood should be inside; when it is outside, it defiles and is impure. If bugs crawl and fish swim, a fish that crawls (like a lobster) is a category violation and is therefore unkosher. Clément glosses Douglas by invoking Lacanian psychoanalytic theory: "To break up, to touch the masculine integrity of the body image, is to return to a stage that is scarcely constituted in human development; it is to return to the disordered Imaginary of before the mirror stage, of before the rigid and defensive constitution of subjective armor." Clément explains that "an entire fantastic world, made of bits and pieces, opens up beyond the limit, as soon as the line is crossed. For the witch (the hysteric), breaking apart can be paradise, but for another it is hell."[15]

Woman's laughter (her heaven, his hell), Clément implies, is a category violation in our culture. The monstrous laughter associated with hysterics and witches brings Clément, through Douglas, to the Lacanian Imaginary; that is, to the prelinguistic connection to the Mother, or, if you will, to Matriarchy itself, before the entry of the child into the Law before the child is taken over by the Father, law, reason, and logic. The Hebrew Bible contains evidence that ancient ritual since lost to us marked this psychological transition from the chaotic pre-linguistic maternal Imaginary to the more settled state of paternal Law. *Genesis* specifies that Abraham had a great celebration at Isaac's weaning. That weaning does not represents traumatic loss (as Melanie Klein suggests) but a positive movement to cultural containment finds expression in the second verse of Psalm 131: "Enough for me to keep my soul tranquil and quiet like a child in its mother's arms, as content as a child that has been weaned."

These constructions of woman's laughter and the suckling baby remind me of a piece of graffiti from a fraternity bathroom: "Never trust anything that bleeds for seven days and does not die." Why is this slogan as funny as it is disgusting? Because all of us, even women, function within a system in which unstopped bleeding means death. Forgetting the very humanity of women who menstruate for seven days and do not die, this injunction against trusting women (who are implicitly not human, witches) reminds us that women stand outside looking in at the most surprising places, even in the most natural places and even in our own consciousness. Woman's blood, like woman's laughter, is encoded differently than human blood or laughter.

David Biale provides for me a final example, from the literature of twentieth-century Zionism, of the metonymic association of woman, mother, and fluid, and the easy substitution of one fluid for another.[16] Quoting what Biale describes as Nathan Bistritsky's "extraordinary piece of mythology that harkens back to the blood symbolism of the biblical priestly code, he predicts that at the end of history the matriarchy will return. In messianic times, Abraham will suckle from the breasts of Sarah his wife, alternating with his son, Isaac."[17] This is Bistritsky's idealized woman: "She — the mother — stands outside of our circle, the circle of history and a strip of blood stands red behind like a holy, terrifying shadow. She wallows in the blood, her holy blood, the blood of virginity, the blood of first sacrifice, the blood of childbirth. Humanity washes in the blood of its heroes, but the dove of the holy spirit descends only on the fountain of blood that flows from the woman."[18] So we move with relative ease from laughter to women to hysteric to witch to mother to blood to milk and around again.

Blood and milk, murmuring and laughter, have a long association with women in the Western tradition of art and literature. Biblical literature offers early representations of associations that have become part of the Western mythology of the feminine. Whether the connotations are positive or negative in a particular context, certain fluids and articulations of voice have accrued meanings that contribute to something like a code of woman's mystery and power in our cultural heritage. When Jewish feminists strain to locate women using classification systems typically associated with the study of Judaism (with categories such as law, ritual, and theology) to the exclusion of classifications that may offer the figure of Woman a more comfortable fit (and here I have talked about laughter as one such possibility), we may miss opportunities to reread woman in the Jewish tradition in ways that are finally recuperative, empowering, and even redemptive.

Cixous begins "The Laugh of the Medusa" promising to speak about women's writing and enjoining Woman to "write herself" because women have been driven from writing "as violently as from their own bodies—for the same reasons, by the same law, with the same fatal goal." Implicitly, Woman claims writing by reclaiming her body. It is a dangerous, compelling enthusiasm. Cixous promises: "Now, I-woman am going to blow up the Law; an explosion henceforth possible and ineluctable; let it be done, right now, in language." I am suggesting that a theory of Jewish feminism might begin with a chapter called "laughter" and would have others called "milk" and "blood," in keeping with Cixous's ultimate reminder that woman "writes with white ink."[19]

NOTES

1. See the opening chapter of Ilana Pardes, *Countertraditions in the Bible: A Feminist Approach* (Cambridge: Harvard University Press, 1992). As a footnote, I also offer Alicia Suskin Ostriker's observation that God's excessive punishment of Moses, who may not enter the promised land, demands interpretation. Miriam is a prophetess; God shames her with the divine "spit" (as He calls it) of leprosy, and her brothers intervene on her behalf with unusual vigor. The people refuse to go anywhere without her, and when she dies, they wish to return to Egypt for fear of thirst, a fear expressed in Moses's striking the rock, an expression of doubt in God's power to provide for them without Miriam. Apparently the people believed, and the text censors, that Miriam had unique access to a Divine water pipe.

2. Judith Plaskow, "Halakhah as a Feminist Issue," *Melton Journal* 22 (Fall 1987): 3–5.

3. My objection to Carol Gilligan's *In a Different Voice: Psychological Theory and Women's Development* (Cambridge: Harvard University Press, 1982) is the special attention it gives to feminine difference.

4. Nina Auerbach's important study of images of women in Victorian literature, *Woman and the Demon: The Life of a Victorian Myth* (Cambridge: Harvard University Press, 1982), is problematic in this regard as well: Auerbach locates power in the representations of heroines, but this power, it seems to me, is no better than the power of the Hegelian slave in the master-slave relationship: the master imagines that the slave upon whom he depends for his mastery will be powerful if unchained.

5. For fuller discussions see my "When Lilith Becomes a Heroine: Midrash as a Feminist Response," *Melton Journal* 23 (Spring 1990): 5-8; and "Coats and Tales: Joseph Stories and Myths of Jewish Masculinity," in *A Mensch among Men: Explorations in Jewish Maculinity*, ed. Harry Brod (Freedom, CA: Crossing Press, 1988), 19–29.

6. In Howard Eilberg-Schwartz, ed., *People of the Body: Jews and Judaism from an Embodied Perspective* (Albany: SUNY Press, 1992), 101.

7. Denise Riley, *Am I that Name?: Feminism and the Category of "Women" in History* (Minneapolis: University of Minnesota Press, 1990), 108.

8. Ilana Pardes, *Countertraditions in the Bible: A Feminist Approach* (Cambridge: Harvard University Press, 1992) , 4.

9. Ibid., 58–59.

10. Sarah is, to be sure, not treated with unequivocal respect in the stories in the *Midrash Rabbah*: because of her, we learn, all women are eavesdroppers just as we learn with reference to Dinah, the rape victim, that all women are gadabouts. And besides the more predictable God-affirming speculations about why Sarah was childless for so long is the envious suggestion that Abraham was blessed with a wife whose beautiful body was not disfigured by the work of pregnancy and childbearing until her old age.

11. Laughter as the defining feature of humanity is the central conceit of Umberto Eco's novel *The Name of the Rose*.

12. Carol P. Christ, *Laughter of Aphrodite: Reflections on a Journey to the Goddess* (San Francisco: Harper & Row, 1987) , 6. Kathleen Norris, "A Prayer to Eve, " *Paris Review* No. 115 (Summer 1990), 199. Hélène Cixous, "Laugh of the Medusa," *New French Feminisms: An Anthology*, ed. Elaine Marks and Isabelle de Courtivron (Amherst: University of Massachusetts Press, 1980).

13. In Hélène Cixous and Catherine Clément,eds., *The Newly Born Woman*, trans. Betsy Wing (Minneapolis: University of Minnesota Press, 1986) , 33.

14. Mary Douglas, Purity and Danger: *An Analysis of Concepts of Pollution and Taboo* (New York: Routledge and Kegan Paul, 1966) quoted in Cixous and Clément, The Newly Born Woman , 33.

15. Cixous and Clément, *The Newly Born Woman*, 32–33.

16. David Biale, "Zionism as an Erotic Revolution," in Eilberg-Schwartz's *People of the Body*, 283–307.

17. Ibid., 296.

18. Nathan Bistritsky's *Days and Nights* (Jerusalem, 1926), 197, quoted in Biale, " Zionism as an Erotic Revolution," 296.

19. Hélène Cixous, "Laugh of the Medusa," *New French Feminisms: An Anthology*, ed. Elaine Marks and Isabelle de Courtivron (Amherst: University of Massachusetts Press, 1980), 245–64.

Chapter 12

Mass Culture and the City in the Works of German-Jewish Novelists: Claire Goll, Veza Canetti, Else Lasker-Schüler, and Gertrud Kolmar

Dagmar C. G. Lorenz

German literature authored by Jewish women has traditionally been city literature. One of the foremost texts dating back to the pre-emancipation epoch, the famous memoirs of Glikl of Hameln (1646–1724), written in Yiddish, are set in Hamburg and Strasbourg in an exclusively Jewish urban environment. Glikl's digressions about the fate of her extended family also provide insights into Jewish life in other major cities such as Berlin, Vienna, and Leipzig. As a businesswoman, a jewelry dealer, and money lender, Glikl had professional contacts with Gentiles. However, she viewed non-Jews with suspicion, always conscious of the possibility of individual attacks on Jewish merchants traveling cross-country and the threat of persecution and pogroms.[1]

In the early nineteenth century the abolition of the ghettos was completed and the relative isolation of the Jewish communities ended. Contacts between Jews and Gentiles on a social and personal basis became more frequent, particularly among the privileged and underprivileged classes, but less so in the middle class. Men and women of the avant-garde—such as the memoir and letter writers Rahel Levin Varnhagen; Henriette Herz; the author Dorothea Mendelssohn Schlegel; and the notorious adventuress Pauline Wiesel, lover of the Prussian Prince Louis Ferdinand and Rahel Varnhagen's correspondent and confidante—crossed the boundaries into Gentile society. Some eventually married Gentiles. Because civil ceremonies did not exist marriages between Christians and non-Christians were illegal and conversion from Christianity to Judaism was outlawed; this step necessitated apostasy on the part of the Jewish partner. Whereas de facto these prominent Jewish-born women abandoned their faith and culture of origin, their identity problems and self-definition suggest their continued entanglement with Judaism and the Jewish community on a subjective level. For this reason Steven Beller and Robert Wistrich consider assimilation and conversion a part of Jewish history. Even if it was the goal of the individuals who assimilated themselves to become non-Jewish, they did continue to belong to a group that for historical reasons developed its own particular patterns and remained easily identifiable.[2]

The multiculturalism characteristic of the salons established by Jewish women was only possible in cities such as Berlin and Vienna, and even there it proved to be fragile and short-lived. In 1807-8, during the Napoleonic occupation, the cultural coexistence of Jews and Gentiles and men and women in these ephemeral circles came to an abrupt end when, as the salonnière Henriette Herz put it, "The educated classes put aside French literature for the sake of German books." The outbreak of nationalism that fueled the Wars of Liberation had its effects well beyond the late Romantic era.[3]

Also in the twentieth century, the European metropolitan and cultural centers were the domain of German Jewish women writers and intellectuals. Their perspective on the ever more complex social processes set in motion by the industrial revolution and rapid urbanization differed distinctly from that of Gentile and most male Jewish authors. For example, the Berlin-based novelist Fanny Lewald discussed in her novels not only the problems engendered by the emancipation and assimilation of German Jews in an anti-Semitic environment, but also the situation of women in a disintegrating patriarchy. Her call for the emancipation of women through job training and education preceded Bertha Pappenheim's passionate advocacy of women's economic independence and self-determination by more than a generation.[4]

At the turn of the century, Jewish women writers and intellectuals explored the modern urban world from various points of view and positioned themselves in it. The parameters of their nonconformist texts differ from those of the male-dominated literary and critical establishment; there are, for example, no women Expressionists, Dadaists, or writers of popular dramas. Jewish women authors did not reject modernity and industrialization as categorically as did most other authors at the turn of the century, but they did not hail progress as a panacea either. However, it is precisely because of their unique representation of reality that Jewish women authors were often misunderstood and underrated. In the wake of the political developments in Germany and Austria during the 1930s, the works of all Jewish authors were suppressed. Many of them were forgotten for good. In contrast to Jewish men such as Hermann Broch, Alfred Döblin, or Elias Canetti, who experienced a revival in the postwar era, the works of some women writers of the same generation are only now slowly being re-discovered and reprinted—most recently Claire Goll, Gertrud Kolmar, and Veza Canetti.

Like the authors of the Romantic era, a number of Jewish women writers had adopted a bohemian life-style. They perpetuated the dissident tradition associated with names such as Rahel Levin Varnhagen, Dorothea Mendelssohn Schlegel, and Henriette Herz. Else Lasker-Schüler and Claire Goll were known to be eccentric to the point of notoriety. In the anonymity of Berlin and Paris, they lived among like-minded artists and intellectuals, enjoying a measure of mobility and freedom of expression. To a degree, the modern mass culture worked to their advantage. Until the Nazi takeover, intellectual and artistic movements had converged in the cosmopolitan culture of these European capitals, putting those who lived and worked there at the cutting edge of intellectual and artistic life. At the same time, these cities were also centers of Jewish culture. The daily contact with Jewish culture, mostly secularized, diminished the alienation commonly experienced by Jews living in provincial Germany and Austria. Yet, the works of Else Lasker-Schüler, Claire Goll, Gertrud Kolmar, and Veza Canetti still reflect the experience of double marginalization that shaped the authors' world view and their literary expression.

For Jewish women intellectuals of the nineteenth century the only livable environment had been the city. This situation remained unchanged in the twentieth century, for example, for Lasker-Schüler, Goll, Kolmar, and Canetti. At the same time, since the turn of the century, the literary and essayistic works of Jewish women writers indicate an increasing awareness of the dangers inherent in the only milieu where they could hope to achieve a measure of self-realization. The magnitude of the external and internal obstacles facing Jewish women who wanted to write is suggested by the fact that Gertrud Kolmar and Nelly Sachs were as hesitant to break their anonymity as Fanny Lewald had been in the mid-nineteenth century. Jewish women writers were more cognizant of the impasse arising from racist and economic anti-Semitism than their generally more optimistic male colleagues. Generated in reaction to the almost complete assimilation of German Jews, modern anti-Semitism had become a major threat at a time when members of the older generations could still remember the last pogroms in Germany.[5] In every generation of Jewish women writers born after 1860, a greater awareness of vulnerability is manifest. The authors knew they were at risk for political and social reasons and conveyed this realization in their texts.

Their female protagonists die tragic deaths; they suffer physical and emotional abuse as well as attacks on their integrity and safety. City life is shown to be increasingly threatening to women because they are socially and economically disadvantaged. At the same time, the authors suggest that leaving the city is no alternative. They portray the situation in the country as even more unsafe for those who live on the margins of the patriarchal capitalist society. Women whose background and aspirations do not conform with the middle-class paradigm are especially at risk.

Claire Goll lived and worked in Paris, Zürich, and New York; Gertrud Kolmar lived in Berlin, and Veza Canetti lived in Vienna. Even before her and her husband's emigration to London in 1938, Canetti had stopped publishing because the presses in Germany and Austria were inaccessible to her as a Jewish woman. Else Lasker-Schüler had moved from her hometown of Elberfeld, near Wuppertal, to Berlin at the turn of the century and become the friend of artists and intellectuals such as Peter Hille, Franz Marc, Gottfried Benn, Franz Werfel, Martin Buber, Gershom Sholem, and Karl Kraus. In 1933 she sought asylum in Switzerland and later traveled through Egypt and Palestine. She finally settled in Jerusalem. It is no coincidence that Lasker-Schüler, who as the oldest of these four authors had experienced the exuberance of a broad-based anarchist and socialist movement, the messianic awakening of early expressionism, and turn-of-the century feminism, was the most conspicuous German-speaking Jewish woman author of her time. She transformed herself into a provocative public personality. Only Claire Goll, who had left her native country before World War I, comes close to the flamboyant, defiant style and manner of Lasker-Schüler; Kolmar and Canetti at least outwardly conformed to the social expectations.

All four authors thematized the social and emotional problems created by the social upheavals engendered by the industrial revolution. Lasker-Schüler's works reflect her own philosophy and experience, her own anarchistic life-style following her divorce from the conservative small-town dermatologist Berthold Schüler, and her inventing and re-inventing of ever new personae. Lasker-Schüler belonged to the

German bohème that prior to World War I had celebrated matriarchy and free love, advocating single motherhood and the unrestricted expression of passion and desire on the part of women. She perceived the same social phenomena as did, for example, the bourgeois Jewish Feminist Bertha Pappenheim, who fought against promiscuity, prostitution, and child abuse. Rather than condemning these phenomena as criminal or morally wrong, Lasker-Schüler usually portrays them in a value-neutral fashion and occasionally makes them positive. Insofar as social chaos and transgression against middle class morality contribute to the collapse of the patriarchal values and social structures, Lasker-Schüler seems to welcome them.

Lasker-Schüler's *Die Wupper* (1906) is an example of these proclivities. The drama is set in a working-class neighborhood in an industrial town in the West of Germany, which is likely a reflection of the author's hometown of Wuppertal. In a mixture of poetry and realism, the drama integrates fairy-tale motifs and social concerns.[6] The author, herself marginalized, represents the class struggle, sexual exploitation of women, particularly of proletarian women by upper-class men, and the plight of the homeless and handicapped in such a way as to empower the marginalized. She lends them a voice by portraying the class barriers as permeable. The central character, the matriarch Mother Pious—half a witch, half an earth-mother figure—has an impact on the lives of everyone around her, her relatives as well as the family of the industrialist Sonntag.

Lasker-Schüler, who lived most of her life at the poverty level in a state of near-homelessness, empathizes with the suffering but also rejoices in the glory of unbound transient life, a major motif in turn-of-the century culture.[7] These facets are most apparent in the characters of three vagrants, who are as disgusting and pathetic as they are admirable and poetic. Lasker-Schüler illuminates these and similar figures from within, intimating that even exhibitionism may be a path to spiritual glory. The truly vital and poetic qualities of the play reside with the characters of Mother Pious, the three vagrants, and the sleep-walker Lieschen, a seductive child-woman. They possess forces against which the members of the bourgeoisie—even the aggressive, sensual, and young former officer, Heinrich Sonntag—are powerless. The middle classes are portrayed as morally and spiritually bankrupt, lacking the vitality to oppose the parvenu Simon who is taking over the domain of the old establishment. In *Die Wupper* neither they nor the Socialists, who appear on stage in the light of the full moon, marching and singing, are forces to be reckoned with in the future. The victory of opportunism and irrationality convey an apocalyptic feeling of impending doom and destruction.

Die Wupper has been performed in the sober, abstract *Bauhaus* style and in Expressionist settings reminiscent of Fritz Lang's film *Metropolis* and Chagall's and Kokoschka's paintings. Whereas the former approach underscores Lasker-Schüler's social concerns, the latter more appropriately accentuates the charismatic aspects of her play by showing the river banks of the river Wupper as a magic organism that, no matter how hard human beings try to control it, retains a life of its own. This emphasis on surrealist and fantastic elements places *Die Wupper* next to Alban Berg's opera version of Georg Büchner's *Woyzek*.

The play acknowledges the irrationality of everyday life and the futility of human plans and projects. In an environment in which everything is in flux, exhibitionists, youthful prostitutes, incestuous grandfathers, voyeurs, and upper-class lechers—in other words, the wretchedness and the squalor—come to suggest hope and vitality, because they defy superimposed patterns and laws, but most of all the cold bureaucratic mind of a man like Simon, the lawyer. In the context of *Die Wupper*, everything that shakes up bourgeois society or undermines its bureaucracy, be it debauchery, or substance abuse, is a manifestation of rebellion while the would-be revolutionaries who march in formation miss their mark in two ways: they organize themselves i.e., (they reproduce the system), and they claim to be rational while they themselves are a part of a demented universe. In Lasker-Schüler's works, the middle-class establishment and the technocrats it created appear as humanity's most dangerous enemy by far. Their conventions and values are shown to be the most confining and destructive elements of modern society, more destructive than open chaos and anarchy.

The views expressed by Claire Goll, an uncompromising pacifist who opposed World War I from its very beginnings, are similar to those of Lasker-Schüler. Unlike most of the anti-war protesters, Goll made her criticism public long before the extent of the destruction and the German defeat could be foreseen. In a series of articles, she appealed to German women to prevent their husbands and sons from obeying the draft orders.[8] She passionately rejected the gender stereotypes upheld by the middle-class women's movement, particularly the notion that women were constitutionally more peaceful and caring than men. Instead, Goll exposed the complicity of women and men, denouncing women's passivity as self-imposed. Without a mother's cooperation, Goll argues, no man would be raised to become a soldier, and without women's supporting the war effort, wars could not be fought.

Goll's Paris experience is reflected in her novels, thematizing the multifaceted culture of the French capital, which the author had thoroughly investigated as a journalist. Race and gender, ethnicity and class, are the central issues in her novels *Der Neger Jupiter raubt Europa* (1926) and *Ein Mensch ertrinkt* (1931).[9] A clearly defined assessment of racial, class, and gender issues emerges from Goll's two novels, with the former of which is set in a middle-class environment, and the latter among proletarians. Goll portrays race as the decisive factor in bourgeois circles. Because Goll's middle class protagonist of *Der Neger Jupiter* is a white woman, she escapes unscathed from her tumultuous marriage to a Black diplomat. From the start, public opinion is against Goll's African protagonist who is introduced exclusively from the perspective of white people. Gradually the perceptions of Jupiter change from grotesqueness to a rare, exotic beauty and appeal, and back to the image of a primitive, misogynist tyrant, until in the end Jupiter is shown in his humanity as a suffering man and no longer as the "other." His despair over the loss of his wife, his child, and his dignity arouses the readers' empathy, and his white opponents' cruelty becomes fully visible. Jupiter becomes an icon of the non-white, non-European man, who is duped, exploited, and destroyed by the French bourgeoisie.

In *Ein Mensch ertrinkt* Goll sketches an entirely different milieu, that of the metropolitan slums, where women of no matter which ethnic background are at a disadvantage. With the complete erosion of patriarchal structures, even the minimal amount of protection women used to enjoy has vanished. Goll describes gender relations among proletarians, that class to which Marx attributed the greatest revolutionary potential, as an unequal battle in a social Darwinist jungle. By defining the attitudes most hostile and detrimental to women as characteristic of the urban proletariat, she expresses, as did Lasker-Schüler in *Die Wupper*, her disagreement with Marxist views. Goll's protagonist, Marie, pays dearly for a short period of permissiveness with her child's and, eventually, her own life. The exploitation and abuse that Marie experienced at the hands of her Black lover and her Jewish employer, and the dire consequences she faces as a single mother, are disproportionate with her rare and fleeting moments of gratification.

Goll exposes the supposed freedom of modern women as a fraud, and the apparent acceptance of non-Europeans into middle-class society as illusory. Although numerous themes in her works coincide with those of Lasker-Schüler's *Die Wupper* (1906) and Veza Canetti's novel *Die gelbe Straße*, Goll's novels differ from those of the other two authors in her rejection of the concept of a specifically feminine psychology and her opposition to rigid ideological doctrines.[10] Veza Canetti focuses on the plight of the poor and oppressed, particularly women exploited by men as a result of the blatant social and economic inequities and the widespread disregard for women. Despite the unmitigated suffering depicted by Canetti, there is an optimistic tone in her works, generated by the Socialist framework underlying her texts. Her works are an indictment of the nuclear family, patriarchy, and capitalism. *Die gelbe Straße*, first published in the Viennese *Arbeiter-Zeitung* for which Canetti wrote regularly until 1934,[11] is set in Vienna, the former capital of the Habsburg multinational state. Canetti portrays the ethnically diverse environment of the city's Second District, a center for immigrants, mainly from Eastern Europe. Canetti's views are shaped by Socialist thought. She emphasizes internationalism, suggesting that capitalist propaganda exaggerates ethnic differences to prevent solidarity among different groups of oppressed. Furthermore, she shows that both proletarians and women are affected by poverty and powerlessness.

The loosely structured novel describes an entire milieu.[12] One of its plots revolves around the Igers, a couple who recently moved from Bosnia to the city. Mrs. Iger is killed by her husband, a ruthless wife- and child-abuser, because in the strange anonymous environment she has no recourse, not even to her authoritarian father. The absence of norms and values in this milieu is reminiscent of Goll's Paris. It is a patriarchal system without patriarchs, that is, each man demands the right to dominate women and children without fulfilling the obligations that in a functioning patriarchy are part and parcel of male power. Canetti's drama *Der Oger* features the same *lumpenpatriarchal* environment and the same dramatis personae, but it illustrates that only in the city do women have a chance of liberating themselves.[13] Aided by friends who abandoned their traditional social values, Canetti's protagonist divorces her stingy, tyrannical husband and gets custody of her son.

Lasker-Schüler, and even more so Canetti, show that the disintegration of patriarchal values is ultimately to the advantage of women and other vulnerable groups. Whereas the bohemian Lasker-Schüler, little concerned with political correctness, celebrates a Dionysian, care-free anarchistic life-style as an end in itself, Canetti considers the crumbling of the old structures as a turning point, at which time women can begin to assert themselves and work toward a society where there is room for them as full-fledged social and marital partners.

Goll's *Ein Mensch ertrinkt* portrays life in Paris, a melting pot of ethnic groups and races, as enticing and repulsive at the same time. The pessimism in *Ein Mensch ertrinkt* corresponds with the message conveyed in Gertrud Kolmar's novella *Eine jüdische Mutter*, written in Berlin at the eve of the Nazi takeover.[14] Kolmar's protagonist is a Jewish widow of a Gentile man, a socially and spiritually disoriented woman. Goll's protagonist, a country girl trying to advance herself as a maid in a Jewish household in Paris, and Kolmar's Jewish mother, who lives with her daughter in one of Berlin's proletarian garden colonies, are destroyed by their brutal and indifferent male-dominated environment. Both authors show women of their own time who fend for themselves without male protection. They are exposed and isolated. In *Ein Mensch ertrinkt*, Marie's child dies of disease and malnutrition; in *Eine jüdische Mutter*, Martha Jadassohn's daughter is kidnapped, sexually abused, and left for dead by a man who is never found. After months of futile hospital treatment, Martha, imagining that she acts as a good Jewish mother, poisons her daughter, convinced that euthanasia is the only way to spare her child from further suffering.

As if to preclude the notion that small town or country life offer greater protection, as was suggested particularly by Fascist authors, Goll and Kolmar chose rural settings for other texts.[15] In her novel *Arsenik*, Goll explored the boredom and pettiness of life in a provincial town. Her somewhat extravagant protagonist gets involved in an illicit affair, and, having become the target of vicious gossip, resorts to murdering her rival and ultimately her lover. In her novella *Susanna*, Kolmar chose an equally oppressive rural setting to show how an eccentric Jewish girl is driven to suicide by her own intolerant community.

Despite differences in topic and perspective, the central concerns of all the four authors are strikingly similar. They explore the interaction among different social and ethnic groups from the perspective of the oppressed, be they women, children, or socially unprotected individuals. Lasker-Schüler and Canetti avoid "Jewish" topics; Goll and Kolmar criticize the metropolitan European Jewish communities and their members for compromising their traditional values and abandoning their identity. They maintain that money has become a value in itself. As a result, spiritual values and personal integrity have been lost. In the works of the latter two, Jewish individuals are destroyed as a result of their unprincipled behavior. In Goll's *Ein Mensch ertrinkt* the victim is a lecherous married jeweler, in Kolmar a Jewish mother who assumes the right to judge whether her child will live or die. Lasker-Schüler and Canetti do not address specifically Jewish problems, but they identify the same problems as Goll and Kolmar as the cause of their society's turmoil.

All four authors depict the demise of the nuclear family and the leveling of ethnic and religious difference in the modern mass culture with more or less emotional detachment, perhaps because they are familiar with Gentile society, but do not feel they are an integral part of the mainstream. As Jews they were repeatedly the targets of anti-Semitism and remained outsiders to the powerful nationalist and Fascist movements; as women they were excluded from the centers of political and social power. They were able to retain their objectivity about the developments and events of their time because they had no real stake in them. The irony is that the social and political developments that were in the hands of men and non-Jews ultimately affected Jewish women the most collectively and individually.

Their assessment of these phenomena differs, but all four authors observe that the urban mass culture is created at the expense of society's weakest members: women and children. Lasker-Schüler, Goll, Kolmar, and Canetti expose vividly in their works those elements that many Gentile and male writers conceal or romanticize (promiscuity, prostitution, child abuse, incest, murder, adultery, exhibitionism, abortion, and suicide) as if to counterbalance the hypocrisy and sugar-coating of the literary mainstream. It is little wonder that to this day German readers are taken aback by their subversive texts, so out of keeping with conventional women's literature.

NOTES

1. Glückl von Hameln, *Denkwürdigkeiten*, trans. Alfred Feilchenfeld (Berlin: Jüdischer Verlag, 1913).
2. Steven Beller, "Class Culture and the Jews of Vienna, 1900," *Jews, Antisemitism and Culture in Vienna*, Ivar Oxaal, Michael Pollak, Gerhard Botz, eds. (London: Routledge, 1987): 42; Robert Wistrich, "Social Democracy, Antisemitism and the Jews of Vienna," *Jews, Antisemitism, and Culture*: 111-20.
3. Henriette Herz, *Henriette Herz in Erinnerungen, Briefen und Zeugnissen*, Rainer Schmitz, ed. (Frankfurt: Insel, 1984): 185.
4. Dora Edinger, ed., *Bertha Pappenheim: Freud's Anna O* (Highland Park, IL: Congregation Soleil, 1968) appeared first as *Bertha Pappenheim: Leben und Schriften*, ed. Dora Edinger (Frankfurt a.Main., Ner-Tamid, 1963).
5. Es ist vergeblich, das Volk der Dichter und Denker im Namen seiner Dichter und Denker zu beschwören. Jedes Vorurteil, das man abgetan glaubt, bringt, wie Aas die Würmer, tausend neue zutage.... Er ist ein Jude.... Was sollen die Juden tun? Opfer sind nicht zureichend, Werbung wird mißdeutet," states Jakob Wassermann in his autobiography, *Mein Weg als Deutscher und Jude* (Berlin: S. Fischer, 1921): 103. For

example, Else Lasker-Schüler's *Artur Aronymus* (Berlin: Rowohlt, 1932) in a poetic form recounts the persecution experienced by the author's father in the middle of the nineteenth century in Westphalia.

6. Else Lasker-Schüler, *Die Wupper. Schauspiel in fünf Aufzügen* (Suhrkamp, 1986).

7. Here the *Wandervogel* movement and the poet-vagabonds Waldemar Bonsels and Hugo Sonnenschein (Sonka) should be mentioned.

8. Claire Goll, *Der Gläserne Garten. Prosa 1917-1939*, Barbara Glauert-Hesse, ed. (Berlin: Argon, 1989).

9. Claire Goll, *Der Neger Jupiter raubt Europa* (Berlin: Argon, 1987); *Ein Mensch ertrinkt* (Berlin: Argon, 1988).

10. Veza Canetti, *Die gelbe Straße*, Elias Canetti, ed. (München: Carl Hanser, 1989).

11. Albert Einstein, Yvan Goll, Jura Soyfer, Theodor Plivier, and Robert Neumann as well as translations of international authors such as Jack London and Schalom Asch were published in *Arbeiter-Zeitung*.

12. In this regard, *Die Gelbe Straße* is surprisingly similar to the city novels of other contemporary Jewish novelists such as Alfred Döblin's *Berlin Alexanderplatz*, Israel Joshua Singer's *The Family Carnovsky*, and Isaac B. Singer's prose works about life in the Warsaw Jewish quarter.

13. Veza Canetti, *Der Oger*, Elias Canetti, ed. (München: Carl Hanser, 1990).

14. Gertrud Kolmar, *Eine jüdische Mutter* (München: Kösel, 1965).

15. Gertrud Kolmar, "Susanna," *Das leere Haus*, Hans Otten, ed. (Stuttgart: Cotta, 1959).

Chapter 13

Pauline Wengeroff and the Voice of Jewish Modernity

Shulamit S. Magnus

In 1898, Pauline Wengeroff began writing her memoirs on a small bench under an oak tree in a wood outside of Minsk.[1] Widowed, her three surviving children grown and scattered far from her, Wengeroff looked back on an eventful, often difficult life, writing of the memories that gripped her, "the wish stir[ring] in me to record for my children, as a keepsake of their mother, all that I once lived through."[2]

Wengeroff lived in tumultuous times. Born in 1833 in Bobruisk, Belorussia, she died in Minsk in 1916, her long life spanning the era of the Russian Jewish *haskalah* (Enlightenment movement) and vast transformations in Russian Jewish society. Wengeroff tells us much about her experiences and doubtless did wish to leave her children a memory of her life. As she records elsewhere, she also wrote to assuage loneliness in her old age.[3] Yet, Wengeroff's memoirs are less a personal or family chronicle than the epic tale of Jewish modernity as it emerged in eastern Europe. Or rather, they are the tale of Russian Jewish modernity told through the microcosm of one family's experiences and one woman's gender-tinted reflections.

Contemporary testimony is a rare and precious resource, but Wengeroff's is particularly so. In an era that saw the emergence of an autobiographical genre among Jews and the proliferation of *maskilic* memoirs, autobiographies and autobiographical novels,[4] to my knowledge, Wengeroff's is the only such writing by a woman. Because she lived in societies bifurcated by gender—as both traditional and modernizing Jewish societies were in the nineteenth century—her writing necessarily reflects female experience, about which we know lamentably little in this period. Wengeroff, moreover, writes quite self-consciously as a woman, of women's lives; she is a unique voice in the literature of her age.

But her writing is not only a source for Jewish women's history or their literary expression, as important as this is. It is a striking new perspective on Jewish modernity as a whole, achieved by telling the story of modernity through the experience of women—the first instance I know of when a major epoch of Jewish history is refracted through a female lens.[5]

All self-reflective writing is gendered. Gender is too basic a component of identity for it to be otherwise. Thus, the autobiographical writing of the *maskilim*, the "enlighteners" who were Wengeroff's contemporaries, is as gendered as hers. They, like all male writers, tell the story of their age through male experience. Mordechai Aron Guenzberg, Avraham Ber Gottlober, and Moshe Leib Lilienblum wrote extensively and intimately of this experience—of early, arranged marriages; premature sexuality; impotence; fatherhood; traumatic relationships with in-laws, particularly mothers-in-law; of frustrated, unhappy relationships with wives; divorces; inability to find, or sexually consummate, satisfying relationships with other women; of male bonding with other *maskilim*.[6]

Yet in the absence of a female perspective and the use of gender as an analytical tool, the maleness of these accounts has not been visible. Even when scholars have recognized the non-representativeness of *maskilic* writing—the fact that the *maskilim* were an elite whose experiences, certainly whose writing, were far from typical—*maskilic* autobiography has been taken as the expression of Jewish, not just male Jewish modernity in eastern Europe.[7] Wengeroff's writing not only adds a female voice to this canon; it puts the maleness of *maskilic* accounts into sharp relief and opens the whole question of gender in the experience, and telling, of Jewish modernity.

The *maskilim* made the traditional family, and traditional women in particular, a central focus of their autobiographical inquiry and a chief object of proposed reform. Such women figure prominently but most problematically in *maskilic* accounts. They are manipulative, overpowering, abusive mothers-in-law, into whose clutches the future *maskilim* fall when, as child-husbands, they go to live in their in-law's homes.[8] Wives are fertile traps, people with whom they share no meaningful relationship yet who will, unless resisted, anchor the *maskilim* in the suffocating world of tradition and familial responsibility.

The chief ills of traditional society are the *cheder* (elementary school), in which mere (male) babes were thrust into the keeping of often-demented *melamdim* who terrorize them, and childhood, arranged marriages. The remedies are reforms in the content and pedagogy of Jewish education; the addition of secular studies to the (revised) traditional curriculum; embrace of physical life and renunciation of the intellectual shackles of the ghetto; and companionate marriage with enlightened, modern women.

The perspective in all this is wholly male, and unselfconsciously so. There is no gender analysis of the power relationships in the traditional family or society—nor, of course, would we expect one—only victims, villains, and occasional (male) saints (like the enlightened Jewish doctor who cured Guenzberg of his impotence).

Maskilic writing has stamped our impressions of the passage from traditionalism to modernity in eastern Europe. Wengeroff's work, although published and widely read, yet never systematically analyzed, offers a rather different version of that odyssey.

Pauline Wengeroff was born into a pious Jewish home. Her father was a successful merchant and government contractor, someone who respected certain secular learning. Yet, foremost, she tells us, he was a Talmud scholar, the author of several *halakhic* works. Her mother was the stern matriarch of a large household and something of a religious fanatic, lording it over servants in her kosher kitchen, meticulously observing every scintilla of Jewish law and custom. In sharp contrast to the tone and content of *maskilic* autobiographies, Wengeroff devotes much of her first volume to a loving, sentimental account of the cycle of the Jewish year as lived out in her parents' home—crucially, however, as experienced by a girl, largely (though not exclusively) in the company of intensely religious and ritually active women.

As a girl in a culture with strictly differentiated gender roles, Wengeroff experienced the world of women from the inside. Women in this world mastered the legal intricacies of the kosher kitchen and made these female domains temples of ritual, domains of the holy. Not only were vast amounts of time spent there; the kitchen was the scene of unchallenged female power: over servants, but also over the religious character of the home. Certain foods, prepared with ritualistic precision—peppered fish, for instance for the Sabbath—signaled the nature of the holiday. Men might announce this in synagogue prayers and in home rituals like the holiday-specific *kiddush*, (sanctification of the wine). Women proclaimed it from the kitchen.

While the men of Wengeroff's family were in synagogue on the Ninth of *Av*, the day of mourning for the destruction of the Temple, the women evoked the drama and anguish of Jewish exile with ash-marked carpets at home. They sat on the prescribed footstools of mourning to read the *Book of Lamentations*, with Wengeroff's mother leading the women (Pauline, her sisters, maids) in weeping. In the days preceding *Yom Kippur*, the Day of Atonement, Wengeroff's mother would be visited by a semi-official female spiritualist called a *Gabete*, who officiated at a solemn, awesome ceremony of remembrance and penance—a non-rabbinic, purely female exercise. *Gabetes* also determined the needs of the poor in the community and solicited charity from wealthy women; one such *Gabete* was a fixture in Wengeroff's house.[9]

Wengeroff's mother was part of a rich Ashkenazic subculture of female ritual and spirituality, which was allowed its own sphere in Jewish as in other traditional, gender-divided societies.[10] In the synagogue, Wengeroff saw women, seated in a special section detached from the main sanctuary, led in prayer by other women, semi-official religious functionaries called *Sogerkes*. When a girl became a bride, she was visited by a *Gollerke*, Wengeroff says, who performed the ritual shaving of her head. If her marriage meant leaving her hometown, the bride bade farewell to friends and relatives accompanied by a *Reisele*, an honorary escort.[11]

Like the *maskilim*, then, Wengeroff depicts a powerful female realm in traditional Jewish society. But while the *maskilim* felt victimized by female power, Wengeroff felt groomed for it, entitled to it.

She did not come into this inheritance. Married to the son of *Hasidim*, she went to live in his parents' home (a reversal of the more typical matrilocal marriage arrangement). But her husband, Chonon, soon experienced a shattering loss of faith while on pilgrimage to his *rebbe*. His learning and observance became perfunctory where once they had been fervent. He trimmed his beard and began dressing in Western clothing. No reproach, no pleading, affected him. For the first of what would be many times, he answered her appeals with a claim of male authority: in her words, "seigneurial rights" (*Herrenrechte*), demanding "obedience and submission to his will."[12]

After four years of living with his parents following the wedding, Chonon decided to strike out on his own business, having received a liquor concession from his parents. He and Pauline began years of wandering in and outside the Jewish Pale of Settlement (areas between the Baltic and Black seas to which Jewish residence was confined by law) in a quest for material success. He had lost his own faith, and he saw his wife's faith as an impediment to upward mobility and social acceptance. He began to pressure her to abandon traditional Jewish observance: her marriage wig and, most painful, her kosher kitchen. She eventually did both; the latter, in a paroxysm of grief to which she gives voice in an entire chapter of the memoirs.

Children were born, but the family often found itself in places where no Jewish education was available (Helsinki, for instance). But even when it was, it was she and not Chonon who searched for tutors; traditional education, the bedrock of Jewish continuity, was no longer a shared value. On the contrary, Judaism, she says, became a marital battleground of greatly mismatched opponents. Chonon, having removed the family from the confines of traditional Jewish society, armed with the vocabulary of secularism, modernity and male authority, decried her attachment to tradition as anachronistic, outlandish, and embarrassing. She, without a cultural context for her behavior, lacked a plausible ideology with which to justify its persistence. Finally, she yielded in order, she says, that the children not identify Judaism with marital strife. Two sons would eventually convert to Christianity when confronted with antisemitic educational quotas. It was the greatest tragedy of Wengeroff's life.

Significantly, in depicting all this, Wengeroff consistently portrays personal tragedy as characteristic of broader processes in modernizing Jewish society, in which, she claims, upwardly aspiring husbands coerced more traditional wives to abandon observance. Thus, far from being merely a personal predicament, the strife over Judaism in her marriage, she asserts, was part of a marital disease widespread among Jewish couples. Women as a class were fighting to preserve tradition against men who would jettison much or all of it in the name of progress and acceptance in the world outside the ghetto.

Why the gender disparity? Wengeroff offers a psychological explanation—for male behavior, at least: weak and disadvantaged in the hostile world of non-Jews, they sought to penetrate, Jewish men, she claims, saw their homes and wives as one area they could dominate. Her husband's never-satiated grasping for success exacerbated their conflict over Judaism. "At least in his own family circle," she wrote, "he wanted compensation for this injustice [of elusive success]. He wanted to be a total master and he was, too, in the fullest sense."[13]

She proposed a compromise to him. The home, her domain, should be "Jewish"; his behavior outside was his own affair. But Chonon refused, as did his fellow Jewish husbands of the age. According to Wengeroff

> Most of the Jewish women of the time [she wrote] were so suffused with tradition that violating these caused almost physical pain. . . The wife who still clung to tradition with every fiber of her being, wanted to impart it to her children, too—the ethics of Judaism, the traditions of its faith, the solemnity of the Sabbath and festivals, Hebrew, the study of the Bible. . . *together* with the lessons of European enlightenment and the innovations of west European culture. . . . . But to all requests and protests, their husbands always had the same answer: "The children need no religion!" The young men of that time knew nothing of moderation and wanted to know nothing of it. In their inexperience, they wanted to make the dangerous leap from the lowest rung of culture directly to the highest. Many demanded of their wives not just assent . . . but submission.[14]

Although Wengeroff dwells primarily on women's loss of a spiritual and ritual domain, she also sketches their forced removal from the world of gainful employment. As historians have shown, "privatizing" women was a key element in the bourgeois ethic emerging in industrializing Europe. Having an "idle" woman at home mimicked the nobility; crucially, it signaled that the male of the household earned enough to dispense with the earnings of a wife or daughters.[15] As modern Jewish historians have stressed, when European Jews left the ghetto, they did not enter European society as a whole but joined the middle class.[16] Because women in all classes of Jewish society, including the wealthy, had always been economically active—witness Gluckel of Hameln and the wives of the Court Jews—"privatizing" women was not only a signal of economic success. It was an act of acculturation to modern, bourgeois non-Jewish norms.[17]

Once again, Wengeroff tells us, Chonon breached tradition, this time in a secular sphere. Wengeroff was familiar with the running of a large-scale business from her parents' home; she had also worked in her in-laws' inn. Yet, when Chonon began to do business, he excluded her, calling her advice "interference and [wanting] to hear nothing of it." He was of the opinion, she wrote, "that a wife, especially his wife, had no ability in this area and experienced my involvement as degrading"—this she notes pointedly, after he had lost her entire dowry in a business venture and despite the example of his own grandmother, who ran an inn and was a much sought-after healer and midwife.

Here too, Wengeroff insists that what happened in her marriage was part of a larger social phenomenon, adding that "at this time, this opinion was widespread among most of the Jews of the Ukraine, especially, though, among the concessionaires, who in their arrogance considered themselves autocrats (*Selbstherrscher*), and would tolerate no advisors."[18] As if this were not enough, Chonon—and again, she claims, other Jewish husbands—then used the fact that they were the ones earning the living to demand religious "reform" of the household they now claimed to control.[19]

As in the ritual sphere, here too, women were losing status, function, and power because, as she sees it, Jewish men blinded by ambition were rushing headlong into modernity, recklessly abandoning one culture for another. Wengeroff writes bitterly of the double-standard practiced, she says, by Jewish men, who sought the benefits of hoped-for liberalism in society while refusing to practice liberal values in their domestic relationships, once again, grounding her personal situation in a larger social reality.

> Preaching modern ideas like freedom, equality and fraternity in *society*, these young men were at home the greatest despots toward their wives, demanding ruthlessly the fulfillment of their wishes. . . . Quite a few wives did not want to give way. . . [but] the spirit of the age won in this struggle and the weaker yielded, with bleeding hearts. This is what happened to others, and to me.[20]

"Despots, autocrats"—elsewhere she refers to "lord-husbands" (Herr Gemahl);[21] while women are "weaker," "yielding with bleeding hearts." Wengeroff was no weak personality. That much is clear from the details of her life story but more fundamentally from its very existence: self-effacing people do not write 450 pages of memoirs, much less publish them. Nor does she regard women as inherently weak. But no amount of personal strength can counter overwhelming social forces, which is what, in Wengeroff's telling, happened to her and to other Jewish women in her time.

While Wengeroff does not state this explicitly, I believe that her juxtaposition of powerful female types in traditional Jewish society with the impotence she portrays in women of modern Jewish society, bespeaks a powerful, aggrieved, critique of Jewish modernity. Rather than being a time of grand dreams, increased opportunity, and widened horizons, modernity to Wengeroff signifies constriction and loss. Traditional Jewish society marked distinctly separate and unequal spheres for men and women, but at least women had a recognized sphere: the home. Modernity, in Wengeroff's telling, restricted women to a home sphere recognized as theirs, yet that nevertheless was men's domain: Chonon could dictate the character of her kitchen, something neither of her parents (or his) would have found imaginable.   No wonder, according to her, women as a class were wedded to traditional ways, escorting "one beautiful custom after another. . . to the last gate of [the] home with sobs."[22]   In modernity, women were to be contained in homes whose course they could not set. Modernity had made them captains without rudders.

In her telling, this loss is a core element of Jewish modernity. Although her story, her refraction of reality, can no more be taken as representative than that of the *maskilim*—its basis in social reality, and her consciousness in telling it are yet to be explored—it is also no less a voice of modernity than theirs.

The full title of Wengeroff's work is *Memoirs of a Grandmother: Scenes from the Cultural History of Russian Jewry in the Nineteenth Century*. By coupling two themes, a grandmother's life and the history of Russian Jewry, Wengeroff performed a radical act of consciousness and presented the story of Jewish modernity in a provocative new trope.

NOTES

1 . The following is based on a forthcoming full-length study of the memoirs of Pauline Wengeroff. Many thanks to Steven Zipperstein for meticulous observations on drafts of this work.   Thanks too to Edie Gelles for incisive comments on a talk I gave on Wengeroff at the Stanford Jewish Studies Colloquium; to the *Yad-Hanadiv-Barecha* Foundation, Jerusalem, which funded a year of my research on Wengeroff; and to the Leo Baeck Institute, New York, for a Fritz Halbers fellowship and for supporting my participation in a session of the 1992 meeting of the American Historical Association focusing on women's writing.

2 . Pauline Wengeroff, *Memoiren einer Grossmutter* (Vol. 1 Berlin, 1908; Vol. 2 Berlin, 1910), 28. All subsequent references are to this edition. I will treat publication history of the memoirs in my forthcoming study.

3 . Ibid., 1:1.

4 . I will not enter here into a theoretical discussion of the distinction between autobiography and memoirs and how this pertains to Wengeroff's writing. On the emergence of autobiographical writing among the Jews, see Israel Zinberg, *A History of Jewish Literature* vol. 11, *The Haskalah Movement in Russia*, trans. Bernard Martin (New York: Ktav, 1978); Alan Mintz, "Guenzberg, Lilienblum and the Shape of the *Haskalah*

Autobiography, " *Association for Jewish Studies Review*, 4 (1979: 71-110); Mintz, *"Banished from Their Father's Table"*: *Loss of Faith and Hebrew Autobiography* (Bloomington: Indiana University Press, 1989); Marcus Moseley, "Jewish Autobiography in Eastern Europe: The Pre-History of a Literary Genre" (Ph.D. dissertation, Oxford University, 1990).

5. Gluckel of Hameln's memoirs, for instance, although they may provide rich information about women's spirituality and their traditional knowledge, and about spousal, parental, and other family relationships, do not aim at telling the story of her time through her own experiences, or those of women, in general. Indeed, Gluckel never intended her memoirs to be read by anyone outside her family circle, much less published. *The Life of Glukel Hameln, 1646-1742, Written by Herself*, trans. Beth Zion Abrahams (New York, 1963). Some important writing by women who are survivors of the Holocaust, and scholarship about women's experiences in that era, attests or consciously reflects on the gendered nature of Holocaust experiences. See, for instance, Sara Nomberg-Przytyk, *Auschwitz, True Tales from a Grotesque Land* (Chapel Hill, North Carolina, 1985); Halina Birnbaum, *Hope Is the Last to Die: A Personal Documentation of Nazi Terror*, trans. David Welsh (New York: Twayne Publishers, 1971); Fania Fenelon, *Playing for Time*, trans. Judith Landry.(New York: Atheneum, 1977); Olga Lengyel, *Five Chimneys* (Chicago, 1947); Germaine Tillion, *Ravensbruck* (Paris: Anchor Press, 1973, 1988); Miriam Novitich, *Sobibor* (New York: Holocaust Library, 1980); Vera Laska, *Women in the Resistance and the Holocaust: Voices of Eyewitnesses* (Westport, CT: Greenwood Press, 1983); Andreas Lixl-Purcell, ed., *Women of Exile: German Jewish Autobiographies since 1933* (New York: Greenwood Press, 1988); Marion Kaplan, "Jewish Women in Nazi Germany: Daily Life, Daily Struggles," *Feminist Studies* (Fall 1990: 579-606); Marion Kaplan, "Sister Under Siege—Feminism and Anti-Feminism in Germany; and Sybil Merton, "Women and the Holocaust—The Case of German and German-Jewish Women," both in *When Biology Became Destiny*, ed. Renate Brindentahl et al. (New York: Monthly Review Press, 1984); Joan Ringelheim, "Women and the Holocaust: A Reconsideration of Research," in *Jewish Women in Historical Perspective*, ed. Judith R. Baskin (Detroit: Wayne State University Press, 1991); Esther Katz and Joan Ringelheim, eds. *Proceedings of the Conference on Women Surviving: The Holocaust* (New York, 1983); Carole Rittner and John K. Roth, eds. *Different Voices: Women in the Holocaust* (New York: Paragon House, 1993).

6. Mordechai Aron Guenzberg, *Aviezer* (Tel Aviv, 1967, photoreproduction of first ed., Vilna, 1864); Avraham Ber Gottlober, *Zikhronot u'massa'ot*, ed. R. Goldberg, 2 vols. (Jerusalem, 1976); Moshe Leib Lilienblum, *Ketavim autobiographi'im*, ed. Schlomo Breiman (Jerusalem, 1970). For a discussion of the problems *maskilim* had developing satisfying sexual relationships and their male friendships, see David Biale, *Eros and the Jews: From Biblical Israel to Contemporary America* (New York: Basic Books, 1992: 149-75).

7. Raphael Mahler, *Hasidism and the Jewish Enlightenment: Their Confrontation in Galicia and Poland in the First Half of the Nineteenth Century* (Philadelphia: Jewish Publication Society, 1985), stresses the middle class origins of the *maskilim* at a time when most of Russian-Polish Jewry was poor. Mintz and Moseley, in stressing how the *maskilim* patterned their autobiographies after Rousseau's *Confessions*, effectively illustrate how rarefied a genre *maskilim* writing was in a society still overwhelmingly traditional, with few Jews literate in western European languages.

8. In arranged marriages, the parents of the bride often obligated themselves to house and feed the couple for several years after marriage, during which time the groom was to

engage in traditional study. The system was called *kest*; most of these marriages, therefore, were matrilocal.

9. Wengeroff, 1: I, 99ff.; 1: I, 113ff.
10. See Chava Weissler, "The Traditional Piety of Ashkenazic Women," *Jewish Spirituality*, ed. Arthur Green. (New York, 1987): 2: 245-75; "The Religion of Traditional Ashkenazic Women: Some Methodological Issues, " *Association for Jewish Studies Review* 12 (1987):73-94; "Prayers in Yiddish and the Religious World of Ashkenazic Women, "*Jewish Women in Historical Perspective*, ed. Judith R. Baskin (Detroit: Wayne State University, 1991).
11. Wengeroff, 1: 106; 1: 183; 2: 61
12. Ibid., 2: 100-101.
13. Ibid., 2: 171
14. Ibid., 2: 135-36
15. See Priscilla Robertson, *An Experience of Women* (Philadelphia, 1982); Judy Lown, *Women and Industrialization* (Cambridge: Cambridge University Press, 1990); Leonore Davidoff and Catherine Hall, eds. *Family Fortunes: Men and Women of the English Middle Class* (Chicago: University of Chicago Press, 1987); Bonnie Smith, *Ladies of the Leisure Class* (Princeton, 1981). As historians have also shown, middle class women continued to contribute to family income in many ways, often in back rooms or offices. A husband's business might also be conducted partially at home, with the women hosting business guests, thus breaching the strictness of gendered "public" and "private" spheres; hence, some caution about this concept. Whatever the reality, the *appearance* of being able to dispense with female earnings was crucial.
16. Jacob Katz, *Out of the Ghetto: The Social Background of Jewish Emancipation* (New York, 1978); Marion A. Kaplan, *The Making of the Jewish Middle : Women, Family and Identity in Imperial Germany Class* (New York: Oxford University Press, 1991).
17. On the economic activities of the wives of Court Jews, see Selma Stern, *The Court Jew* (New Brunswick, NJ: Jewish Publication Society, 1950, Original edition 1895).
18. Wengeroff 2: 114.
19. Ibid., 2: 170-71.
20. Ibid., 2: 36.
21. Ibid., 2: 171-72.
22. Ibid., 2: 137. There may have been other reasons for Wengeroff's insistence that her situation was part of a broader social reality; I will explore this in my larger work on her memoirs.

Chapter 14

Traced in Ink: Women's Lives in "Qotzo shel Yud" by Yalag and "Mishpachah" by D. Baron

Zilla Jane Goodman

In the nineteenth century, if Hebrew literacy were taken into account, Jewish men were proportionately the most literate group in Eastern Europe.[1] Not so Jewish women, whose literacy, such as it is, was mostly in Yiddish, and whose lives were circumscribed by that high proportion of Hebrew male literacy. The Hebrew and Aramaic letters in which Jewish Law was formulated, contributed to the domination of Jewish women and determined communal Jewish life in a median hold.[2] The Law contained various items of legislation which were unfavorable to women, and the language of the Law (Hebrew and Aramaic) was usually not taught to women. In principle, all Jewish males were active participants in the life of the letter with which they engaged in active daily communion, if, most centrally, by way of pronouncement, decision making, and dialogue, or, more peripherally, by way of articulation and daily expression in prayer and ritual. Women, as a gender-bound constituency, were not even marginal to this word-constructed grouping. They stood outside of its community, yet were appended to and dominated by it. Thus Yalag's much studied poem "Qotzo shel Yud," and Baron's story "Mishpacha," which focus on the effects of the Law/Letter on the lives of women, have an added meaning in this context.[3]

The letter served as the main reference point for communal class structures of meritocracy. Thus women, who were allowed scant entry into the world of the letter, were set quite outside the class movements of the group, and were joined to it only by way of their fathers or husbands. This is equally true of women, who, through no initiative of their own, found themselves placed higher in the social order by dint of paternal financial success that bought them partners of more elevated social standing.[4]   Whatever level of literacy existed within the community of Jewish women,[5] and if indeed that literacy expressed itself in women's liturgical creativity,[6] it was a literacy and liturgy outside the bounds of the Hebrew letter with its class-determining consequences, and was sealed by its Yiddish and feminine character in a woman's capsule, and was without societal consequences.

But a no-class status did not mean freedom from the tyranny of class—quite the opposite. Groups that cannot initiate their own class mobility may be defined as subaltern.[7] They are most vulnerable to the exigencies and dictates of the mainstream. The stasis imposed on them makes them victim to the caprice of anything that is capable of movement at all.   They are most prey to those elements that are paramount in the fixing of hierarchical classification, which in this case were the written word of the sources, the later codifications of the Law, and any contemporary decrees and responsa uttered in their name.

The letter's tyrannical status dominated its initiates as well as those it excluded.   Yet although the initiates had, by virtue of an available discourse, the ability at times to circumvent and manipulate the letter's authority, the excluded (Jewish women) had no entry into this realm. A literal domination overarched their lives in a general way and chartered the conventions of their daily living. Its force could demote them to the nether reaches of society, putting them out in the cold and relegating them to their "natural" level, quite outside the realm of community.[8]

This power of the letter is the subject of Y. L. Gordon's satirical poem "Qotzo shel Yud" and Devorah Baron's story "Mishpachah." From the perspective of this central theme, the two tales speak to each other with Baron's narrative serving as expanded commentary on Yalag's poem. In both texts a letter qua letter, placed in the hands of male representatives of the Letter, inscribes a woman's life: one with tragedy and the other with happiness. An interesting exchange occurs between the poetic saga, written by a man who was undoubtedly very sympathetic to women, and Baron's story which was written around essentially the same topic by a woman. The very different ways in which the two writers make use of the sources, name attribution, references to sexuality, love, and woman's position in society, as well as their character choices and representations and their manipulation of literary devices serve, paradoxically, to bring their texts into closer alignment even while they are expressive of a discrepancy in sensitivity.

In the summer of 1875, Yehudah Leib Gordon, arguably the most prominent Haskalah poet, withdrew to Marienbad where he completed what in Michael Stanislawski's words, "he — and hosts of later readers — would come to regard as his best poem, the mock epic 'The Tip of the Yud' ('Qotzo shel Yud')."[9] It is certainly his most famous poem, and its impact on the Jewish world was such that after its first appearance in *haShachar* in 1875[10] it was not only translated into Yiddish in 1904 (as "Iber a Pintele," by Yoel Linski), but crossed cultural boundaries and was translated into Ladino in prose form in Cairo in 1901.[11]

"Qotzo shel Yud" is the story of a beautiful young Jewish woman (Bat-shua), who is betrothed at the age of fifteen by her well-to-do father to Hillel, who excels in learning but cannot support his family. He leaves Ayalon (the location of the tale; its name a deliberate metathesis — because of governmental censorship — of Vilna) in search of a livelihood and disappears, leaving Bat-shua an *agunah*[12] with two small children. She sells her jewelry and opens a shop. Her father dies impoverished, but the newly constructed railway line in town brings a new man, Feibe, the railway supervisor, into her life. He contacts Hillel who is in Liverpool and pays him to grant Bat-shua a *get*. When the document reaches Ayalon four weeks later it is declared *pasul* (invalid) by the leading voice in the triumvirate of Rabbis in the local religious court, because he disagrees with the orthography used by Hillel, before a rabbinical court in London, in signing his own name. The matter cannot be remedied for in the intervening period Hillel has drowned at sea (being lost in "waters without end," his death cannot be verified), and cannot sign another. Bat-shua accepts her fate, refuses Feibe's offers of help, falls sick as a result of the shock and thus loses her business. The poem ends with her utter impoverishment and destitution.

The story-line is framed by a lengthy opening chapter composed of cumulative adductions about the condition of Jewish Woman, which are proclaimed in a tone of sustained pathos. Within the plaintive cries of pity, whose melodramatic tenor and rhythmic regularity vitiate, to late twentieth century ears, the tragedy they contain, are enumerated, in detail, the ills a Jewish woman is heir to. These are presented by a thick overlaying of direct source references drawn from the Bible, the Talmud, the liturgy, and later Rabbinic codifications and decrees. The allusions used and the customs cited are among the most potent examples of women's degradation in the tradition. Yalag dilates their effects by individualizing the quotes by way of direct address, by the addition of words more suggestively extreme than in the original, and by means of proximity and layering.

The story of Eve and the snake, drawn from Genesis 3, is augmented by Talmudic explication (e.g. *Sotah* 9)[13] in the verse "*zuhamat haNachash meAz bakh rovezet*" (the filth of the snake has crouched in you from the start),[14] where Woman's Primal Sin—which as narrated by the Bible, is the essential cause of humankind's misery and loss of Eden—is amplified in the later texts referred to in the poem, where the snake's primordial filth adheres forever to all women. The obvious sexual component of this construal is underscored by the hint at the bestial entailed in the verb *rovetzet* and by the preceding question/answer line where, speaking in the voice of the Letter, the poetic voice turns to Woman and asks "And what are you? The whole of you?" and in the same voice answers "Hot blood and excretions." By coalescing filth, hot blood, and excretions, all references to the concerns of religious texts pertaining to women, Yalag selectively points to a conception of Woman that is clearly one of repugnance.

The Talmudic pronouncement "*Kol beIsha erva*" and its parallel "*Sei'ar shebeIsha erva*" (A woman's voice is lewd—or foul or unchaste; like nakedness—and similarly a woman's hair) becomes personalized by the form of address derived by appending the second person pronominal suffix to "voice" and "hair" ("*kolekh erva uSei'ar roshekh mifletzet*"),[15] while the tradition's revulsion at woman's sexuality, evident in the lines quoted earlier, is emphasized by the use of the word *mifletzet*, which makes her hair a hideous idol (or monstrous) in the present context and a taboo in terms of the Law.

The Mishnaic admonition to fathers—"Whoever teaches his daughter Torah, it's as if he taught her impropriety" (or folly; vanity; something unsavory) (*Sotah* 3:4)—is turned into an address to contemporary women, "*Hen Torah lakh tiflah*," prefaced by the exclamatory "*Hen*" (surely; for indeed), whose axiomatic force undermines the Mishnaic text and points to its absurdity.

The liturgical statement of gratitude to the Divine, proclaimed by Jewish men daily, who assert the superiority of their Jewish and masculine form by thanking God with three negations: "for not making me a gentile, for not making me a slave, for not making me a woman," is presented in the poem in an inverted manner. The stanza in which it appears begins with two verses that at first glance apparently commend, albeit in a suspect and patronizing manner, Jewish woman's exclusion from the world of the Letter: "It's good for you that you know not the language of your fathers / That they shut your God's house in your face."[16]

But the explanatory verses immediately following leave no doubt as to the actual tenor of the opening lines: "for now you won't hear your deriders praises / 'For not making them Woman' daily they bless. / To them you are as a gentile and slave."[17]

The repeated use of the third-person plural pronoun, counterpointed by the singular second-person address to the Hebrew Woman of the poem, inverts the negative polarization of women in the prayer, by setting men on the negative pole.

The first chapter which began with the rhetorical sigh "Oh Hebrew woman who knows your life?"[18] ends with the couplet "This is the story of every Hebrew woman-/ This is the story of the beautiful Bat-shua."[19] Thus Bat-shua is fixed right at the start of the epic as a Jewish anywoman, and her story is the story of all Jewish women.

Bat-shua's flawless and unrivaled beauty, which pointedly contradicts the aforementioned examples about woman's impurity, is made much of in the poem. Alongside her complacency it is highlighted as her greatest virtue. Many stanzas are devoted to her external description, but they are not set in the form of plain and simple praises. Rather, they subvert their explicit statement by way of the allusive networks in the poem itself, by embodying little stings in their very own tails or by complex fields of meaning and context. Bat-shua's beauty is extolled with the love language of the Song of Songs,[20] where the biblical sentiments are quite the opposite of those mentioned in the first section of the poem. These are presumably anathema to Rabbinic attitudes which insist that men not look at women.[21] Gordon sneaks in a reference to this prohibition when he says that Hillel and Bat-shua did not meet prior to their wedding, and speaking in the name of the letter, offers as justification for this custom the case of Avraham and Sarah mentioned in the Talmud.[22] The verse used to illustrate Bat-shua's perfection pronounces that "This rib was built of perfect stones," where the metonymic item accorded her derives from a biblical assertion about woman's nascence, which, viewed from a contemporary and nonreligious perspective, is an inversion contingent upon naught but womb envy, and carries with it a statement of the primary dependence of woman on her immediate vehicle of creation, man. Man was worthy of being created by God, in His image, but woman was created via man.

Just as she is a picture of physical perfection, she also incorporates all the gentle and genteel qualities of "pure and noble womanhood." A halo surrounds her, she is made in God's image purified seven-fold, and all about her is innocence and spring. But her gentility is not so perfect, for it reaches absurd proportions. When denuded of all at the end of the saga, she passionately declares in answer to a question asking if God wrought her awful fate:

> No, kind folk. Heaven forfend that there be any
> wickedness in God;
> For my Rock and my Lord graced me with good talents,
> And success once shone its face upon me.
> I almost had all that is good, me and my children
> I almost lived like a woman of bounty
> But I was slain by the tip of a Yud.[23]

She cannot see that it is the men of the Letter who brought her to her end. She has so fully bought into the claims of the established authorities that they are equated with the Divine when she refuses Feibe's offers of help after the *get*'s invalidation, saying: "God does not wish me to live with you / My Lord He is—He may do as He desires."[24]

The only image that disrupts Bat-shua's angelic purity is powerful in its antithetical elements. It has her suckling at the breast of the she-wolf who nursed "*romel vakhoresh*" the founder of Rome and the Emperor of Persia, respectively. This bestial (sexual) note is expanded by the comment that "God, her father, taught that creature to be a nurse without peer."[25] One can only wonder at the intentionality inherent in calling up the image of the she-wolf, attaching it to figures emblematic of mighty foreign powers who have dominated Israel, juxtaposing it with the oh-so-pure Bat-shua and then sanitizing it by the attribution of sublime and holy maternity to the she-beast. It could be read in two ways. The first reading would have the poet speaking these words as unmediated, albeit set in satirical intent. Here the verses would merely constitute an expansion on the work of hyperbole, satirical and excessive at core, but reliable within its own terms. A second reading would attribute a higher level of intentionality and suggest a deeper level of satire. Here the use of the bestial in apposition with Bat-shua, and the negation of this fabrication in the following couplet, could stand as a statement about the power and quality of woman's sexuality—even in so vanqished a person as Bat-shua—and the manner in which it is routinely neutralized into the motherly and sacred all at once.

The second reading would seem to better fit other parts of the poem. Speaking of arranged marriages, arranged for the Jewish woman by "*alufa hamezaveg zivugim*" (her Champion [God] who matches couples),[26] forty days before her birth, the poem reiterates in a number of ways that "love is not for a daughter of Israel" in a stanza that ends "Our mothers did not know love—Shall we make our sister like a whore?", here the mother and whore are juxtaposed and both are placed under a biblical umbrella, with the allusion to the Matriarchs and to Dinah, who was raped by Shekhem. The echoes of the second reference are particularly harsh: Romantic love for the Jewish woman is so unthinkable that it is seen as a sign profligacy. Yet the example of that profligacy—Dinah—was a victim, not a perpetrator. The echoes of the biblical story reverberate in the poem and make all Jewish women victims as well; victims of men's fear of them which deprives them of any autonomy. In another stanza even the ascetic, "the dry tree, steals a glance at her (Bat-shua)—for he too has, in secret, a lusting soul." And the couplet that responds to this says that "and God's *Shekhinah* luxuriates on her, when her upright stance moves forward her legs."[27] Again lust or desire, interwoven with religion, is imbued with the holy and thereby neutralized.

Although Gordon's sympathies are not in question, and the revolutionary nature of his text is unquestionable, his choice of satire as a genre, and his manipulation of that genre for the purposes of a tirade against the repressive hegemony of *Halakhah*, afford him a distance from its subject and compel him to lead his protagonist to her bitter end. But his poem is as much a railing against Rabbinical oppression, and about the transition from medievalism to modernity (the building of the railway; the redemptive possibilities of the telegraph; Feibe, the modern man, as a figure of potential redemption), as it is a protest song about the lot of women in a traditional Jewish society constructed on the bones and sinews of ossified and over dominant religious authority structures.

Bat-shua is the only individualized woman to appear in this text and she is cast in the mold of a "modest and compliant Daughter of Israel" and never oversteps its boundaries.[28] The depiction of her extreme submissiveness (see her refusal to accept Feibe's offer of support, and her closing remarks regarding the cause of her downfall, quoted earlier) is both parodic and satirical: God does not wish her to live with Feibe, but nonetheless will not abandon her and "Heaven forfend that there be any wickedness in God," for she was "slain by the tip of a Yud." Thus the *yud*, the Letter of the *Halakhah*, has an independent agency so powerful it is capable of overriding the positive power of the Divine.

But the greatest parody in the poem revolves upon the nature of Rav Vafsi's objection to the signature. Even in terms of the letter itself, his protest is untenable, and in this lies Gordon's ultimate sting. The first *lamed* in the name Hillel is written with a dagesh forte and therefore should not, in correct grammatical orthography, be preceded by a *yud*. Thus Vafsi's conclusion, built on centuries of discussion on the subject, is entirely fallacious[29] and makes a mockery not only of him, but of all the Rabbinic debates on the subject. In a note attached by Yalag to the poem, after providing a summary of assorted opinions pertaining to the correct spelling of the name, he comments that "shame would cause anyone's heart to break on seeing our Great Lights fumbling around a simple matter that any toddler understands, that the letters in the heavy paradigm take a dagesh in the second root consonant, and if this is the case there is no place for a yud; and it seems that they also did not know that the name Hillel appears in the Bible (Judges 12:13-15)."[30] His charges are dire and would appear that he uses this specific name to illustrate his perception of Rabbinical inflation, which uselessly argues the unarguable as if in ignorance of the most basic facts.[31]

Gordon knits a matrix with the names in the poem that supports its conceptual weave. Vafsi's name is the name of the father of one of the twelve spies sent to investigate the Land of Israel in Exodus 13. The Talmud, in *Sotah* 34b, comments on this name, saying Vafsi "(was so named) because he suggested God. . . was weak" and "because he stepped over (*pasa*) the attributes of the Holy One, blessed be He." The commentary interprets "stepping over" as misrepresentation.[32] The second part of his epithet *haKuzari* fulfills a double function. It is a sound play, with Kuzari approximating the Hebrew *akhzar* (cruel) and a reference to the Kuzars—many of whom converted to Judaism in the eighth century—who were considered cruel and evil by the Russians.[33] Thus Vafsi's character and behavior are embodied in his name.

The root of the name Chefer (Bat-shua's father), *ch:f:r*, appears in verbal form in the same passage from *Sotah* that discusses the name Vafsi, as a quote from Isaiah 24:23, where it carries the meaning of eternal shame and the condition of being ashamed.[34]

The name Feibe, accorded the representative of the modern world, who brings the light of modernity to the town (the Railroad), and the light of possible salvation to Bat-shua, reverberates in a number of ways. Popular etymology has it that the name is a Yiddish version of Phoebus (Apollo, the sun god). As such it was associated with light, and light-giving, and often served as a synonym to Sheraga (Aramaic, "candle, lamp") in the double-barreled name Sheraga-Feive. In its later in the poem—Feibish—contains the semantic content of the Yiddish adjective *Vaibish*, an appellation that no doubt would be deemed fitting in that society for a man who is sympathetic to women. Another reading has the name split in two, with *vai* denoting a cry of sorrow, and *bish* holding the meaning of bad.[35]

Bat-shua's name means daughter of a cry or of a cry for help. The letters *shin*, *vav*, and *ayin* also stand as an acronym for the *Shulchan Arukh*. Thus the name represents her suffering and helplessness and is also a reference to the way her life is determined by the exigencies of *Halakhah*. Bat-shua is also the name of Yehudah's wife in Genesis 38, and is thus attached to the figure of Tamar, another woman who suffers by way of the dictates pertaining to women and marriage. She is a levirate widow, who is not given *Chalizah*, and her position therefore is much like that of the *agunah*. In contradistinction to Bat-shua though, Tamar takes matters into her own hands and rebels by claiming her own sexuality so foreign to Jewish women, according to Yalag's poem— when she seduces Yehudah, her father-in-law and oppressor. Bat-shua is also an alternate name given to Bat Sheva (Chronicles 1, 2 and 3), who is associated with forbidden desire. In her case, King David (the supreme emblem of male authority) overcomes any problems of *aginut* by energetically ascertaining that her husband is dead and is known to be dead. These stories of attempted and realized male dominance serve as foil to Bat-shua's saga by way of correspondences and antithetical parallels.

The title of Gordon's poem, which serves as its thematic kernel, is drawn from a Rabbinic source (*Menahot* 29a) that declares the importance of each little mark of Holy writing. "Rabbi Akivah would in the future extrapolate reams upon reams of *Halakhah* upon each tip" and "each letter that does not have parchment surrounding it on all four sides is *pasul*" for "even the right hand tip of a yud that does not have parchment around it, is stuck to another letter" (Rashi)—"and is thus stuck to it and delays it."[36] The poem thus states its direct relationship to the *Halakhah* and to the *Halakhah's* obsession with the letter in its minutest traces. This relationship is reinforced by the mosaic made of abundant quotes from the sources that comprise a major part of the poetic weave. The text is replete with commentary, articulated in blown tones by the poetic voice. Given that the work is intentionally satirical, these forms are appropriate.[37]

Devorah Baron's story "Mishpachah," first published in 1933, is, like Yalag's poem, the tale of a woman whose life is determined by ink in a *get*. Unlike the poem, however, this story has a happy ending. The locus of the story is a Shtetl, not the city. The story is Dinah's story. She is married off to Barukh, his father's only son, so that the male line of succession can continue. For ten years she does not bear a child, and a reluctant Barukh, as per custom, sets out to divorce her. Just as the *get* is being inscribed, a letter in the document goes astray, skips out of the line, and the divorce is declared invalid. The couple stays together and within the year Dinah gives birth to a healthy male child. The story seems to end on a note of jubilant sentimentality.

Although the title of the story does not bear the mark of the Letter, the word "Mishpachah" is tinged with a dissident quality when it is subordinated to the notion of family in the story wherein, in biblical fashion, it denotes the line of male succession alone. The narrative opens with a reference to "the chain of the generations" represented in the Bible. This style of genealogical recounting is then exemplified in the text by a retelling of Genesis, with one male "begat" following another. The biblical form is then transferred to the Shtetl in the tale, where male names are repeated in the successive generations of one of its families. From the nominal chronicles of this family, the narrative moves to the family into which Dinah marries. Thus a line is drawn — much like the recurring refrain throughout the text exhorting that the chain not be broken — from biblical male succession to the fictive present,[38] and it is this line that, in society's view in the story, comprises Dinah's sole raison d'être.

The note of protest in "Mishpachah" is subdued and subtly drawn, but its presence is insistent. The women are more numerous than in Yalag's poem and they are certainly more active. But their activity seems, for the most part, to be the result of internalized gendering, where they buy into the status-quo and even trumpet its cause and abet it. Liebke the orphan girl, who serves Dinah and Barukh shamelessly, throws herself at Barukh when she knows the time for his divorce is near. She does not question the justice of it all, but merely sees this as her chance to attain some borrowed status via a man. Batyah, the family matriarch, has learned from her father, the traveling *Maggid* (preacher), to speak in those parables that she uses so cruelly against women (she compares Dinah, within her hearing to a fruitless tree that must be felled).[39] She has appropriated the male voice *en tout*.[40]

Unlike Yalag, Baron does not make any explicit statements about women being banned from study but elucidates this practice with repeated references to *"bnei mikra bnei ivri v'bnei alef bet"* (boys who are of the ages of Bible learning, the learning of Hebrew and the learning of the alphabet),[41] who are mere children and are contextually counterpointed to the grown women who nurture and educate them, but do not have access to what they learn and by a throwaway memory of evenings in her father's house when, after cleaning (i.e., taking care of his needs), she sat listening to him examining her youngest (his youth is emphasized) brother's biblical knowledge.[42]

Sexuality in this story is alluded to only in reference to child-bearing possibilities and is transposed onto household objects and circumstances or expressed by similes drawn from the plant world. Libke is described as "filling the whole bed,"[43] much as Batyah pronounces Dinah and Barukh's bedroom empty and notes that their house is too clean and shiny.[44] Seeds, plants, fertile ground, frozen rivers, and thawing reeds appear in various places in the texts, at times as similes and at others as metaphoric transpositions signifying sexuality or emotions and events. Dinah's physical aspects that receive mention do so in conjunction with her orphaned (and thus deserted) condition. Her face is the face of "an infant that has not been nurtured,"[45] her head is an orphan's head.[46] Thus womanly sexual features are hinted at delicately and subsumed under the mantle of motherhood and domesticity. Despite a similar intertwining in Yalag's work, the harsh dichotomies—as in the reference to she-wolf—spoken there are indicative of a very different sensibility that does not stop at excess in proffering its convictions.

Whether it's modesty and submission that win Dinah's day is open to question. If the words of the Holy Man she visits in search of a remedy for her barren condition are to be taken as prophecy, then in him the letter operates as oracle. When the entire narrative is taken into account, the advice articulated through his voice—that she further quell her almost nonexistent voice; lower her kerchief even further; accept all insults that come her way and light a third candle on the Sabbath[47] — adds to the parodic tone of the text by overenlarging the pathos appended to her. She who is already overly submissive is ordered an extra dose of submission as cure. It is as though it is actually her fault and that she need repent for the condition to change. As though only total passivity and absolute silence can save a Jewish woman from her travails.

"Mishpachah" is full of biblical quotations, but with scant Talmudic allusions. The voice that speaks the biblical phrases most often, using them as similes and metaphors for all and any situations, is the voice of the family elder, Shelomo. He is described as "wise in the Torah, as finding the correct verse for everything."[48] But at the end of the narrative his adeptness is shown to be something he hides behind, a way in which to avoid responsibility.

The story, unlike the poem, ends with the illusion of safety and with an apparent affirmation of religious bounty. Things turn out well for Dinah, who finds herself embraced by the warmth of family. A comprehension of the happy resolution is summarized by Shelomo, who declares that "the cup of sorrow was filled and therefore God had mercy on Dinah."[49] And Shelomo seems incapable of asking if maybe it was not God who had mercy, but society that was cruel. His proclamation is an example of Devorah Baron's quiet cry of resistance that sounds throughout the text. The narrative comment introducing Shelomo's announcement is wonderfully tongue-in-cheek. It translates as follows: "And that one, (Shelomo) in his integrity (literally 'innocence of heart'), showed nearly no signs of amazement."[50] Shelomo, the learned family elder, by whose sanction the *get* is initiated in the first place, is ascribed the virtue of integrity, but what he is really doing is using religious statement to blind himself to his own behavior.

In the wake of her visit to the Holy Man, after Batyah has insulted her in the synagogue, Dinah prays silently at home (after Barukh marks the appropriate passages for her in the correct order). Her manner of praying is likened to the childless Chana's prayers in Samuel I, 1:13: "Her lips move and her voice is not heard." Her agony thus becomes part of the age-old suffering of the childless Jewish woman, who is harassed and shamed by society for her barrenness.

Dinah offers to take one of Musha's girls into her home. This in itself is a condemnation of society. She wishes to express pure maternity, in whatever manner available, whereas society demands she give birth to a child, and preferably a son. By inserting this incident into the tale Baron highlights, by way of implied comparison, the ruthless nature of society's norms, which in this case are inferred from the Letter's mandates, and take no account of individuals and feelings.

Baron's use of allusive names is not as evocative as Yalag's. It is worth mentioning though that Shelomo the Elder is anything but wise, that Dinah is a victim, that Batyah's lack of compassion is indicative of an essentially alien nature (the biblical *Bityah* [Chronicles I 4:18] is a foreign king's daughter, and not a daughter of the Divine) and that it is as if Barukh ben Neiriyah, Jeremiah's scribe (Jer. chapter 36 and elsewhere) lends the present Barukh his power which muddles the present scribe's hand and causes the letter to lengthen.

The figure that is most clearly in sympathy with Dinah is the Rabbi, the narrator's father, which is in direct contradiction to Yalag's Rav Vafsi and the role he plays in Bat-shua's life. The Rabbi in this story is most fond of those passages in the Talmud that are compassionate toward women.[51] The narrator introduces this tendency of his by saying that the day before a *get* he would fast all day and pore over his books all night, possibly trying to ascertain names (his hesitancy in this opposite to Vafsi's bulldozing certainty) or maybe studying the matter of divorce in general, to which is added the narrative comment "for it is known that the opinions of the ancient ones differed." The attitude illustrated and this narrative comment voice a quiet indignation at the relativity of Rabbinic interpretation, whose dicta are anything but relative in their effects on the world.

Barukh, his weakness notwithstanding, is quite the opposite of Hillel, who escaped a wife and family. But in the story there is no potentially redemptive male figure such as Feibe, and no potentially redemptive power such as modernity. The text is contained in a time that is almost static, in a Shtetl life that seems to be unchanging.

The overt criticism in the narrative is saved for the women. It is most apparent when dealing with Batyah and her sharp tongue and malicious personality. Leibke, who is also ascribed an innocence at the end of tale, attempts to stake her claim to Barukh in a brazen manner. Her action escapes direct comment, but she is depicted as "charging" toward Barukh to call him to dance.[52]

In a reversal of the unvoiced woman in Jewish society, it is the women who have most voice in the text. Yet this reversal is illusory. Despite their overall absence, the men preside over the text, with their voices clearly entering it when it comes to such matters as deciding a woman's fate. Even Barukh's weak voice, which is heard only once, has a determining power over Dinah's life as it answers untruthfully in the affirmative that he is willing to grant the divorce. This power is emphasized by the fact that this is his one and only utterance in the tale. But the primacy of the written letter is demonstrated at the same time. Barukh's incorrect answer (the double yes) can be rectified, the misconstrued letter cannot.

And finally, Dinah's happiness at the end of the story is contingent upon its fairy-tale ending, which conjures up the birth of a son to continue the coveted male line that extends from Adam and Abel and

Cain to Avner ben Barukh, her own son. But this happy ending might not be so happy if we consider Leibke, for instance. She is now relegated to the position of servant, which, we are informed, "she accepted with innocent joy."[53] Thus the story ends with what looks like resolution, but is in fact merely a perpetuation whose marks can be discerned in the circularity of the text and the oversentimentalized content of its closure.

Both texts stretch the construct of the submissive woman to parodic lengths, and both use manifold intertextual allusions. But whereas Yalag's satire derives in large measure from direct declarations that need be antonymically read, Baron's critique obtains in a delicately nuanced and modest satirical woof. And both texts, Yalag's poem and Baron's story, end with two women demoted by the vagaries of the Letter's hierarchical vicissitudes to the status of subaltern, from where movement, even in shadow, is well nigh impossible.

NOTES

1 . For a discussion on Jewish literacy in Russia see Joel Perlman, "Russian Jewish Literacy in 1897: A Reanalysis of Census Data," *Papers in Jewish Demography*, ed. V. O. Schmelz and S. DellaPergola, (Jerusalem: The Hebrew University, 1993). Perlman's conclusion on a reevaluation of the 1897 census is that earlier analyses of this data, which rate Jewish male literacy much lower than expected, were biased in terms of their definitions of literacy inasmuch as it was defined as the ability to read Yiddish texts; those Jewish men who could read the *Siddur* were not included in the "literate" grouping. Perlman concludes that "substantial minorities of Jewish men apparently fell into a peculiar category with regards to literacy," and that "these men could not move from their ability to follow the Siddur to literacy in another medium." His closing remarks adduce that "in this interpretation, Russian Jewry was more literate than most groups before the transformations of industrialization, urbanization, and new forms of schooling fully affected them. And in this interpretation nearly all Russian Jewish males were characterized by the peculiarity of being able to read the *Siddur*. But that peculiarity is different from being literate in the usual meanings of the term," which adduction supports the present discussion.

2 . For a discussion of the normative character of Jewish society (which pertains equally to traditional societies of the later period) see Jacob Katz, *Tradition and Crisis: Jewish Society at the End of the Middle Ages* (New York: Free Press, 1966).

3 . For an alternative comparison of these texts, together with the stories" Fradel" and "Keritot" by Baron, see Nurit Govrin, *Ma'agalim* (Ramar-Gan: Sifriyat Maqor, 1975), 280–87.

4 . This comes more into play from the time of early modernity onward as the result of a class intersection between intellectual determinants and material resources, brought about by changing economic conditions (which revolve both on impoverishment — and thus greater need — and an opening mobility — and thus the possibility of wealth accrual.)

5 . And it is being examined and brought to the fore more and more at present.

6 . For some discussion on women's prayers see Taitz, E. "Women's Voices, Women's Prayers," and Sh. Z Berger,. *Tehines:* "A Brief Survey of Women's Prayers" in S. Grossman, and R. Haut, eds., *Daughters of the King* (Philadelphia: Jewish Publication Society, 1992).

7 . For a discussion on the subaltern see Gayatri Spivak and elsewhere . "Thinking Academic Freedom in Gendered Post-Coloniality." 32nd T. B. Davie memorial Lecture, Capetown: University of Capetown, 1992:1.

8 . As their status was familialy derived and dependent on either parental or spousal standing, the loss of these (depending on the manner in which they were lost) could cause the woman to all but be excluded from society. This is especially true of the *agunah* and the woman divorced because of an attribution of barrenness.

9 . Michael Stanislawski, *For Whom Do I Toil? Judah Leib Gordon and the Crisis of Russian Jewry* (New York: Oxford University Press, 1988), 125.

10 . Ibid.: 242, note 47.

11 . Note in appendix in Y. L. Gordon *Kitvei Yehudah Leib Gordon* (Hebrew) (Jerusalem: Dvir, 1956), 259. The translations are my own.

12 . The *agunah* is somewhat analogous to the English "grass widow," but only in the broadest terms. For the question of the *agunah* see *Encyclopaedia Judaica* (Jerusalem: Keter, 1971), 2: 429-33. An *agunah* is defined there as a "married woman who for whatsoever reason is separated from her husband and cannot remarry, either because she cannot obtain a divorce from him . . . or because it is unknown whether he is still alive. The term is also applied to a *yevamah* (' a levirate widow') . . , if she cannot obtain *chalizah* from the *levir* or if it is unknown whether he is still alive (Git. 26b, 33a; Yev. 94a; and Posekim). The problem of the *agunah* is one of the most complex in halakhic discussions and is treated in great detail in halakhic literature (no less than six volumes of *Ozar ha-Posekim* are devoted to it." Despite all attempts to ameliorate the situation of the *agunah* and the potential *agunah*, this construction is one that has caused the most dire suffering to Jewish women. Important to the present poem is the statement that a husband cannot be declared dead if the husband has drowned "in waters that have no end," i.e., the ocean, unless a witness can testify to his burial or has found one of his limbs in the place where he went down, and that this is the one instance where the relaxation rules pertaining to witnesses, which are applied to the declaration of the demise of the husband to include the wife, does not apply. *haEnziqlopedia halvrit* (Hebrew) (Jerusalem: Chevra leHoza'at Enziklopediyot, 1974), 26: 722-24.

13 . See Gordon's comments on this in his note in *Kitvei Yehudah Leib Gordon*: 350.

14 . Ibid.: 130.

15 . Ibid.: 130.

16 . Ibid.: 130.

17 . Ibid.: 130.

18 . Ibid. : 129.

19 . Ibid. : 130.

20 . Ibid. : 131.

21 . And note the persistent attempts to interpret this book allegorically.

22 . Ibid. : 350. See Gordon's note on this subject.

23 . Ibid.: 140.

24 . Gordon, *Kitvei Yehudah Leib Gordon*: 139.

25 . Ibid.: 131.

26 . Ibid.: 130.

27 . Ibid.: 132.
28 . Despite any allusions to an unrealized sexuality, she only once acts out of character for "a pure daughter Israel." (This when she kisses Fiebe when he asks her to marry him.)
29 . Stanislawski, *For Whom Do I Toil*: 127, argues that the debates about the *Halakhic* correctness of Vafsi's decree are irrelevant, but in the sense it is looked at here it is extremely important, as it leavens the satirical aspect of the poem by depicting (a) Vafsi's stubbornness, and (b) the contemporary power of a dominant and boorishly cruel personality in the application of the letter, where its authority supersedes both greater quality (the Ari and Caro) and larger quantity (the other two *dayanim* and the Rabbinical court in London that had authorized the document). See footnote 28 in this paper.
30 . Gordon, *Kitvei Yehudah Leib Gordon*: 350.
31 . It is worth noting in this context that the authorities Vafsi invokes in support of his argument are the *Shulchan Arukh* and later commentators expanding on its codes, whereas the other two *dayanim* quote the authority of the earlier and greater Ari and Joseph Caro (the writer of the *Shulchan Arukh* itself, who revises the discussion in an extension to the *Arukh*). The incident addresses the theme of spiritual and intellectual degeneration, which is buttressed by the introduction to Rav Vafsi. He is ushered in by a stanza describing this process of deterioration in terms of the claims made by Rabbis as to their own greatness:

> Before, in Israel, when the Torah was light,
> And not used as an ax to grind, or a rod of pride,
> There were a few Geonim in every generation,
> All of them holy, and that title was their glory;
> Now — as many Rabbis as there are, so are there Geonim
> Till even the young ones boast of that title,
> And we even have a variety of types of Geonim:
> Real Geonim and Mighty Geonim
> And Geonic Geonim, and of the second and third degrees,
> And Great Lights and Eagles, Pillars and Hammers (Ibid.: 138.).

As the claims grow greater and greater, the stature shrinks and withers. Witness Vafsi himself who is introduced with a derision that marks him as an extreme example of this corruption: "And in Ayalon there is a Rav of superior standing, Not a simple Gaon but a Wondrous Gaon, Unique and special even among the few chosen and the name of the name of His Glory: Rav Vafsi the Khuzari" — and who cruelly and incorrectly quotes the Letter so as to assert thereby his awesome (and non-existent) competence. For a comprehensive discussion on the name Hillel in the Talmud, see M. Bar Asher *Qovetz Ma'amarim biLeshon Chazal* (Jerusalem: The Hebrew University, 1972): 12-13.
32 . I. Epstein ed., *The Talmud* (London: Soncino Press, 1985). Glossary and indices, B. D. Klein.
33 . Gordon, *Kol Kitvei*: 360 (note).
34 . Ibid.
35 . Ibid.: 361, where the name is explained in two ways: as a play on the words *vai* (a cry of distress) and *bish* (bad, in Hebrew), and alternatively as *vaybish*, viz., one who has fallen into the hands of a woman, and see Gordon's comments, ibid: 350.
36 . I. Epstein, *The Talmud*.
37 . Stanislawski, *For Whom Do I Toil?*: 126-27, stresses the satirical nature of the work, saying that "Gordon strove not to depict a typical, or even likely, scene in Russian—

Jewish life, but to satirize the treatment of women in traditional Jewish society." and calls the denouement "tragic, if avertible and nonsensical." The satirical intent is not in doubt, and the tragic inflation of the text and, the active existence of the textual references in Jewish life is unquestionable. Their voice can be trusted as examples of direct representation, albeit quoted in the poem for unreliable purposes. The satiric tenor is more the result of phraseological cumulation and of the excessive bent of the fabula and its melodramatic expression in the poem.

38 . Devorah Baron, *Parshiyot* (Hebrew) (Jerusalem: Bialik Institute, 1968):11-12. The translations are my own. Dan Miron. *Devorah Baron: Mivchar Ma'amarim al Yetziratah*, ed. A Pagis (Tel Aviv: Am Oved, 1974) and Dan Miron, *Kivvun Orot* (Jerusalem: Schocken, 1979), sees this genealogical account – and the biblical references in stories in general – as expressive of Devorah Baron's perception of cyclical and unchanging temporality, which imbues even apparently singular historical events with "mythological value. "

39 . Baron: 29.

40 . Musha, who shows compassion toward Dinah, is an exception.

41 . Baron, *Parshiyot*: 16 and elsewhere.

42 . Ibid.: 18.

43 . Ibid.: 20.

44 . Ibid.: 27.

45 Ibid.: 14.

46 . Ibid.: 18.

47 . Ibid.: 28.

48 . Ibid.: 13.

49 . Ibid.: 35.

50 . Ibid.

51 . The night before he is due to officiate in a divorce he pores over the words of Rabbi Eliezer in Sanhedrin 22a: "For him who divorces the first wife, the very altar sheds tears against whom thou has dealt treacherously. Epstein, *Talmud*.

52 . Ibid.: 30.

53 . Ibid.: 35.

Chapter 15

On Becoming Female: Crossing Gender Boundaries in Kabbalistic Ritual and Myth

Elliot R. Wolfson

Despite the acknowledged fact that the trend of medieval Jewish mysticism known as theosophic kabbalah is distinguished in the religious history of Judaism by the explicit and repeated use of gender symbolism to characterize the nature of the divine, the state of research in this area is still somewhat rudimentary.[1] Indeed, previous studies of gender in the relevant kabbalistic literature have been marred by a conspicuous lack of sophistication. Most scholars who have written on such issues have taken for granted that the occurrence of gender images should be interpreted within a framework of what may be called a naive biologism, that is, the presumption that the differences between male and female are linked essentially and exclusively to biological functions. Needless to say, such an orientation fails to recognize that the latter in and of themselves are indicators of sexual but not gender differentiation. Although there obviously is a correlation between biological sex and gender identity, the two are not equivalent, as recent scholars in the fields of cultural anthropology and feminist psychology have emphasized. Gender identity is engendered by cultural assumptions concerning maleness and femaleness that interpret the body. In that respect we may speak of gender as a sociocultural construction that is a matter of semiology (reading cultural signs) rather than physiology (marking bodily organs). The body is a sign whose signification is determined by the ideological assumptions of a given society. There is no body without culture as there is no culture without body.[2]

Elsewhere I have examined the issue of the feminine in theosophical kabbalah by exploring in detail the philosophical implications of the divine androgyne.[3]   I attempted in that study to introduce some measure of concern for the cultural dimension of gender as it is employed in the kabbalistic materials. In short, I argued that the theosophic myth that informs kabbalistic symbolism and ritual reflects the androcentric and patriarchical norms of medieval society in general and that of rabbinic culture more particularly. I suggested, therefore, that notwithstanding the fact that kabbalists consistently speak of the unity and perfection of God in terms of the union of masculine and feminine, the idea of the ultimate wholeness or oneness for the kabbalists is predicated on a reconstituted male androgyne. That is, the androgynous nature of God is not based on two independent forces of equal value, but rather on one force that comprises both masculine and feminine traits, and that one force is the male who represents the ideal *anthropos*. Hence, the union of male and female is predicated ultimately on the absorption or containment of the left side (passive, judgmental, constraining female) in the right side (active, merciful, overflowing male). Indeed, the negative valorization of the feminine is underscored by the fact that when the female potency is separated from the masculine the potential exists that she will evolve into a demonic force. The task of *homo religiosus* is to restore the feminine to the masculine, to unite the two in a bond that overcomes gender differentiation by establishing the complete male who embodies masculine and feminine.

I argued, moreover, that in the engendering myth of kabbalistic theosophy the locus of the feminine is the phallus (i.e., the aspect of the divine that is the ontic source of both masculinity and femininity corresponds to the male organ). The point is made quite simply in one of the first kabbalistic works to surface in twelfth-century Provence, the *Sefer ha-Bahir*: in one passage we read that the letter *ṣaddi* (which stands for the *Ṣaddiq*, the Righteous one who is in the position of the phallus in the divine *anthropos*) orthographically can be broken into a *yod* on top of a *nun*, the former symbolizing the male potency (the sign of the covenant of circumcision) and the latter the female (perhaps related to the word *neqevah*).[4]   Contained within the one letter is the duality of male and female. One should speak, therefore, of an androgynous phallus. To put the matter in slightly different terms, we have here another example of a one-sex theory: the feminine is but an extension of the masculine.[5]   Thus, according to an anonymous, thirteenth-century kabbalistic text, the rite of circumcision "alludes to the perfect unity, and the matter of the androgyne (*du-parṣufim*) is explained in it; examine and discover with respect to the exposure of the corona."[6] The corona of the penis symbolically corresponds to the feminine *Shekhinah*, a correlation facilitated by the fact that the word '*aṭarah*, crown, is the technical name of the corona as well as one of the designations of the *Shekhinah*.[7] Insofar as the male organ is the ontic source of both male and female, the religious significance of circumcision lies in the fact that by means of this ritual the androgynous unity of God is established. Within the symbolic representation of theosophic kabbalah, the biological woman is not only overlooked but erased insofar as the gender system adopted by kabbalists locates the feminine in the male's reproductive organ. Even in those passages that treat the female as something distinct from the male, the phallocentric orientation is evident, for the feminine is portrayed as a receptacle that receives the seed from the male.[8] The experience of genderedness imparted by the mythic symbols of kabbalistic theosophy is such that the feminine is judged exclusively from the vantage point of the phallus.

I also criticized Scholem's attempt to contrast the kabbalistic viewpoint with that of the encratist tendency of ancient Gnosticism on the grounds that the former involves the conjunction of male and female, as opposed to the latter, which advocates the overcoming of sexual differentiation by reestablishing an original androgynous state.[9] A more nuanced understanding of gender in the kabbalistic sources does not warrant such a distinction. On the contrary, the goal of *gnosis* expressed in the Gnostic source mentioned by Scholem, the *Gospel of Thomas*, to "make the female male,"[10] is indeed an entirely appropriate slogan for the kabbalists. The union of God is predicated on the unity of male and female, but that unity is determined further by reintegrating the female in the male such that the primary male androgyne is reconstituted.

Gender imagery in the kabbalistic sources reflects the binary ideology of the general medieval culture, as well as the specific rabbinic society that reinforced the division of the sexes along hierarchical lines, delegating a subservient role to the female. The male is valorized as the active, dominant, primary sex and the female is the passive, dominated, and secondary one.[11] Reinterpreting the myth of the androgynous human articulated in rabbinic sources, the kabbalists depict God as comprising male and female, the former representing the front and the latter the back. The otherness of the feminine (by a play on words the expression '*aḥor*, the back, is transposed into '*aḥer*, the other) is overcome when the male and female face one another in the moment of sexual unification. In this facing, however, the feminine is effaced.

According to the standard kabbalistic symbolism, judgment is associated with the feminine and mercy with the masculine. Hence, the symbolic import of sexual union is the sweetening of judgment by mercy. What is really implied by this amelioration is that the distinctive quality of the feminine aspect of the divine is expunged as she is contained in the male. Gendered differences are transcended when the female divests herself of her essential femininity, that is, when she becomes part of the male because the latter embodies the generic anthropos and hence represents the most basic elemental force of the divine. Although it is certainly the case that the kabbalists emphasize time and again that the complete human being comprises masculine and feminine, and indeed the messianic era is understood precisely in terms of the erotic union of the male and female aspects of the divine—the "secret of faith"[12] or the "perfection of everything"[13] —the nature of the feminine is such that this union entails the overcoming of the femaleness of the female. Redemption is a state wherein male and female are conjoined, but in that union the female is enfolded back into the male whence she derived.[14] Scholem's distinction between the conjunction of male and female and the re-establishment of a primordial androgyne cannot be upheld.

When the complex theosophic discourse is applied to the anthropological sphere, it is evident that here too it is the task of the female to become male, especially through sexual union. In this context I would like to cite one passage conveying the idea that the movement from femaleness to maleness represents the ideal for the earthly woman, emulating thereby the progression in the divine realm. The text is an anonymous kabbalistic exposition on the commandment of levirate marriage, *sod ha-yibbum*, whose provenance, I surmise, is thirteenth-century Catalonia:

> It is written in *Sefer ha-Bahir*[15] that the Holy One, blessed be He, created seven holy forms, and the forms are divided into two hands, two legs, a head and the body. Thus there are six, and these six [are male]. [It is written] "male and female He created them" (Gen. 1:26) the seventh form is the female. Thus the woman completes the seven forms. When the Holy One, blessed be He, created Adam, He combined all seven forms together, and afterward He separated the seventh so that the woman would be the seventh form of the man, and the man is not

complete without her, as it is written, "it is not good for man to be alone,"[16] and it is written, "they will be as one flesh."[17] Just as Sabbath is rest for the six days so too the woman is rest for the six forms, for without her a man is not stationary, he wanders to and fro. As the rabbis, blessed be their memory, said, "the one who dwells without a wife dwells without goodness."[18] And this is what the rabbis, blessed be their memory, said, "a person is not exempt from [the commandment] to procreate until he has a boy and a girl,"[19] so that what is born to him corresponds to the seven forms. This is also what they alluded to by the fact that a man and not a woman is commanded with respect to procreation, for most of the forms and their essence are in the male, and the woman is but the completion. This is what the rabbis, blessed be their memory, said, "a woman who produces seed first gives birth to a male,"[20] for the seed of the man, in which there are the six forms, annuls the seed of the woman which has but one form. The male comes by way of the male and the female by the power of the female.[21]

The feminine potency is here portrayed as the seventh form that completes or perfects the other six. That this completion involves the female being reintegrated into the male is obvious from the examples adduced in the realm of human relationships. The lack of autonomy of the feminine gender is underscored in the continuation of the text that elaborates on the biblical law that the male child and not the female inherits the property of the father. Most significantly, the woman is depicted as the vehicle that allows the man to produce offspring. While the Talmudic opinion that a man fulfills his obligation of procreation by having a child of each sex is theosophically reinterpreted,[22] it is clear from the end of the passage that having male children is privileged, for the female ontically is only the completion of the masculine. Indeed, the act of *coitus* replicates the structure above: the seminal fluid alludes to the six male forms and the vaginal secretion to the seventh female form. Following the rabbinic view, which in turn reflects the Hippocratic and Galenic standpoint,[23] conception requires the mixing of two seeds, but the desired situation involves the domination and superiority of the male so that a male child is conceived. By secreting her fluids first, the woman allows the sperm of the man to dominate and thus the embryo that is conceived is male. The woman's task to complete the male structure is accomplished through the production of male progeny.

By giving birth in general, and to male offspring in particular, gender boundaries are crossed, because the female assumes the role of the engendering male. The point is alluded to in the following zoharic text: "R. Yose said: from the time a woman gets pregnant until the day she gives birth there is nothing in her mouth but that her child should be a male. Thus it says, 'When a woman brings forth seed and bears a male' (Lev. 12:2)."[24] The intention of the woman expressed verbally to bear a male child has the effect of masculinizing her so that she produces seed like a man and gives birth to a boy. According to the zoharic exegesis, the bringing forth of the male seed on the part of the woman is accomplished through the orifice of the mouth which corresponds to the procreative organ of the male; this parallelism is a foundational structure in Jewish esotericism. The woman takes the place of a male who procreates by uttering her desire to have a boy.

It can be shown from still other zoharic sources that the female who gives birth is depicted as male. In his discussion of the feminine element of divinity in kabbalistic symbolism, Scholem already noted that one must distinguish between two aspects of femininity—corresponding to the upper and lower *Shekhinah*—the active energy and creative power, on the one hand, and the passive receptivity, on the other. The former is associated more specifically with the image of the "upper mother," the third gradation or *Binah*, and latter with the "lower mother," the tenth gradation or *Malkhut*.[25] Scholem comes close to realizing the complex inversion of gender that this symbolism presupposes when he remarks that the "male symbol" of the Creator or Demiurge (applied to *Binah*) "represents that aspect of the feminine that is in principle denied to the lower *Shekhinah*."[26] Analogously, Scholem remarks that "when the *Shekhinah* functions as a medium for the downward flow of life-giving energies, it is understood in male symbols."[27] In spite of these momentary insights, however, Scholem's analysis in general (as most other scholars who have written on the subject) suffers from a lack of attentiveness to the dynamic of gender metamorphosis. That is, he too readily describes the symbolic valence of motherhood as a feminine trait, assuming that the biological function reflects the meaning of the theosophic symbol. Thus, when describing the active forces of the *Shekhinah*, Scholem speaks of the "maternal, birth-giving, and creative element that comes about as a result of the very act of receiving." The dual role of giving and receiving is designated by Scholem as the "dialectics of femininity."[28] In my view, the idea of motherhood in kabbalistic symbolism is decidedly masculine, for the womb that gives birth is valorized as an erectile and elongated phallus.[29] One would do better, therefore, to refer to the creative and maternal element of the female as the transvaluation of the feminine into the masculine.[30]

In light of this gender transformation one can appreciate the active characterization of the divine gradation that corresponds to the upper mother. Indeed, in zoharic literature and other texts influenced thereby, *Binah*, the feminine counterpart to the second emanation, *Ḥokhmah*, is called the world-of-the-masculine ('alma' di-dekhura') as opposed to the lower *Shekhinah*, which is called the world-of-the-feminine ('alma' de-nuqba'), for *Binah* is the womb whence the other emanations that constitute the divine anthropos derive.[31] Many of the images and symbols employed in the *Zohar* and in related sources to depict the ninth gradation—*Yesod*, which corresponds to the divine phallus—are used as well in relation to *Binah*, the gradation referred to as the mother or the womb that receives the seed from *Ḥokhmah*, the father. To be sure, the attribute of *Binah* is empowered to give birth by virtue of the semen she receives from *Ḥokhmah*, but that reception transforms her phallically into a spring that overflows. The uterus that contains the fecundating phallus is thereby transmuted into an instrument of the male principle.

In the zoharic corpus, the very concept of motherhood is shaped by the parallelism set between the divine grades of *Binah* and *Yesod*. Thus, for instance, another designation of *Binah* in zoharic literature is the "concealed world" ('alma' de-itkkaseya'), a term that relates specifically to the character of *Binah*, the divine mother, as that which encompasses and encloses her offspring.[32] The aspect of concealment, frequently associated with the phallic *Yesod*, is linked to the image of *Binah* as the mother who sits upon her children.[33] The masculine element is especially highlighted in those contexts where the image of the mother hovering over her children is combined with that of the mother nursing her babes.[34] Breast-feeding too is valorized as a phallic activity (the milk obviously taking the place of the semen) insofar as anything that sustains by overflowing is automatically treated as an aspect of the phallus.[35] The point is underscored in one zoharic passage that reflects on the word 'eḥad in shema' yisra'el yhwh 'elohenu yhwh 'eḥad (Hear, O Israel, the Lord is our God, the Lord is one) (Deut. 6:4). In line with earlier kabbalistic sources,[36] the zoharic authorship interprets the three letters of this word as a reference to the ten *sefirot*,—that is, the 'alef corresponds to the first *sefirah*, *Keter*, the letter *ḥet* the eight *sefirot* from *Ḥokhmah* to *Yesod*, and the *dalet* the *Shekhinah* who is the impoverished (dal) emanation. According to the masoretic orthography, however, this *dalet* is enlarged and theosophically signifies that the *Shekhinah* cleaves to the upper gradations. In this state the *Shekhinah* is "augmented and all the world is nourished from her, and the breasts 'were like towers, so I became in his eyes as one who finds favor' (Song of Songs 8:10)."[37] The *Zohar* contrasts the ontic situation of the *Shekhinah* in exile, on the one hand, and the state of blessing and augmentation, on the other: the first instance is depicted by the verse, "We have a little sister, whose breasts are not yet formed" (Song of Songs 8:8), whereas the latter is conveyed in the aforecited verse, "My breasts are like towers, so I became in his eyes as one who finds favor" (ibid., 10). The maturation of the *Shekhinah* from a woman without breasts to one with full grown breasts in effect symbolizes her gender transformation from a female to a male.[38] Thus the breasts are described in the obvious phallic image of a tower whence all beings are sustained.[39] The phallic function of the breasts is alluded to as well in the expression *ke-moṣ'et shalom* (as one who finds favor), the term *shalom* serving in zoharic literature as in standard kabbalistic symbolism as one of the designations for the divine phallus.

The motherly quality of brooding over the offspring is also connected with the concept of *Teshuvah*, literally, return (i.e., the emanations are in stationary position in relation to their source).[40] This too is the theosophic symbolism of *Yom Kippur*, the Day of Atonement, wherein all things return to their ontic source to be sustained by the overflowingness of the primal concealment. Thus, on that very day there is an aspect of disclosure for the fifty gates of *Binah* open up to every side, but there is also an aspect of concealment because the Mother remains covered and hidden. The latter motif is connected with the prohibition of uncovering the nakedness of the father and mother (Lev. 18:7), the precise *Torah* portion that is read in the afternoon service of *Yom Kippur*.[41] In a profound inversion of symbolism, the concealment of the Mother enables her to sustain her offspring, and in that act of nourishing she is masculinized. Theosophically interpreted, the sin of disclosing the genitals of the mother creates a blemish above that separates the Mother from her children; repentance is, quite literally, causing the Mother to return to her place wherein she continues to assume the masculine role of feeding and sustaining the offspring in a manner that is concealed.[42]

That the divine Mother is described in the same or proximate terms used to describe the phallus indicates that the female who gives birth is valorized as a male, for the act of birthing is treated as a form of expansion or ejaculation that is characteristically masculine.[43] The act of procreation is decidedly phallic. Hence, the tenth of the emanations, the *Shekhinah*, which is feminine vis-à-vis the upper emanations, is masculine in relation to what is beneath her, and indeed is referred to frequently as *malkhut* on account of this procreative quality. According to one text in the *Zohar*, interpreting the verse, "Drink water from your cistern, running water from your own well" (Prov. 5:15), when the *Shekhinah* receives the influx from the upper masculine divine potencies she is transformed from an empty cistern (*bor*) that has nothing of its own into a well (*be'er*) that is full and overflows to every side: the impoverished *dalet* becomes an open *he'*.[44]   In the aspect of overflowing the queen becomes king; thus one of the most common and influential symbols of the feminine Presence is King David. The appropriateness of this symbol is not due to a feminization of David, but rather the masculinization of the *Shekhinah*.[45]

In this connection it is of special interest to note the interpretation of the verse, "On the third day, Esther put on royal apparel and stood in the inner court of the king's palace, facing the king's palace, while sitting on his royal throne in the throne room facing the entrance of the palace" (Esther 5:1), in the following zoharic passage: "'On the third day,' when the power of the body was weakened and she existed in spirit without a body, then 'Esther put on royal apparel' (*wa-tilbash 'esther malkhut*). . . She was adorned in the supernal, holy *Malkhut*; she most certainly was clothed in the Holy Spirit."[46] The text goes on to record that Esther was granted to be clothed in the Holy Spirit as a reward for her reticence to disclose information about her upbringing to Ahasuerus (see Esther 2:20). The significant point for this context is that Esther takes on, or is united with, the aspect of God referred to as *Malkhut*, the tenth emanation that corresponds to the feminine *Shekhinah*, only when she overcomes her own physical status. To become the divine feminine involves a denial of biological womanhood. The underlying conceptual point here is identical to the issue that I raised before, namely, the engendering aspect of the *Shekhinah*, designated as *Malkhut*, is related to the masculine potency of God; hence, only when the distinctive bodily characteristics of the woman are subjugated by the spirit that is related to the masculine can she receive the overflow (or the Holy Spirit) from the divine realm. Ironically enough, according to the complex gender system of theosophic kabbalah, impregnation, birthing, and mothering are seen as male traits.

A perfect homology exists between the divine and mundane spheres: just as the divine feminine can assume the qualities of the male, so too can the earthly biological woman be gendered as masculine. One may speak, therefore, of a kind of spiritual transvestism that is logically implied by kabbalistic myth: a woman actualizes her fullest potential qua human when she is adorned with the qualities of the male, realized principally through the act of generation.   But do we have evidence for movement in the opposite direction, that is, crossing gender boundaries such that the male becomes female? Is it ever appropriate, according to the kabbalists, for the male to divest himself of his maleness and adopt the gender of the feminine?   Given the hierarchical nature of the gender attribution in these sources one would not expect to find such a reciprocal process. Yet, there is precisely a dynamic of this sort that is most fully articulated in the kabbalistic theosophy of the sixteenth-century master, Isaac Luria, as transmitted by his various disciples.   In the remainder of this chapter I would like to explore in some detail the theme of the male becoming female in the myth and ritual of Lurianic kabbalah. Although it is obviously the case that many of the motifs in this corpus are exegetical elaborations of earlier sources, especially zoharic passages, I can only mention briefly some of the background ideas and images from the *Zohar* that are indispensable for a proper appreciation of the later material.

The motif that serves as the basis for my reflections is that of the upper and lower waters, the former depicted as masculine and the latter as feminine.   This motif is expressed already in classical rabbinic sources,[47] perhaps reflecting some form of Gnostic speculation,[48] where the dual waters have an exclusively cosmological reference. In later kabbalistic literature, especially the *Zohar*, this motif is developed further and assumes as well a theosophic connotation.[49]   The obvious gender symbolism associated with these waters, based on the model of orgasmic secretions, is drawn quite boldly in the following zoharic passage:

> The upper water is male and the lower female, and the lower is sustained by the male. The lower waters call out to the upper like a female who opens up for the male, and she spills water corresponding to the male water that produces semen. The female is nourished by the male.[50]

Perhaps the most interesting development of this motif in zoharic literature involves the idea of the souls of the righteous entering into the *Shekhinah*, wherein they are integrated into the lower female waters, the *mayyin nuqbin*, that arouse the upper male water, *mayyin dukhrin*.   To cite one representative text:

The desire of the female for the male is not realized except when a spirit enters into her and she discharges fluid corresponding to upper masculine waters. So too the Community of Israel [the *Shekhinah*] does not arouse the desire for the Holy One, blessed be He, except by means of the spirit of the righteous who enter into her. Then the fluids flow within her corresponding to the male fluids, and everything becomes one desire, one bundle, one bond. This is the will of everything, and the stroll that the Holy One, blessed be He, takes with the souls of the righteous.[51]

In an extraordinary reversal of gender symbolism, the penetration of the souls of the righteous into the feminine Presence results in their stimulating and becoming part of the fluids secreted by the female, which, in turn, arouse the seminal fluids of the upper male potency of the divine. The ontic status of the righteous is determined precisely by this role: "Rachel gave birth to two righteous individuals, and this is appropriate, for the sabbatical year is always situated in between two righteous individuals, as it is written, 'The righteous (*ṣaddiqim*, i.e., in the plural) shall inherit the land' (Ps. 37:29), the righteous above and the righteous below. The supernal waters flow from the righteous above and from the righteous below the female flows with water in relation to the male in complete desire."[52]

Moreover, it is clear from any number of passages that the zoharic authorship sees this task as the purpose of the nocturnal ascent of the righteous[53]: "When the soul rises it arouses the desire of the female toward the male, and then the fluids flow from below to above, and the pit becomes a well of flowing water. . . for this place is perfected by the soul of the righteous, and the love and desire is aroused above, and it becomes one."[54] The entry of the righteous soul into the *Shekhinah* entirely reverses the gender roles normally associated with each of the relevant agents in this drama, for the masculine soul becomes feminine as it is integrated as part of the feminine waters and the feminine aspect of the Godhead becomes masculine insofar as the pit is transformed into a well of flowing waters. The feminization of the righteous accounts as well for the image of God taking a stroll with the souls of the righteous, an obvious euphemism for sexual intercourse, based ultimately on the phallic understanding of the feet.[55] This image is entirely appropriate because the souls of the righteous are female partners in relation to the masculine deity. Underlying this relationship may be an implicit homoeroticism that necessitates the feminization of the human male vis-à-vis the divine who is depicted as masculine. If there is a latent homoeroticism in the zoharic symbolism, it should be noted that it is still expressed within a purely heterosexual context, that is, the male righteous constitute the feminine waters that arouse the overflow of the masculine waters upon the divine feminine. The issue is rendered much more complex by the fact that, as I have argued, the divine feminine is itself part of the male organ.

The ideas expressed in the zoharic corpus are elaborated in the kabbalistic materials deriving from the circle of Isaac Luria in sixteenth-century Safed.[56] Most importantly, in the Lurianic literature this motif is applied to specific rituals wherein it is clear that the goal of the male adept is to become female. Thus, for example, in *Sha'ar ha-Kawwanot* Ḥayyim Vital offers the following explanation for the gesture of shutting the eyes[57] that is required when the *Shema'*, the traditional proclamation of divine unity, is recited:

> Before you say "Hear O Israel [the Lord, our God, the Lord is one]" (Deut. 6:4) you should close your two eyes with your right hand and concentrate on what is written in the [zoharic section] *Sabba de-Mishpaṭim* [regarding] the beautiful maiden that has no eyes.[58] We have explained in that context that the meaning [of this expression] is Rachel who ascends at this point [of the prayer] in the aspect of female waters in relation to the Father and Mother.[59]

To appreciate the complex symbolism underlying this comment it is necessary to bear in mind that, according to the Lurianic interpretation of the liturgical order, the mystical significance of the *Shema'* is "to raise the female waters from the Male and Female to the Father and Mother so that the Father and Mother will be united and the [influx of the] consciousness (*moḥin*) will come down to the Male and Female."[60] The worshipper thus joins the feminine hypostasis so that he may rise with her in the aspect of the female waters to facilitate the union of the lower two masculine and feminine configurations (*parṣufim*) in the Godhead, *Ze'eir' Anpin* and *Nuqba' di-Ze'eir*, which, in turn, stimulate the union of the upper masculine and feminine configurations, the Father ('*Abba'*) and Mother ('*Imma'*).[61] The latter union results in the overflowing of the male waters (*mayyim dukhrin*) from *Ze'eir 'Anpin* to *Nuqba' di-Ze'eir* during the moment of coupling that is consummated during the *'Amidah*, the standing prayer of the eighteen benedictions. It is most significant for the theme of my discussion that, according to the Lurianic interpretation, the male adept ritually covers his eyes to transform himself into that divine grade symbolized by the zoharic image of a beautiful maiden without eyes, namely, the configuration (parṣuf) called Nuqba' di-Ze'eir, which corresponds to the last of the ten sefirot, the Shekhinah. One may speak of a process of effeminization of the male, a motif that has not been sufficiently noted in discussions of Lurianic symbolism and ritual. It lies beyond the concerns of this chapter to engage this important topic in full, but it is necessary to remark that the motif of the males becoming integrated into the female waters is part of this larger phenomenon of gender metamorphosis. To be sure, the union of the righteous souls with the Shekhinah is based on the fact that they correspond to the male aspect of the divine, the membrum virile. However, once these souls enter into the Shekhinah, they become incorporated as part of her and constitute the female waters that further stimulate coitus in the higher grades of the divine realm.[62]

The assimilation of the male into the female is characterized as the male closing his eyes in emulation of the beautiful maiden without eyes. The ritual gains its mystical valence from the fact that the eyes function as a symbol for the male sexual organs while still remaining eyes or, to put the matter somewhat differently, the eyes are the aspect in the head that function like the genitals in the lower region of the body. Hence, the female persona of the divine is depicted as the beautiful maiden without eyes.[63] The male worshipper must partake of the character of the feminine by emasculating himself, a procedure that is ritually fulfilled through the shutting of the eyes.

The interpretation that I have offered is confirmed by a second passage in Sha'ar ha-Kawwanot that deals more generally with the closing of the eyes during prayer.[64] In this text Vital has imputed new theosophic meaning to a well-established prayer gesture that has as its purpose the augmentation of intention during worship[65]: by closing his eyes, the male worshipper becomes the beautiful maiden without eyes. According to this passage, the mystical significance of prayer in general, enacted by means of this gesture, is connected to the fact that the male is assimilated into the female in order to arouse the unity of the masculine and feminine above.

The mandate for the male worshipper, therefore, is not simply to act as a stimulus to arouse the secretions of the female but rather to be integrated into them.[66] It is evident, however, that the crossing of gender boundary implied here is not predicated on any ambiguity regarding or open challenge to the status accorded the respective genders in kabbalistic thought. On the contrary, the hierarchy of gender roles in classical kabbalah is only reinforced in the Lurianic material. That is, the male's becoming female is necessary so that the female may become male through the activation of the masculine principle of beneficence.   Vital expresses this in the context of describing the supplication prayer (*nefillat 'appayim*), which succeeds the '*Amidah* in the traditional morning liturgy on Monday and Thursday:

> Now is the time of the descent of the drop of male waters of grace into the female Rachel. One must first raise the female waters in order to receive afterwards the male waters, according to the secret, "When a woman brings forth seed and bears a male" (Lev. 12:2). And the rabbis, blessed be their memory, said,[67] "a woman who produces seed first gives birth to a male."[68]

Without entering further into the complicated symbolism articulated in the continuation of the previous passage, related specifically to the descent of the righteous into the realm of the demonic shells to liberate the entrapped sparks,[69] suffice it to say that for Luria the male fulfills an essential religious task by becoming female, by being assimilated into the female waters that rise to stimulate the male waters that in turn inseminate the female so that she gives birth to a male. To translate this web of symbols grammatologically: he becomes she so that she arouses he to turn she into he. This circular process of reconstituted masculinity is referred to in Lurianic kabbalah as the secret of impregnation ('*ibbur*). To cite one textual witness: "Just as the souls of the righteous elevate the female waters each night during sleep to *Malkhut*, and she renews them, according to the secret, 'They are renewed every morning' (Lam. 3:23), and the explanation of this renewal is that she illuminates them in the aspect of expanded consciousness (*moḥin de-gadlut*) so too when *Ze'eir 'Anpin* ascends in the secret of the female waters he is renewed by means of the Father and Mother."[70]   The stimulation of the female waters has the sole purpose of assisting in the rebirth of the male through the masculinized feminine in a state of increased consciousness. In the final analysis, the androcentric and phallocentric orientation adopted by kabbalists is so pervasive that even the positive values normally associated with the feminine are assigned to the male. This is captured in the brief comment of Vital that "there are five aspects of grace (*ḥasadim*) of the Mother and five aspects of grace of the Father, and the aspects of grace of the Mother are the acts of strength of the

Father."[71]   As noted earlier, according to standard kabbalistic symbolism, grace is associated with the masculine and strength with the feminine. It follows, therefore, that the male attributes in the Mother must be transposed into female attributes of the Father.

In conclusion, it can be said that there is a model in theosophic kabbalah of the male becoming female just as there is one of the female becoming male. It is indeed appropriate, in fact mandatory, for the male to divest himself of his maleness and assume the posture of the feminine. For the followers of Lurianic kabbalah, this gender transformation is the essential dynamic enacted in the structure of the liturgy. This movement, however, reifies the standard binary hierarchy of gender symbolism: the male becomes female only in order to add strength to the female to renew herself as male. The female must either be restored to the male or turned into a male. From the vantage point of kabbalists, this is the secret that establishes the covenant of unity.

NOTES

1. This chapter is part of a larger study, "Crossing Gender Boundaries in Kabbalistic Ritual and Myth," to appear in a forthcoming collection of my essays, *Circle in the Square: Studies in the Use of Gender in Kabbalistic Symbolism* (Albany: SUNY Press, forthcoming).

2. C. Walker Bynum, "Introduction: The Complexity of Symbols," in *Gender and Religion: On the Complexity of Symbols*, ed. C. W. Bynum, S. Harrell, and P. Richman (Boston: Beacon Press, 1986), 7; J. Epstein and K. Straub, "Introduction: The Guarded Body," in *Body Guards: The Cultural Politics of Gender Ambiguity* (New York: Routledge, 1991), 3.

3. E. R. Wolfson, "Woman—The Feminine as Other in Theosophic Kabbalah: Some Philosophical Observations on the Divine Androgyne," in *The Other in Jewish Thought and History*, ed. R. Cohn and L. Silberstein (New York: New York University Press, 1994).

4. *Sefer ha-Bahir*, ed. R. Margaliot (Jerusalem: Mosad ha-Rav, 1978), § 61. For discussion of this critical passage see E. R. Wolfson, "The Tree That Is All: Jewish-Christian Roots of a Kabbalistic Symbol in *Sefer ha-Bahir*," *Journal of Jewish Thought and Philosophy* 3 (1993): 71.

5. For discussion of this phenomenon in Western culture, see T. Laqueur, *Making Sex: Body and Gender from the Greeks to Freud* (Cambridge: Harvard University Press, 1990).

6. MS Paris 843, fol. 39b.

7. See, e.g., *Zohar* 1:162a. For other references to this motif, see E. R. Wolfson, "Circumcision, Vision of God, and Textual Interpretation: From Midrashic Trope to Mystical Symbol," *History of Religions* 27 (1987): 205, n. 53, to which many more sources could be added.

8. See, e.g., *Zohar* 1:162a-b.

9. G. Scholem, *Origins of the Kabbalah*, trans. A. Arkush, and ed. R. J. Zwi Werblowsky (Princeton: Princeton University Press, 1987), 142. A similar position is taken by C. Mopsik, *Lettre sur la sainteté: Le secret de la relation entre l'homme et la femme dans la cabale* (Paris: Verdier, 1986), 324-25, n. 218, and M. Idel, "Sexual Metaphors and Praxis in the Kabbalah," in *The Jewish Family: Metaphor and Memory*, ed. D. Kraemer (New York:

Oxford University Press, 1989), 211. See also the formulation of Y. Liebes, *Studies in the Zohar*, trans., A. Schwartz, S. Nakache, and P. Peli (Albany: SUNY Press, 1993), 106: "the dual sexuality of the divinity is the very foundation of all the doctrine of the Kabbala." To evaluate this statement more precisely one must take into consideration the cultural construction of gender in the relevant sources. When that is done it becomes evident that the feminine is part of the masculine, and hence the dual sexuality of the divinity is reduced to one sex that comprises two elements, the merciful male and the judgmental female.

10 . See K. Vogt, "'Becoming Male': A Gnostic and Early Christian Metaphor," in *Image of God and Gender Models in Judaeo-Christian Tradition*, ed. K. E. Børresen (Oslo: Solum Forlag, 1991), 172-87.

11 . Cf. the summary account given by C. Walker Bynum, "'And Woman His Humanity': Female Imagery in the Religious Writing of the Later Middle Ages," in *Gender and Religion: On the Complexity of Symbols*, 257: "Male and female were contrasted and asymmetrically valued as intellect/body, active/passive, rational/irrational, reason/emotion, self-control/lust, judgment/mercy, and order/disorder."

12 . See *Zohar* 1:49b.

13 . See *Zohar* 3:163b.

14 . See, e.g., *Zohar* 3:145b.

15 . *Sefer ha-Bahir*, § 172.

16 . Gen. 2:19.

17 . Gen. 2:25.

18 . B. Yevamot 62b.

19 . Ibid., 61b.

20 . B. Berakhot 60a; Niddah 25b, 28a, 31a.

21 . MS Vatican 236, fols. 76a-b. See also MS Parma 2704 (De Rossi 68), fol. 87a.

22 . Cf. *Zohar* 3:7a discussed in I. Tishby, *The Wisdom of the Zohar*, trans., D. Goldstein (Oxford: Oxford University Press, 1989), 1361.

23 . See A. Preus, "Galen's Criticism of Aristotle's Conception Theory," *Journal of the History of Biology* 10 (1977): 65-85; M. Boylan, "The Galenic and Hippocratic Challenge to Aristotle's Conception Theory," *Journal of the History of Biology* 17 (1984): 83-112.

24 . *Zohar* 3:42b.

25 . G. Scholem, *On the Mystical Shape of the Godhead: Basic Concepts in the Kabbalah*, trans., J. Neugroschel, ed., and rev., J. Chipman (New York: Schocken, 1991), 174-75.

26 . Ibid., 176.

27 . Ibid., 186.

28 . Ibid., 187.

29 . On portrayals of the uterus as the penis in Renaissance anatomical material, see evidence adduced by Laqueur, *Making Sex*, 79-98. The kabbalistic transformation of motherhood into a masculine ideal is predicated on a one-sex model as well that viewed the female genitals as internal analogues to the male genitals. The womb, therefore, is characterized in terms of a penislike extension.

30 . On the androgynous character of the archetype of the Great Mother, see E. Neumann, *The Origins and History of Consciousness*, trans., R. F. C. Hull (Princeton: Princeton University Press, 1954), 46. On the phenomenon of the phallic mother, or the uroboric snake woman that combines begetting and child-bearing, see Neumann, *The Great Mother: An Analysis of an Archetype*, trans., R. Manheim, 2nd ed. (Princeton: Princeton University Press, 1963), 13, 170, 308-10.

31 . For discussion of this terminology, see G. Scholem, "On the Development of the Concept of Worlds in the Early Kabbalah," *Tarbiz* 2 (1931): 39-41 (in Hebrew).

32 . See, e.g., *Zohar* 1:219a, and *The Book of the Pomegranate: Moses de León's Sefer ha-Rimmon,* ed. E. R. Wolfson (Atlanta: Scholars Press, 1988) 138 (Hebrew section): "Behold I will reveal to you a true secret. Know that there is no male in Israel who is married that does not stand between two women, one hidden and the other revealed. When a man is married the *Shekhinah* above his head becomes in relation to him a hidden world, and his wife stands next to him in the matter that is revealed. Thus, he stands between two women, one hidden and the other revealed, to be in the pattern that is above." The biblical model recalled in this context is Jacob who stands between his two wives, Leah and Rachel, symbolically corresponding to *Binah* and *Malkhut*. See parallel in *Zohar* 1:50a, already noted by Y. Liebes, "The Messiah of the Zohar," in *The Messianic Idea in Jewish Thought: A Study Conference in Honour of the Eightieth Birthday of Gershom Scholem* (Jerusalem,1982), 205, n. 402. In line with the gender dynamic operative in this text, the upper female in relation to the male is a concealed world and the lower female is the revealed world. The upper feminine, however, in this posture is valorized as male.

33 . See *Zohar* 1:158a.

34 . *Zohar* 2:9a.

35 . See *Zohar* 1:184a, where the image of nursing from the mother's breast (cf. Song of Songs 8:1) is interpreted as a reference to the unity and love between *Yesod* and *Shekhinah*. In that context, therefore, breast-feeding assumes a sexual connotation. The breasts can also symbolize masculine and feminine potencies; cf. *Zohar* 1:44b and 2:253a (both interpreting Song of Songs 4:5).

36 . See M. Idel, *Kabbalah: New Perspectives* (New Haven: Yale University Press, 1988), 55.

37 . *Zohar* 1:256b.

38 . In the continuation of the zoharic text the growth of the breasts is linked more specifically to the righteous and meritorious activities of Israel. That is, when the Jewish people cleave to the Torah and go in a truthful path, then the *Shekhinah* is fortified like a wall and develops towering breasts. The allegorical depiction of Israel's deeds as the breasts of the *Shekhinah* is found as well in *Zohar* 2:80b. See also 1:45a, where the beauty of a woman is tied especially to her breasts.

39 . The phallic signification of the mature breasts is evident as well in *Zohar* 3:296a ('Idra' Zuta'): "The beauty of the female is entirely from the beauty of the male. This female [*Shekhinah*] is called the smaller wisdom in relation to the other one, and thus it is written, 'We have a little sister, whose breasts are not yet formed' (Song of Songs 8:8), for she tarries in the exile. 'We have a little sister,' certainly she appears as little, but she is big and great, for she is the completion of what she has received from everyone, as it is written, 'I am a wall, my breasts are like towers' (ibid., 10). 'My breasts' are filled to nurse all things. 'Like towers,' these are the great rivers that issue forth from the supernal mother."

40 . *Zohar* 2:85b; cf. *The Book of the Pomegranate*, 163. The nexus between the motif of returning and the role of *Binah* as that which overflows in blessings is underscored in the anonymous kabbalistic text, influenced by zoharic traditions and the writings of Moses de León, the *Sefer ha-Ne'elam*, MS Paris, BN 817, fol. 57a.

41 . *Zohar* 3:15b. On the paradoxical nature of this passage, see the marginal notes in *Gershom Scholem's Annotated Zohar* (Jerusalem: Magnes Press, 1992), 2232.

42 . The nexus of Repentance, Yom Kippur, and illicit sexual relations, especially uncovering the genitals of the father and mother, in the zoharic text is evident as well in

the following comment of Joseph of Hamadan in his commentary on the *sefirot*, MS Oxford-Bodleian 1628, fol. 67b (concerning this work see M. Idel, "Commentary on the Ten *Sefirot* and Fragments from the Writings of Joseph of Hamadan," *Alei Sefer* 6-7 [1979]: 74-84; in Hebrew): "From there [*Binah*] begins the drawing-forth of the genitals (*yeniqat 'arayot*), and thus on Yom Kippur we read at the time of Minḥah [the afternoon service] the matter of illicit sexual relations ('*arayot*), for they draw forth from the attribute of *Binah* which is called *Teshuvah* in every place. On Yom Kippur we stand in the strength of *Teshuvah*, and you find that the beginning of the [section on] illicit sexual relations is 'the nakedness of the father and mother' (Lev. 18:7), which is the attribute of *Binah* on account of the beginning of the secret of illicit sexual relations (*sitre 'arayot*)." For a parallel to this explanation, see Joseph of Hamadan's *Sefer Ṭa'ame ha-Miṣwot*, positive commandments (no. 48) in M. Meier, "A Critical Edition of the *Sefer Ta'amey ha-Mizwoth* ("Book of the Reasons of the Commandments") Attributed to Isaac Ibn Farhi/Section I—Positive Commandments/With Introduction and Notes," Ph.D. dissertation (Brandeis University, 1974), 196: "We read the section on '*arayot* in the Minḥah prayer on Yom Kippur because we comprehend [at that time] the attribute of *Binah*, and from there we begin to draw forth the '*arayot*, the secret of the wife and her husband, the secret of unity." For a slightly different formulation, see J. Zwelling, "Joseph of Hamadan's *Sefer Tashak*: Critical Edition with Introduction," Ph.D. dissertation, Brandeis University (1975), 109, where it is emphasized that from *Binah* is the drawing-forth of the golden bowl (*yeniqat golat ha-zahav*),—the phallus that overflows to all the attributes. Cf. Joseph of Hamadan's *Sefer Ṭa'ame ha-Miṣwot*, negative commandments (no. 30), MS Paris, BN 817, fol. 155a, where a connection is made between the custom to read the section on '*arayot* during the afternoon service of Yom Kippur and the tannaitic treatment of illicit sexual relations as an esoteric discipline (according to M. Ḥagigah 2:1). In that context, moreover, Hamadan offers a slightly different nuanced explanation for this commandment: "Know that the matter of the '*arayot* all relates to the fact that one should not make use of the sceptre of the glorious king, for he who has intercourse with his mother it is as if he actually had intercourse with the *Shekhinah* for she is the mother of all living things. Therefore, [in Lev. 18:7] it is written 'your mother' twice, corresponding to the mother above and the mother below. Not for naught did the rabbis, blessed be their memory, say [B. Berakhot 57a], the one who has intercourse with his mother in a dream should anticipate understanding. This is the attribute of *Binah* that is called mother. Therefore, he who has intercourse with his mother makes use of the sceptre of *Binah* who is called mother, and he who makes use [of the sceptre] of the glorious king is guilty of death. Therefore the Torah says, 'Your father's nakedness and the nakedness of your mother, you shall not uncover,' corresponding to Ṣaddiq and *Malkhut* who are called father and mother, and [the continuation of the verse, 'she is your mother—you shall not uncover her nakedness') corresponds to *Binah*." According to an alternative symbolic explanation, on Yom Kippur there is a reunion of mother and daughter, i.e., *Binah* and *Malkhut* are conjoined in a union that has no precise analogue in the anthropological sphere. On the contrary, sexual relations between husband and wife are prohibited precisely because in the divine realm this mating occurs. Cf. *The Book of the Pomegranate*, 162-63; *Sefer ha-Ne'elam*, MS Paris, BN 817, fol. 57b.

43 . With respect to this quality of motherhood, there is an obvious discrepancy between the social and religious duty of the woman and the theosophic symbolism. That is, the symbolic valorization of the mother as masculine stands in marked contrast to the

exclusive (secondary) social and religious role accorded the woman related to the biological functions of motherhood.

44 . *Zohar* 1:60a. In other contexts a distinction is made between *be'er* and *be'erah*, the former referring to the *Shekhinah* before she receives water from the masculine attribute of *Ḥesed* and the latter once she has received it. See, e.g., *Zohar* 3:183b. The former expression is used in particular in contexts that describe the relationship of Isaac, who represents the attribute of Judgment, and the *Shekhinah*. See *Zohar* 1:60b, 135b; 3:103a, 115a, 156b.

45 . See, e.g., *Zohar* 1:60b, 3:84a.

46 . *Zohar* 3:183b.

47 . See *Genesis Rabbah* 13:13, ed. J. Theodor and C. Albeck, 2nd ed. (Jerusalem, 1965), 122.

48 . See A. Altmann, "Gnostic Themes in Rabbinic Cosmology," in *Essays in Honour of the Very Rev. Dr. J. H. Hertz, Chief Rabbi on the Occasion of his Seventieth Birthday*, ed. I. Epstein, E. Levine, and C. Roth (London, 1944), 23-24.

49 . See Scholem, *On the Mystical Shape*, 187-88; Liebes, "The Messiah of the Zohar," 179, n. 314; English translation in *Studies in the Zohar*, 53 and 185, n. 157. Although Scholem duly noted that the concept of the female waters involved the active force of the feminine, his attempt to distinguish between the zoharic and Lurianic usage of this motif cannot be upheld. The developments that occur in the Lurianic material must be seen as exegetical transformations of the earlier passages occasioned by distinctive psychological orientations.

50 . *Zohar* 1:29b.

51 . *Zohar* 1:60b. Cf. 3:79b: "Praiseworthy are the righteous for several supernal secrets are hidden for them in that world, and the Holy One, blessed be He, takes delight in them in that world."

52 . *Zohar* 1:153b.

53 . Concerning this theme, see E. R. Wolfson, "Forms of Visionary Ascent as Ecstatic Experience in the *Zohar*," in *Gershom Scholem's Major Trends in Jewish Mysticism: 50 Years After*, ed. J. Dan and P. Schäfer (Tübingen: Mohr, 1994), 209-35.

54 . *Zohar* 1:135a.

55 . See E. R. Wolfson, "Images of God's Feet: Some Observations on the Divine Body in Judaism," in *People of the Body: Jewish and Judaism from an Embodied Perspective*, ed. H. Eilberg-Schwartz (Albany: SUNY Press, 1992), 143-81.

56 . In a passage reportedly written by Luria himself, the zoharic conception is reformulated. See *Sha'ar Ma'amere Rashbi* (Jerusalem, 1898), 29a and 30c.

57 . A *locus classicus* for the ritual of closing the eyes during prayer in kabbalistic literature is *Zohar* 3:260b, where it is connected specifically with the prohibition of looking at the *Shekhinah*. Regarding this gesture during prayer, cf. E. Zimmer, "Poses and Postures during Prayer," *Sidra* 5 (1989): 92-94 (in Hebrew). On shutting the eyes as a contemplative technique in kabbalistic sources, see also M. Idel, *Studies in Ecstatic Kabbalah* (Albany: SUNY Press 1988), 134-36. For discussion of some of the relevant sources and the reverberation of this motif in Hasidic texts, cf. Z. Gries, *Conduct Literature (Regimen Vitae), Its History and Place in the Life of Beshtian Hasidism* (Jerusalem, 1989), 220-22 (in Hebrew).

58 . Cf. *Zohar* 2:95a, 98b-99a. Concerning this motif see E. R. Wolfson, "Beautiful Maiden without Eyes: Peshaṭ and Sod in Zoharic Hermeneutics," in *The Midrashic Imagination: Jewish Exegesis, Thought, and History*, ed. M. Fishbane (Albany: SUNY Press, 1993), 155-203.

59 . Sha'ar ha-Kawwanot (Jerusalem, 1963), 21c; cf. Peri 'Es Hayyim (Jerusalem, 1980), 168.

60 . Sha'ar ha-Kawwanot, 20c. Cf. Y. Avivi, "R. Joseph ibn Tabul's Sermons on the Kawwanot," in Studies in Memory of the Rishon le-Zion R. Yitzhak Nissim, ed. M. Benayahu (Jerusalem: Yud ha-Rav Nissim, 1985), 4: 82-83 (in Hebrew).

61 . Cf. 'Es Hayyim (Jerusalem, 1910), 29:2, 84a; Sha'ar Ma'amare Rashbi, 53a-b. See also Sha'ar ha-Kelalim, ch. 1, printed in 'Es Hayyim, 5c. The work is associated with three of Luria's disciples: Moses Yonah, Moses Najara, and Joseph Arzin. According to Y. Avivi, however, the text was authored by Hayyim Vital on the basis of compositions written by the aforementioned kabbalists. Cf. R. Meroz, "Redemption in the Lurianic Teaching," Ph.D. dissertation (Hebrew University, 1988), 90-91 (in Hebrew).

62 . Cf. 'Es Hayyim 39:1, 65a; 49:1, 112d; Qehillat Ya'aqov (Jerusalem, 1992), 3.

63 . Cf. the marginal note of Jacob Zemah in Hayyim Vital, Mavo She'arim, 2:2:6 (Jerusalem, 1892), 8c, according to that the eyes are said to correspond to the consciousness of Knowledge which is in the head (moah ha-da'at she-ba-ro'sh). Here too one sees the specific linkage of the eyes to a masculine potency, albeit displaced from the genital region of the body to the cranium. In that context the zoharic reference to the beautiful maiden without eyes is also mentioned.

64 . Sha'ar ha-Kawwanot, 59c.

65 . In the Lurianic material one can still find evidence as well for the more standard kabbalistic approach to the closing of the eyes as a technique to enhance mental concentration. See, e.g., Sha'ar Ruah ha-Qodesh (Jerusalem, 1874), 42d, 46d; Sha'ar ha-Kawwanot, 4a (regarding Luria's own practice of shutting his eyes during the private and public recitation of the eighteen benedictions).

66 . The point is underscored with respect to the righteous in the following Lurianic text in MS Oxford-Bodleian 1551, fol. 135b: "The secret of the female waters is the merit of our prayers. And also the souls of the righteous that ascend they arouse these male waters, i.e., the consciousness (mohin) of Ze'eir and his Nuqba'. After they arouse the male waters of Ze'eir they too are called female waters in relation to the 'Abba' and 'Imma', Yisra'el Sabba' and Tevunah, which are also joined together."

67 . See n. 20, this chapter.

68 . Sha'ar ha-Kawwanot, 46d.

69 . In this context, then, the female waters comprise demonic forces, aspects of judgment, that need to be purified. See I. Tishby, The Doctrine of Evil and the "Kelippah" in Lurianic Kabbalah (Jerusalem: Magnes Press, 1942), 89-90 (in Hebrew).

70 . 'Es Hayyim 29:3, 21d. Cf. Sha'ar Ma'amere Rashbi, 17d-18a. According to that complex passage, Ze'eir 'Anpin constitutes the female waters that are also identified as the encompassing light ('or ha-maqif). The male is contained in the female in the secret of impregnation (sod ha-'ibbur). This containment signifies the masculinization of the feminine rather than the feminization of the masculine.

71 . 'Es Hayyim 39:11, 76a.

Part IV

The Social Fabric of Gender and Judaism

Chapter 16

The Geopolitics of Jewish Feminism

Alice Shalvi

As one who travels frequently between Israel, Western Europe, and North America, as I have been doing during the past fifteen years, I cannot fail to be impressed by the enormous difference in kind and quantity of Jewish women's activity in each of these three regions.[1] In the United States, the Women's Liberation Movement of the late 1960s, many of the pioneers and leaders of which were Jewish, led increasing numbers of women to seek self-fulfillment in paid employment rather than devoting themselves to the home and family—the traditional focus and sphere of women's and most particularly (due to family pressures, social norms, and peer rivalry) of Jewish women's lives.

Feminism found expression not only in changing lifestyles but also in academic research, which illuminated areas of knowledge in history, sociology, psychology, and literature previously deemed unworthy of academic inquiry, while also bringing new perspectives to bear on areas previously addressed only from a male viewpoint. Feminist interpretation gradually attained legitimacy and perhaps nowhere has its impact been more revisionary and revolutionary than in the areas of religious knowledge, spiritual experience, and ritual practice.

Fortunate in the overall high educational level of U.S. Jewry, the rich diversity and the essential pluralism of U.S. Judaism, where the reform and conservative movements gained supremacy long before the Women's Movement arose, American Jewish women entered areas which were previously all-male preserves, demanding the right to study and be ordained as rabbis and cantors, donning *tallitot* (prayer shawls), putting on *tefillin* (phylacteries) and changing the language of traditional liturgy both to embrace the female sex and to eliminate gender specification. Even within the Orthodox sector of U.S. Jewish society, women devised new rituals and revived old, forgotten customs, celebrating *Rosh Hodesh*, marking *bat mitzvah*, performing girl baby naming ceremonies, reciting *tehinnah* (supplication).

Even enumerating only a select number of key events and presents milestones of U.S. Jewish feminism introduces an impressive and varied list:

1971	The founding of *Ezrat Nashim*.
1972	Ordination of the first woman Reform rabbi.
1973	First National Conference of Jewish Women.
1973	Special edition of *Response*, emanating from previous conference.
1976	Elizabeth Kolton, ed. *The Jewish Women*; Baum, Hyman, and Michel, eds. *The American Jewish Women*.
1981	Blu Greenberg, *On Women and Judaism*.
1982	The Women's *Tefilla* Network founded.
1983	Susannah Heschel, ed. *On Being a Jewish Feminist*; Susan Weidman Schneider, *Jewish and Female*.
1984	Rachel Biale, *Women and Jewish Law*.
1985	Jewish Theological Seminary decision to ordain women.

More recently there has been a true plethora of publications, conferences, catalogues, and films. Between February and April 1993 there were at least three major conferences on themes related to Jewish women, one sponsored by CLAL, another at Brandeis University, and another under the auspices of the Melton Center for Jewish Studies at Ohio State, intended inter alia to mark the twentieth anniversary of the first National Conference of Jewish Women.

The most revolutionary and radical element in all this activity was the questioning not only of the patriarchal nature of Judaism but even its very androcentricity, the masculinity of the godhead — acts involving revisioning and revising the basic tenets and premises that have underlain Judaism for over three millennia. To a large extent, I believe, this particular aspect of Jewish feminist activity was made possible by comparable work on other religions. An audaciously radical work such as Judith Plaskow's *Standing Again at Sinai* could, I submit, have been written nowhere but in the country of Mary Daly.

Women's infiltration of the male-dominated sphere of Jewish communal life has, however, been slower and less significant, possibly because this, rather than the synagogue, is where the true power of U.S. Jewry lies — a power that derives as much, if not more, from wealth as from ability or intellect. One Shoshana Cardin hardly makes an egalitarian summer, and although a few women serve in key positions in local and regional federations and even in national bodies, the number of women Combined Jewish Philanthropy (CJF) and United Jewish Appeal (UJA) leaders and decision-makers remains totally out of proportion to the vast number active at a lower and more menial level.

Significantly, to my mind, Hadassah — the largest women's Zionist organization — is distinctly non-feminist in its policy and activities, although in recent years its Jewish Studies department has begun to deal with feminist issues. The largest Jewish women's organization in the United States., the National Council of Jewish Women, is not Zionist and is primarily concerned with general social issues, not with Jewish ones. In other words, no large Jewish women's national organization combines a feminist outlook with primarily Jewish or Zionist activities.

In Western Europe the only numerically significant Jewish community today is in France, where the tremendous influx of Jews from North Africa has brought about a remarkable renaissance of Jewish life and religious practice, far exceeding what was previously achieved by the Ashkenazim. New and vibrant communities have sprung up where none previously existed, while older ones, such as those in Paris, Nice, and Lyon, have been resuscitated and augmented.

What is most significant about the younger generation of women in the community is that, having obtained a far better education than that which would have been theirs had they remained in Algeria, Tunisia, or Morocco or even come to Israel, many are choosing to do research precisely on the anthropology and sociology of their now-defunct communities. This was brought home to me most forcibly when I attended a conference on the Jewish Woman in Paris in December 1988. *Halakhah*, ritual, and women's status in Judaism at large were addressed only by the two guest speakers from abroad, Blu Greenberg and myself. Almost all the other presentations dealt with customs and traditions in the "old country." Actually, two works on women and Judaism had just been published, one by Janine Gdalya (the organizer of the conference), the other by journalist Renee David; but these were not the themes that interested the younger women, few if any of whom were religiously observant.

In Switzerland there is currently (Spring 1993) an interesting dispute that in many ways reflects that country's backwardness in admitting women into political and public life. The Basel *kehillah* is debating whether a woman may be elected president of the community. Following the submission of material sent by the Israel Women's Network on the status of this debate in Israel, where the High Court has ruled on the subject, the local rabbi has agreed that in principle an outstandingly gifted woman might be eligible for this totally non-*halakhic* post, but the implication is that no sufficiently remarkable creature has as yet appeared on the communal scene.

The United Kingdom provides a fascinating example of the debilitating nature of an essentially nonpluralistic community, over which a monolithic rabbinical establishment holds sway. Though there is a fairly strong ultra-orthodox presence in London and in certain cities in north-east England, and whereas a growing number of Jews are joining the Reform and Masorati (Conservative) movements, the vast majority of affiliated Jews belong to the establishment United Synagogue, not least because only through synagogue membership can one ensure burial in one of the country's Jewish cemeteries.

The United Synagogue is headed by the Chief Rabbi of Great Britain, a post which because of the favor in which Margaret Thatcher held the previous incumbent, Rabbi Immanuel Jacobovits led to this elevation to a peerage and seat in the House of Lords, like the Archbishop's of Canterbury and York, who head the establishment Church of England. Although he is an outspoken dove as far as the Israeli-Arab conflict is concerned and has done important work in medical ethics, he is not noted for his sympathy for women's ambitions in the area of reform or ritual participation. His (communally very active) wife is emphatic in her criticism of what she perceives as unseemly feminist tendencies.

Although, in common with trends in the general population, a smaller percentage of Jewish women achieve higher education in the United Kingdom. than in the United States, in the mid-1980s a growing number of university-educated women began to feel disenfranchised. Several of them were professionally engaged in Jewish education and increasingly dissatisfied at their inability to apply their considerable knowledge of Judaism and Judaic studies to their advancement within the synagogue or even the community at large. Just before Purim 1988, I introduced a group of them to the notion of *Rosh Hodesh* as a regular focal point for study, discussion, and possibly even ritual revival. When I was invited to the same home on *Rosh Hodesh* Tammuz over a year later, I was amazed and delighted to discover that the seed sown at that first meeting had fallen on fertile ground and, carefully tended by a few dedicated leaders, it had produced in the greater London area alone a whole crop of *Rosh Hodesh* groups that met regularly and worked diligently. In September 1992 these groups held a Shabbaton, with full prayer and Torah reading, expertly conducted by the women, who omitted those "sacred sayings" (*devarim she'be'kedusha*) for which a *minyan* (prayer quorum) is required.

Following this weekend, the women of the Stanmore community in northwest London received permission from their rabbi to hold a similar all-women's service on the synagogue premises, but news of their plans leaked out to the Chief Rabbi, who promptly forbade holding the service. He later permitted it to take place in a private home, with Torah reading from a book but not from a Torah scroll. The women acceded to his ruling, but the entire incident had stirred up an enormous controversy within the Anglo-Jewish community, which seems set to further weaken the increasingly shaky authority of the Chief Rabbi.

The current Chief Rabbi, Jonathan Sacks, in 1992 established a commission to report on the status and role of women in the community, which is due to submit its report in September 1993. If, as seems highly likely, this report is critical of the current state of affairs, he may well find himself at an impasse, caught between his alleged commitment to implementing the commission's recommendations and the conservatism of a reactionary all-male *bet din*.

Meanwhile, in June 1993, the Traditional *Rosh Hodesh* group joined forces with the Reform Movement's women's group, *The Half-Empty Bookcase*, to establish a Jewish Women's Network. At the some time, a Women's Aid Society has been established to help victims of domestic violence. So Jewish women in the United Kingdom are clearly on the move, at last.

And so to Israel, to contemplate a veritable *Via Dolorosa* of women's liberation. Let me begin by confessing that for the first twenty five years of statehood the myth of equality between the sexes held the majority of Israeli women in thrall, so that we complacently believed we were in no need of a liberation movement. That myth had its source in such potent symbols as women pioneers and kibbutz members ploughing the land, women soldiers fighting alongside men, and Golda Meir. The fact that an unduly large proportion of the neo-feminists who became active in the early 1970s were Anglo Saxons further encouraged the widely held belief that this was a foreign import that had no place in Israeli society.

At the beginning of 1973 the Jerusalem branch of the Association of University Women launched a series of study sessions on the status of women in Judaism. This was at the initiative of Priscilla Fishman, whose daughters Talya and Leora were then involved in U.S. Jewish feminist activities. I joined the group because I had just experienced an eye-opening instance of discrimination at the University of the Negev, where I was denied a senior administrative post (for which I was the best candidate) solely on the (explicitly stated) grounds that I was a woman. That experience led me to compare notes with female colleagues at the Hebrew University and, in turn, to the establishment of a caucus of women faculty members who demanded and obtained important changes in policy (e.g. the abolition of anti-nepotism rules discriminating against women; a longer trial period in which to publish adequately, for mothers of young children; equity in grants for the spouses of male and female faculty on research fellowships abroad, etc.) It also led me to deliver what, in retrospect, I see as the first piece of Israeli feminist literary criticism—a paper on *Sexual Politics in "Troilus and Cressida,"* the reception of which further heightened my awareness of how deeply embedded traditional notions of sex-based divisions and differences are in Israel.

The Yom Kippur War of 1973-74 shocked the government into an awareness of the extent to which women had been relegated to secondary roles in the Israel economy and the concomitant danger of this in times of national emergency, when all the (male-only) reserves were conscripted. One result of this (belated) recognition of reality was the establishment in 1975 (U.N. International Year of the Woman) of a commission of inquiry, headed by M. K. Ora Namir, which for the first time collected and collated reliable data on women's status in Israel. Significantly and perhaps predictably (as the remainder of my account will further clarify) the only one of the ten working committees into which the commission was divided that failed to function and was rapidly disbanded was that on women and *halakhah*, composed primarily of rabbis and lawyers, the latter of whom included Shulamit Aloni, already an outspoken opponent of *halakhic* authority.

The fall of the Labor government in 1977 was the primary, though not the sole, reason for the non-implementation of the majority of the commission's 241 recommendations, once these were submitted in February 1978. But consciousness had been raised and complacency irrevocably dispelled, particularly among the members of the commission, which comprised most of the leading women members of the community — professionals, politicians and activists in the various women's organizations.

Meanwhile, and subsequently, a number of events occurred of greater and lesser importance on both the personal and public level. In 1975 I became principal of the *Pelech School for Religious Girls*, which I rapidly turned into an even more progressive establishment than it had already been when the oldest of my three daughters joined it in 1973. The only religious school in which Talmud was a compulsory subject for girls, in 1977 it became the first to employ a woman to teach this subject — Beverly Gribetz, a new immigrant from the United States, who gave me the names of *Ezrat Nashim* activists Judith Hauptman and Arlene Agus as people I must meet on my first visit to New York that year. In them I found kindred spirits, religiously observant women who had dared to challenge conventions and premises developed over many centuries, and from them I gained courage to try to follow suit upon my return to Israel.

In 1978, Bar-Ilan University devoted its annual Contemporary Jewry Conference to Women and Judaism and this was my first encounter with Cynthia Ozick and Blu Greenberg. It also provided the setting for an amusing example of rabbinical evasion when Judy Hauptman gave a Talmud *Shi'ur* on Shabbat in the *bet ha — midrash* at Kibbutz Lavie, through the open windows of which we could see Rabbi Shear-Yashuv Cohen (now Chief Rabbi of Haifa) pacing up and down on the balcony, obviously with at least one ear open to the proceedings, while behind him Judy's husband wheeled their baby carriage!

In 1981 the Hebrew University's Senate finally approved the establishment of a unit of Gender Differences in Society. In 1982 Haifa University established a unit for Women's Studies and hosted the first international, intercultural, interdisciplinary "Women's Worlds" conference, which has since been held trienially, each time in a different country. In 1983 the Jerusalem Drama Workshop, an all-women theater group, first performed *Ma'seh Bruria*, the fruit of a long period of Talmud study on the part of the playwright, Aliza Israeli-Elyon; the two actresses; and the woman director, Joyce Miller, and the first of what have become a series of text-based productions. In spring 1984 Susannah Heschel delivered two lectures on Women and Judaism at Van Leer Institute in Jerusalem and, to the ill-concealed astonishment of the academic director of this august institution, drew capacity audiences.

In August 1984, the topic of the American Jewish Congress' annual U.S.-Israel Dialogue was "Woman as Jew, Jew as Woman: An Urgent Enquiry." To the surprise of the organizers, this was to prove a landmark in the development of Israeli feminist activity. It brought together a group of Jewish feminists from the United States (including Betty Friedan, Blu Greenberg, Cynthia Ozick, Elizabeth Holtzman, Cynthia Fuchs Epstein, Jacqueline Levin and other luminaries) to meet with a group of Israelis, primarily academicians expert in various areas of women's studies (such as Galia Golan, Frances Raday, and Dafna Izraeli), but also including Brigadier General Amira Dotan, head of the Women's Corps in the IDF, and one or two lawyers from Na'amat and WIZO, who were chosen for their professional expertise rather than on the basis of organizational membership.

Never in the twenty years of these annual dialogues had there been so electric an atmosphere; never had so many (women) members of the general public demanded to be allowed to attend what were normally closed dialogue sessions; never before had the normally rather innocuous discussions resulted in a series of action-oriented resolutions. Nor did any such dialogue before or since 1984 end with a march through the streets of Jerusalem, as we marched (or rather, walked as unobtrusively as possible for group of about 100 women) to the King David Hotel, whence we refused to be ejected until we had delivered our list of demands to Shimon Peres and Yitzhak Shamir, who were even then debating which of the two should have first turn at being prime minister after the "hung" Knesset elections of the previous month. That afternoon, glowing with euphoria at having actually achieved our immediate goal, a number of us decided to act on Frances Raday's suggestion that we establish a women's lobby, an organization that would be affiliated to no one party, but would have as its overall aim the furthering of women's status and the ultimate achievement of equality between the sexes. And so the Israel Women's Network was born, the direct outcome of vibrant interaction between American and Israeli feminists.

Following a series of "speak-outs" around the country, we rapidly concluded that reform of the rabbinical courts must be a top priority, but this was to take on a deeply entrenched, all-male and on the whole religiously fundamentalist establishment and to engage in a struggle that has reached its apex in 1993-94, in the international Year of the Agunah and the establishment of International Coalition of Agunah Rights (ICAR), which, uniquely, has brought together a very wide range of Jewish women's organizations in Israel and abroad.

Other conflicts with the rabbinical establishment were less directly concerned with *halakhah* and more with preconceptions regarding the role of women in public bodies that form part of the religious establishment in Israel. Thus, it took a High Court decision in 1987 to enable Leah Shakdiel, a highly knowledgeable and religiously observant woman, to take her seat on the Religious Services Council in Yeroham, to which she had been democratically elected, and a further High Court decision, also in 1987, to enable two women municipal councilors to serve on the electoral board that chose the Chief Rabbi of Tel Aviv-Jaffa. It is worth noting that in 1993 there was no need for court action when two women were included on the electoral board to choose the Chief Rabbis of Israel, even though one of the candidates was the same one who six years earlier had threatened to withdraw his candidacy if there were women on the electoral board in Tel Aviv.

In December 1987, Pnina Peli, a pioneer of women's prayer groups in Israel, organized a conference on Women and *Halakhah*, at which most of the presenters were U.S. women and Israeli men. Once again, divorce law proved a focus for acrimonious charges and countercharges and many noted with considerable indignation the patronizing tone of the few orthodox rabbis who deigned to address the plenary sessions.

A year later, the First International Jewish Feminist Conference was held in Jerusalem. Co-sponsored by the American Jewish Congress and the Israel Women's Network, it led to sharp conflict between the Israelis and Americans regarding agenda and content: the Americans didn't want to discuss the *intifada*, whereas the Israelis were offended by the "pre-emptive strike" that led to a pre-conference demonstration on the "Who is a Jew?" issue. Instead of the postconference establishment of international Jewish women's network, as was rather grandiosely proposed, there were two totally unplanned outcomes: the physical assault by ultra-orthodox men on the group of conference participants who held a service at the Western Wall led to the establishment of the *Women of the Wall*, on whose petition to be permitted to pray publicly at this national site the High Court has yet to rule; and the exclusion of the Israel-Arab conflict from the conference agenda led to a postconference meeting of Israeli and Palestinian Women, which in turn brought about the establishment of the *Women's Peace Network* (*Reshet*). (My active involvement in the Peace Net led to my resignation from *Pelech* in July 1990. The Religious Branch of the Ministry Education found my "pro-Palestinian" activities coupled with my anti-clerical feminism too much to swallow and threatened to withdraw accreditation if I remained in my job.)

Women's spirituality and women's religious ritual, so prominent in Jewish feminist discourse and activism in the United States, and now in the United Kingdom, are not the acknowledged agenda of Israeli feminists. There has been a significant increase in advanced Torah study among modern orthodox women, spearheaded by mothers of *Pelech* pupils who wished to emulate their daughters. This has resulted in the establishment of a number of institutions where orthodox women study Talmud or other texts (e.g. Bruria College and the Woman's Institute for Torah Studies, MATAN). Aviva Zornberg has emerged as an outstanding teacher of the Bible, but she also teaches only in English and has hence acquired a smaller number of disciples than the renowned Nehama Leibowitz.

Increased study and subsequent knowledge have led to a certain increase in celebratory ritual: *Simhat Bat* to mark the birth of a girl; *bat mitzvah* involving study and often a *drasha*, not merely a party; *Rosh Hodesh* groups; and women's *ushpizin*. Some academic research has been done: by Susan Sered on rituals among Kurdish women; by Tamar Elor on women in the *haredi* community; and by Ilana Pardes on the Bible, but there are no university courses related to women and Judaism, nor were we able to elicit the required support for an international conference on women theologians (which I proposed in 1986). However, in 1992 the Progressive Movement in Israel ordained its first woman rabbi, Na'ama Kelman, and this year the Masorati Movement in Israel has finally decided to follow the Jewish Theological Seminary's suit and ordain women.

What is of supreme importance in Israel and is at last having a very real impact on women's status in the country is political action. The Gulf War of 1991, like the Yom Kippur War almost twenty years earlier, brought home to women most forcibly the extent to which they were expected by society at large and by the government in particular to bear the double burden of homemaking on the one hand, and active participation in the workforce on the other; that is, to fulfill two roles that, at time of war and given the total closure of the school and child-care system, proved irreconcilable with each other. Coupled with a sharp increase in domestic violence and spousal murder, which that year reached an unprecedented forty-one women killed, the Gulf War experience led women to realize they must be more actively engaged in the actual decision-making process. A Women Voters' Registration Operation conducted by the Israel Women's Network led to a marked increase in women's membership in political parties and to vociferous demands for greater representation of women in each party's list of candidates for the Knesset elections in June 1992. As a result, the number of women MKs increased from eight to eleven, all of whom openly declare themselves feminists and are working together across party lines to improve women's status through legislation.

The fight for greater rights for women inevitably encounters the opposition of the religious parties and the religious establishment. Thus one cannot avoid the melancholy conclusion that so long as religion and politics are inextricably intertwined and the state-sanctioned (and state-financed) religious establishment remains exclusively orthodox, with no official possibility of pluralism, the majority of Israelis will remain alienated from Jewish religious tradition and women will remain marginal in everything pertaining to that tradition. The only hope for change lies in an influx from North America of Conservative and Reform Jews who care passionately for religious pluralism and will constitute a substantial portion of the electorate favoring separation of religion and state.

It appears to me to be the inescapable conclusion of the (albeit superficial and personal) account presented here that, in accordance with the well-known dictum *Wie es Christelt sich, azoy Yidelt's sich* (roughly translated: When in Rome, do as the Romans do), what occurs within Jewish society is profoundly influenced by and approximates what occurs within the host society. When the latter is pluralistic in nature, with no central religious establishment or ruling religious caste, the Jewish minority can be equally pluralistic and decentralized. This explains the extraordinary vigor of U.S. Jewry (despite the prevalence of intermarriage and assimilation) and, within U.S. Jewry, of Jewish feminism. In the United Kingdom, an official rabbinical establishment hampers comparable development, and there is not as strong a general feminist tradition to encourage Jewish feminism; consequently it lags behind that in the United States. Most depressing of all is the situation in Israel, where a strong, fundamentalist religious establishment, enjoying increasing political power in the legislature and the government, is able to strangle at birth any nascent religious feminism and even to frustrate women's fight for equal rights in secular life wherever that impinges in any way on religious "principles" or *halakhah*, as in the case of abortion.

Nevertheless, incorrigible optimist that I am, I have a strong feeling that, with feminism and egalitarianism alive and well in Israel today, Israeli Jewish feminism (i.e., feminist activity related to women's role and status within Jewish religion in a Jewish State) is waiting to be born.

Perhaps *you*—the feminists of North America—will be its surrogate parents?

NOTE

1. What follows is not an academic survey, but rather a personal account of an ongoing process that I have observed over the past twenty years and of which I have been privileged to some extent to be a part. Hence the overly-profuse use of the first-person singular. It seems I just had the good luck to be in the right place at the right time.

Chapter 17

From Equality to Transformation: The Challenge of Women's Rabbinic Leadership

Laura Geller

Twenty years ago some people thought we had come to the end of a journey, that we had reached the promised land of equality for Jewish men and women. After all, a revolution had occurred in Jewish life. Women could be rabbis.

Twenty years ago I was a rabbinic student at Hebrew Union College-Jewish Institute of Religion (HUC-JIR) in New York. I studied in the old building on West 68th Street, which was around the corner from where Sally Priesand was serving as the first woman rabbi. I was the only woman in my class, one of only two women rabbinic students in the New York school. My classmates were supportive and friendly; generally my teachers, all of whom were men, were rooting for my success. Most of them believed that because there were women rabbis and women rabbinic students, we had already succeeded in reaching equality and equal opportunity.

Few of them understood the particular pressures and the unique challenges that I experienced in my years at the College. Only other women understood the pain of patriarchal texts, the confusion of finding myself absent in the stories that shape our tradition, the desperate need to re-envision a Judaism that includes the experience of all Jews. Only other women understood the pressure of being a pioneer, of wanting to be considered as capable as the men without being forced to give up my own sense of balance, of wanting a life where work is a blessing within the context of other blessings—family, commitments, friends.

Although these were problems only women understood twenty years ago, there were hardly any other women with whom to share these feelings. I felt as though I was wandering in the wilderness, lonely for the dancing of Miriam and the women.

What a difference two decades make! As of this June 1993 there were 219 women ordained as Reform rabbis, and women now comprise almost half the students at HUC-JIR. Also by June 1993, there were 52 women rabbis ordained by the Reconstructionist Rabbinical College and 50 from the Jewish Theological Seminary. Our lives as women who are rabbis are full of blessings: work that challenges and stimulates us; colleagues, both women and men, to share our struggles and our successes; partners, children, friends, community. We have much to celebrate.

Women rabbis have changed the face of Judaism. At the simplest level, the change is obvious. As Rabbi Ellen Lewis wrote a few years ago: "When I first assumed my present pulpit, I tried to do everything just like my predecessor did. I had great respect for his work in the congregation and was not looking to be revolutionary. I just wanted to be the rabbi. What I found was that, even if I did the same things he did, when I did it it looked and sounded different." At her first Bat Mitzvah as a student rabbi, the young thirteen-year-old girl looked up at Rabbi Lewis as they practiced on the pulpit and asked: "At my Bat Mitzvah do you think we can wear matching dresses?"

Other similar stories abound. Rabbi Deborah Prinz tells the story of her first Shabbat on the pulpit of Central Synagogue. Rabbi Sheldon Zimmerman had for years been changing the language of the prayerbook to make it gender neutral. Rabbi Prinz read the prayerbook the same way. But at the end of the service a congregant came up to Rabbi Zimmerman to complain: "See, you hire a woman and the first thing she does is change the prayerbook!"

At the conclusion of my first High Holy Days services as the rabbi at the University of Southern California, two congregates rushed up to me. The first, a middle-age woman, blurted out:

Rabbi, I can't tell you how different I felt about services because you are a woman. I found myself feeling that if you can be a rabbi maybe I can be a rabbi too. For the first time in my life I felt as if I could learn those prayers, I could study Torah, I could lead this service, I could do anything you could do. Knowing that made me feel much more involved in the service, much more involved with Judaism! Also the service made me think about God in a different way, I'm not sure why.

The second congregant had something very similar to say, but with a slightly different emphasis. He was a man in his late twenties.

Rabbi, I realized that if you could be a rabbi then *certainly* I could be a rabbi. Knowing that made the service somehow more accessible for me. I didn't need you to do it for me. I could do it, be involved with Jewish tradition, without depending on you.

In each of these anecdotes, and there are hundreds more, the theme is the same: people experience women rabbis differently from the way they experience male rabbis. And that difference changes everything: the way they experience prayer, their connection to the tradition, and even their image of divinity.

When women function as clergy, the traditional American division between clergy and lay person begins to break down. A woman who is an Episcopal priest told me that when she offers the Eucharist, people take it from her differently from the way they would take it from a male priest, even though she follows the identical ritual. People are used to being fed by women, and so the experience is more natural, and hence less mysterious.

People don't attribute to women the power and prestige often attributed to men. Therefore when women become rabbis, or clergy of any kind, there is often less social distance between the congregant and the clergy. The lessening of social distance and the reduction of the attribution of power and status leads to the breakdown of hierarchy within a religious institution. "If you can be a rabbi, then certainly I can be a rabbi!" "Can we wear matching dresses?"

Women rabbis have had an profound impact on the way many Jews experience divinity. Although most of the systematic work in the area of Jewish feminist theology has been done by women scholars who are not themselves rabbis, the very presence of women rabbis has forced many congregants to confront God in different ways. For some Jews, there is an unconscious transference that they make between their rabbi and God. As long as their rabbi is male, they are not even aware that they associate him in some way with a male divinity. But when the rabbi is female, they can't make that unconscious transference. And so they begin to confront directly their images of God and perhaps even open themselves to ask "who is the God I experience and how can I speak toward God in prayer?" Here too, although much of the most creative work in prayer and liturgy is being written by feminists who are not themselves rabbis, it is often women rabbis who are on the front line when it comes to liturgy.

Rabbis are on the front line of ritual work as well. Congregants come to rabbis for help in negotiating the transitions of their lives-the joys and the losses. Women rabbis have created ceremonies and rituals to meet the real-life experience of the Jews they serve, and many of those rituals are for women. Covenant ceremonies for daughters, b'not mitzvah, weddings, divorces, ceremonies of healing from loss, miscarriage, abortion, infertility, adult survivors of childhood incest, becoming fifty, and sixty, children leaving home...are all actual transitions in the lives of Jews that have led women rabbis to create ritual. Along with other feminists—scholars, educators, cantors, lay people—women rabbis have been part of the transformation of Judaism. After twenty years, we do have much to celebrate.

But, we also have reason to be concerned. Those who believed that the ordination of women itself was enough to bring us to the promised land of an egalitarian Judaism were wrong. Even after twenty years, after over two hundred women have been ordained by the Reform Movement, there are still significant differences between the careers of men and women rabbis. This difference is of great concern to me, so I would like to try to understand it. I will focus my remarks on the Reform Movement because it is the movement I know best, but I suspect that similar observations could be made about the Reconstructionist and Conservative Movement as well.

Of the 189 Reform women rabbis already ordained, none serve as the head of a thousand-member congregation. This is particularly troubling given that the traditional measure of success for rabbis in the Reform Movement is the size of their congregations. What explains the fact that women rabbis are not assuming positions that Reform Judaism has defined as powerful? There are two different ways that this phenomenon has been addressed until now. The first way, what I would call the "different voice" theory, is best illustrated in an article by Rabbi Janet Marder published in the Summer 1991 issue of "Reform Judaism." Rabbi Marder suggests that women have not assumed positions that are considered powerful because women are choosing a different path. She describes how some women see themselves as agents for change, consciously attempting to redefine rabbinic leadership.

Through conversation with different women rabbis, she argues that many women rabbis share a commitment to three fundamental values that are central to their rabbinate: balance, intimacy, and empowerment.

The value of balance was repeatedly mentioned to Rabbi Marder in her interviews with women colleagues. Over and over again, women challenged the conventional view that the rabbinate must be an all-consuming lifetime calling. In the past, male rabbis have often tended to take pride in how many hours they devote to their work. Rabbi Marder found that many women emphasized the ways they have made room in their life for other priorities and have been willing to limit the hours spent in work. Some have chosen to work part time, or serve smaller synagogues or in rabbinic positions that require fewer evening or weekend commitments; others have accepted a lower salary for lighter responsibilities.

Given the high priority these women place on balance, it is not surprising that some women seem to be choosing different career paths from the one the Reform Movement holds out as the "success track." Rabbi Marder quotes Rabbi Arnold Sher, director of the Reform Movement's Rabbinic Placement Commission: "I have no statistical way of proving it, but my gut feeling is that most men in A congregations (up to 120 members) aspire to move into larger ones. It's very clear that women in AB congregations (166-300 members) are not seeking larger pulpits." Some women are choosing smaller congregations that not only grant the rabbi more control over her time and her schedule, but also provide the opportunity to form intimate relationships and create community.

Many women rabbis echo the words of Reconstructionist Rabbi Sandy Sasso: "Women come to the rabbinate with a different set of experiences. Women's center of focus is on people rather than principles. Women's version of reality is not a hierarchical model where one's goal is to move up, to be alone at the top, but rather a network model where the goal is to connect with others, to be together at the center."

The "different voice" theory is compelling because it seems to describe the personal choices of many women rabbis I know. In each individual case it makes sense why a particular women has chosen a particular "alternative" career path. But viewed as an aggregate, as a class of rabbis, the difference between men's and women's careers is stunning-and depressing. Are we freely choosing this voice? Or is the "different voice" argument a justification for keeping some of us out of positions that have been defined as powerful?

An alternative way to understand the discrepancy in the career paths of men and women is to argue that there remains discrimination against women in the rabbinate, that is, a glass ceiling. This argument takes into account the obstacles to equality that women rabbis still face. First, there are significant salary discrepancies between women and men. Rabbi Mark Winer has been monitoring salary data for the Central Conference of American Rabbis (CCAR) for the past fourteen years. His data show an alarming disparity in wages between men and woman in the rabbinate, with the wage gap getting larger the further one is removed from entry-level positions. At the middle-size congregation, over three hundred families, for example, there is no woman even close to the median salary. It is hard to understand this discrepancy in any other way than as evidence of endemic discrimination in the compensation of women rabbis around the country. Although both the CCAR and the Union of American Hebrew Congregations (UAHC) have gone on record deploring this salary gap, to date little has been done to remedy the problem.

A second problem relates to the specific pressures on women rabbis who become mothers. In the early years after the ordination of the first woman, there was a great deal of talk among woman rabbis about maternity leave. We were advised back then to handle each situation as individuals, and to wait until we had a solid and sure relationship with our congregation or community before we raised the question. The advice from the leadership of the Reform Movement in those old days was that whereas a congregation would never refuse their beloved rabbi her maternity leave, they might not hire the rabbi in the first place if maternity leave was part of the rabbi's negotiation for the position. Now, twenty years later, the Reform Movement has taken a proactive stance. The most recent guidebook for Rabbinic Congregational Relations includes a recommendation of two months paid maternity leave plus accrued vacation. It is far from perfect, and often congregations ignore it, but it is the beginning of the Reform Movement's attempt to address the reality that in our society childcare is still viewed as primarily the responsibility of women.

The decision on the part of the CCAR and the UAHC to articulate the norms for how women must be treated concerning maternity leave could provide an important precedent for the Reform Movement to take real leadership in the other areas where women rabbis are concerned. But, at least until now, there does not seem to be an attempt to confront other areas of inequality.

There are many women who, given their years since ordination, are qualified for consideration as rabbis of thousand member family congregations. Thus far, the Reform Movement has left them alone to decide whether or not to apply for these positions. Most don't apply. Part of the problem may be a failure of imagination. Many women colleagues have difficulty imagining being a senior rabbi because there are no models of women senior rabbis. Some women acknowledge that their own experience as assistant rabbis, particularly the ways they were treated by their seniors, discouraged them from even considering it. Other women rabbis have stated that they believe women are hired more quickly than men as assistants because male senior rabbis believe that women are more docile and easier to manage. The perception that success as an assistant requires docility may make it hard for women who have succeeded as assistants to imagine themselves as the one in charge. Recently, a very talented women colleague who had been serving as an associate rabbi was invited by her congregation to apply for the position as senior when it became vacant. She turned down the invitation to apply, preferring instead to serve as interim senior rabbi until an appropriate successor could be found. Among her concerns was the sense that she would not be able to handle the senior rabbi's job. However, after the year as interim rabbi, she was able to imagine herself as the senior rabbi. And by then it was too late.

Perhaps the Reform Movement should have intervened as it finally did on the issue of maternity leave, interrupting the "normal" course of events to encourage the woman to apply by suggesting that the congregation wait for a year before beginning its search. In order for this kind of affirmative action or differential treatment to be considered, the Reform Movement must first view women rabbis as a class and acknowledge that the structures that presently exist favor men by definition. Synagogues, and other Jewish institutions as they presently exist, assume, for example, that the rabbi is not the primary caretaker of a preschool child. Women who are mothers are, as a class, frustrated when they imagine themselves as rabbis of institutions that claim to be gender neutral but in fact assume a male standard. Gender then becomes a question of power, with maleness the norm and femaleness the other.

These obstacles to equality are ultimately about power. A fourth critical issue, which is also about power, is the representation of women in the structure of our movements. After twenty years there are still very few women faculty at the Hebrew Union College-Jewish Institute of Religion. Just a few months ago the Cincinnati campus hired its second woman faculty member in the Rabbinical School. Los Angeles has one and New York has none. Only one woman holds the rank of academic head, and women constitute only ten to fifteen percent of the Board of Governors. Only one regional director of the UAHC is a woman. The relative absence of women in the academic and professional branches of Reform Judaism supports the reality that the institutions favor men by definition.

Finally, women will remain powerless to crash through the glass ceiling until we are free to talk about the full reality of being a woman in the working world, and this includes being a woman working as a leader in a Jewish institution or congregation. The fifth, and perhaps the most difficult obstacle to women rabbis is the reality of sexual harassment and violations of sexual boundaries. Many women colleagues have stories that are shared only in private conversations with other women. Some experiences relate to inappropriate comments made to us during interviews about physical appearance, clothes or even breast size. Other experiences relate to women rabbis being threatened by inappropriate sexual advances by board members. Some women rabbis even have memories (some distant and some recent) of inappropriate advances made by faculty or administrators at the Hebrew Union College.

The 1992 and the 1993 Pacific Association of Reform Rabbis Conventions included sessions on sexual harassment. This is a good beginning. But there is still pressure on women rabbis to join a conspiracy of silence about violations of boundaries committed by male colleagues with congregants or staff. Therefore it is particularly welcome that the CCAR Journal has published Rachel Adler's important work about the complicated issues of power involved in violations of sexual boundaries between rabbis and congregants, thereby opening up a public conversation about our power as counselors and the devastation that occurs when we violate sexual boundaries.

For women rabbis to feel safe we must see the official agencies of all of our movements reacting strongly to condemn all these violations, between senior rabbi and assistant, between rabbis and congregants, between powerful congregant and woman rabbi, between professor or administrator and student. All of the movements of American Jewish life must mandate effective education and training of all rabbis, investigate complaints, and develop and monitor a disciplinary procedure. The old message that these movements just look the other way and even reward violators with better jobs is a threatening message to women rabbis and congregants.

So how should we understand the difference between the careers of men and women rabbis? Ought we, along with Carol Gilligan, to explain the different choices women make in light of women's different experience that propels them to seek connection rather than hierarchy?[1] Or ought we, along with Catharine MacKinnon,[2] to counter that because women lack power and don't participate in making the rules, we have no alternative but to seek other, less powerful, opportunities? Are women rabbis' choices affirmatively challenging the rabbinic establishment's view that bigger is better, that moving up and moving on is the way to define success, or are women not being given a chance to play on the same field? Are these different choices attributable to a different women's voice or to women being excluded from the dominant conversation?

The past twenty years show evidence of both possibilities: exclusion and of different choices. Perhaps both are true. Or perhaps there is a third possibility: we can't even talk about the possibilities of different choices until we even out the playing field and acknowledge that the structures themselves must be transformed to make room for women's participation.

The experience of the past two decades has made it clear that the ordination of women was just the beginning of our journey. Just as it took our people forty years of wandering in the desert to reach a rich and fertile promised land, the journey toward the promised land of an egalitarian Judaism is far from over. But the years of wandering have provided a glimpse into the future, the opportunity to revolutionize old ways of thinking, and to begin to shift the paradigm from equality between men and women to the transformation of Judaism itself. We are clearly not there yet. But even as the struggle for equality continues, we can begin to see the questions raised by transformation.

The impact of women rabbis on Judaism begins with the revolutionary idea that women's experience ought to be acknowledged and valued. This idea poses fundamental challenges to rabbinic Judaism. It means that women are subjects as well as objects, that women are fully part of the story of our tradition. It means we must wrestle with our sacred texts to hear the voices of women just as we need to wrestle with the structures of our modern Jewish institutions to make room for women's commitments and styles. It means that we must listen to the views of the others who have been silent or invisible in our tradition. It means that those texts and those institutions will change as they are shaped in response to these different voices.

What would Jewish institutions look like if they were shaped in response to the values that seem to be shared by so many women-balance, intimacy, and empowerment? Already the impact of women has been felt by the men who have been their classmates and colleagues. Rabbi Sher told me that, in his view, women rabbis have "humanized" male rabbis, that women have taught men about balance. He argues that the definition of success is starting to change as men as well as women are choosing more often to stay in middle-size congregations, preferring continuity and intimacy and the pleasures of organic growth to the more traditional rewards of prestige and power. These kinds of changes may well change the shape of synagogues and raise new kinds of questions. What would a synagogue look like if success were defined not as climbing to the top of a hierarchy, but rather as being at the center of a web of connections? What will careers in the rabbinate look like when maleness is no longer assumed to be the norm, when rabbis are partners rather than seniors and associates, when job sharing is a real possibility, when parental leave is equally accessible to men as to women? What will salaries be like when men as well as women choose to trade some money for more flexible schedules? What will Jewish communities be like when rabbis stop being surrogate Jews and instead enable their communities to take responsibility for their Jewish lives? What will Jewish institutions be like when we make room for the many different kinds of Jews we know there are: Jews in different kinds of families, Jews searching for community and spirituality? And what will the rabbinate be like when we value the diversity among us rabbis: women and men; married and single; lesbian, gay, and heterosexual; parents and non-parents; scholars and activists; rabbis who serve in congregations and Hillels and organizations and hospitals and schools—and the list goes on.

These questions of transformation are the most important questions posed by women's rabbinic leadership after twenty years. These are the questions that will shape the next twenty years of our journey. And these are the questions that will lead us out of the wilderness to a Judaism that truly embraces both women and men. [3]

NOTES

1. Carol Gilligan, *In a Different Voice* (Cambridge: Harvard University Press, 1982).
2. Catharine MacKinnon, *Feminism Unmodified: Discourses on Life and Law* (Cambridge: Harvard University Press, 1987).
3. I wish to thank the participants of the Jewish Feminist Research Group of the American Jewish Congress' Jewish Feminist Center (including Professors Tamara Eskenazi and

David Ellenson, Rabbis Sue Levi Elwell and Janet Marder, Marcia Spiegel, Diane Schuster, Nurit Shein, Carol Plotkin, Marleen Marks, Linda Thal, Rachel Adler, Yaffa Weisman, and Michele Lenke) for the invaluable discussion about the first draft of this chapter. In addition, I would also like to thank Rabbis Mark Winer, Debra Hachen, Deborah Prinz and Arnold Sher for their helpful conversations about these issues and Rabbis Emily Feigenson and Patricia Karlin Newman, Professor Judith Resnik, and Ben Bycel for their thoughtful and critical readings of earlier drafts.

Chapter 18

Triple Play: Deconstructing Jewish Women's Lives

Sylvia Barack Fishman

Introduction

When a navigator or astronomer is having difficulty getting her bearings on the position of a distant object, she can employ a mathematical technique called triangulation. By measuring the angles between the points of a triangle, she can determine the exact position of the elusive object. The farther apart the points of the triangle, the more reliable the technique, and the more exactly will the object be located. Triangulation is a technique in the social sciences as well, in which multiple methods of information gathering are employed in order to more accurately pinpoint and explore social trends.

Feminists and other contemporary social scientists have urged greater permeability of boundaries between social science research and historical analysis.[1] I'd like to suggest just this type of triple play, or triangulation, using an interdisciplinary approach to describe, analyze, and interpret contemporary American Jewish life. By using data from quantitative, statistical studies together with qualitative data and literary analysis, we create an interdisciplinary framework for interpretive analysis. The use of these three disciplines serves as a corrective for methodological shortcomings that may occur when one particular method is used exclusively. The resulting analysis can be richer as well as more representative.

This chapter uses the tools of quantitative and qualitative social science and literary analysis to explore changing behaviors and attitudes among American Jewish women, and manifestations of connectedness to and alienation from Judaism, the Jewish people, and Jewish institutions among this group. One of the great lacunae in much writing about Jews and Judaism has been the tendency to analyze the actions and cultural artifacts of men alone and call such studies a "history" or "sociology of the Jews." During the past fifteen years, scholars analyzing the roles, contributions, and experiences of women in every period of Jewish history have done much to ameliorate this situation. However, as Lynn Davidman pointed out following the publication of her book on newly Orthodox Jewish women,[2] although gender has emerged as a significant factor in understanding the behaviors and attitudes of social groups, sociological studies of contemporary American Jewish women are rare. Women are the subject of this case study, but this interdisciplinary method is appropriate and useful for studying all areas of contemporary American Jewish life, including transformations in Jewish family life, intermarriage, and Jewish organizational and philanthropic behavior.

When we study contemporary Jewish life, we stand in the center, as participant-observers, in the flux of change, as eminent social psychologist Simon Herman remarked in his landmark study of Jewish identity.[3] In order to study contemporary life effectively, we use, in addition to the tools of the historian, specialized tools of information gathering and analysis that enable us to examine a constantly changing world. Thus, the study of contemporary life is a little like putting together a jigsaw puzzle in which the shapes of the pieces are constantly shifting, even as the study and analysis proceed.

Qualitative Data

One important new data base for quantitative research is the first national survey of the American Jewish community in two decades, the 1990 National Jewish Population Survey (NJPS), a cooperative study supervised by the Council of Jewish Federations.[4] It involved initial screening of some 125,813 adult Americans, locating 5,146 households that could be identified as Jewish. Further screening selected 2,441 households and administered lengthy questionnaires to respondents in those households, asking not only about the respondent, but also about each member of the household.

Marriage and Identity

National data from the 1990 NJPS show relatively high rates of singlehood and rising rates of divorce, with the result that fewer than two-thirds of American Jews are currently married. Even among Jews from age 35 to 64, traditionally the most married of all groups, 25% of women are not currently married. This marks a dramatic break with the recent past. In 1953 almost two-thirds of Jewish women were married by age 22 and more than three-quarters were married by age 25. Today, Jewish women, as they always have, still marry slightly later than other white women—and all Americans marry later now than they did 40 years ago. However, Jewish rates of marriage and divorce today more closely match those of the general population than they do those of American Jews in the past.[5]

Today facts change rapidly, and yesterday's accepted truths are tomorrow's untruths. For example, in the 1940s, 1950s, and 1960s, Jewish women as a group had distinguished themselves by their punctilious use of family planning and birth control, and as a result expected family size among Jews was almost identical to actual completed family size. When Jews said they wanted a family of 3 children, they almost always ended up with 3 children. During the 1980s, prominent Jewish demographers insisted that despite the fact that Jewish women were significantly postponing marriage and childbirth, these women would eventually give birth to the number of children they said they wished to have, an average of 2.2 children, which is considered adequate fertility level to prevent the shrinkage of the Jewish population.[6] I argue against equating expected family size with actual family size, because of delayed marriage. Effective use of contraception is a salient factor only when one is trying to prevent conception. Given medical reports that demonstrated the strong correlation between infertility and the aspiring mother's age, I hypothesize that demographers should no longer assume expected family size would be equal to completed family size.[7]

Data from the 1990 NJPS show that changes in marriage patterns have indeed affected both the timing and the size of today's families. In 1990, more than half of women age 25 to 34 (55%), and one-quarter of those age 35 to 44 had no children. Although almost all American Jewish women age 45 or over reported having children, either biological or adopted, it is not clear that all or even most of one out of four childless women in the age 35 to 44 group will in fact achieve the status of motherhood.

But there is a gap between fertility expectations and completed family size among Jewish women today. Jewish women are less likely than any other religious or ethnic groups to state that they wish to remain childless. Most American Jewish couples hope to have children "some day." Calvin Goldscheider and Francis Kobrin Goldscheider point out that among Jewish populations—unlike among Protestants and Catholics—"educational attainment is directly rather than inversely related to the fertility expectations." Thus, "Jews with doctorates expect 2.2 children and only 11% expect to be childless; Jews with college degrees expect only 1.8 children and 21% expect to be childless." In contrast, the reverse pattern is true of highly educated Protestant and Catholic women.[8]

However, highly educated Jewish women do not actually have as many children as they once expected. Although Jewish career women are more committed to the idea of having families than any other group of career women, they are at least as likely as other white middle class women to postpone the onset of childbearing until they have reached what they consider to be an appropriate level of financial or occupational achievement. Expectations do not always give way to reality. As Frank Mott and Joyce Abma point out, Jewish women age 16 to 26 years old who were interviewed in the national study in 1969-70 expected to have an average of 2.5 children; that same cohort, today age 35 to 44, have in fact born an average of 1.5 children and expect an average of 1.7 children when their families are completed.[9] Contrary to their own expectations, the Goldscheiders conclude that "as education increases among both Jewish men and women, the proportion with no children increases." Indeed, "among those with a masters degree . . . Jews have significantly higher levels of childlessness than non-Jews."[10]

Labor Force Participation

Another enormous change in the lives of American Jewish women centers around patterns of employment. The majority of American Jewish women today continue to work for pay outside the home throughout their childbearing and child-rearing years. Among American Jewish women age 44 and under, only 17% are homemakers, 11% are students, 70% work for pay (59% work fulltime and another 11% work parttime), and 4% are not employed (1990 NJPS Jewish female respondents). These changes have affected women across the religious spectrum, and few differences are seen between women who call themselves Orthodox, Conservative, or Reform/Reconstructionist in terms of the likelihood that they will work.

In contrast, until very recently, Jewish women were distinguished by the pronounced plummeting pattern of their participation in the labor force. In 1957, only 12% of Jewish women with children under age 6 worked outside the home, compared to 18% of White Protestants. As recently as 15 years ago, it was still true that Jewish women were likely to work until they became pregnant with their first child, and then to drop out of the labor force until their youngest child was about junior high school age.

Jewish Communal Involvement

The Jewish and contemporary American secular lives of women are closely related. The data show that secular education is not, as many have portrayed it, a factor that undermines strong Jewish identification. Despite widespread Jewish communal anxiety about the impact of higher education and careerism upon the communal activities of American Jewish women today and tomorrow, the data show that the "enemy" of the dynamic involvement of Jewish women in American Jewish communal life is not higher education for women or careerist aspirations, but rather a weak Jewish life in other areas as well— socially, culturally, and religiously—regardless of educational or occupational profile.[11]

As in the past, single women are much less likely to volunteer time for Jewish causes than married women. This is a long-standing pattern, but it is of much more concern to Jewish communal leaders today because the single years make up a much larger segment of women's lives. Among married women, the most likely group to volunteer, mixed marriage—rather than education, occupation, age, presence of children in the home, or any other factor—marks the single greatest difference in levels of female volunteerism for Jewish causes. Jewish women who are married to non-Jewish men have drastically lower rates of volunteerism for Jewish causes than other married Jewish women. Among American Jewish women age 44 and under, 5% of mixed married Jewish women volunteer time for Jewish organizations, compared to 42 % of Jewish women who are married to Jewish men.

Persons critical of the phenomena of working Jewish mothers have sometimes charged that careerism leads women away from a Jewish social life—and ultimately away from Jewish involvements. Friendship circles are a very significant factor in whether or not Jewish women volunteer time for Jewish causes. Jewish women who say that none of their best friends are Jewish almost never volunteer for Jewish causes, although 40% of them volunteer for non-Jewish causes. Thirteen percent of Jewish women who have some Jewish friends volunteer for Jewish causes and 40% volunteer for non-Jewish causes only. However, among Jewish women who have mostly Jewish friends, 35% volunteer for Jewish causes and 19% volunteer for only non-Jewish causes.

In the past, popular impressions were that the most traditional Jewish women would be at home with their children and have the most predominantly Jewish friendship circles, whereas less traditional Jewish women would work outside the home for pay and have more non-Jewish friends, presumably persons they may have met at work. However, data on American Jewish women age 18 to 44 does not support these stereotypes. The religious makeup of women's friendship circles is not dependent on employment status.

Jewish Education

Friendship circles, are, however, closely tied to extent of Jewish education among younger American Jewish women. The combination of years and type of Jewish education has a statistically significant positive relationship to every aspect of Jewish life — Jewish philanthropic behavior, emotional attachment to Israel, Jewish organizational participation, levels of religious ritual performance, desire to live in a Jewish milieu — as well as a negative relationship to levels of intermarriage. This analysis shows that intermarriage is not affected today by higher levels of secular education or by gender — two areas that used to be thought very relevant — but that one of the most important indicators for Jewish behaviors among American Jews today, both men and women, is the extent of their formal Jewish education. Indeed, formal Jewish education is one of the best indicators of whether Jewish women will marry Jews, volunteer for Jewish causes, and give their children Jewish education.[12]

Orthodox women are the most likely to have received some formal Jewish education and non-observant or "just Jewish" women the least likely, although significant numbers of older Orthodox women did not receive any formal Jewish education — reflecting the opinion of some Orthodox thinkers that girls need not know the holy tongue. Orthodox Jews are more likely to provide their daughters with a rigorous Jewish education than any other wing of Judaism. Half of all born-Jewish respondents age 18 to 44 who were raised as Orthodox Jews received day school education. And among those Jews the percentages of boys and girls in day school were virtually identical. The gender gap in Jewish education today is seen primarily among supplementary school students and primarily among persons whose households of origin were Conservative or Reform/Reconstructionist. Jewish education for girls rises in Conservative and Reform settings among younger women who are presumably more likely to have been affected by the growing popularity of the *Bat Mitzvah* ceremony.

Thus, we learn from quantitative data about large patterns of change in the lives of American Jewish women. We learn that Jewish women today are more likely than Jewish women in the past or than non-Jewish American women today to work toward complicated combinations of educational, occupational, and personal aspirations. Jewish women are likely to receive high levels of education, to work through their adult lives, and to express a desire for children. We learn that these complex lifestyles are not necessarily associated with attenuated Jewish connections, but weak levels of Jewish identification are associated with minimal levels of Jewish education and with personal definitions of identity that exclude "Jewish by religion."

Limitations of Quantitative Research

We often prize quantitative research because it seems to be a way around the subjectiveness of human perceptions. It is sometimes assumed that because emotional factors supposedly do not enter into the historical or scientific analysis of a given society or historical period, the descriptions proposed by historians and social scientists represent objective facts. However, the scholar who transforms raw materials into an analysis of experience also shapes one's understanding of that experience. By selecting for analysis certain facts and not others, by analyzing those facts with a distinctive interpretive framework, and by presenting those facts in a particular context, analysts create a view of reality that wittingly or unwittingly bears his or her own personal imprint.

As Simon Herman forthrightly states:

> Social scientists, like other men and women, have their biases. . . these beliefs and valuations, which shape the social scientists approach to any social problem, often remain hidden even to the scientist . . . their operation is accordingly unchecked. It is not sufficient . . . that the conscientious researcher seeks out

facts with scrupulous honesty and care . . . it behooves him, in addition, to make explicit . . . the underlying value premises on which the conclusions he predicted are predicated.[13]

Moreover, even setting aside the researcher's bias, measuring human behaviors and attitudes through survey research techniques is not like weighing out a pound of pistachio nuts. All of the information gathered through survey research on Jewish populations is based on the reporting of information by respondents.

Quantitative studies such as the NJPS are absolutely critical for analysis. Numerical studies and statistics can provide a panorama, a broad picture of the outlines of an entire culture or society. The information they provide is, quite simply, the best, indeed the only way we have of understanding the large-scale movements of American Jewry. However, like all methods, it has its limitations. By looking for broad-based information, researchers often do not focus on acquiring detailed information about significant subgroups.

Moreover, because the subjects of survey research only respond to previously determined question, no information is gathered beyond those questions. Respondents generally will not stay on the phone for more than a 45-minute interview, so researchers must make choices about which questions to ask. Unfortunately, research choices are sometimes made that ignore important developments in American Jewish life, and especially in the lives of Jewish women.

An example of two areas that are closely involved with Jewish feminist transformation of women's lives, and which have not been included in the 1990 NJPS or in most studies of Jewish populations in major metropolitan areas, are the *Havurah* movement and the life cycle celebration. Despite the growth and influence of the *Havurah* movement in the United States, the NJPS questionnaire only asks if the respondent currently belongs to a synagogue or ever belonged to a synagogue as an adult. Women and men who support and attend the many nonsynagogue-connected *Havurah* services are computed the same way as persons who never step into a synagogue, even if they attend *Havurah* worship services every week. The proliferation of *Havurah*-style services has been especially significant for women during the past two decades, because the participatory nature of the *Havurah* service has made it the locale for dramatic growth in women's participation in public Judaism.

Similarly, as ways of measuring connectedness to Jewish religious rituals, the NJPS questionnaire asks a battery of questions about traditional observances, including the following: do you light candles on Friday night; buy kosher meat; use separate meat and dairy dishes; light Hanuka candles; have a Christmas tree; attend a Purim celebration; fast on Yom Kippur; celebrate *Yom Ha-Atzmaut* (Israeli Independence Day); refrain from handling money on the Sabbath; or fast on the day before Purim, called *ta'anit Esther*? However, the questionnaire does not ask about most rituals connected with life cycle events: the *Brit Milah* (ritual circumcision) or *Shalom Bat*; rituals surrounding the wedding; and rituals surrounding death, such as observance of a *shiva* period or reciting *kaddish*. How widespread are these emotionally powerful experiences today? Anecdotal evidence seems to indicate that these life cycle rituals have far more salience for most American Jewish men and women than such traditional observances as separating meat and dairy dishes or fasting on *ta'anit Esther*. Moreover, much creative religious activity on the part of Jewish feminists has focused on Jewish life cycle events. Because questions were not asked about life cycle events, we have no answers in that area from what is currently our most comprehensive data base.

Ironically, unless researchers start with a comprehensive knowledge of trends in the lives of Jewish men and women as they begin new research, they often don't elicit as much useful information and as complete and accurate a picture of Jewish behaviors and attitudes. A sensitivity not only to Jewish life in the past but to the flux of current Jewish life, including issues of gender, is an indispensable component of the intellectual equipment of a competent researcher of contemporary Jews. Quantitative research is especially useful when the researcher wishes to depict and analyze what sociologist C. Wright Mills calls "public issues of social structure." These "issues transcend the individual and the range of [her] . . . inner life." Quantitative research gives us meaningful pictures of the "larger structures of social and historical life."[14]

Qualitative Research

A Breath of Life: Feminism in the American Jewish Community uses a combination of qualitative and quantitative data as well as literary data to provide a multi-faceted picture. In writing this book, I used data elicited from the as yet largely untapped wealth of data in the NJPS. In addition, I conducted interviews for two and a half years: from January 1990 through September 1992, with 120 women age 18 to 80 living in diverse communities across the United States.[15] Women were selected for these interviews with the aim of providing maximum diversity among women who have a connection to and interest in some aspect of contemporary Jewish life. The women interviewed included 15 female rabbis and Jewish educators, 20 students, 30 writers and professors of Judaica, 12 Jewish communal professionals and 12 Jewish communal volunteers, 14 professionals in nonsectarian spheres, and 16 women's prayer group participants. Although I constructed and used a questionnaire as a guideline for these interviews, our discussions were designed to and did range far beyond the standard questions, following each woman into her own special area of concern and expertise. Several outstanding questions were added to the questionnaire at the suggestions of the interviewees themselves. The dialogue reported consists of direct quotations.

In moving from an analysis of the NJPS quantitative data to this qualitative research on contemporary American Jewish women, I was, in effect, moving from an exploration of transformations in large, social structures (e.g., as shifts in marital status, endogamy, and labor free participation) into a consideration of the ways in which new tendencies played themselves out in the lives of women in a variety of social situations. The following quotes are from qualitative research that shed light on which experiences tend to make women feel more connected to Judaism and to Jewish life, and which experiences are alienating. They help us to understand how American Jewish women actually experience the changes in their lives. They also help us to fill in the gaps and answer questions that were not asked in the quantitative survey data. Quantitative data, for example, indicated that large numbers of American Jewish women are juggling three identities: as professionals, as family-oriented women, and as Jews. Women across the religious spectrum are now likely to work outside the home. In the interviews, some women describe how they successfully integrate their deep Jewish concerns with the rest of their lives. Despite potentially conflicting roles, they report a sense of well-being. Here is a vignette of the positive and family-nurturing ways in which some contemporary women combine these three roles:

> I had a special opportunity. When I was 39 I was diagnosed
> with breast cancer. I spent days thinking deeply about the way
> I had lived my life, what I had done and what I wanted to do.
> And I realized that I would not have wanted to change one
> minute of my life. When my husband and I were young, we
> knew we had to help each other. When my children were very

small, I spent a lot of time volunteering for Jewish organizations. My career grew from a one person public relations firm in 1966 to a national agency employing 28 people [Image Dynamics in Baltimore], with international accounts. As my children were growing up, they were always involved with my work and I was always involved with them. They used to help me collate and staple reports on the dining room table and I used to rush home from work to get them from one activity to another. They all got a good Jewish education. They're all grown now, and they have remained tied to the Jewish community, and they all say those growing up years were wonderful years.[16]

However, the growing number of women who do not fit the normative Jewish family pattern often feel the Jewish community is not responsive to their special needs. Many of them express the opinion that the Jewish communal and religious worlds are not keeping pace with a Jewish community in which one out of four adults will be divorced at some point in life. This perceived lack of communal responsiveness creates in them feelings of anger and alienation. Here is what one young Orthodox divorcee said:

When we get to synagogue on Saturday morning and my little boys go to the other side of the *mekhitzah*, no one takes an interest in them. They run around wild, and everyone says, tsk, tsk how come she doesn't discipline her children better—but no man calls them over and says, here sit down near me, I'll show you what we're doing now. I think that providing the male children of divorced women with male role models is something the whole community should be concerned with, rather than leaving us on our own this way.[17]

Another Orthodox woman, herself happily married and a successful attorney in Chicago, does *pro bono* work on behalf of *agunot*, women whose husbands refuse to give them a *get*, or religious divorce. She describes the recalcitrance of many in the rabbinic world as follows:

The Jewish communal consequences of *mamserut* are irrevocable. Unequal bargaining power yields lots of opportunities for exploitation. There are no statistics on the number of women who end up giving in to blackmail. The

community has to deal with this on a case by case basis—
[because] no policy decisions have been made. Lots of rabbis
encourage women to "pay off" their husbands—They say, "It's
only $50,000, your father is rich—pay him off!"

She says, "As a feminist, I try to be goal oriented and I try not to get
distracted by disturbing details. If they ask me to sit at a separate table,
I sit there, but I won't let anyone dislodge me from my ultimate goal of
getting fair treatment of these women."[18]

The Reform rabbinic establishment also came under fire for its lack
of sensitivity to the realities of divorced women's lives in some
interviews. One woman insisted:

The Reform movement should not allow itself to be used as a
haven for men who won't give their wives a get—but want
religious ceremonies when they themselves get remarried.
Many men would come around if their Reform rabbis would
only insist that they give a previous wife a get before they can
have a ketubah for their new wife.[19]

But by far the most universal alienating experiences that Jewish
women found in the Jewish world centered around the death of a
parent and the exclusion of women from the recital of Kaddish in many
traditional settings. One woman told the following story:

We were sitting shiva in our living room, when all of a sudden
there was this invasion of men in suits and ties, sweaty, on their
way home from work, men from our conservative shul
(synagogue) I hardly knew and my mother had never met.
They ordered my mother and me and all our female friends out
of the room—and I mean ordered. "We have to daven (pray),"
they said. "Your husband has to say kaddish." "What do you
mean my husband?" I asked them in tears. "My father was
buried this morning. My husband's parents are alive and well.
I'm saying kaddish for my father." "No you're not!" barked the
gabbi (sexton). `You can say kaddish till you're blue in the face
but it won't count. If you want your father's soul to go to
heaven, you better get a man to say kaddish for him three times a
day."[20]

Some women found particular styles of synagogue worship alienating, and a substantial proportion were deeply disturbed by prayer with separate seating. A writer from a Moroccan Jewish background said:

> The first time I went to a Sephardi synagogue, I was flooded by feelings of both profound joy and profound anguish. I wept. It was wonderful to be worshipping in my own tradition—at last. And yet I was furious at being stuck up in a balcony. Sitting up in the balcony of that synagogue gave me a different concept of the nature of sin. Do you know what sin is—it is the hypocrisy of men. Women are locked away and segregated in synagogues so that men don't have to deal with their fear. . . . Sephardi Jews lived in and resemble Moslem society. I was always enraged growing up. . . . Father said, you're rebelling against nature. Because of feminism I began to understand not just why I was angry but what I should do about it. For me the medium was language.[21]

Others, however—even some who are not especially observant religiously—feel more comfortable with the traditional synagogue. Many find themselves caught betwixt and between, full of conflict. Among aspects of American Jewish life that have been virtually untouched by quantitative research, is the enormous creative ferment that is going on today among Jewish women who are involved in trying to make the Jewish community more responsive to their changing needs. A highly educated Conservative woman in her 50s, for example, is involved in the effort to construct new prayers for moments such as pregnancy and birth, which she describes as:

> the most religious episodes in my life. Five times from an act of love I have felt life growing inside of me. I know what a miracle is. Crossing the Red Sea is nothing compared to that. . . . I'd like to retrieve and reuse many of the beautiful, traditional . . . *techinot* utilized by our grandmothers to provide us with at least the beginnings of liturgical responses to our own bodies.[22]

A Reform woman in her seventies describes the profound positive impact that evolutions in Jewish life have had on her feelings of connectedness with Judaism:

I would say that three kinds of days were the highlights of my life—the day I got married, the days when my four children were born, and the day 10 years ago when I had my *Bat Mitzvah*, read from the *Torah*, and helped to put the *Torah* back into the ark. Every time I handle the *Torah* I want to weep with joy. I realize how much it means to me. All my life I have been Jewish, and at last I have a way to express my Jewishness.[23]

A twenty-two-year-old rabbinical candidate at the Jewish Theological Seminary, who grew up in a weakly identified Reform Jewish home, has the following to say about the evolution of her own Jewish life:

This *Rosh ha-Shanah* for the first time I began to use a *talit*. Now I use it daily when I pray. It shuts out the whole external world, and it also shuts out interfering thoughts and feelings. It envelops me in thoughts of God and the words of my prayers.[24]

And an Orthodox adolescent describes the forging of powerful links with Judaism through the enfranchisement she felt when she celebrated her *Bat Mitzvah* at an all-female worship and *Torah* reading group:

I know on *Shabbes* when I was *davening* [praying, here—leading the female group in prayer] and I was *layning* [chanting the portion of the week from the *Torah*], I felt when people talk about being close to *Hashem* [the Name, respectful Hebrew euphemism for God], this is what they mean. I felt awe...A *Bat Mitzvah*'s about taking a new role in Jewish society. Since then, I've been a lot more aware of what I should and shouldn't do. It used to be that I wouldn't care too much if what I did was right and wrong. Now I know that this is my responsibility, not anyone else's. No one else is watching me, no one's going to fix my mistakes.[25]

Qualitative research demonstrates powerful, simultaneous trends toward continuity and change in the lives of American Jewish women today. As they juggle multiple roles, Jewish women frequently have high expectations of the Jewish community, and are disappointed when the community does not seem to provide communal and religious support systems that are responsive to their new lifestyles. Perhaps more consciously than ever before, Jewish women today explore their

Jewish heritage and their own spirituality in modes that are sometimes built on patterns derived from past Jewish cultures and sometimes depart from prior patterns. Among a limited but very diverse subgroup of women, Jewish feminism has created powerful feelings of connectedness to Judaism and Jewish life.

Using Literary Texts

Through qualitative research we can learn a lot about what it means to be an American Jew, about as yet unquantified changes in Jewish life, and about the complexities that gender adds to the experience of being an American Jew. However, even in such interviews the researcher is dependent on information that the informant wishes to reveal. A very different type of "handle" on reality is provided by literature. Fiction can give the researcher valuable insight into things that are usually unrevealed and unquantifiable—the hearts, minds, and souls of contemporary American Jews. It is in this exploration, the exploration of what experience feels like from the inside, "where the meanings are" that literature can help us most. And, as we struggle to understand transformations in the American Jewish notion of what it means to be a Jewish woman or a Jewish man, this is an area perhaps more revealing than many have realized in the past.

One contemporary school of literary criticism concentrates on the concept that literature is embedded in the cultural context out of which it grew.[26] The converse is also a powerful and important approach to contempory social sciences: We can learn much from literature about the complex matrix in which feelings about Judaism and Jews are embedded. In the literature briefly dealt with in the this chapters, women have confused and angry feelings about Judaism that are interwoven with their confused and angry feelings about other aspects of their lives. This kind of conflict is seldom expressed quite so clearly in sociological research. Whereas the respondent is sometimes inhibited by the desire to please, to tell a coherent and consistent story, the good fiction writer fearlessly illuminates the inner workings of a character's mind.

The intersection between feminist literary criticism and the experience of contemporary American Jewish women, as depicted by Jewish female writers, is particularly instructive. Sandra Gilbert and Susan Gubar describe the evolution of a monster-woman character as a result of "patriarchal socialization." They point out that any young girl, but especially a lively or imaginative one, is likely to experience her education in docility, submissiveness, selflessness as in some sense sickening. . . . The girl learns anxiety about, perhaps even loathing of, her own flesh. . . . It is debilitating to be any woman in a society where women are warned that if they do not behave like angels they must be monsters.[27]

For the female author, the stakes can be especially high, and the tendency to see herself as a "monster-woman" is especially strong:

As Elaine Showalter has suggested, women writers participate in a quite different subculture from that inhabited by male writers. . . . At its best, the separateness of this female subculture has been exhilarating for women. . . . While male writers seem increasingly to have felt exhausted by the need for revisionism which Harold Bloom's theory of the anxiety of influence accurately describes, women writers have seen themselves as pioneers in a creativity so intense that their male counterparts have probably not experienced...its like since the Renaissance or the Romantic era.[28]

At its worst, however, female authors are subject to a gender-distinctive "anxiety of authorship," in which the very act of authorship is consciously or unconsciously perceived by the female writer to be inappropriate to her sex. Thus, by the very act of writing, she feels herself to be a monster-woman. Poet Adrienne Rich makes this image into a powerful symbol for the discomfort of the intellectual, creative woman in her poem, "Planetarium,"

> A woman in the shape of a monster
> a monster in the shape of a woman
> the skies are full of them.[29]

These are the women who feel monstrous precisely because they are brilliant and creative.

Female Jewish writers in the United States today often depict women being manipulated by society to reject intrinsic aspects of their personhood. In different societies the objectionable—or monstrous—portions of the female psyche change, but the dynamic of deconstructing one's own life, of displacing pieces of oneself, and of creating within and yet outside oneself a "dark sister"—a *golem*—to embody the "monstrous" elements remains the same.

Cynthia Ozick's playful short story about a similar theme, "Puttermesser and Xanthippe," deals with these issues by turning stereotypes on their heads. The protagonist, Puttermesser (Yiddish for butterknife—Puttermesser is not very sharp) is a female *Luftmensch* (Yiddish expression for and absent-minded intellectual type, almost always male; a sky-man; a person who does not relate to the exigencies of daily life) and devotes herself exclusively to the matters of the mind. Semiconsciously, she literally creates a female *golem* to house the pieces of herself with which she cannot cope.[30] Just as the male *golem* of Jewish legend—a maleness unmediated by reason—becomes more and more destructive and must eventually be destroyed by his creator, the female *golem*, Xanthippe, represents a femaleness unmediated by reason. Xanthippe fulfills male anxieties about the fully sexual adult female and becomes a monster of sexuality. Her voracious sexual predatoriness, which reduces all of New York's male civil servants into mere shells of men is meant to be humorous. It suggests that only a *golem* could be as mindlessly sexual as some misogynists think all women are. It also suggests that some relentlessly "intellectual" feminists misguidedly deny a whole segment of their own selves, a physicality that they may subconsciously fear and repress as much as men do.

These themes pervade literature by American Jewish women, even when they are not the main focus of the novel. For example, in Lynn Sharon Schwartz's *Leaving Brooklyn*, Audrey, a young woman growing up in Brooklyn in a lower-middle-class Jewish home, can see the world the way her solid, mainstream parents and their friends see it—with her one good eye. She often retreats to her other eye, an eye badly damaged during birth, which shows her a very different world indeed; it is a random and dizzy world with unlimited opportunity and unlimited danger. Her mother and her good eye warn her to be a good girl, to follow the beaten path, to live an orderly existence and stay "in Brooklyn" and out of danger. Her wayward eye leads her across the bridge to the sinister clamor of Manhattan, that world that is not Brooklyn, to dark and thrilling sides of human nature—her own and that of others.

The fourteen-year-old Audrey is seduced by her Manhattan ophthalmologist. Their long, voluptuous affair eventually enables her to see Brooklyn and herself with new eyes. Much to Audrey's surprise, she discovers that her parents and their card-playing cronies and their

seemingly ordinary and unexciting friends have braved the very real
dangers and threats of the McCarthy era with unpretentious and
unsung courage. She sees that people may dwell in Brooklyn and
partake of greater, more dangerous, and more noble adventures in
living than she had ever imagined. She thinks, "There was life in
Brooklyn. Passion. Conflict. Thought. An ample scene for both my
eyes. . . . I left Brooklyn. I leave still, every moment. For no matter
how much I leave, it doesn't leave me."[31]

Rebecca Goldstein's fiction often explores in the *Mind-Body Problem*,
the need that some men have to divide humanity into mind and body,
and the destructive ways in which women have internalized these false
dichotomies. Renee Feuer, the protagonist, is pulled between Judaism
and secularism. Her mother first castigates her for being too pretty, and
therefore not *edel* (refined) and later "greets each announcement of my
educational plans with 'Nyu, Renee, is this going to help you find a
husband?' so that the consequence of all my academic honors, Phi Beta
Kappa, *summa cum laude*, scholarships, fellowships, prizes, was only a
deepening sense of guilty failure." When Renee calls to tell her mother
that she has become engaged to a world-famous mathematician, her
mother uses this happy occasion to strip Renee even further:

> You should be very proud, Renee, that such a man should love
> you. Of course, I know you're not just any girl. Who should
> know if not me? This is why God gave you such good brains, so
> that you could make such a man like this love you.

Pursuing a doctorate in philosophy at Princeton University, she is not
taken seriously by her professors because she is too pretty to be smart
and too smart to be pretty.

It is not only Renee's Orthodox mother and her atheistic professors
who have trouble dealing with the concept of a beautiful but brainy
woman. Women feel that way about themselves too. Her best friend
from undergraduate days at Barnard, a fiercely antireligious physicist
named Ava, is convinced women must make themselves both
androgynous and ugly to be taken seriously as intellectuals.[32]

Goldstein's more recent female protagonists feel even more
compelled to reject parts of themselves. A hulking, brilliant, reclusive
woman named Hedda, who behaves like an all-mind *golem*, writes a
novel in which a very conventional and proper woman imagines that
she has an unconventional *dark sister*. This unconventional sister, who is
an astronomer, appears only by day. Eventually, the separation

between the two parts of herself breaks down, and the protagonist is flooded by her own unacceptable feelings and interests.[33]

Literary texts reinforce the observations of social scientists that modern Jewish men and women, who often cope with one set of assumptions in secular workplaces and another set of assumptions in Jewish social, religious, and communal settings, have found the technique of compartmentalization especially useful in reducing the discomfort of cognitive dissonance between their secular and Jewish worlds. Along with other Jewish women writing today, Rebecca Goldstein suggests that American Jewish women approach their own lives as a text, deconstructing, rewriting, and interpreting chaotic experience so that it appears to have a narrative flow and inner coherence. She indicates that women have often come to regard large segments of their personhood as alien, as a fifth column, as "the dark sister" to their more politically correct, acceptable public personae.

Fiction by Goldstein and others indicates that for Jewish women, there is often another layer of conflicting values and behaviors. Not only do Jewish women have to cope with the conflict between Jewish and non-Jewish values systems, but also with the conflict between society's prescriptions for correct feminine behavior and their own innate talents, energies, and preferences. They often find themselves indulging in "triple play" compartmentalizing on three levels: separate eyes, for seeing Jewish bourgeois propriety and the wild outside world; separate sisters; and *golems*, to embody the rejected pieces of women's selves.

Utilizing Multiple Approaches

The description and analysis of objective experience emerges as a very elusive goal. Each method of gathering and analyzing information has particular limitations. Quantitative studies, although absolutely critical to our understanding of contemporary life and sometimes thrilling in the information they can provide, present numbers that are always a blend of the experiences of many individuals and are never the actual experiences of any one individual. Moreover, quantitative studies seem to lend themselves more easily to exploring the way people act, rather than the way they feel. From quantitative research, we learn that American Jewish women today enjoy unprecedented levels of secular education and formal Jewish education, but we do not learn about the ways in which their secular and their Jewish learning and lives either fit well together or are experienced as a conflict.

Qualitative studies can provide valuable insights about a given group. They give us the flesh and blood voices of the men and women behind the statistics and fill in many gaps in statistical data. However, they do not always place that particular group within the larger picture or tell us about the influence or importance of the group being studied within the larger matrix of society. From qualitative research, we learn that some Jewish women find the synagogue and Jewish communal world has been supportive to them, whereas others have had profoundly alienating experiences. But we do not learn how those experiences affect them at the core of their being or how they affect their perceptions of themselves as human beings and as Jews.

Fiction, memoirs, poetry, and essays do not aim to convey a broad picture of all the different ways in which people can behave or think. Moreover, successful fiction needs dramatic tension. By its very nature, fiction tends toward individualized pictures of idiosyncratic people. From fiction by American Jewish women we have learned that women can be alienated from their inner selves as Jewish women. Their feelings about Jews and Judaism are sometimes embedded in fears that they are also unacceptably intellectual, artistic, scientific, mystical, violent, angry, or nonmaternal—any of these pieces of themselves can potentially be viewed as "other."

Qualitative research, quantitative research, and literary analysis are each valuable tools when we are trying to reconstruct the truths of lives of American Jewish men and women, and when we are trying to understand the changing shape of the American Jewish community. Used alone, each can lead to and reveal important insights, but each used alone can lead to significant distortions of the whole picture. Used together, they can illuminate both the broad outlines and the inner workings of American Jewish life today. Most scholars of the current American Jewish scene will choose to focus their energies primarily in one of these areas. However, I believe that to the extent that we can make simultaneous use of these three type of analysis, we will enrich our understanding of contemporary American Jewish life, and we will enrich the field of the sociology of American Jews as well.

There is often a tendency to regard quantitative research, including descriptive or analytical materials based on numbers, as scientific or factual; and conversely, there is often a tendency to regard evidence from literary texts with suspicion. I would like to suggest that we need to see the "facts" within fiction, and to see what may be "fictional" about putative "facts." It is also important that we learn to regard quantitative material with educated suspicion, valuing it, but understanding the ways in which the pieces of numerical picture may be represented or distorted.

By this, I do not suggest that we lose sight of the differences between fact and fiction. I agree with historian Dan T. Carter that the act of blurring this line can be intellectually dangerous:

> Over the last 40 years, humanists and social scientists alike have been acutely aware of the limitations of "knowing"—the problems that philosophers have always grouped under the term epistemology. Influential scholars in many fields have moved beyond the "hermeneutics of suspicion" toward a skepticism so pervasive that it severs the connections between reality and language. Pushing the argument to its limit, they embrace the complete contingency of language and treat all knowledge as "texts" that are divorced from reality, totally dependent upon the prejudice and preconceptions of the author (and the reader), and thus subject to infinite interpretation. Even social scientists, who traditionally have prided themselves on their commitment to search for forms of objective, verifiable truth, have suddenly found that the very foundations of their enterprise are in doubt.[34]

We can take our cue from Philip Roth, who, after years of arguing with readers about the issue of representativeness in art, produced a tricky but magnificent novel that reveals volumes about what it means to be an American Jew today, and called it *The Counterlife*.[35] He also wrote a memoir that provides the outlines of his life and slyly called it *The Facts*.[36] There are more facts about the Jewish heart in *The Counterlife* than there are in *The Facts*. Researchers of contemporary Jewish life need to explore the counterlives of American Jewish women and men, or they will not understand the facts either.[37]

NOTES

1. Shulamith Reinharz, *Feminist Methods in Social Research* (New York: Oxford University Press, 1992), 159.
2. Lynn Davidman, *Tradition in a Rootless World: Women Turn to Orthodox Judaism* (Berkeley: University of California Press, 1991).
3. Simon Herman, *Jewish Identity* (New Jersey: Transaction Publishers; 2nd Ed., 1989); 20.
4. The first national study of American Jews undertaken since 1970, the 1990 NJPS, conducted by the Council of Jewish Federations, studied households representing Jews across the country living in communities of diverse sizes and composition. A summary

of the findings is provided by Barry A. Kosmin, Sidney Goldstein, Joseph Waksberg, Nava Lerer, Ariella Keysar and Jeffrey Scheckner, *Highlights of the CJF National Jewish Population Survey* (Council of Jewish Federations, 1991).

5. For earlier discussions of these changes, see Sylvia Barack Fishman, "The Changing American Jewish Family in the Eighties,"*Contemporary Jewry* 9, No. 2 (Fall 1988), 1-34, and "Family Ties: Serving Today's Jewish Households," in *Changing Jewish Life: Service Jewry and Planning in the 1990's*, eds. Lawrence Sternberg, Gary A. Tobin, and Sylvia Barack Fishman (New York: Greenwood Press, 1991), 57-85.

6. Calvin Goldscheider, *Jewish Continuity and Change: Emerging Patterns in America* (Bloomington: Indiana University Press, 1986), 92-98.

7. See my extended argument of this issue in "Choosing Jewish Parenthood," Sylvia Barack Fishman, *A Breath of Life: Feminism in the American Jewish Community* (New York: Free Press, 1993), 45-64.

8. Calvin Goldscheider and Francis K. Goldscheider, "The Transition to Jewish Adulthood: Education, Marriage, and Fertility," paper for the Tenth World Congress of Jewish Studies, Jerusalem, Aug. 1989, 17-20.

9. Frank L. Mott and Joyce C. Abma, "Contemporary Jewish Fertility: Does Religion Make a Difference?" *Contemporary Jewry*, 1992, 13: 74-94.

10. Goldscheider and Goldscheider, "The Transition to Jewish Adulthood," 17-20.

11. These issues are explored at more length in "Women: Their Education, Work, and Jewish Communal Participation," *American Jewry: Portrait and Prognosis*, procedings of the Hollander Colloquium of the Willstein Institute at the University of Judaism, Los Angeles, July 1991.

12. For a more extended discussion of the impact of Jewish education, see Sylvia Barack Fishman and Alice Goldstein, *When They Are Grown They Will Not Depart; Jewish Education and the Jewish Behavior of American Adults* (Waltham, MA: CMJS, Brandeis University, 1993).

13. Herman, *Jewish Identity*, 20.

14. C. Wright Mills, *The Sociological Imagination* (New York: Oxford University Press, 1959), 8-13.

15. Ann Arbor, Atlanta, Baltimore, Berkeley, Boston, Brooklyn, Bronx, Cambridge (MA), Cherry Hill (NJ), Chicago, Columbus (OH), Columbia (MD), Denver, Encinatas, Gainesville (FL), Los Angeles, Miami, Norfolk (VA), Orefield (PA), Philadelphia, Pittsburgh, Portland (OR), Providence, New Haven, Newton (MA), Rockland County (NY), Rockville (MD), San Diego, San Francisco, Sharon, St. Louis, Silver Springs (MD), Teaneck, Tuscon, and Westchester County (NY).

16. Fishman, *A Breath of Life*, 40-41.

17. Ibid., 35.

18. Ibid., 36.

19. Ibid., 37.

20. Ibid., 140.

21. Ibid., 156.

22. Ibid., 128.

23. Ibid., 131.

24. Ibid., 133, quoting from Nicky Goldman, "The Celebration of *Bat Mitzvah* within the Orthodox Community in the United States Today," unpublished paper for the Hornstein Program in Jewish Communal Service, Brandeis University, Spring 1991.

25. Fishman, *A Breath of Life*, 133.

26. See especially Stephen Greenblatt, *Learning to Curse: Essays in Early Modern Literature* (New York: Routledge, 1990), for a coherent discussion of his theories of "cultural poetics" or "new historicism."

27. Sandra M. Gilbert and Susan Gubar, *The Madwoman in the Attic: The Woman Writer and the Nineteenth Century Literary Imagination* (New Haven: Yale University Press, 1979), 53-54.

28. Elaine Showalter, *A Literature of Their Own* (Princeton: Princeton University Press, 1977), cited by Gilbert and Gubar, *Madwoman*, 50-51. See also Lynette Carpenter and Wendy K. Kolmar, eds., *Haunting the House of Fiction: Feminist Perspectives on Ghost Stories by American Women* (Knoxville: University of Tennessee Press, 1991).

29. Adrienne Rich, "Planetarium."

30. Cynthia Ozick, "Puttermesser and Xanthippe," quoted in Sylvia Barack Fishman, *Follow My Footprints: Changing Images of Women in American Jewish Fiction* (Hanover, NH: University Press of New England, 1992), 440-94.

31. Lynne Sharon Schwartz, *Leaving Brooklyn* (Boston: Houghton Mifflin, 1989).

32. Rebecca Goldstein, *The Mind-Body Problem* (New York: Dell, 1983).

33. Rebecca Goldstein, *The Dark Sister* (New York: Viking Penguin, 1991).

34. Dan T. Carter, "The Academy's Crisis of Belief," *Chronicle of Higher Education* 39, No. 13 (18 Nov 1992).

35. Philip Roth, *The Counterlife* (New York: Penguin Books, 1986).

36. Philip Roth, *The Facts: A Novelist Autobiography* (New York: Farrar, Straus, and Giroux, 1988).

37. Another version of this chapter appeared in *Contemporary Jewry* 14 (1993), 23-47.

Chapter 19

Of Mice and Supermen: Images of Jewish Masculinity

Harry Brod

This chapter explores certain cultural images of Jewish men, focusing particularly on the dynamics of power and powerlessness and, closely related to this, of heroism and victimization. [1] As one would expect in any analysis of forms of masculinities, issues of violence and of sexuality will come to play pivotal roles here. The discussion begins with the examination of some well-known images in popular culture, some of them not usually associated with Jewish themes, before it turns to incorporate into the discussion depictions of Jewish men within the Jewish tradition. The first popular culture icon to be discussed is paradigmatically non-Jewish, and one of the questions posed is that of the relationship between representations of the quintessentially non-Jewish and the quintessentially Jewish man.

Heroism and Survival

First consider the fruits of the creative energies of two young Jewish men who lived in Cleveland, Ohio, during the Depression. They enjoyed reading the Sunday comic strips, and decided they would like to try to create a character of their own. Jerry Siegel and Joe Shuster tried to market this character, but found no takers. Finally, somebody decided to accept this character and introduce him in a comic book. The character these two Jews created eventually made his debut on the cover of the first issue of *Action Comics* in June 1938, heralding the first appearance of Superman, who originated the superhero genre.[2] (Prior to that, the heroes were nonsuperpowered figures such as detectives, cops, pirates, etc.)

We don't usually think of Superman, the first and still prototypical superhero, as a Jewish character. Nonetheless, it will be my thesis that we should do so, the counterintuitiveness of such an idea notwithstanding. In fact, much of what I wish to explore is the question of why it goes so much against the grain to imagine Superman as Jewish.

By no means is this the first time such a question has been raised. The cover of the 4 August 1992 issue of the New York *Village Voice* highlights a picture of Superman in his traditional pose leaping into the air, above which, in large red letters, is written "SuperJew!" The cover article's title is "Is Superman Jewish?: The Chosen Heroes from the *Golem* to Alan Dershowitz" (this being not long after the publication of Dershowitz's book *Chutzpah*). The title as given inside is "Up, Up and Oy Vey!"[3]

Jeff Salamon notes some stereotypically Jewish things about Superman. Kryptonians are superintelligent, and Superman's father Jor-El was a scientist. (I would add that in the Superman canon one never learns what his mother Lara actually did. Her role seems to be to tearfully watch baby Kal-El fly off to Earth in his rocket as the planet Krypton explodes around him). As the sole survivor of his race, he lives in a permanent diaspora. Henry Louis Gates stresses this theme of Superman as an immigrant when he writes of "Superman, the hero from Ellis Island, personified as an (undocumented) alien who had been naturalized by the ultimate American couple, Eben and Sarah Kent."[4]

A striking puzzle arises regarding the relationship between Superman and his alter ego Clark Kent. Perhaps the best way to explain the puzzle is to contrast Superman with another comic book hero, Batman. Batman's secret identity is Bruce Wayne, a real person who predates and grounds the Batman identity, which is a fictional creation. But with Superman, the matter is reversed. Superman is the real person. He really is a being from another planet. Clark Kent is the fiction. There really is no such person, especially in the sense that there is really no such personality as the Clark personality. (He was raised by the Kents, but he left his hometown and went to the big city where nobody knew him, so it is not clear why he needed to maintain this identity when he left Smallville for Metropolis.)[5] Although Bruce Wayne certainly has to maintain fictitious elements of his character and prevaricate in order to preserve his secret identity, he does not create out of whole cloth a personna completely opposite to his real nature, as Clark's personality is to Superman's. The problem, then, is why Superman goes to such great lengths to preserve the Clark personna. And, especially, why does he want Lois Lane to fall in love with Clark rather than with Superman? Why does he want Lois to fall in love with a lie?

An enlightening answer is given by another cartoonist in the Jewish tradition. In the Introduction to *The Great Comic Book Heroes*, Jules Feiffer writes that this is Superman's joke on the rest of us.[6] Clark is Superman's vision of what other men are really like. We are scared, incompetent, and powerless, particularly around women. Though Feiffer took the joke good-naturedly, a more cynical response would see here the Kryptonian's misanthropy, his misandry embodied in Clark and his misogyny in his wish that Lois be enamored of Clark (much like Oberon takes out his hostility toward Titania by having her fall in love with an ass in Shakespeare's *A Midsummer-Night's Dream*).

At this point recall some of the contemporary villains faced by popular heroes, villains who at first glance appear to be unconnected to Jewish issues, and then relate them to what I have already said. Shortly after the film *Batman Returns* came out, an Op-Ed piece in the *New York Times* called attention to the anti-Semitic stereotypes embedded in the film's villain, the Penguin.[7] He is an evil, ugly, greedy, conspiratorial, smelly, unkempt, ill-mannered, hook-nosed, claw-handed fishmonger out to rule the world and destroy Christmas. Consider this alongside other villainous characters from the *Star Wars* films. I quote from Paul Hoch's *White Hero, Black Beast: Racism, Sexism and the Mask of Maculinity*:

> Two other stereotypical dark beasts appear. The first, the "filthy jawa" is a short, "extraordinarily ugly," "rodent-like" and "shrouded" being who "scurries" about "collecting and selling scrap jabbering in low, guttural croaks and hisses" and giving off offensive odors. Such "vermin" are "disgusting creatures," cringing "hereditary cowards," wandering "migrants" whose "covetous hands" produce nothing but try to pawn off inferior merchandise on the hard-working farmers who are their customers, while these underhand operators "bow and whine with impatient greed." Significantly, "hygiene was unknown among the jawas," for these "travesties of men had long since degenerated past anything resembling the human race." The jawa is the only race in the entire book whose name is not capitalized throughout. Moreover, the chance of a two

consonant name having just the two consonants "j" and "w" of
the word Jew in precisely that order is only 21 x 20 (in fact less
than one in a million if the extreme infrequency of these
particular consonants in English usage is taken into account).
The jawa is an anti-Semite's dream! The novel's other dark
desert beasts are the Tuscan Raiders, or Sandpeople:
"outrageous mahouts" who "pursue a nomadic existence,"
"vicious desert bandits" who "make sudden raids on local
settlers."   These "marginally-human" murderers "wrapped
themselves mummylike in endless swathings and bandages"
and emitted "terrifying grunts of fury and pleasure." In short,
the usual stereotype of the marauding Arab. Lest we be in any
doubt about these two sets of desert sub-men who squabble so
bitterly among themselves, we are told that some scientists
believe "they must be related" and "the jawas are actually the
mature form."[8]

We have, then, these two negative images of Jews, and in particular
Jewish men, in the culture: the evil, dark image of the Penguin and the
jawas, and the also negative, but not evil, Clark Kent-type character.
Clark is a sort of quintessential characterization of the Jewish *nebbish*.
He's a quasi-intellectual. He's a writer; he wears glasses; he's inept,
timid, and cowardly; and he is described as mouselike.
   And speaking of mice, one of the reasons I've begun and remained
with the theme of comic books is that one of the most extraordinary
Jewish books of recent years — indeed one of the most extraordinary
books of recent years — is Art Spiegelman's comic book, *Maus*, about
Holocaust victims and survivors and their families in the postwar
United States.[9] In *Maus*, the Jews of the Holocaust are drawn as mice,
the Germans are cats, the Poles are pigs and, when the tale moves to the
contemporary scene, non-Jewish Americans are dogs, and American
Jews are drawn with masks of mice on their faces. Spiegelman usually
draws himself as a mouse, but occasionally as wearing the mask of a
mouse. So his own identity is ambivalent.
   I find this a very effective symbolization of the ambivalence of post-
Holocaust American Jewish male identity. Spiegelman's self-portrait is
particularly striking in that it embraces ambiguity, precisely what most
depictions of Jewish men in popular culture avoid, engaging rather in
the sort of rigid dichotomous polarization evident in Superman/Clark
Kent. On the one hand, Superman is so super that the principal
problem his writers have is coming up with a threat to him credible

enough to add any suspense to the plot. On the other hand, Clark Kent is such a complete *nebbish* that he's also an unbelievable character. As to the effectiveness of his "disguise," here is an explanation offered by one of the editors of Superman's comic book appearances, E. Nelson Bridwell: "It may surprise the sophisticate of today that she [Lois Lane] took so long to penetrate the simple disguise of a pair of glasses. But in a day when people accepted the chestnut about the girl whose attractions are never noticed until she is seen without her glasses, Superman's camouflage worked."[10] The principle behind the disguise, then, is the old saw that men don't make passes at girls who wear glasses. To the extent that the disguise works, it thus also marks Clark as feminized.

It is precisely the extremism of the polarization between Superman and Clark that makes him such a paradigmatically Jewish American male character. I am here indebted to Paul Breines's *Tough Jews: Political Fantasies and the Moral Dilemma of American Jewry*.[11] Breines argues that the image of the Jewish male as a super-schlemiel is so accepted, even by Jews who want to counter it, that when Jews create a Jewish hero — a tough Jew — he turns out not to have Jewish characteristics at all. Hence, I believe, this Superman created out of the depths of the powerlessness felt by Siegel and Shuster, and hence many other characters cast in the same mold. Herein lies the dilemma: to create a heroic Jewish male image one must abandon the Jewish component and rely on the dominant culture's version of the heroic male. Jewish male heroes must be non-Jewish Jews, to borrow Isaac Deutscher's phrase. This is why it is so impossible to see Superman as a Jewish character. My purpose here is not to explain the circumstances under which Jewish men may have been said to be either mice or Supermen; it is to critique the dichotomized way in which the question is posed, and furthermore to look for alternatives to this inadequate approach to Jewish masculinity.

In *Tough Jews*, Breines discusses Leon Uris's *Exodus*, especially the film version, which defined Jewish heroism for a generation of American non-Jews. Its hero is Ari Ben Canaan, whose name tells us that he is a lion, but also a Canaanite, played in the film by Paul Newman, complete with blue eyes and all. Because the ethos of heroism has changed in recent years, and we now make heroes out of gangsters, instead of Ari ben Canaan played by Paul Newman we now have Bugsy Siegel played by Warren Beatty; but the principle remains the same. Jews have to out-Gentile the Gentiles in order to make it. The point is made in Breines's book by Arthur Koestler, who was a member of a *Burschenshaft*, a Jewish fraternity, in Vienna in the early part of this century. Koestler writes that the member was

> to demonstrate that "Jews could hold their own in dueling, brawling, drinking and singing just like other people. According to the laws of inferiority and overcompensation," Koestler adds, "they were soon out-Heroding Herod once more"—practicing dueling for hours each day, eventually becoming the "most feared and aggressive swordsmen at the University."[12]

The dichotomization of Jewish masculinity appears again in the following passage from *Tough Jews*, in which Breines quotes from Philip Roth's *The Counterlife*. A male Jewish "not altogether disillusioned, left-leaning, Zionist intellectual" says the following about American Jews in Israel.[13]   Note the counterpoint of a feminized Yiddish culture and language against a masculinized Hebrew and Israeli language and culture, and the need for American Jews to achieve a clear positive Jewish identity through vicarious identification with Jews elsewhere, whether they be Israeli Jews as in this case or the Jews of the Holocaust, as in *Maus*:

> The American Jews get a big thrill from the guns. They see Jews walking around with guns and they think they're in paradise. Reasonable people with a civilized repugnance for violence and blood, they come on tour from America, and they see the guns and they see the beards and they take leave of their senses. The beards to remind them of saintly Yiddish weakness and the guns to reassure them of heroic Hebrew force.[14]

The difficulty of coming to terms with the question of what constitutes heroism and courage in Israel and in the Holocaust emerges again in Lawrence Langer's *New York Times* book review of Tom Segev's *The Seventh Million: The Israelis and the Holocaust*, in which Langer writes:

> Segev offers an illuminating account of how "Holocaust" and "heroism" came to be associated in the public imagination, especially through the naming of the Yad Vashem Holocaust Martyrs' and Heroes Remembrance Authority and the Ghetto Fighters' Museum (and kibbutz). He observes provocatively that because of this association, many surviving victims

Holocaust but had not rebelled. The myth of heroism was a heavy burden, at odds with their memories and experiences.[15]

It seems to me that in speaking of the Holocaust, to put the word "merely" in front of the word "survived" is itself a crime against humanity. But according to this book, at least some of the survivors have come to feel this about themselves. The slander of having gone like lambs to the slaughter weighs particularly heavily on Jewish men because of the history of expectations of male heroism. We very much need a more nuanced understanding of the relationship between victimization and heroism, able to overcome the dichotomy between being either a total victim or a total hero. Discussions of the nature of survival in the Holocaust have been distorted by the exaggerated dichotomies between heroism and victimization I have argued to be endemic to discussions of Jewish men.[16]

Sexualities and Their Discontents

Jewish men being seen as powerless, as victims, means they are seen as effeminate in our culture. And effeminacy here signals homosexuality. There are indeed important historical structural parallels between anti-Semitism and the oppression of lesbians and gays in that they share certain essential characteristics. Unlike forms of oppression like racism and sexism, one cannot by and large tell by just looking who is or is not Jewish or lesbian or gay. However, in both anti-Semitism and lesbian and gay oppression there are stereotypes that say you can tell who is who just by appearance and behavior. These two forms of oppression are therefore uniquely suited to terrorize the population as a whole, to have everyone policing themselves lest they appear to be "one of them." Heterosexism has accordingly played the role in the United States in the 1980s that anti-Semitism played in Europe in the 1930s, functioning as pivotal in "law and order" campaigns to intimidate and isolate the population as a whole. The connections between these two phenomena come further into view when one realizes how much of the current wave of Jewish feminism has been Jewish lesbian feminism. In accordance with the Jewish precept of paying one's intellectual debts and honoring one's teachers, we must keep at the forefront of our consciousness how impoverished Jewish feminism would be without those very important contributions.

The common or analogous marginalization of Jews and other "Others" is also discussed in Michael Kimmel's essay "Judaism,

Masculinity, and Feminism," in which Kimmel talks about walking down the streets of New York City in an anti-Vietnam War parade when someone yells from the sidewalk "Drop dead, you commie Jew fag!"[17] Kimmel wonders why that combination of epithets rolls so trippingly off the tongue. What do they have in common? He answers that all three are perceived as being less than real men, as threatening the nation's national and sexual security.

The issue of Jewish men being seen as effeminate within the Jewish tradition is discussed by Lori Lefkovitz in "Coats and Tales: Joseph Stories and Myths of Jewish Masculinity," in which Lefkovitz examines the history of the interpretation of the story of Joseph.[18] The text says little more about Joseph's appearance than that he is beautiful. But at a certain historical moment this becomes an interpretive problem for the rabbis. Perhaps he is too beautiful. Why did he resist the sexual advances of Potiphar's wife anyway? Maybe something's wrong; maybe he is not sufficiently masculine? The story becomes problematic, and various midrashic solutions emerge to try to solve the problem. Some argue that Potiphar's wife was unattractive, whereas others alternatively marvel at Joseph's ability to control his manly lusts. Joseph also partakes of the pattern in which, as Lefkovitz points out,

> It is the younger son, often the child of the more beloved but less fertile wife, the physically smaller, less hirsute, more delicate, more domestic son, the son closer to the mother, a hero of intellect rather than of brawn, who will be chosen by God over his brothers. An awareness of this pattern may have contributed to an image of the Jews as a feminized people ruled by their women.[19]

Feeling themselves under continual threat of feminization, many Jewish men bristle at any suggestions of homosexuality. For example, consider the recent uproar when Labor Party Israeli Knesset member Yael Dayan began speaking of David's love for Jonathan as homosexual in the context of a debate over the rights of gays and lesbians in Israel's military.[20]

The dominant contemporary image of Jewish male heterosexuality in our culture is of sexual incompetence, like Clark Kent or the early Woody Allen. In stark contrast to this contemporary American image Andrea Dworkin's essay "The Sexual Mythology of Anti-Semitism" very usefully reminds us that in Nazi ideology the Jewish male was the rapist, cast in images very similar to the myths of African-American men in the United States.[21]   Stereotypes of the sexuality of Jewish men have been much more varied than we often realize.

Circumcision and Rebirth

If there is any quintessential issue of Jewish masculinity, it would have to be circumcision, which raises in a different context many of the issues discussed here. But anyone looking for current discussions of this issue among men in the Jewish community will be met by an almost deafening silence. I have been told more than once that when this subject comes up in rabbinic training, men begin to giggle. The classic theological interpretation of circumcision, of course, treats it as the mark of the covenant. Kabbalistic interpretation regards circumcision as symbolic feminization.[22]   Were one to ask most Jews what the significance of circumcision was, one would most likely hear an explanation about the sublimation of sexuality and the suppression of instinct. These accounts look at the effect of circumcision on the male who is circumcised, as it might seem obvious to do. In contrast, I wish to consider the other male most prominently involved, the father, whom the tradition holds responsible for performing the circumcision.

Various anthropological theories attempt to explain circumcision rituals in many cultures, most of which perform the rite at puberty rather than infancy. The extent to which these theories are applicable to the Jewish case is therefore questionable. Though the theory I wish to apply is in my view better suited to explain circumcision at puberty than infancy, it will nonetheless be useful to follow a certain line of thought.

In tribal cultures, anthropologists tell us, at the stage in life in which he is called upon to have his son circumcised, the father, the patriarch, traditionally faced competition to his authority from two different directions. One is from the tribe. By this point in life, one has established oneself as head of one's own family, presumably with some accumulated wealth. So why, then, would it not be more advantageous to go off and start one's own clan? What keeps one bound to one's tribe of origin? At the birth of a son the tribe has reason to worry that a new competing clan may be inaugurated. The tribe therefore looks for tests by which it might assure itself of the father's loyalty. The father also faces a future potential threat from the son's impending ascension to power. There is now going to be a new male rival, not only for the mother's affections but eventually also for power and authority.

The hypothesis that many anthropologists have come to endorse is that in many cultures circumcision represents the father's making a symbolic sacrifice of the son to the tribe, thereby reassuring the tribe of his loyalty and binding him to the tribe by the sacrifice. Furthermore, it sublimates the father's aggression toward the son. The father might be experiencing impulses to rid himself of this potential rival, to perhaps commit infanticide.

The hostility of fathers toward sons is present in the founding myths of many cultures. In the Greek tradition, and the Freudian tradition that adopts it, prior to the Oedipus complex lies the Laius complex. The story starts because Laius fears his son is going to kill him, so he launches a preemptive strike to get rid of him before he becomes a threat. In the Christian story, the Christian God the Father allows his son Jesus to die on the cross. The Jewish tradition has the Akedah, the story of Abraham and the binding of Isaac. Of those three founding stories, the Jewish case is the only one where the murderous intention is not carried through (Laius did not succeed, but he never changed his intention to kill his son). I would argue that one can link circumcision to the halting of that sacrifice. The symbolic act of cutting replaces Abraham's descending knife.

The halting of Abraham's murderous act is also the birth of the Jewish people, because it reaffirms God's commitment to found a nation, a promise called into question by the possible death of Isaac. This moment is thus a rebirth, specifically a masculine rebirth. The first birth, into the body, was given to Isaac by Sarah. But the rebirth into the covenant, into the spirit rather than the body, is conferred by Abraham. This fits a pattern common in many cultures in which women's birthing powers are appropriated by men, whether by rituals of circumcision or baptism. Men confer the more important life of the soul, whereas women confer merely the life of the body. Sarah's absence from this story is therefore not just an omission in the text. Rather, it is a fundamental part of what the story is about, a story about a male-to-male conferring of life.

This idea of male birth, male creation of life, is very powerful and visible in many cultures. Sometimes the role of women in giving birth is bypassed by a myth of birth coming directly from the land. For example, one of the founding fathers of modern political theory, Thomas Hobbes, in developing the foundations for his new science of politics instructs his readers "to consider men as if but even now sprung out of the earth, and suddenly, like mushrooms, come to full maturity, without all kind of engagement with each other."[23]

If one were in the grip of this male appropriation of birth, when one arrived in a new land one might come to think that one had a direct relationship to it, unmediated by any other person. So to Europeans arriving on the shores of America, Native Americans were simply invisible. One plants one's flag pole directly in the earth (I choose to retain all the Freudian connotations here) and claims the land as one's own, simply not registering the presence of other people who were there before your arrival. And when Zionists come to Israel to give birth to the new state, the presence of prior inhabitants might also not sufficiently register, were one under the sway of a male vision of giving birth directly from the land, unmediated by any other presence. One cannot then bring under one's purview the people present prior to one's own birth. One lacks the umbilical cord that might connect one back through the generations. I therefore wish to argue that its masculinity has proven to be the Achilles heel of Zionism, its tragic flaw of being unable to adequately recognize the people present on the land before Israel's own birth.

On numerous occasions I have encountered the term "feminist Judaism," by which is meant not simply an egalitarian role for women within Judaism, what some call "Jewish feminism," but rather a Judaism transformed as a whole by the full inclusion of women's perspectives. However, I have never heard a discussion of feminist Zionism and what that might look like. It seems to me that feminist Zionism would not only be egalitarian Zionism, but a Zionism that would have at the center of its vision a consciousness of the needs of other peoples already on the land when modern Zionism began the work of giving birth to the state of Israel.

Conclusion

I shall close by returning to Superman, now as discussed in Arthur Flannigan-Saint-Aubin's essay "The Male Body and Literary Metaphors for Masculinity," in which he cites an interview with Superman's creators to the effect that they "were never able to imagine the Man of Steel with a penis."[24] His interpretation is that Superman's whole body is phallic, and one can't very well have one penis atop another. He argues further that the Freudian model of masculinity has conceptualized the male genitals as synonymous with the phallus, thereby ignoring the testicles, constituting a massive displacement and denial. Freudians have spoken for generations about castration anxiety as being anxiety about the loss of the phallus. Actual castration, however, involves the testicles, not the penis. This misidentification goes remarkably untreated.

Flannigan-Saint-Aubin sees a model for a desirable masculinity in the new character of Clark Kent. The once familiar characters have undergone major revisions of late in the comic books and even more recently in the ABC television series "Lois & Clark: The New Adventures of Superman." Superman now has his share of existential anxieties—he is a stranger in a strange land, worried about adjusting to terrestrial culture.[25] And Clark is no longer the timid mouse of old. He now has adventures in his own right. Both Superman and Clark are now more complete, integrated personalities. Seeing Clark as a model of masculinity is thus not to adopt a completely passive stance. Rather, this endorses a mode of masculinity designed to overcome the dichotomous polarizations I earlier argued were endemic to portrayals of Jewish men. In his search for a new embodied metaphor to symbolize this new masculinity, Flannigan-Saint-Aubin comes to envisage testicular as opposed to phallic imagery. As opposed to the phallus, understood as hard, aggressive, and linear, the testicles just sort of "hang loose." They are vulnerable, sensitive, plural rather than singular, and even generative of life, as the source where semen is produced.[26]

Flannigan-Saint-Aubin's image for a more positive masculinity of course refers to men in general, not specifically to Jewish men. I close with a cautionary note about contemporary culture's use of images of Jewish men to embody changes in men along these lines. Some have seen as a sign of progress the presence of a number of positive Jewish male characters on U.S. network television in recent years, including Michael on "thirtysomething," Stuart on "L. A. Law," Joel on "Northern Exposure," and Jerry on "Seinfeld" (who now that he is a comedy writer for a TV show should be seen as a successor to Buddy on the old "Dick Van Dyke Show" whose ambivalent Jewishness is evidenced by his appearance on the "Alan Brady Christmas Show" without comment, while having his Bar Mitzvah in another episode).

The choice of Jewish men to represent such nice, sensitive, "new" men might therefore be seen as an occasion for Jewish pride, especially because they are so identified as Jews, in contrast to what Donna Perlmutter called the "blatant de-Jewification" carried out when such works as Nora Ephron's *Heartburn* and Neil Simon's *Brighton Beach Memoirs* made their transitions to the screen in the eighties.[27] However, I would argue that the choice of Jewish men to embody this type represents a strategy whereby the producers of these shows minimize their risks. Since Jewish men are already seen as feminized by the culture, using them to embody the more "sensitive" traits stereotypically associated with women is therefore both less threatening and more plausible to the audience than if these characters were blond, blue-eyed WASPS. In the same vein a generation ago, the first commercial film released by a major studio to focus on a gay relationship, John Schlesinger's 1971 *Sunday Bloody Sunday,* starred Peter Finch as the bisexual Jewish doctor. While these characterizations certainly do contain positive traits, the common use of Jewish male characters to embody characteristics usually considered "softer" thus presupposes the culture's negative valuation of Jewish men as already feminized, and is thus implicated in this characterization constructed by the culture to be disparaging. Thus, despite what may be initial appearances to the contrary, images of Jewish men continue to incorporate the ambiguities usually present in such images.

NOTES

1. I wish to express my thanks to the organizers of the Melton Center's "Gender and Judaism" Conference for inviting me to speak, and thus giving me the opportunity to develop the ideas herein expressed, and to the reviewers of this volume for helping me to refine them. Because I am acutely aware of how it has been women's struggles that have made possible the discussion of gender within Judaism, I greatly appreciate the generosity of spirit shown by devoting a plenary session to the subject of Jewish masculinity.
2. *Action Comics,* No. 1, June 1938, Detective Comics, Inc.
3. *The Village Voice,* 4 August, 1992, 1 & 86.
4. Henry Louis Gates, Jr., "A Big Brother from Another Planet," *New York Times,* 12 September 1993, Section H, 51.
5. The writers and editors of Superman comics were aware of the problem. Among several stories exploring the issue, the cover story of the October 1963 issue of *Action Comics,* No. 305, is "Why Superman Needs a Secret Identity," told as "An Imaginary Story" picturing various catastrophes that would befall Superman and those closest to him were he to lose his secret identity (ed. Mort Weisinger [Sparta, IL: National Periodical Publications], 1-14). The last panel of the story carries an invitation: "Readers, can you figure out some more reasons why a secret identity is so vital to Superman? We'll print the best letters."
6. Jules Feiffer, ed., *The Great Comic Book Heroes* (New York: Dial Press, 1965), 18-21.
7. *Batman Returns,* Tim Burton, Dir. (Warner Bros., 1992).
8. Paul Hoch, *White Hero, Black Beast: Racism, Sexism, and the Mask of Masculinity* (London: Pluto Press, 1979), 49-50. Hoch is quoting from the novelization of the film.
9. Art Spiegelman, *Maus: A Survivor's Tale,* Vols. 1-2 (New York: Pantheon, 1986, 1991).
10. E. Nelson Bridwell, ed., *Superman: From the Thirties to the Seventies* (New York: Crown, 1971), 13.
11. Paul Breines, *Tough Jews: Political Fantasies and the Moral Dilemma of American Jewry* (New York: Basic Books, 1990).

12 . Breines, *Tough Jews*, 141.

13 . On the conflict between the "Jewboy" vs. the "nice Jewish boy" in Roth see Barbara Gottfried, "What Do Men Want, Dr. Roth?", *A Mensch among Men: Explorations in Jewish Masculinity*, ed. Harry Brod (Freedom, CA: Crossing Press, 1988), 37-52. In citing this and other essays from a book I edited I do not wish to engage in self-promotion but rather to acknowledge those whose work has influenced my own.

14 . Breines, *Tough Jews*, 22.

15 . Lawrence L. Langer, "Zion's Response to the Holocaust," *New York Times Book Review*, 18 April 1993, 37.

16 . One of the possible sources of a more nuanced understanding of the dialectic of victimization and resistance is recent scholarship on Jewish women's resistance in the Holocaust. I do not wish to assert here that women's actual behavior was necessarily different from men's, but merely that our understanding of the dynamics of survival has greatly benefited from a particularly sophisticated understanding of the dialectic of victimization and heroism provided by feminist scholars working on this subject. See for example Marlene E. Heinemann, *Gender and Destiny: Women Writers and the Holocaust* (New York: Greenwood Press, 1986) and Carol Rittner and John K. Roth, eds., *Different Voices: Women and the Holocaust* (New York: Paragon House, 1993).

17 . Michael Kimmel, "Judaism, Masculinity, and Feminism," in Brod, *Mensch*, 153-56.

18 . Lori Lefkovitz, "Coats and Tales: Joseph Stories and Myths of Jewish Masculinity," in Brod, *Mensch*, 19-29.

19 . Lefkovitz, "Coats and Tails," 20-21. See Arthur Waskow, *Godwrestling* (New York: Schocken, 1978).

20 . Michael Parks, "A New View of David Stirs Goliath-Size Roar," *New York Times*, 11 February 1993, Section A2, Cols. 1-2.

21 . Andrea Dworkin, "The Sexual Mythology of Anti-Semitism," in Brod, *Mensch*, 118-23.

22 . Wolfson, Elliot R. "On Becoming Female: Crossing Gender Boundaries in Kabbalistic Ritual and Myth," paper presented at the Gender and Judaism Conference, Melton Center for Jewish Studies, Ohio State University, Columbus, Ohio, April 26, 1993.

23 . Thomas Hobbes, "The Citizen: Philosophical Rudiments Concerning Government and Society," *Man and Citizen: Thomas Hobbes' De Homine and De Cive*, ed. Bernard Gert (Garden City: Doubleday, 1972), 205. Quoted in Christine Di Stefano, "Masculinity as Ideology in Political Theory: Hobbesian Man Considered," *Women's Studies International Forum* 6:6, 1983, 637.

24 . Arthur Flannigan-Saint-Aubin, "The Male Body and Literary Metaphors for Masculinity," *Theorizing Masculinities*, eds. Harry Brod and Michael Kaufman (Newbury Park, CA: Sage Publications, 1994), quoting R. Greenberger, J. Byrne, and M. Gold, eds., *The Greatest Superman Stories Ever Told* (New York: D. C. Comics, 1987).

25 . The anxiety-ridden comic book superhero was created by Stan Lee (born Stanley Lieber) at Marvel Comics in the 1960s. Spiderman, secretly Peter Parker, was guilt-laden over failing to stop the criminal who then murdered his Uncle Ben, with whom he and his Aunt May lived in Forest Hills (where I grew up) in New York City. Peter's personality was that of a teenage Clark. The role of Jewish men in the comic book industry is a subject worthy of discussion in its own right.

26 . Flannigan-Saint-Aubin's approach may perhaps best be understood as an application to men of the sort of approach taken by Luce Irigaray in *This Sex Which Is Not One*, trans. C. Porter (Ithaca: Cornell University Press, 1985).

27 . Donna Perlmutter, "Jewishness Goes Back in Closet on the Screen", *Los Angeles Times*, 12 April 1987, Calendar Section, 20-24.

Chapter 20

An Anthropological and Postmodern Critique of
Jewish Feminist Theory

Maurie Sacks

Introduction

Anthropologists believe that cultures operate as whole systems and that
subsystems, such as religions, cannot be understood outside the context
of the larger culture in which they operate. Religion, then, is simply an
analytical category that bounds certain behavior clusters, but does not
encompass the totality of a culture.[1]   Postmodernists espouse "a
wariness toward generalizations which transcend the boundaries of
culture and reason."[2]   Together, these two methods of inquiry suggest
that it is not possible to separate religion from culture or knowledge
from the particular "knower."

Postmodern thought insists attention be paid to multiple realities
that exist on the ground in time and space. Applied to Jewish feminist
scholarship, it demands that we understand the relationship between
Jewish-American feminism and Judaisms (even feminisms) that exist,
and have existed, in history. Postmodernism requires that we make
contemporary Jewish feminism an object of study and relinquish the
comfort of a "God's eye view"[3] that privileges our ideal egalitarian
Judaism as morally superior. In order to construct a postmodern Jewish
social science we must not only interject history into our cultural
imagination of Judaism, but we must also shape methodologies capable
of describing Judaisms as they exist for their carriers, methodologies
that allow Jewish women as well as men to be voiced members of

Jewish societies. This may mean abandoning the assumption that constructs such as dominance and subordination, public and private, power and impotence, derived from western liberal philosophy are useful concepts in the study of gender cross-culturally. Anthropology has gone a long way toward developing a postmodern social science. This chapter examines how it has done this, and how anthropological methods and thought have been useful in examining Jewish gender systems and Jewish feminist theory.

Anthropological Methods and Feminist Social Scientists

Anthropology offers three approaches to the study of human behavior that are useful in the pursuit of a social science that recognizes both men's and women's roles in constructing society and culture as well as the particularism of each local culture: ethnography, holism, and reflexivity.

Ethnography. Ethnographic research documents people's lives through the use of qualitative research methods like interviews, life histories, and participation in the daily activities of informants. These methods have only recently been applied to the study of Jewish women's lives.[4] Ethnography is an important strategy for ending the age-old "silence" of Jewish women cited in Jewish feminist literature of the 1970s–1980s.[5] Sered's work on elderly Middle Eastern Jewish women in Jerusalem as ritual experts,[6] Davidman's and Kaufman's work on *ba'alot t'shuva*,[7] and my own work on *shalach mones* exchange among modern Orthodox Jews in New Jersey[8] are examples of the ethnography of gender. Ethnographic knowledge of Jewish women is further enhanced through ethnohistorical scholarship that employs analysis of heretofore unexamined documents to throw light on women's roles in constructing Jewish society and culture. Weissler's work on *tehines* or women's vernacular prayers of the sixteenth through nineteenth centuries[9] is a major contribution along these lines, as are Baum, Hyman and Michel's work on Jewish Women in America, Berkowitz's on women's roles in the development of European Zionism,[10] and Baskin's *Jewish Women in Historical Perspective*, along with many others. Taken together, these works document the fact that Jewish women have, over the centuries, actively constructed Jewish culture and have not simply been victims of it.

Holism. The holistic approach that anthropology takes to the study of society and culture contrasts with the strategy of many Jewish scholars interested in gender issues. Paula Hyman, at a recent

American Anthropological Association meeting, noted that some Jewish scholars have jokingly referred to their own work as the study of texts addressing texts.[11] Anthropological holism insists that no subarea of culture such as religion or written texts, no matter how hoary, can be isolated from any other in the pursuit of ethnographic knowledge. From this perspective, a social scientific understanding of gender roles in the historical enterprise of Jewish culture cannot be divorced from insight into the material conditions of life, social structure, and folk culture. Textual evidence alone, whether religious or more comprehensively historical, fails to illuminate, for anthropological purposes, the meaning of gender for Jewish men and women, nor can analysis of public religious behaviors, nor even attention to avowed values. Sanday demonstrates that understanding the meaning of gender systems from an anthropological point of view demands knowledge of the broader contexts of men's and women's social and economic lives.[12] She proposes that gender values derive from, and are symbolized by, origin myths that in turn are demonstrably associated with the manner in which societies make a living. Limiting inquiry to those behavior clusters commonly known as "religion" is insufficient to achieve a social scientific understanding of gender systems.

Reflexivity. Furthermore, anthropological reflexivity, or critical anthropology, meshes with other postmodern lines of inquiry, such as feminist criticism, that question the nature of how we know what we know. This line of thinking criticizes the notion that researchers, laden as we are by both our enculturated and gendered views of what positivists presume to be "reality," can possibly be "objective" in our assessment of observed phenomena. Young-Eisendrath notes that the biased nature of the gendered researcher as data collector requires "constant examination of assumptions and motivations."[13]

During the 1970s a genre of feminist ethnography appeared that questioned and contradicted the texts as established by male anthropologists and women influenced and trained in the male manner of generating and questioning ethnographic data.[14] The very existence of this feminist discourse required a re-examination of the assumptions upon which the discipline of anthropology was based, and a literature addressing these issues was soon forthcoming.[15]

Freed from positivism, one of the contributions anthropologists have made to gender studies is the exploration of the possibility that, in some cultures, men and women have different cognitive maps of the reality in which they both live as bearers of a single culture. Ardener, in what in 1975 was ground-breaking work, suggested that we need to question the very idea that social discourse is monological, that there is one "truth" that can be elicited from any member of a culture regardless of gender.

The concept that there could be different gendered realities in one sociocultural system was being explored, at the same time, by French feminist thinkers Helene Cixoux and Luce Irigiray. Working from Lacan, they proposed that the very discourse of Western culture that seeks to determine who is dominant, who subordinate, is male-centered.[16] These notions of relative power relations have been developed mostly by male thinkers. Deconstruction of these male concepts, then, opens the way for the demystification of patriarchy and legitimizes serious investigation of a female way of being.

In the mid-1980s, literary critic, Elaine Showalter, a followed up on this line of thinking by proposing a "female" phase of women's writing that frees itself of "both imitation [of] and protest [against male discourse]—two forms of dependency—and turn[s] instead to female experience as the source of an autonomous art."[17]

Chava Weissler suggests that pursuing the concept of an independent female mode of experiencing Judaism can "transform" our understanding of Judaism by bringing to the fore women's experiences and relegating men's Judaism to the background. Recently, Susan Sered has proposed that female Judaisms, nonliterate and undocumented, have survived through the ages and that to understand the true balance of power in Jewish gender systems we must learn to value women's folk Judaism equally with male-dominated formal Judaism. In my fieldwork among Turkish Muslims and Orthodox American Jews, I corroborated the presence in these cultures of a shared female experience that does not support the common-knowledge belief in clear-cut female subordination and male dominance. To my knowledge, few Jewish feminist scholars have been investigating the constructed nature of our own feminist beliefs.

The Concept of Power in Feminist Discourse

Anthropologists have contributed to the debate on the nature of power that is central to feminist concerns about gender relationships. Scholars like Annette Weiner, Beverly Chinas, and Jane Goodale examine different definitions of power and look at patriarchal cultures from a female point of view.[18] Weiner argues that women's power can be experienced only when the concept "power" is defined to include women's influential behavior in reproducing the relationships that constitute society.[19]   This aspect of "power" is not usually included in the modern Western concept, and is generally ignored by Jewish feminists.

Weiner also argues that women's material wealth often goes unrecognized by Western researchers because we value men's wealth more. A major goal of American feminism is to acquire equal access for women to material wealth.   Jewish feminists have, among other concerns, the exclusion of women from professional Jewish opportunities, especially those offering the highest remuneration. However, in Jewish culture women have often been the breadwinners of the family or, if not, the purse-keepers.   Jewish women's overrepresentation in the American feminist movement could be related to the fact that they have the cultural expectation that women will be engaged in the marketplace and have material power. Could the fact that the American feminist movement has moved resolutely in the direction of women's equal access to the marketplace and public statuses, rather than in the direction of establishing support for women's traditional activities as have third-world feminisms, be related to the Jewish women's economic position in Eastern European *shtetlach*?

Further, in Jewish feminist discourse, women's material wealth in the form of ritual objects, heirlooms, even control over daily expenses and food has often been overlooked as a source of power. If women control domestic culture, then, according to Jenna Joselit they "have exerted a powerful influence on the way American Jews lived their lives, not only guiding their consumption of food and uses of space but also shaping their relationship to the larger society and to one another."[20] Joselit also shows that women have even been instrumental in inventing the ceremonies that take place within the home, like the American Hanukah, a response to the American Christmas for Jewish children attending secular schools with their Christian counterparts, the likes of which does not exist in other Judaisms.[21]   Barbara Kirshenblatt-Gimblett analyzes the role of women in creating Jewish-American cuisine, and concludes that American Jewish women, through their cookbooks and shared gastronomical experiences, invented American Jews who, ultimately, are what they eat.[22]   Kirshenblatt-Gimblett's paper on torah binders[23] is another exception to the general dearth of acknowledgments of women's construction of Jewish culture.

Power and the Private-Public Debate

Another aspect of feminist discourse that has not been adequately explored by Jewish feminists is the public-private dimension of power. It is assumed by many American feminists that public power is superior to power in the private sphere and therefore if women are barred from participation in public statuses, then they must be inferior in value in a society. Some Jewish feminists have only recently discovered the work of anthropologist Michele Rosaldo, published in 1974, in which she examined the public/private concept and reached precisely this conclusion.[24]   However, anthropologists have come to question the utility of the public/private construct, and its applicability cross-culturally. Again, by defining the private as inferior, and somehow not organically necessary to the functioning of the public spheres, Western thinkers are able to disempower women conceptually by devaluing precisely what they do.

Beverly Chinas, in the 1970s, did some important work on the power inherent in "private" sphere, feminine, functions. In her work on the Isthmus Zapotecs, a patriarchal culture in Mexico, Chinas observed that women frequently controlled men, but there were no formal, publicly, and openly named status roles that acknowledged the behaviors involved. Women, in roles as "peace keepers," might physically steer a drunk and potentially violent man to a safe place to dry out, for example. Because they could freely visit neighbors or kin, women were capable of gathering information unavailable to men, who could be blocked from social intercourse with certain households because of publicly known animosities to which women did not have to defer. In these roles of "peacekeeper" or "information gatherer," women limited or influenced men's decisions and actions, but were not acknowledged by status-names.[25]   Likewise, in Jewish culture, there are no named statuses for "reproducer of social relations" or "inventor of folk (unofficial) ritual," or "mediator between Jewish and secular culture," or even "manager of major traditional rituals" such as *bar mitzvah*,[26] the Passover *seder*, or the *Shabbos* meal. Because men's statuses are named openly—like "rabbi," "scholar," "member of the minyan"—they appear to receive more value. Little work has been done, after Chinas, on the role of "covert" statuses in social organization, and understanding of Jewish women's culture has suffered from this omission.

Anthropologists have pointed out that, in fact, domestic behaviors have great bearing on public institutions and the behaviors of men in public places. Joselit's observation that domestic culture determines not only the daily content of Jewish lives, but also shapes Jews' relationships to the larger society and to one another, is an insight along these lines. My own fieldwork revealed that modern Orthodox women in New Jersey are extremely conscious of their roles in building the very communities that supported the institutions in which they are supposedly subordinated.[27]

Contemporary American Jewish Feminism in Context

In contemporary America, Jewish women are among the most educated, most likely to be in responsible and well-paid positions in the marketplace, latest to marry, and least likely to have many children.[28] With a life expectancy of nearly fourscore years, Jewish-American women are devoting less time to domestic responsibilities than ever before; many remain single for large portions of their lives. Those wishing to live lives in which Judaism has great significance are almost forced to look to Jewish professions or to performance of public ritual roles if they reject the alternative of the Orthodoxies that support separate male and female gender roles. As women used to being educated with men, getting into the best secular colleges, and achieving in publicly acknowledged statuses, these women have experienced exclusion from what they perceive to be the seats of power and personal satisfaction in Judaism: the synagogue, the house of learning, and the professional Jewish power structure. Jewish feminist scholars and writers are, being high achievers, probably even more likely than other professional women to be uncomfortable about traditional Jewish gender roles. Being published, with or without sanction of a doctorate, gives us an aura of knowledgeability and "objectivity" in the minds of students and readers that, from the point of view of reflexivity, is unwarranted. Far from being "scientific," our work is colored by our own subjective experience. This experience is shaped as much by American feminist discourse as it is by the nature of gendered Judaism. It is, I would submit for example, our Western experience and not our Jewish experience that rejects domesticity as an equally highly valued subculture as the cultures of the synagogue, the Seminary, or Federation. It is our eighty-year life expectancy, coupled with our penchant for having no more than 1.8 children, that causes our lives to loom bereft of Jewish focus unless we find roles for ourselves in worship services or Jewish professionalism.

Our personal needs to construct lives that are Jewishly meaningful drive some of us to participate in the *Havurah* movement, an egalitarian and informal alternative to organized Jewish practice that brings worship into the home, or at least into a milieu that more resembles the extended families of our cultural imagination than do our real families, which are separated by divorces or scattered all over the country. Egalitarian Judaism, from this point of view, is not an evolutionary progression to a superior form of Judaism, but an adaptation to the specific needs experienced by a particular class of Jewish-American women of a certain age who have had common life experiences. As such, it is not different in kind from other Jewish adaptations to historical circumstances. Support for this interpretation may be derived from the evidence that American-style egalitarian Judaism has not caught on in other contemporary world Jewrys.

It is important to understand that a postmodern reading of contemporary American Jewish feminism does not in any way diminish the meaning egalitarian Judaism has for many American women. It meets our needs for individual expression as scholars, professional Jews, and religious Jews. This is a very personal experience, however, not based on scientific facts or a generalizable moral superiority. Postmodern scholars wishing to contribute to a Jewish social science need increasingly to make the distinction between our personal perceptions and our subjective selves, on the one hand, and our Judaism, as objects of our inquiry, on the other. In this way we can distinguish our Judaism from other Judaisms such as Orthodox Judaism, which answer to the needs of other people, and are equally valid and moral forms of Jewish practice from postmodern and anthropological perspectives.

In Jewish studies, both in the humanities and social sciences, scholarship has been used to support political positions, especially those espousing a morally superior "egalitarian" Judaism without much thought having been given to the subjectivity of the scholars themselves. Political correctness, in the context of the American academy, calls for belief in the moral superiority of an androgenous gender system in which equality is equated with identity: differences between men and women are minimized as much as possible. Little reflection has been given to the fact that the Jewish feminist agenda for achieving an egalitarian and thus morally superior Judaism is based on a theory of gender constructed within the context of the American feminist movement of the 1970s. This theory is ahistorical, assuming a generalized and timeless subordination of women to men in Judaism that is captured in the written texts, public behaviors, and openly avowed values of a hypothetical Jewish culture that embraces and represents all Jewish cultures that have actually existed in specific times and places. In short, this theory recapitulates the nomothetic concerns of the Enlightenment and subsequent modern thought, but does not transcend them.

In conclusion, a Jewish social science that strives to understand what motivates persons who identify themselves as Jews to behave in certain ways, could not limit itself to the study of religion, but must examine the broader contexts of Jewish cultures, even the contexts of wider sociocultural systems in which Jews live. From this perspective it is more useful to consider contemporary American Jewish feminist scholarship, as well as Jewish feminist political action, as aspects of late twentieth-century Jewish-American culture themselves, rather than to take at face value feminist discourse concerning the nature of "Judaism" and its gender hierarchy. A Jewish social science must deconstruct the manner in which the American feminist discourse has influenced perceptions of gender in Judaism before it can provide a rational, as opposed to mainly emotional, basis for an agenda of social action.

NOTES

1. This chapter has evolved over a period of years. Acknowledgment is due to many colleagues who have discussed these ideas with me, including Neil Gillman and Barbara Kirshenblatt-Gimblett; and the scholars, Paula Hyman, Ellen Umansky, and Riv-Ellen Prell, who have responded to different versions. Montclair State College gave me released time during two different semesters to work on these ideas. Parts of this chapter will appear in the introduction to my book, *Women in Jewish Culture: Active Voices* which is forthcoming from the University of Illinois Press. This article appeared in *Jewish Political Studies Review*, vol. 6, no. 1-2 (1994).

2. L. J. Nicholson, *Feminism/Postmodernism* (London: Routledge, Chapman & Hall, 1990), 5.

3. Ibid., 3.

4. To date most ethnographies of Jewish communities concentrate on male institutions or ignore gender issues entirely. For example see F. K. Furman, *Beyond Yiddiskeit: The Struggle for Jewish Identity in a Reform Synagogue* (Albany: SUNY Press, 1987), S. C. Heilman, *Synagogue Life: A Study in Symbolic Interaction* (Chicago: Chicago University Press, 1973), and W. Toll, *The Making of an Ethnic Middle Class: Portland Jewry over Four Generations* (Albany: SUNY Press, 1983). An exception would be Riv-Ellen Prell, *Prayer and Community: The Havurah in American Judaism* (Detroit: Wayne State University, 1989).

5. See R. Adler, "The Jew Who Wasn't There: Halakhah and the Jewish Women" in S. Heschel, ed. *On Being a Jewish Feminist: A Reader* (New York Schocken, 1983); P. Hyman, "The Other Half: Women in Jewish Tradition," in E. Koltun, ed., *The Jewish Women: New Perspectives* (New York: Schocken, 1976); P. Hyman, "Lilith Interview: After a Decade of Jewish Feminism the Jewry Is Still Out," *Lilith*, 11(1983): 20-24.

6. Susan Sered, *Women as Ritual Experts: The Religious Lives of Elderly Jewish Women in Jerusalem* (New York: Oxford University Press, 1992).

7 . L. Davidman, *Tradition in a Rootless World: Women Turn to Orthodox Judaism* (Berkeley: University of California Press, 1991); D. R. Kaufman, *Rachel's Daughters: Newly Orthodox Jewish Women* (New Brunswick, NJ: Rutgers University Press, 1991).

8 . Maurie Sacks, "Competing Community at Purim," *Journal of American Folklore* 102, no. 405 (1989): 276–91.

9 . C. Weissler, "Prayers in Yiddish and the Religious World of Ashkenazic Women," in J. Baskin, ed., *Jewish Women in Historical Perspective* (Detroit: Wayne State University, 1991); "'For Women and Men Who Are Like Women': Construction of Gender in Yiddish Devotional Literature" *Journal of Feminist Studies in Religion* 5 no. 2 (1989): 7–24; "The Religion of Traditional Ashkenazic Women: Some Methodological Issues," *Association for Jewish Studies Review* 12 no. 1 (1987).

10 . C. Baum, P. Hyman, and S. Michel, *The Jewish Woman in America* (New York: Dial Press, 1976); M. Berkowitz, "Transcending 'Tsimmes and Sweetness': Recovering the History of Zionist Women in Central and Western Europe, 1897–1933," in M. Sacks, ed., *Women in Jewish Culture: Active Voices* (Champaign: University of Illinois Press, forthcoming), J. Baskin *Jewish Women in Historical Perspective.* (Detroit: Wayne State University Press, 1991).

11 . P. Hyman, commentary on the panel discussion "Jewish Women: Spirituality, Politics, and Identity" at the American Anthropological Association Meeting in San Francisco, December 1992.

12 . P. Sanday, *Female Power and Male Dominance: On the Origins of Sexual Inequality* (New York: Cambridge University Press, 1981).

13 . P. Young-Eisendrath, "The Female Person and How We Talk about Her," in M. M. Gergen, ed., *Feminist Thought and the Structure of Knowledge* (New York: New York University Press, 1988), 155.

14 . See for examples: A. Weiner, *Women of Value, Men of Renown: New Perspectives in Trobriand Exchange* (Austin: University of Texas Press, 1976); J. Goodale, *Tiwi Wives* (Seattle: University of Washington Press, 1982); B. Chinas, *The Isthmus Zapotecs: Women's Roles in Cultural Context* (New York: Holt, Rinehart and Winston, 1973).

15 . S. Ardener, *Perceiving Women* (New York: Halstead Press, 1975); R. Reiter, *Toward an Anthropology of Women* (New York: Monthly Review Press, 1975); S. Rodgers, "Women's Place: A Critical Review of Anthropological Theory," *Comparative Studies of Society and History*, vol. 29, no. 1 (January, 1978): 123–93; M. Z. Rosaldo and L. Lamphere, *Women, Culture and Society* (Stanford: Stanford University Press, 1974).

16 . H. Cixous, "Laugh of Medusa," *Signs* vol. 1, no. 4 (1976): 875–93; L. Irigiray, *Ce Sexe qui n'en pas un* (Paris: Editions de Minuit, 1977).

17 . E. Showalter, *The New Feminist Criticism: Essays on Women's Literature and Theory* (New York: Pantheon, 1985), 137–38; brackets added.

18 . Weiner, Chinas, and Goodale op cit.

19 . "A. Weiner, Trobriand Kinship From Another View: The Reproductive Power of Women and Men," *Man* (N.S.) 14 (1979): 159–81.

20 . J. Joselit, "'A Set Table': Jewish Domestic Culture in the New World, 1880–1950," in S. Braunstein and J. Joselit, eds., *Getting Comfortable in New York: The American Jewish Home, 1880–1950* (New York: Jewish Museum, 1992).

21 . Ibid.

22 . B. Kirshenblatt-Gimblett, "Kitchen Judaism," in S. Braunstein and Joselit, op. cit.

23 . B. Kirshenblatt-Gimblett, "The Cut That Binds: The Western Ashkenazic Torah Binder as Nexus between Circumcision and Torah," in V. Turner, ed., *Celebrations: A World of Art and Ritual* (Washington, D. C.: Smithsonian Institution, 1982), 136–46.

24 . Rosaldo and Lampere, op. cit.

25 . Chinas, op cit.

26 . J. Davis, "The *Bar Mitzvah Balabusta*: Mother's Role in the Family's Rite of Passage," in M. Sacks (Forthcoming), op. cit.

27 . M. Sacks (1989), op. cit.

28 . S. Cohen, J. Woocher, and B. Phillips, *Perspectives in Jewish Population Research* (Boulder, CO: Westview Press, 1984); S. B. Fishman, *A Breath of Life: Feminism in the American Jewish Community* (New York: Free Press, 1993); S. Goldstein and C. Goldscheider, *Jewish Americans: Three Generations in a Jewish Community* (Landham, MD: University Press of America, 1985); C. Waxman, *America's Jews in Transition* (Philadelphia: Temple University Press, 1983).

About the Editor

Tamar Rudavsky is Yassenoff Associate Professor of Philosophy and Jewish Studies in the Department of Philosophy, The Ohio State University, and Director of the Melton Center for Jewish Studies. She received her Ph.D. from Brandeis University, and is the editor of *Divine Omniscience and Omnipotence in Medieval Philosophy: Islamic, Jewish, and Christian Perspectives*. Her articles on medieval Jewish philosophy have appeared in *Da'at, The Journal of the History of Philosophy, Franziskanische Studien, The New Scholasticism,* and *Maimonidean Studies,* as well as in edited volumes and encyclopedias. Her current research involves an examination of conceptions of time and temporality in medieval Jewish philosophy. As a secondary research interest, she has continued to work on conceptions of gender in medieval metaphysics.

About the Contributors

Howard Adelman is Associate Professor and Director of the Program in Jewish Studies at Smith College. His current research projects include gender in early-modern Italian Jewish history, the life and thought of Leon Modena of seventeenth-century Venice, wife-beating in Jewish history, and Jewish-Christian relations, with a particular interest in martyrdom. He has published articles, taught courses, lectured, and organized conferences in these areas, and is now preparing books about them.

Harry Brod is editor of *The Making of Masculinities: The New Men's Studies* and *A Mensch among Men: Explorations in Jewish Masculinities* (with Michael Kaufman), and author of *Hegel's Philosophy of Politics: Idealism, Identity, and Modernity*. He teaches in the Philosophy Department at the University of Delaware.

Sylvia Barack Fishman is Assistant Professor of Contemporary American Jewish Life in the Near Eastern and Judaic Studies Department, and Senior Research Associate of the Cohen Center for Modern Jewish History, both at Brandeis University. She has published numerous articles and three books: *A Breath of Life: Feminism in the American Jewish Community* (Free Press/Macmillan, 1993); *Follow My Footprints: Changing Images of Women in American Jewish Fiction* (University Press of New England, 1992); and *Changing Jewish Life: Service Delivery and Planning in the 1990s*, ed., with Lawrence Sternberg and Gary Tobin (Greenwood Press, 1991). Her monograph on *Changing Lifestyles of American Jewish Women and Men* will be published by SUNY Press in 1994.

Harriet Pass Freidenreich is Professor of History at Temple University in Philadelphia. She is the author of *The Jews of Yugoslavia: A Quest for Community* and *Jewish Politics in Vienna, 1918-1938*. She is currently writing a collective biography of Jewish women who studied at universities in Germany and Austria before the Nazi era.

Laura Geller is Senior Rabbi of Temple Emanuel in Beverly Hills and the first woman to head a large American synagogue. She has also served as Executive Director of the American Jewish Congress, Pacific Southwest Region. Among her accomplishments at AJ Congress are the creation of the AJ Congress Feminist Center and the AJ Congress Jewish Urban Affairs Center. Her articles on Jewish feminism have appeared in *Tikkun, Sh'ma, Reform Judaism* and other journals and she has written chapters in many books. Presently she is at work on a book about traditional and innovative life-cycle rituals.

Zilla Jane Goodman is a Finkelstein Fellow at the University of Judaism in Los Angeles. She has published articles in modern Hebrew literature, concentrating on the work of S. Y. Agnon and N. Y. Berdichewski. Her current research deals with the fiction of David Grossman.

Leonard D. Gordon has recently accepted a rabbinical position at the Germantown Jewish Centre in Philadelphia. He has taught courses in the history of rabbinic literature at the Jewish Theological Seminary, at Kenyon College, and at The Ohio State University. His writing on gender and Judaism includes a contribution to *The Seminary at 100* and articles in *Kerem, Journal of the American Academy of Rabbis, Jewish Currents,* and *United Synagogue Review.*

Naomi Graetz teaches English at Ben Gurion University of the Negev, Beersheba. She was on the board of the Israel Women's Network and is a founding member of MASLAN (the Women's Support Center of the Negev). Among her publications is *S/He Created Them: Feminist Retelling of Biblical Tales.* In 1992, she was a Research Associate at the Five College Women's Studies Research Center at Mount Holyoke College. Her current research deals with attitudes toward wife-beating in the Jewish tradition, metaphor and *halakhah.*

Susannah Heschel holds the Abba Hillel Silver Chair in Jewish Studies in the Department of Religion, Case Western Reserve University. She has written extensively on Jewish-Christian relations in Germany, and has held the Martin Buber Visiting Professorship in Jewish Religious Philosophy at the University of Frankfurt. She is the editor of *On Being a Jewish Feminist: A Reader,* and is currently coediting *The Encyclopedia of Women and Religion*

Lori Hope Lefkovitz is Associate Professor of English at Kenyon College. She is the author of *The Character of Beauty in the Victorian Novel* and articles about Victorian fiction, literary theory, pedagogy, and feminism and Judaism. Her current projects include an edited collection, *Textual Bodies: Changing Boundaries of Literary Representation* (SUNY Press), and a book about the representation of biological sisters in literature and film.

Alan T. Levenson is Assistant Professor at the Cleveland College of Jewish Studies where he teaches modern Jewish thought and history. He has published articles in the *Leo Baeck Institute Yearbook, Studies in Zionism, Judaism: A Quarterly Journal,* and *Journal of Reform Judaism.*

Laura S. Levitt is an Assistant Professor of Jewish Studies in the Department of Religion at Temple University. She teaches graduate and undergraduate courses in both the Department of Religion and the Temple Women's Studies Program. Her recent publications include *Jewish Feminist Identity/ies: What Difference Can Feminist Theory Make?* She is currently working on a book on Jewish feminist identity/ies.

Jane Rachel Litman is currently Director of Curriculum and Faculty of the University of Judaism's Department of Continuing Education and is a member of the Jewish Studies and Women's Studies faculty at California State University at Northridge. She has written widely on issues of women's history, creative ritual and liturgy, and Jewish ethics and continuity. Her work has been published in *Sh'ma, Lilith, Plexus, The Reconstructionist, Womanspirit,* and other Jewish and women's magazines.

Dagmar C. G. Lorenz is Professor of German at The Ohio State University in Columbus. Her books include: *Ilse Aichinger, Franz Grillparzer- Dichter des sozialen Konflikts, Verfolgung bis zum Massenmord, Diskurse zum Holocaust in deutscher Sprache, Insiders and Outsiders,* and *Jewish and Gentile Culture in Germany and Austria.* Her current research deals with German, Austrian, German-Jewish, and women's literature.

Shulamit S. Magnus is Acting Assistant Professor of History at Stanford University. She is author of *Jewish Emancipation in a German City: Cologne, 1798-1871* (forthcoming), and articles about modern German Jewry and Jewish women's history. She is currently working on an analysis and translation of the memoirs of Pauline Wengeroff.

Rochelle L. Millen is Associate Professor of Religion at Wittenburg University, Springfield, Ohio. She has published widely in the area of women and *halakhah*. Her current research deals with the methodology of *halakah* and its relationship to social context. She is presently working on a manuscript on the intellectual world of Martin Buber and has been the recipient of Lilly Foundation grants for research and for international study.

Jody Myers is Associate Professor of Religious Studies and Coordinator of the Jewish Studies Program at California State University, Northridge. Her writings, which deal with the modern permutations of traditional Judaism, include "Attitudes toward the Resumption of Sacrificial Worship in the Nineteenth Century" and "The Messianiac Idea and Zionist Ideologies." She is currently completing a study of the religious activism of Zevi Hirsch Kalischer.

Pamela S. Nadell is Associate Professor of Jewish Studies at The American University and co-chair of the Jewish Women's Caucus (Association for Jewish Studies). In addition to her articles on Jewish immigration and American Jewish women, she is the author of *Conservative Judaism in America: A Biographical Dictionary and Sourcebook.* Her current research examines the movements for female rabbinic ordination.

Maurie Sacks is Associate Professor of Anthropology at Montclair State College in New Jersey. Her publications include *Women in Jewish Culture: Active Voices* which is forthcoming from the University of Illinois Press, and "Computing Community at Purim," *Journal of American Folklore* 102, 405, (July-Sept. 1989).

Alice Shalvi is Professor Emeritus of English Literature at the Hebrew University of Jerusalem, is the founding Chairwoman of the Israel Women's Network. Among her publications are *Shakespeare: The Man and his Art* (Hebrew and English); *Renaissance Concepts of Honour in Shakespeare's Problem Plays; Women in Israel;* and numerous articles on drama, education, and women-related issues.

Elliot R. Wolfson is Associate Professor and Director of Graduate Studies in the Skirball Department of Hebrew and Judaic Studies at New York University. He is the author of *The Book of the Pomegranate: Moses de Léon's Sefer ha-Rimmon* (Brown Judaica Series, 1988) and *Through a Speculum That Shines: Vision and Imagination in Medieval Jewish*

Mysticism (Princeton University Press, 1994). He has also published widely in scholarly journals and anthologies in the area of Jewish mysticism and philosophy. Two collections of his essays—*Along the Path: Studies in Kabbalistic Myth, Symbolism, and Hermeneutics* and *Circle in the Square: Studies in the Use of Gender in Kabbalistic Symbolism*—will appear in 1995. In addition, he is the editor of *The Journal of Jewish Thought and Philosophy* and co-editor of the *Series in Judaica: Mysticism, Hermeneutics, and Religion* for the State University of New York Press, as well as co-editor of *Études sur le judaisme médiéval* for E. J. Brill.

Bibliography

Abramov, Tehilla. 1983. *Devar Schmuel* no. 39. (Reprint of first ed., Venice, 1702).

———. 1988. *The Secret of Jewish Femininity: Insights into the Practice of Taharat HaMishpachah*, Malka Touger, trans. Southfield, MI: Targum Press.

Adelman, Howard. 1991. "Rabbis and Reality: The Public Roles of Jewish Women in the Renaissance and Catholic Restoration." *Jewish History* 5 (1): 27–40.

———. 1992. "Wife-Beating in Jewish History." *Association for Jewish Studies: Twenty-Fourth Annual Conference.* Boston.

———. forthcoming. "Finding Women's Voices in Italian Jewish Literature," *Women of the World: Jewish Women and Jewish Writing*, Judith Baskin, ed. Detroit: Wayne State University Press.

———. 1994. "Custom, Law, and Gender; Levirate Union among Ashkenazim and Sephardim after the Expulsion from Spain," *The Expulsion of the Jews: 1492 and After*, R. Waddington and Arthur H. Williamson, eds. New York: Garland.

Adler, Rachel. 1973. "*Tum'ah* and *Toharah*: Ends and Beginnings," *Response* 18, Summer: 117–27.

———. 1983. "The Jew Who Wasn't There: *Halakhah* and the Jewish Women," *On Being a Jewish Feminist: A Reader*, Susannah Heschel, ed. New York: Schocken.

———. 1991. "A Question of Boundaries: Toward a Jewish Feminist Theology of Self and Others," *Tikkun* 6 (3): 43–45.

Agus, Irving. 1947. *Rabbi Meir of Rothenburg.* Philadelphia: Jewish Publication Society.

Alcalay, Reuben. 1965. *The Complete Hebrew-English Dictionary.* Tel Aviv: Massadah Publishing.

Alt, Franz. 1989. *Jesus: Der erste neue Mann.* Munich: Piper Verlag.

Altmann, A. 1944. "Gnostic Themes in Rabbinic Cosmology," *Essays in Honour of the Very Rev. Dr. J. H. Hertz, Chief Rabbi on the Occasion of His Seventieth Birthday*, I. Epstein, E. Levine, and C. Roth, eds. London: Edward Goldston, 23–24.

Ardener, S. 1975. *Perceiving Women.* New York: Halstead Press.

Asis, Tom Yov. 1981. "'Herem derabbenu gershom'," *Tzion* 46: 267–69.

Auerbach, Nina. 1982. *Woman and the Demon: The Life of a Victorian Myth.* Cambridge: Cambridge University Press.

Avivi, Y. 1985. "Joseph ibn Tabul's Sermons on the *Kawwanot*," *Studies in Memory of the Rishon le-Zion Yitzhak Nissim*, M. Benayahu, ed. Jerusalem.

Baader, Maria. 1993. "Zum Abscheid: Über den Versuch, als jüdische Feministin in der Berliner Frauenszene einen Platz zu finden," *Enfernte Verbindungen: Raissismus, Antisemitismus, Klassenunterdrückung*, Ika Hügel, Chris Lange et al. , eds. Berlin: Orlanda Frauenverlag, 82–94.

Bal, Mieke. 1987. *Lethal Love: Feminist Literary Readings of Biblical Love Stories.* Bloomington: Indiana University Press.

Bar-Asher, M. 1972. *Qovetz Ma'amarim biLeshon Chazal.* Jerusalem: Hebrew University.

Baron, Devorah. 1960. *Agav Orcha.* Merchavia: Sifriyat Poalim.

———. 1968. *Parshiyot.* Jerusalem: Bialik Institute.

———. 1969. *The Thorny Path*, Joseph Schachterk, trans. Jerusalem.

Baskin, Judith, ed. 1991. *Jewish Women in Historical Perspective.* Detroit: Wayne State University Press.

———, ed. forthcoming. *Women of the World: Jewish Women and Jewish Writing.* Detroit: Wayne State University Press.

Baum, C., Hyman, P., and Michel, S. 1976. *The Jewish Women in America*. New York: Dial Press.

Baumgardt, David. 1957. "The Ethics of Lazarus and Steinthal." *Leo Baeck Institute Yearbook* 2: 205–17.

Belke, Ingrid. 1971. *Moritz Lazarus und Heymann Steinthal: Die Begruender der Voelkerpsychologie in ihren Briefen*, Vol. 1. Tübingen: J. C. B. Mohr.

Beller, Steven. 1987. "Class, Culture and the Jews of Vienna, 1900," *Jews, Antisemitism and Culture in Vienna*, Ivar Oxaal, Michael Pollak, and Gerhard Boltz, eds. London: Routledge.

Benedict, Libbian. 1926. "Jewish Women Headliners—XLVIII: Clarice M. Baraight—Magistrate," *American Hebrew* 1, January.

Berger, Sh. Z. 1992. "*Tehines*: A Brief Survey of Women's Prayers," *Daughters of the King: Women and the Synagogue*, S. Grossman. and R. Haut, eds. Philadelphia: Jewish Publication Society.

Berkowitz, Michael. forthcoming. "'Transcending *Tsimmes* and Sweetness': Recovering the History of Zionist Women in Central and Western Europe, 1897–1933," *Women in Jewish Culture: Active Voices*, Maurie Sacks, ed. Champaign: University of Illinois Press.

Berman, Saul. 1973. "The Status of Women in Halakhic Judaism," *Tradition*. 14 (2), Fall: 12.

Berstein, Susan David. 1992. "What's 'I' Got to Do with It?," *Hypatia* 7 (2): 120–47.

Biale, David. 1992. *Eros and the Jews: From Biblical Israel to Contemporary America*. New York: Basic Books.

_____. 1992. "Zionism as an Erotic Revolution," *People of the Body: Jews and Judaism from an Embodied Perspective*, Howard Eilberg-Schwartz, ed. Albany: SUNY Press.

Biale, Rachel. 1984. *Women and Jewish Law: An Exploration of Women's Issues in Halakhic Sources*. New York: Schocken.

Birnbaum, Halina. 1971. *Hope Is the Last to Die: A Personal Documentation of Nazi Terror*, David Welsh, trans. New York: Twayne Publishers.

Bistritzky, Nathan. 1926. *Days and Nights*. Jerusalem.

Blumenthal, David. 1993. "Who Is Beating Whom?," *Conservative Judaism* 45 (3), Spring: 72–89.

Bock, Gisela. 1986. *Zwangssterilisation im Nationalsozialismus: Studien zur Rassenpolitik und Frauenpolitik*. Opladen: Westdeutscher Verlag.

Boksenboim, Yacob, ed. 1987. *Iggerot beit rieti*. Tel Aviv: Chaim Rosenberg School of Jewish Studies, Tel Aviv University.

Bonfil, Robert. 1984. "The Historian's Perception of the Jews in the Italian Renaissance: Towards a Reappraisal," *Revue de études juives* 143: 71–75.

Boylan, M. 1984. "The Galenic and Hippocratic Challenge to Aristotle's Conception Theory," *Journal of the History of Biology* 17: 83–112.

Breiman, Schlomo, ed. 1970. *Moshe Leib Lilienblum, Ketavim autobiographi'im*. Jerusalem.

Breines, Paul. 1990. *Tough Jews: Political Fantasies and the Moral Dilemma of American Jewry*. New York: Basic Books.

Brereton, Virginia Lieson, and Klein, Christa Ressmeyer. 1979. "American Women in Ministry: A History of Protestant Beginning Points," *Women of Spirit: Female Leadership in the Jewish and Christian Traditions*, Rosemary Ruether and Eleanor McLaughlin, eds. New York: Simon and Schuster, 301–32.

Bridwell, E. Nelson, ed. 1971. *Superman: From the Thirties to the Seventies*. New York: Crown Publishers.

Broder, Henryk M. 1987. *Der Ewige Antisemit: Über Sinn und Funktion eines beständigen Gefühls*. Frankfurt am Main: Fischer Taschenbuch.

Broner, Esther. 1983. "Of Holy Writing and Priestly Voices," *Massachusetts Review* 24: 254–69.

Brooke, Christopher. 1991. *The Medieval Idea of Marriage.* Oxford: Oxford University Press.

Browning, Christopher. 1992. *The Path to Genocide: Essays on Launching the Final Solution.* Cambridge: Cambridge University Press.

Brumberg, Joan J., and Tomes, Nancy. 1982. "Women in the Professions: A Research Agenda for American Historians," *Reviews in American History* 10, June: 275–96.

Brumlik, Micha. 1991. *Der Anti-Alt.* Frankfurt am Main: Eichborn Verlag.

Brundage, James A. 1987. *Law, Sex and Christian Society in Medieval Europe.* Chicago: University of Chicago Press.

Buber, Martin. 1951. *Two Types of Faith.* New York: Macmillan.

Bulkin, Elly; Pratt, Minnie Bruce; and Smith, Barbara. 1984. *Yours in Struggle: Three Feminist Perspectives on Anti-Semitism and Racism.* Brooklyn: Long Haul Press.

Bynum, C. Walker. 1986. "Introduction: The Complexity of Symbols," *Gender and Religion: On the Complexity of Symbols,* C. W. Bynum, S. Harrel, and P. Richman, eds. Boston: Beacon Press.

Canetti, Elias, ed. 1990. *Der Oger.* Munich: Carl Hanser.

Carpenter, Lynette, and Kolmar, Wendy, eds. 1991. *Haunting the House of Fiction: Feminist Perspectives on Ghost Stories by American Women.* Knoxville: University of Tennessee Press.

Carter, Dan T. 1992. "The Academy's Crisis of Belief," *Chronicle of Higher Education* 39 (13), 18 November.

Chafe, William H. 1991. *The Paradox of Change: American Women in the Twentieth Century.* New York: Oxford University Press.

Chinas, B. 1993. *The Isthmus Zapotecs: Women's Roles in Cultural Context.* New York: Holt, Rinehart and Winston.

Christ, Carol P. 1987. *Laughter of Aphrodite: Reflections on a Journey to the Goddess.* San Francisco: Harper & Row.

Cixous, Hélène. 1980. "Laugh of the Medusa," *New French Feminisms: An Anthology,* Elaine Marks and Isabelle de Courtivron, eds. Amherst: University of Massachusetts Press.

_____. 1986 "Sorties: Out and Out: Attacks/Ways Out/Forays," *The Newly Born Woman,* Hélène Cixous and Catherine Clément, eds.; Betsy Wing, trans. Minneapolis: University of Minnesota Press, 63–131.

Clar, Reva, and Kramer, William M. 1986. "The Girl Rabbi of the Golden West: The Adventurous Life of Ray Frank in Nevada, California and the Northwest," *Western States Jewish History* 18: 99–111, 223–36, 336–51.

Cohen, Ed. 1991. "Who Are 'We'? Gay Identity as Political (E)motion (A Theoretical Rumination), *Inside/Out: Lesbian Theories, Gay Theories,* Diana Fuss, ed. New York: Routledge.

Cohen, S., Woocher, J., and Phillips, B. 1984. *Perspectives in Jewish Population Research.* Boulder, CO: Westview Press.

Cohen, Shaye J. D. 1987. *From the Maccabees to the Mishnah.* Philadelphia: Westminster Press.

_____. 1984. "The Significance of Yavneh: Pharisees, Rabbis and the End of Jewish Sectarianism," *Hebrew College Annual* 55.

Cohon, Samuel S. 1950. "The History of the Hebrew Union College," *American Jewish Quarterly* 40: 25–26.

Cuddihy, John Murray. 1974. *The Ordeal of Civility: Freud, Marx, Levi-Strauss, and the Jewish Struggle with Modernity.* New York: Basic Books.

Davidman, Lynn. 1991. *Tradition in a Rootless World: Women Turn to Orthodox Judaism.* Berkeley: University of California Press.

Davidoff, Leonore, and Hall, Catherine, eds. 1987. *Family Fortunes: Men and Women of the English Middle Class.* Chicago: University of Chicago Press.

Davis, J. forthcoming. "The *Bar Mitzvah Balabusta:* Mother's Role in the Family's Rite of Passage," *Women in Jewish Culture: An Active Voice,* Maurie Sacks, ed. Champaign: University of Illinois Press.

DeBeauvoir, Simone. 1974. *The Second Sex,* H. M. Parshley, trans. New York: Knopf.

Decke, Bettina. 1988. "Christlicher Antijudaismus und Feminismus," *Der sogenannte Gott,* Albert Sellner, ed. Frankfurt am Main.

Degler, Carl. 1980. *At Odds: Women and Family in America from the Revolution to the Present.* New York: Oxford University Press.

Diena, Aziel. 1977. *Sheelot uteshuvot* no. 138, Yacob Boksenboim, ed. Tel Aviv: Chaim Rosenberg School of Jewish Studies, Tel Aviv University.

Dilliard, Heath. 1984. *Daughters of the Reconquest.* Cambridge: Cambridge University Press.

Di Stefano, Christine. 1983. "Masculinity as Ideology in Political Theory: Hobbesian Man Considered," *Women's Studies International Forum* 6 (6), 633–644.

Douglas, Mary. 1966. *Purity and Danger: Analysis of Concepts of Pollution and Taboo.* London: Routledge.

Dworkin, Andrea. 1988. "The Sexual Mythology of Anti-Semitism," *A Mensch among Men: Explorations in Jewish Masculinity,* Harry Brod, ed. Freedom, CA: Crossing Press, 118–23.

Edelstein, Alan. 1982. *An Unacknowledged Harmony: Philo–Semitism and the Survival of European Jewry.* Westport, CT: Greenwood Press.

Edinger, Dora, ed. 1968. *Bertha Pappenheim: Freud's Anna O.* Highland Park, IL: Congregation Soleil.

Eilberg-Schwartz, Howard, ed. 1992. *People of the Body: Jews and Judaism from an Embodied Perspective.* Albany: SUNY Press.

Ellenson, Elikim. 1975. *Nissuim shelo kedat moshe veyisrail.* Tel Aviv: Devir.

Ellinson, Elyaleim. 1989. *Haishan Vehamitzvoth.* Jerusalem: Torah Education Department of the WIZO.

Elior, Rachel. 1989. "HaBaD: The Contemplative Ascent to God," *Jewish Spirituality: From the Sixteenth Century Revival to the Present,* Arthur Green, ed. New York: Crossroad Publishing.

Encyclopaedia Judaica. 1972. *Apologetics.* Jerusalem: Keter Publishing.

_____. 1972. *Purity and Impurity, Ritual.* Jerusalem: Keter Publishing.

Endelman, Todd. 1987. "The Social and Political Context of Conversion in Germany and England, 1870–1914," *Jewish Apostasy in the Modern World,* Todd Endelman, ed. New York: Holmes and Meier.

Epstein, Julia, and Straub, Kristina. 1991. "Introduction: The Guarded Body," *Body Guards: The Cultural Politics of Gender Ambiguity,* Julia Epstein and Kristina Straub, eds. New York: Routledge.

Epstein, Louis M. 1927. *The Jewish Marriage Contract.* New York: Jewish Theological Seminary.

Epstein, I., ed. 1985. *The Talmud.* B. D. Klein. Glossary and indices. London: Soncino Press.

Evans, Richard J. 1976. *The Feminist Movement in Germany, 1894–1933.* London: Sage.

Feiffer, Jules, ed. 1965. *The Great Comic Book Heroes.* New York: Dial Press.

Fenelon, Fania. 1977. *Playing for Time,* Judith Landry, trans. New York: Atheneum.

Finkelstein, Louis. 1964. *Jewish Self-Government in the Middle Ages.* New York: Philipp Feldheim.

Fishman, Sylvia Barack. 1988. "The Changing American Jewish Family in the Eighties," *Contemporary Jewry* 9 (2), Fall: 1–34.

———. 1991. " Family Ties: Serving Today's Jewish Households, " *Changing Jewish Life: Service Jewry and Planning in the 1990s*, Lawrence Sternberg et al., eds. New York: Greenwood Press, 57–85.

———. 1993. *A Breath of Life: Feminism in the American Jewish Community*. New York: Free Press.

Fishman, Sylvia Barack, and Goldstein, Alice. 1993. *When They Are Grown They Will Not Depart: Jewish Education and the Jewish Behavior of American Adults*. Waltham, MA: CMJS, Brandeis University.

Fishman, Talya.1992. "A Kabbalistic Perspective on Gender-Specific Commandments: On the Interplay of Symbols and Society," *AJS Review* 17 (2) Fall: 199-245.

Flannigan-Saint-Aubin, Arthur. 1994. "Removing the Steel Fig Leaf: Toward a Testicular/Testerical Masculinity," *Theorizing Masculinities*, Harry Brod and Michael Kaufman, eds. Newbury Park, CA: Sage.

Frankenthal, Käte.1981. *Der dreifarhe Fluch; Jüdin, Intellelctuelle, Sozialistinl*. Frankfurt: Campus Verlag.

Frankiel, Tamar. 1990. "Sex and the Spirit," *Tikkun* 5 (6), November/December: 33–35, 106– 7.

———. 1990. *The Voice of Sarah: Feminine Spirituality and Traditional Judaism*. New York: Harper & Row.

Friedfertig, Raizel Schnall, and Shapiro, Freyda, eds. 1981. *The Modern Jewish Woman: A Unique Perspective*. Brooklyn: Lubavitch Educational Foundation for Jewish Marriage Enrichment.

Friedman, Maurice. 1988. *Martin Buber's Life and Work: The Early Years, 1878-1923*. Detroit: Wayne State University.

Friedman, Mordechai A. 1986. *Ribbui hasim beisrael*. Jerusalem: Mosad Bialik.

Frishtik, Mordechai. 1992. "Physical and Sexual Violence by Husbands as a Reason for Imposing a Divorce in Jewish Law," *Jewish Law Annual* 9: 145–69.

Frymer-Kensey, Tikva. 1992. *In the Wake of the Goddess: Women, Culture and the Biblical Transformation of Pagan Myth*. New York: Fawcett Columbine.

Funke, Hajor. 1986. "Bitburg, Jews, and Germans: A Case Study of Anti-Jewish Sentiment in Germany during May 1985," *New German Critique* 38, Spring/Summer: 57–72.

Furman, F.K. 1987. *Beyond Yiddishkeit: The Struggle for Jewish Identity in a Reform Synagogue*. Albany: SUNY Press.

Gates, Henry Louis, Jr. 1993. "A Big Brother from Another Planet," *New York Times*, 12 September, Section H, 51 & 64.

Gesenius, William. 1836. *Hebrew and English Lexicon of the Old Testament*. Boston: Crocker and Brewster.

Gilbert, Sandra M., and Gubar, Susan. 1979. *The Madwoman in the Attic: The Woman Writer and the Nineteenth Century Literary Imagination*. New Haven: Yale University Press.

Gilligan, Carol. 1982. *In a Different Voice: Psychological Theory and Women's Development*. Cambridge: Harvard University Press.

Ginsburg, Elliot. 1989. *The Sabbath in Classical Kabbalah*. Albany: SUNY Press.

Glatzer, Nahum, ed. 1965. *On Jewish Learning*. New York: Schocken.

Glauert-Hesse, Barbara. 1989. *Der Gläserne Garten: Prosa 1917–1939*. Berlin: Argon.

Glazer, Myra, ed. 1989. "Introduction," *Burning Air and a Clear Mind: Contemporary Israeli Women Poets*. Athens: Ohio University Press, xv–xxviii.

Glazer, Penina Migdal, and Slater, Miriam. 1987. *Unequal Colleagues: The Entrance of Women in the Professions, 1890–1940*. New Brunswick, NJ: Rutgers University Press.

Goldberg, R., ed. 1976. *Avraham Ber Gottlober, Zikhronot u'massa'ot*. 2 vols. Jerusalem.

Goldberg, Robin. 1991. "Imagining History as Herstory through the Story of Esther: Restoring and Restorying the Feminine among HaBaD Women," unpublished manuscript of paper delivered at the 1991 Association for Jewish Studies Annual Conference.

Goldman, Nicky. 1991. " The Celebration of the *Bat Mitzvah* within the Orthodox Community in the United States," unpublished paper for the Hornstein Program in Jewish Communal Service, Brandeis University, Spring.

Goldscheider, Calvin. 1986. *Jewish Continuity and Change: Emerging Patterns in America*. Bloomington: Indiana University Press.

Goldscheider, Calvin, and Francis, K. 1989. "The Transition to Jewish Adulthood: Education, Marriage and Fertility," paper for the Tenth World Congress of Jewish Studies, Jerusalem, August.

Goldstein, Rebecca. 1983. *The Mind-Body Problem*. New York: Dell.

_____. 1991. *The Dark Sister*. New York: Viking Penguin.

Goldstein, S., and Goldscheider, C. 1985. *Jewish Americans: Three Generations in a Jewish Community*. Landham, MD: University Press of America.

Goll, Claire. 1987. *Der Neger Jupiter raubt Europa*. Berlin: Argon.

_____. 1988. *Ein Mensch ertrinkt*. Berlin: Argon.

_____. 1989. *Der Gläserne Garten. Prosa 1917-1939*, Barbara Glauert-Hesse, ed. Frankfurt: Aragon.

Goodale, J. 1982. *Tiwi Wives*. Seattle: University of Washington Press.

Goody, Jack. 1983. *The Development of the Family and Marriage in Europe*. Cambridge: Cambridge University Press.

Gordon, Leonard. 1991. "Law, Theology and Pluralism in Earliest Rabbinic Judaism," *Journal of the Society of Rabbis in Academia*, Summer: 57–60.

_____. 1991. "Who Were the Rabbis and Why Do We Care?," *Reconstructionist*, Summer: 21–23.

Gordon, Lynn D. 1990. *Gender and Higher Education in the Progressive Era*. New Haven: Yale University Press.

Gordon, Y. L. 1956. *Kitvei Yehudah Leib Gordon*. Tel Aviv: Dvir.

Gottfried, Barbara. 1988. "What Do Men Want, Dr. Roth?," *A Mensch Among Men: Explorations in Jewish Masculinity*, Harry Brod, ed. Freedom, CA: The Crossing Press.

Göttner-Abendroth, Heide. 1988. *Das Matriarchat I; Geshichte seiner Frforschung*. Stuttgart: Verlag W. Kohlammer.

Govrin, Nurit. *Ha-machatzit ha-rishona*. Jerusalem: Mossad Bialik.

Graetz, Naomi. 1991. "Miriam: Guilty or not Guilty," *Judaism* 40, Spring: 184–92.

_____. 1992. "The *Haftorah* Tradition and the Metaphoric Battering of Hosea's Wife," *Conservative Judaism* 45 (1) Fall: 29–42.

Greenberg, Blu. 1983. "Judaism and Feminism," *The Jewish Woman*, Elizabeth Koltun, ed. New York: Schocken.

Greenberger, R., Byrne, R. J., and Gold, M., eds., 1987. *The Greatest Superman Stories Ever Told*. New York: D. C. Comics.

Greenblatt, Stephen. 1990. *Learning to Curse: Essays in Early Modern Literature*. New York: Routledge.

Gries, Z. 1989. *Conduct Literature (Regimen Vitae): Its History and Place in the Life of Beshtian Hasidism*. Jerusalem.

Gross, Rita. 1979. "Female God Language in a Jewish Context," *Womanspirit Rising: A Feminist Reader in Religion*, Carol P. Christ and Judith Plaskow, eds. San Francisco: Harper & Row.

Grossman, Avraham. 1991. "Medieval Rabbinic Views on Wife Beating, 800-1300." *Jewish History* 5: 53-62.

Grossman, S., and Haut R., eds. 1992. *Daughters of the King: Women and the Synagogue*. Philadelphia: Jewish Publication Society.

Guenberg, Mordechai Aron. 1967. *Aviezer*. Tel Aviv (photo-reproduction of first ed., Vilna, 1864).

Hackett, Amy. 1976. "The Politics of Feminism in Wilhelmine Germany, 1890-1918." Ph.D dissertation, Columbia University.

_____. 1983. "The Politics of Feminism," *On Being a Jewish Feminist: A Reader*, Susannah Heschel, ed. New York: Schocken.

Halnziqlopedia halvrit. 1974. Jerusalem: Chevra leHoza at Inziklopediyot.

Hajnal, J. 1983. "Two Kinds of Pre-Industrial Households," *Family Forms in Historic Europe*, Richard Wall et al., eds. Cambridge: Cambridge University Press.

Halivni, David Weiss. 1986. *Midrash, Mishnah and Gemara: The Jewish Predilection for Justified Law*. Cambridge: Harvard University Press.

Hall, Stuart. 1990. "Cultural Identity and Diaspora," *Identity, Community, Cultural Difference*, Jonathan Rutherford, ed. London: Lawrence and Wishart, 222-37.

Hameln, Glükel. 1963. *The Life of Glükel Hameln, 1646-1742, Written by Herself*, Beth-Zion Abrahams, trans. London: East and West Library.

Heilman, Samuel, and Cohen, Steven M. 1989. *Cosmopolitans and Parochials: Modern Orthodox Jews in America*. Chicago: University of Chicago Press.

Heilman, S.C. 1973. *Synagogue Life: A Study in Symbolic Interaction*. Chicago: Chicago University Press.

Heine, Susanne. 1987. *Women and Early Christianity: Are the Feminist Scholars Right?* London: SCM Press.

Heinemann, Marlene E. 1986. *Gender and Destiny: Women Writers and the Holocaust*. New York: Greenwood Press.

Herman, Simon. 1989. *Jewish Identity*. 2nd ed. NJ: Transaction Publishers.

Herminghouse, Patricia. 1986. "Women and the Literary Enterprise in Nineteenth-Century Germany," *German Women in the Eighteenth and Nineteenth Centuries*, Ruth-Ellen Joeres, ed. Bloomington: Indiana University Press.

Heschel, Susannah. 1988. "Töteten 'die Jüden' die Göttin?" *Emma*, December.

Heschel, Susannah, ed. 1983. *On Being a Jewish Feminist: A Reader*. New York: Schocken.

Hertz, Deborah. 1989. *Jewish High Society in Old Regime Berlin*. New Haven: Yale University Press.

Herz, Henriette. 1984. *Henriette Herz in Erinnerungen, Briefen, und Zeugnissen*, Reiner Schnitz, ed. Frankfurt: Insel.

Hewitt, Elizabeth C., and Hiatt, Suzanne R. 1973. *Women Priests: Yes or No?* New York: Seabury Press.

Hobbes, Thomas. 1972. "The Citizen: Philosophical Rudiments Concerning Government and Society," *Man and Citizen: Thomas Hobbes' De Homine and De Cive*, Bernard Gert, ed. Garden City: Doubleday.

Hoch, Paul. 1979. *White Hero, Black Beast: Racism, Sexism, and the Mask of Masculinity*. London: Pluto Press.

Holtz, Barry, ed. 1984. *Back to the Sources*. New York: Summit Books.

Hyman, P. 1983. "Lilith Interview: After a Decade of Jewish Feminism the Jewry is Still Out," *Lilith* 11.

Idel, Moshe. 1988. *Kabbalah: New Perspectives*. New Haven: Yale University Press.

_____. 1988. *Studies in Ecstatic Kabbalah*. Albany: SUNY Press.

_____. 1989. "Sexual Metaphors and Praxis in the *Kabbalah*," *The Jewish Family: Metaphor and Memory*, David Kraemer, ed. New York: Oxford University Press.

Irigaray, Luce. 1985. *This Sex Which Is Not One*, C. Porter, trans. Ithaca: Cornell University Press.

Janeway, Elizabeth. 1974. *Man's World Woman's Place: A Study in Social Mythology*. New York: Delta.

Joselit, J. 1992. "'A Set Table': Jewish Domestic Culture in the New World, 1880-1950," *Getting Comfortable in New York: The American Jewish Home, 1880-1950*, S. Braunstein and J. Joselit, eds. New York: The Jewish Museum.

Kanarfogel, Ephraim. 1992. "Rabbinic Attitudes toward Nonobservance," *Jewish Traditions and Nontraditional Jews*, J. J. Schacter, ed. Northvale, NJ: Jason Aronson.

Kaplan, Aryeh. 1976. *Waters of Eden: The Mystery of the Mikveh*. New York: National Conference of Synagogue Youth/Union of Orthodox Congregations of America.

_____. 1983. *Made in Heaven: A Jewish Wedding Guide*. New York: Moznaim Publishing.

Kaplan, Marion. 1979. *The Jewish Feminist Movement in Germany; The Campaigns of the Jüdischer Frauenbund, 1904-1938*. Westport, CT: Greenwood Press.

_____. 1984. "Sister Under Seige — Feminism and Anti-Feminism in Germany," *When Biology Became Destiny*. Renate Brindentahl et al, eds. New York: Monthly Review Press.

_____. 1990. "Jewish Women in Nazi Germany: Daily Life, Daily Struggles." *Feminist Studies*, Fall: 579-606.

_____. 1991. *The Making of Jewish Middle Class: Women, Family and Identity in Imperial Germany*. New York: Oxford University Press.

Karpeles, Gustav. 1889. *Die Frauen in der Jüdischen Literatur: Ein Vortage*. Berlin.

Katz, Esther, and Ringelheim, Joan, eds. 1983. *Proceedings on Women Surviving: The Holocaust*. New York.

Katz, Jacob. 1966. *Tradition and Crisis: Jewish Society at the End of the Middle Ages*. New York: Free Press of Glencoe.

_____. 1973. *Out of the Ghetto: The Social Background of Jewish Emancipation*. Cambridge: Cambridge University Press.

Kaufman, D. R. 1991. *Rachel's Daughters: Newly Orthodox Jewish Women*. New Brunswick, NJ: Rutgers University Press.

Kayserling, Meyer. 1879. *Die Jüdischen Frauen in der Geschichte, Literatur und Kunst*. Leipzig.

Kellner, Menachem. 1991. *Maimonides on Judaism and the Jewish People*. Albany: SUNY Press.

Kimmel, Michael. "Judaism, Masculinity, and Feminism," *A Mensch among Men: Explorations in Jewish Masculinity*, Harry Brod, ed. Freedom, CA: Crossing Press, 153-56.

Kirshenblatt-Gimblett, B. 1992. "Kitchen Judaism," *Getting Comfortable in New York: The American Jewish Home, 1880-1950*, S. Braunstein and J. Joselit, eds. New York: The Jewish Museum.

Knilli, Friedrich, and Zielinski, Siegfried, eds. 1982. *Holocaust zur Unterhaltung: Anatomie eines internationalen Bestsellers*. Berlin: Verlag für Ausbildung und Studium.

Kolmar, Gertrud. 1959. "Susanna," *Dasleere Haus*, Hans Otten, ed. Stuttgart: Cotta.

_____. *The Great Mother: An Analysis of an Archetype*, 2nd ed., R. Manheim, trans. Princeton: Princeton University Press.

_____. *Einer jüdischer Mutter*. Munich: Kösel.

Koltun, Elizabeth, ed. 1976. *The Jewish Woman: New Perspectives.* New York: Schocken.

Kosmin, Barry A., et al., eds. 1991. *Highlights of the CJF National Jewish Population Survey.* Council of Jewish Federations.

Kraemer, David. 1990. *The Mind of the Talmud: An Intellectual History of the Bavli.* New York: Oxford University Press.

Krengel, Shimoneh. 1990. "Exploring the Hidden," *Wellsprings* 31, 6 (3), February/March: 4–7.

Kurzweil, Edith. 1984. "An American in Frankfurt," *Partisan Review* 51 (4); 52 (1): 828–833.

Lampronti, Isaac, ed. fols. 59b–67b.s.v. 1750–1888. *Pachad yitzhakq* 2. Venice–Berlin.

Laqueur, Thomas. 1990. *Making Sex: Body and Gender from the Greeks to Freud.* Cambridge: Harvard University Press.

Laska, Vera. 1983. *Women in the Resistance and the Holocaust: Voices of Eyewitnesses.* Westport, CT: Greenwood Press.

Lasker-Schüler. 1932. *Artur Aronymus.* Berlin: Rowohlt.

_____. 1986. *Die Wupper: Schauspiel in fünf Aufzügen.* Surkamp.

Lazarus, Nahida Ruth. 1898. *Ich Suchte Dich! Biographische Erzaelung.* Berlin: Siegfried Cronbach.

_____. 1899. *The Ethics of Judaism.* Philadelphia: Jewish Publication Society.

Lefkovitz, Lori. 1988. "Coats and Tales: Joseph Stories and Myths of Jewish Masculinity," *A Mensch among Men: Explorations in Jewish Masculinity,* Harry Brod, ed., Freedom, CA: Crossing Press, 19–29.

_____. 1990. "When Lilith Becomes a Heroine: Midrash as a Feminist Response," *Melton Journal* 23, Spring.

Lengyel, Olga. 1947. *Five Chimneys.* Chicago.

Lerman, Rhoda. 1989. *God's Ear.* New York: Henry Holt.

Liebes, Y. 1982. "The Messiah of the Zohar," *The Messianic Idea in Jewish Thought: A Study Conference in Honour of the Eightieth Birthday of Gershom Scholem.* Jerusalem.

_____. 1993. *Studies in the Zohar,* A. Schwartz, S. Nakache, and P. Peli, trans. Albany: SUNY Press.

Lindheim, Irma L. 1928. *The Immortal Adventure.* New York: Macaulay.

_____. 1962. *Parallel Quest: A Search of a Person and a People.* New York: Thomas Yoseloff.

Linville, Susan E. 1992. "The Mother–Daughter Plot in History: Helma Sanders-Brahm's Germany, Pale Mother," *New German Critique* 55, Winter: 53.

Lixl-Purcell, Andreas, ed. 1988. *Women of Exile: German Jewish Autobiographies since 1933.* New York: Greenwood Press.

Lorde, Audre. 1984. "Uses of the Erotic: The Erotic as Power," *Sister Outsider: Essays and Speeches.* Trumansburg, NY: Crossing Press, 53–60.

Lown. Judy. 1990. *Women and Industrialization.* Cambridge: Cambridge University Press.

MacKinnon, Catherine. 1987. *Feminism Unmodified: Discourses on Life and Law.* Cambridge: Harvard University Press.

Mahler, Raphael. 1985. *Hasidism and the Jewish Enlightenment: Their Confrontation in Galicia and Poland in the First Half of the Nineteenth Century.* Philadelphia: Jewish Publication Society.

Maier, Charles. 1988. *The Unmasterable Past: History, Holocaust, and German National Identity.* Cambridge: Harvard University Press.

Marcus, Ivan. 1992. "Jewish Learning in the Middle Ages," *The Melton Journal,* Autumn: 22, 24.

Marcus, Jacob R. 1972. "The First Women Rabbi," *Press Release, Special Topics: Rabbis, Women.* American Jewish Archives.

Marcus, Ralph. 1929. "In Memoriam: Norvin R. Lindheim," *American Jewish Quarterly* 4 (2), January.

Markovitz, Andrei S. 1991. "Germany: Power and the Left: A New Political Configuration," *Dissent* 38, Summer: 354–59.

Meiselman, Moshe. 1978. *Jewish Woman in Jewish Law*. New York: Ktav Publishing.

Mendes-Flohr, Paul. 1981. "Werner Sombart's 'The Jews and Modern Capitalism.'" *Leo Baeck Institute Yearbook* 21: 87–107.

Meroz, R. 1988. "Redemption in the Lurianic Teaching." Ph.D. dissertation, Hebrew University.

Merton, Sybil. 1984. "Women and the Holocaust — The Case of German and German-Jewish Women," *When Biology Became Destiny: Women in Weimar and Nazi Germany*, Renate Brindenthal et al., eds. New York: Monthly Review Press.

Meyers, Michael A. 1976. "A Centennial History," *Hebrew Union College — Jewish Institute of Religion at One Hundred Years*, Samuel E. Karff, ed. Hebrew Union College Press.

Miller, Nancy K. 1991. "Dreaming, Dancing, and the Changing Location of Feminist Criticism," *Getting Personal; Feminist Occasions and Other Autobiographical Acts*, New York: Routledge.

Mills, C. Wright. 1959. *The Sociological Imagination*. New York: Oxford University Press.

Mintz, Alan. 1979. "Guenzberg, Lilienblum and the Shape of the *Haskalah* Autobiography," *Association for Jewish Studies Review* 4: 71–110.

———. 1989. "*Banished from their Father's Table*": *Loss of Faith and Hebrew Autobiography*. Bloomington: Indiana University Press.

Mitscherlich, Margarete. 1985. *Die friedfertige Frau*. Frankfurt: Fischer Verlag.

Modena, Leon. 1988. *Autobiography of a Seventeenth-Century Venetian Rabbi: Leon Modena's Life of Judah*, Mark R. Cohen, ed. and trans. Princeton: Princeton University Press.

Modleski, Tania. 1991. *Feminism without Women: Cultural Criticism in a "Postfeminist" Age*. New York: Routledge.

Mohanty, Chandra Talpade, and Martin, Biddy. 1986. "Feminist Politics: What's Home Got to Do with It?," *Feminist Studies, Critical Studies*, Teresa de Lauretis, ed. Bloomington: Indiana University Press, 191–212.

Moltman-Wendell, Elisabeth. 1992. "Jesus, Die Tabus und das Neue," *Dialog der Religionen*, Fall: 130–45.

Moltmann, Jürgen. 1993. "Verletzt Gewissen," *Publik-Forum* 10, 21 May: 16.

Mopsik, C. 1986. *Lettre sur la sainteté: Le secret de la relation entre l'homme et la femme dans la cabale*. Paris.

Morello, Karen Berger. 1986. *The Invisible Bar: The Woman Lawyer in America, 1638 to the Present*. New York: Random House.

Morrell, Samuel. 1982. "An Equal or a Ward: How Independent Is a Married Woman According to Rabbinic Law?," *Jewish Social Studies* 44: 189–210.

Moseley, Marcus. 1990. "Jewish Autobiography in Eastern Europe: The Pre-History of a Literary Genre." Ph.D. dissertation, Oxford University.

Mott, Frank, and Abma, Joyce. 1993. "Contemporary Jewish Fertility: Does Religion Make a Difference?," *Contemporary Jewry*.

Mulack, Christa. 1988. *Am Anfang war die Weisheit*. Munich: Kreuz Verlag.

———. 1993. "Jesus, die Nazis und die Männer," *Publik-Forum* 4, 26 February: 21–22.

Nadell, Pamela S., and Simon, Rita J. forthcoming. "Sisterhood Ladies and Rabbis: Women in the American Reform Synagogue," *Women in Jewish Culture: An Active Voice*, Maurie Sacks, ed. Champaign: University of Illinois Press.

Neumann, E. 1954. *The Origins and the History of Consciousness*. Princeton: Princeton University Press.

_____. 1963. *The Great Mother: An Analysis of an Archetype*, R. Manheim, trans. 2nd ed. Princeton: Princeton University Press.

Neumark, Yosef. 1984. "Feminism vs. Judaism." *The Jewish Woman's Outlook: A Perspective for the Torah Woman*, April/May-Nissan/Iyar 5744 6 (2): 13–17.

Neusner, Jacob. 1981. *Judaism: The Evidence of the Mishnah*. Chicago: University of Chicago Press.

_____. 1988. *The Mishnah*. New Haven: Yale University Press.

Nicholas, David. 1985. *The Domestic Life of a Medieval City: Women, Children, and the Family in Fourteenth Century Ghent*. Lincoln, NB: University of Nebraska Press.

Nicholson, L. J. 1990. *Feminism/Postmodernism*. London: Routledge, Chapman, and Hall.

Nomber-Przytyk, Sara. 1985. *Auschwitz: True Tales from a Grotesque Land*. Chapel Hill: University of North Carolina Press.

Novitich, Miriam. 1980. *Sobibor*. New York: Holocaust Library.

Ortner, Sherry B. 1993. "Is Female to Male as Nature Is to Culture?"; "Zion's Response to the Holocaust," Lawrence L. Langer. *New York Times Book Review*, 18 April, 3, 37.

Otten, Hans, ed. 1959. *Gertrud Kolmar "Susanna", Das leere Haus*. Stuttgart: Cotta.

Ozick, Cynthia. 1983. "Notes toward Finding the Right Question," *On Being a Jewish Feminist: A Reader*, Susannah Heschel, ed. New York: Schocken, 120–51.

_____. 1992. "Puttermesser and Xanthippe," *Follow My Foot Prints: Changing Images of Women in American Jewish Fiction*. Hanover, NH: University Press of New England, 440–94.

Pardes, Ilana. 1992. *Countertraditions in the Bible: A Feminist Approach*. Cambridge: Harvard University Press.

Parks, Michael. 1993. "A New View of David Stirs Goliath-Size Roar," *New York Times*, 11 February, Section A 2, Cols. 1–2.

Patai, Raphael. 1978. *The Hebrew Goddess*. New York: Avon.

Paulsen, Wolfgang. 1981. "Theodor Fontane—The Philosemitic Antisemite," *Leo Baeck Institute Yearbook* 26: 310–27.

Perlman, Joel. 1993. "Russian Jewish Literacy in 1897: A Reanalysis of Census Data," *Papers in Jewish Demography*, V. O. Schmelz and S. Della, eds., Pergola. Jerusalem: The Hebrew University.

Perlmutter, Donna. 1987. "Jewishness Goes Back in Closet on the Screen," *Los Angeles Times*, 12 April, Calendar Section, 20–24.

Plaskow, Judith. 1987. "*Halakha* as a Feminist Issue," *Melton Journal* 22, Fall: 3–5.

_____. 1989. "Towards a New Theology of Sexuality," *Twice Blessed: On Being Lesbian, Gay and Jewish*, Christie Balka and Andy Rose, eds. Boston: Beacon Press.

_____. 1990. *Standing Again at Sinai: Judaism from a Feminist Perspective*. New York: Harper & Row.

_____. 1990. "Rabbis and the End of Jewish Sectarianism," *Hebrew Union College Annual* 55: 27–53.

_____. 1991. "Feminist Anti-Judaism and the Christian God," *Journal of Feminist Studies in Religion* 7 (2), Fall: 99–108.

Prell, R.E. 1989. *Prayer and Community: The Havurah in American Judaism*. Detroit: Wayne State University Press.

Preus, A. 1977. "Galen's Criticism of Aristotle's Conception Theory," *Journal of History of Biology* 10: 65–85.

Priesand, Sally Jane. 1975. *Judaism and the New Woman*. New York: Behrman House.

Procter, Priscilla and William. 1976. *Women in the Pulpit: Is God an Equal Opportunity Employer?* Garden City, NJ: Doubleday.

Quindlen, Anna. 1988. *Living Out Loud.* New York: Random House.

Raisig, Christoph Mattias. 1992. *Der Rheinische Synodalbeschluss vom 11. Januar 1980, "Zur Erneuerung des Verhältnisses von Christen und Juden": Seine Vorgeschichte, seine Inteiton undie ersten Reaktionen.* Inaugural dissertation, Göthe Universität Frankfurt.

Reinharz, Shulamith. 1992. *Feminist Methods in Social Research.* New York: Oxford University Press.

Reiter, R. 1975. *Toward an Anthropology of Women.* New York: Monthly Review Press.

Remy, Nahida. 1893. *Culturstudien über das Judenthum.* Berlin: Carl Drucker.

_____. 1894. *Prayer in Bible and the Talmud.* New York.

_____. 1895. *The Jewish Woman.* Cincinnati: C. J. Krehbiel.

Rich, Adrienne. 1986. "Compulsory Heterosexuality and Lesbian Existence," *Blood, Bread, and Poetry: Selected Prose 1979–1985.* New York: W. W. Norton.

Riley, Denise. 1990. *Am I That Name?: Feminism and the Category of Women in History.* Minneapolis: University of Minnesota Press.

Ringelheim, Joan. 1991. "Women and the Holocaust: A Reconsideration of Research," *Jewish Women in Historical Perspective,* Judith Baskin, ed. Detroit: Wayne State University Press.

Rittner, Carole, and Roth, John K., eds. 1993. *Different Voices: Women and the Holocaust.* New York: Paragon House.

Robertson, Priscilla. 1982. *An Experience of Women.* Philadelphia: Temple University Press.

Roiphe, Anne. 1987. *Lovingkindness.* New York: Warner.

Rosaldo, M. Z., and Lamphere, L., eds. 1974. *Woman, Culture and Society.* Stanford, CA: Stanford University Press.

Rose, Lawrence. 1990. *Revolutionary Antisemitism in Germany: From Kant to Wagner.* Princeton: Princeton University Press.

Rossiter, Margaret W. 1982. *Women Scientists in America.* Baltimore: Johns Hopkins Press.

Roth, Joel. 1988. "On the Ordination of Women as Rabbis," *The Ordination of Women as Rabbis: Studies and Responsa,* Simon Greenberg, ed. New York: Jewish Society of America.

Roth, Phillip. 1986. *The Counterlife.* New York: Penguin Books.

_____. 1988. *The Facts: A Novelist Autobiography.* New York: Farrar, Straus, and Giroux.

Russell, Letty, ed. 1985. *Feminist Interpretations of the Bible.* Philadelphia: Westminster Press.

Sacks, Maurie. 1989. "Competing Community at Purim." *Journal of American Folklore* 102 (405): 276–91.

Sacks, Maurie, ed. forthcoming. *Women in Jewish Culture: An Active Voice.* Champaign: University of Illinois Press.

Safrai, Shmuel, ed. 1987. *The Literature of the Sages: First Part: Oral Tora, Halakha, Mishna, Tosefta, Talmud, External Tractates.* Philadelphia: Fortress Press.

Sanday, P. 1981. *Female Power and Male Dominance: On the Origins of Sexual Inequality.* New York: Cambridge University Press.

Sander, Helke. 1991. *The Three Women,* Helen Petzold, trans. London: Serpent's Tail.

Sanders, E. P. 1983. *Paul, the Law, and the Jewish People.* Philadelphia: Fortress Press.

Say, Elizabeth. 1990. *Evidence on Her Own Behalf: Women's Narrative as Theological Voice.* Savage, MD: Rowman & Littlefield.

Scarf, Mimi. 1983. "Marriages Made in Heaven?," *On Being a Jewish Feminist: A Reader,* Susannah Heschel, ed., New York: Schocken, 51–63.

_____. 1988. *Battered Jewish Wives.* Lewiston, Queenston: Edwin Mellen Press.

Schaumberger, Christine, ed. 1987. *Weil Wir Nicht Vergessen Wollen: Zu Feministischen Theologie im deutschen Kontext*. Münster: Morgana Frauenbuch Verlag.

Schmitz, Rainer, ed. 1984. *Hennriette Herz in Erinnerungen, Briefen und Zeugnissen*. Frankfurt: Insel.

Scholem, Gershom. 1931. "On the Development of the Concept of the Worlds in Early Kabbalah," *Tarbiz* 2: 39–41.

_____. 1965. *On the Kabbalah and its Symbolism*, R. Manheim, trans. New York: Schocken.

_____. 1987. *Origins of the Kabbalah*, A. Arkush, trans. R. J. Zwi Werblowsky, ed. Princeton: Princeton University Press.

_____. 1991. *On the Mystical Shape of the Godhead: Basic Concepts in the Kabbalah*, J. Neugroschel, ed.; revised by J. Chipman. New York: Schocken.

Schüssler Fiorenza, Elisabeth. 1988. *In Memory of Her: A Feminist Theological Reconstruction of Christian Origins*. New York: Crossroad Publishing.

Scolnic, Benjamin. 1993. "Bible Battering," *Conservative Judaism* 40, Spring: 43–52.

Sered, Susan. 1992. *Women as Ritual Experts: The Religious Lives of Elderly Jewish Women in Jerusalem*. New York: Oxford University Press.

Setel, T. Drora. 1985. "Prophets and Pornography: Female Sexual Imagery in Hosea," *Feminist Interpretations of the Bible*, Letty Russell, ed. Philadelphia: Westminster, 86–95.

Shapiro, Rami M. 1991. *Embracing Esau: A Jewish View of the Deep Masculine and its Reclamation*. Miami: Light House Books.

Showalter, Elaine. 1977. *A Literature of Their Own*. Princeton: Princeton University Press.

_____. 1985. *The New Feminist Criticism: Essays on Women's Literature and Theory*. New York: Pantheon.

Shwartz, Lynne Sharon. 1989. *Leaving Brooklyn*. Boston: Houghton Mifflin.

Siegele-Wenschkewitz, Leonore, ed. 1988. *Verdrängte Verdrängenheit die Uns Bedrängt: Feministische Theologie in der Verantwortung für die Geschichte*. Munich: Christian Kaiser.

_____. 1992. "Die Wiederkehr des antijüdischen Steretoyps in feminstischer Theorie und Theologie," *Metis: Zeitschrift für historische Frauenforschung und feministische Praxis* 1 (2): 29–32.

_____. 1993. "Frauengeschichte im Nationalsozialismus: Eine 'Frauenpraxis aus Liebe'? Zur Diskussion mit Annette Kuhn," *Metis: Zeitschrift für historische Frauenforschung und feministische Praxis* 2 (4), October.

Slater, Miriam. 1984. *Family Life in Seventeenth Century London*. London: Routledge.

Smith, Bonnie. 1981. *Ladies of the Leisure Class*. Princeton: Princeton University Press.

Soelle, Dorothee. 1993. "Warum brauchen wir eine feministische Christologie?" *Evangelische Theologie* 53, (1): 86–92.

Sokol, Morse Z., ed. 1992. *Rabbinic Authority and Personal Autonomy*. Northvale, NJ: Jason Aronson.

Solomon, Barbara Miller. 1985. *In the Company of Educated Women: A History of Women and Higher Education in America*. New Haven: Yale University Press.

Soloveitchik, Joseph B. 1983. *Halakhic Man*. Philadelphia: Jewish Publication Society.

Sorge, Elga. 1989. "Zur Hexe mit dem Antisemitismus" *Emma*, February: 50–51.

Spelman, Elizabeth. 1988. *Inessential Women: Problems of Exclusion in Feminist Thought*. Boston: Beacon Press.

Spero, Shubert. 1978. "Orthodox Judaism," *Movements and Issues in American Judaism*, Bernard Martin, ed. Westport, CT: Greenwood Press.

Spiegelman, Art. 1986, 1991. *Maus: A Survivor's Tale*, Vols. 1 and 2. New York: Pantheon.

Spiel, Hilde. 1989. *Diehellenunddiefinsteren Zeiten; Erinnerungen, 1911-1946*. Munich: List.

Spitzer, Julie. 1974. *When Love Is Not Enough: Spousal Abuse in Rabbinic and Contemporary Judaism.* Stanford: Stanford University Press.
_____. 1985, 1991. *Spousal Abuse in Rabbinic Contemporary Judaism.* New York: National Federation of Temple Sisterhoods.
Stanislawski, Michael. 1988. *For Whom Do I Toil? Judah Leib Gordon and the Crisis of Russian Jewry.* New York: Oxford University Press.
Stern, Frank. 1992. *The Whitewashing of the Yellow Badge: Antisemitism and Philosemitism in Postwar Germany.* William Templar, trans. Oxford: Pergamon.
Stern, Selma. 1950. *The Court Jew.* Philadelphia: Jewish Publication Society.
Sternberg, Lawrence et al., eds. 1991. *Changing Jewish Life: Service Jewry and Planning in the 1990s.* New York: Greenwood Press.
Stone, Lawrence. 1977. *The Family, Sex and Marriage, England 1500–1800.* New York: Harper & Row.
Taitz, E. 1992. "Women's Voices, Women's Prayers," *Daughters of the King: Women and the Synagogue,* S. Grossman and R. Haut, eds. Philadelphia: Jewish Publication Society.
Ticktin, Esther. 1976. "A Modest Beginning," *The Jewish Woman,* Elizabeth Koltun, ed. New York: Schocken.
Tillion, Germaine. 1973, 1988. *Ravensbruck.* New York: Anchor Press.
Tishby, I. 1942. *The Doctrine of Evil and the "Kelippah" in Lurianic Kabbalah.* Jerusalem.
_____. 1989. *The Wisdom of the Zohar,* trans. D. Goldstein. Oxford: Oxford University Press.
Toll, W. 1983. *The Making of an Ethnic Middle Class.* Albany: SUNY Press.
Trible, Phyllis. 1984. *Texts of Terror.* Philadelphia: Fortress Press.
Umansky, Ellen M. 1979." Women in Judaism: From the Reform Movement to Contemporary Jewish Religious Feminism," *Women of Spirit: Female Leadership in the Jewish and Christian Traditions,* Rosemary Ruether and Eleanor McLaughlin, eds. New York: Simon and Schuster, 333–54.
_____. 1991. "Spiritual Expressions: Jewish Women's Religious Lives in the Twentieth Century United States," *Jewish Women in Historical Perspective,* Judith R. Baskin, ed. Detroit: Wayne State University Press, 265–88.
Umansky, Ellen M., and Ashton, Diane, eds. 1992. *Four Centuries of Jewish Women's Spirituality: A Sourcebook.* Boston: Beacon Press.
Verel, Shoshana. 1989. "B'veiteha shel Devorah Baron," *Ha–aretz,* 6.8. 54. New York: Vintage Books.
Vogt, K. 1991. "'Becoming Male': A Gnostic and Early Christian Metaphor," *Image of God and Gender Models in Judeo–Christian Tradition,* K. E. Børresen, ed. Oslo.
Volkov, Shulamit. 1978. "AntiSemitism as a Cultural Code." *Leo Baeck Institute Yearbook* 23:
von Hameln, Glückl. 1913. *Denkwürdigkeiten,* Alfred Feilchenfeld, trans. Berlin: Jüdischer Verlag.
Wacker, Marie-Theres. 1991. "Feminist Theology and Anti Judaism: The Status of the Discussion and the Context of the Problem in the Federal Republic of Germany," *Journal of Feminist Studies in Religion* 7 (2), Fall: 109–16.
Waldenberg, Eliezer. 1985. *Responsa of Ztitz Eliezer,* 2nd ed. Jerusalem.
Walsh, Mary Roth. 1977. "*Doctors Wanted: No Women Need Apply*": *Sexual Barriers in the Medical Profession, 1835–1975.* New Haven: Yale University Press.
Waskow, Arthur. 1978. *Godwrestling.* New York: Schocken.
Wasserman, Jakob. 1921. *Mein Weg als Deutscher und Jude.* Berlin: S. Fischer.
Weems, Renita J. 1989. "Gomer: Victim of Violence or Victim of Metaphor?," *Semeia* 47: 87–104.

Wegner, Judith Romney. 1988. *Chattel or Person: The Status of Women in the Mishnah.* New York: Oxford University Press.

Weiler, Gerda. 1984. *Ich Verwerfe im Landes die Kriege: Das verborgene Matriarchat im Alten Testament.* Munich: Frauenoffensive.

_____. 1989. *Das Matriarchat I: Geschichte seiner Erforschunh.* Stuttgart: Verlag W. Kohlhammer.

Weiner, A. 1976. *Women of Value, Men of Renown: New Perspectives in Trobriand Exchange.* Austin: University of Texas Press.

Weiner, A. 1979. "Trobriand Kinship from Another View: The Reproductive Power of Women and Men," *Man,* 14.

Weisinger, Mort, ed. 1963. *Action Comics,* October No. 305. Sparta, IL: National Periodical Publications.

Weissler, Chava. 1987. "The Religion of Traditional Ashkenazic Women: Some Methodological Issues," *Association for Jewish Studies Review* 12 (1): 73–94.

_____. 1987. "The Traditional Piety of Ashkenazic Women," *Jewish Spirituality: From the Sixteenth Century to the Present,* Arthur Green, ed. New York: Crossroad Publishing, 245–75.

_____. 1989. "'For Women and Men Who Are Like Women': Construction of Gender in Yiddish Devotional Literature," *Journal of Feminist Studies in Religion* 5 (2).

_____. 1991. "Prayers in Yiddish and the Religious Word of Ashkenazic Women," *Jewish Women in Historical Perspective,* Judith Baskin, ed. Detroit: Wayne State University Press.

Wengeroff, Pauline. 1908. *Memoiren einer Grossmutter.* Berlin.

Wertheimer, Jack. 1989. "Recent Trends in American Judaism," *American Jewish Year Book:* 63–162.

Windaus-Walser, Karin. 1988. "Gnade der weiblichen Geburt? Zum Umgang der Frauenforschung mit Nationalsozialismus und Antisemitismus" *Feministische Studien* 6, November: 102–15.

Winkler, Paula. 1901. "Betrachtungen einer Philozionistin." *Die Welt* 6, September.

Wolff, Hanna. 1975. *Jesus der Mann: Die Gestalt Jesu in tiefenpsychologisher Sicht.* Stuttgart: Radius Verlag.

Wolfson, Elliot R. 1987. "Circumcision, Vision of God, and Textual Interpretation: From Midrashic Trope to Mystical Symbol," *History of Religions* 27: 205.

_____. 1992. "Images of God's Feet: Some Observations on the Divine Body in Judaism," *People of the Body: Jewish and Judaism from an Embodied Perspective,* H. Eilberg-Schwartz, ed. Albany: SUNY Press.

_____. 1993. "The Tree That Is All: Jewish-Christian Roots of a Kabbalistic Symbol in *Sefer ha-Bahir,*" *Journal of Jewish Thought and Philosophy* 3: 71.

_____. 1993. Beautiful Maiden without Eyes: Peshat and Sod in Ziharic Hermeneutics," *The Midrashic Imagination: Jewish Exegesis, Thought and History,* M. Fishbane, ed. Albany: SUNY Press.

_____. 1994. "Woman — The Feminine as Other in Theosophic Kabbalah: Some Philosophical Observations on the Divine Androgyne," *The Other in Jewish Thought and History,* R. Cohen and L. Silberstein, eds. New York: New York University Press.

_____. 1994. Forms of Visionary Ascent as Ecstatic Experience in the Zohar," *Gershom Scholem's Major Trends in Jewish Mysticism: 50 Years After,* J. Dan and P. Schäfer, eds. Tübingen.

Wolfson, Elliot R., ed. 1988. *The Book of the Pomegranate: Moses de Leon's Sefer ha-Rimmon.* Atlanta: Scholars Press.

Yagel, Abraham. 1980. *A Valley of Vision*. Philadelphia: University of Pennsylvania Press.

Yerushalmi, Yosef Hayim. 1972. *From Spanish Court to Italian Ghetto*. New York: Columbia University Press.

Young-Eisendrath. 1988. "The Female Person and How We Talk About Her," *Feminist Thought and the Structure of Knowledge*, M. M. Gergen, ed. New York: New York University Press.

Zimmer, E. 1989. "Poses and Postures during Prayer," *Sidra* 5: 92–94.

Zinberg, Israel. 1978. *A History of Jewish Literature. vol. 11: The Haskalah Movement in Russia*, Bernard Martin, trans. Cleveland: Press of Case Western Reserve.

Zwelling, J. 1975. "Joseph of Hamadan's Sefer Tashak: Critical Edition with Introduction." Ph.D. dissertation, Brandeis University.